E 449
.H791

Hopkins, John Henry, bp., 1792-1868
    A scriptural, ecclesiastical, and historical
view of slavery, from the days of the patriarch
Abraham, to the nineteenth century. Addressed
to the Right Rev. Alonzo Potter. New York,
Pooley & Co. c1864s
    376 p.

    1. Slavery. 2. Slavery in the U. S. - Con-
troversial literature - 1864. 3. Slavery -
Justification. I. Potter, Alonzo, bp., 1800-
1865.

E449.H791

013904

A

SCRIPTURAL, ECCLESIASTICAL, AND HISTORICAL

VIEW OF SLAVERY,

FROM THE

DAYS OF THE PATRIARCH ABRAHAM, TO THE NINETEENTH CENTURY.

ADDRESSED TO THE

RIGHT REV. ALONZO POTTER, D.D.,

BISHOP OF THE PROT. EPISCOPAL CHURCH, IN THE DIOCESE OF PENNSYLVANIA.

BY

JOHN HENRY HOPKINS, D.D., LL.D.,

BISHOP OF THE DIOCESE OF VERMONT.

New-York:
W. I. POOLEY & CO., HARPER'S BUILDING, FRANKLIN SQUARE.

JOHN A. GRAY & GREEN,
PRINTERS, STEREOTYPERS, AND BINDERS,
16 & 18 Jacob St., N. Y.

CONTENTS.

———•◦•———

CONTENTS OF THE APPENDIX.

ERRATA.

---•••---

Page 59.—(Sixteen lines from the top,) instead of "Archbishop of Exeter," read Bishop of Exeter.

Page 79.—(Nine lines from the bottom,) instead of "rights" read rites.

Page 100.—(Ten lines from the bottom,) instead of "Colosians" read Colossians.

Page 117.—(Four lines from the bottom,) instead of "and" read nor.

Page 123.—(Fourteen lines from the top,) instead of "McKnight" read Macknight.

Page 170.—(Seventeen lines from the top,) instead of "way" read away.

Page 173.—(Sixteen lines from the bottom,) instead of "There" read These.

Page 224.—(Five lines from the top,) instead of "perpetuate" read perpetrate.

Page 229.—(Nine lines from the top,) instead of "antagonist" read antagonists.

Page 230.—(Three lines from the bottom,) instead of "74" read 77.

Page 230.—(Bottom line,) instead of "75" read 78.

INTRODUCTION FOR THE GENERAL READER.

In the month of December, 1860, I was requested formally, by several gentlemen of New-York, to state in writing my opinion of the Biblical argument on the subject of negro slavery in the Southern States, and also on the constitutional position of the contending parties. I considered it my duty to comply with that request, and the pamphlet was published at their expense in the following month of January. No compensation, pecuniary or otherwise, was offered or expected for my labor. It was asked and given purely as a service to what I deemed to be the truth, at a time when the secession of the Southern States had invested that truth with the highest importance to the peace and safety of our country.

Some gentlemen of Philadelphia, having read this pamphlet, addressed a similar request to me on the fifteenth of April, 1863, with reference to the topic of slavery, and I replied by consenting to the republication of the same Biblical argument on that subject, including the popular objections commonly urged against it. As in the former case, so it was in this—that no pecuniary or other inducement of a personal nature was contemplated. I did not know, and cared not to inquire into the political standing of those gentlemen. The question, in my mind, was above all party considerations, because it involved the authority of the Scriptures, the consistency of the Church, and the morality of the American Constitution. I was sufficiently acquainted with the subscribers of the letter to recognize them as Episcopalians of high character, who had a right to know the sentiments of every bishop in the Church, in answer to any respectful application.   And I should have deemed myself not only unworthy of my office, but unworthy of the name of a Christian freeman, if I could have shrunk from avowing my convictions of the truth, through the love of popular praise or the fear of popular censure.

The letter of request, together with my reply, is here recorded, in order that my readers may have the whole case fully and fairly before them.

THE LETTER OF REQUEST.

PHILADELPHIA, April 15, 1863.

RIGHT REVEREND SIR: Your views on the Scriptural aspect of Slavery, contained in a letter addressed by you to some gentlemen in New-York, shortly before the breaking out of the war, has come to our notice, and been perused with much satisfaction and profit.

We believe that false teachings on this subject have had a great deal to do with bringing on the unhappy strife between two sections of our common country, and that a lamentable degree of ignorance prevails in regard to it.   It is of the deepest importance to the public welfare that a sound public opinion should exist on this topic.   Believing that the communication of your views as a Christian Bishop on the Scriptural aspect of Slavery may contribute to this desirable result, we respectfully venture to beg that you will favor us with them, and permit us to make them public.

We are with great respect your obedient servants,

G. M. WHARTON,   SAMUEL JACKSON, M.D.,
A. BROWNING,   CHAS. J. BIDDLE,
JOHN STOCKTON LITTELL, P. McCALL.

To the Rt. Rev. JOHN HENRY HOPKINS, Burlington, Vt.

THE ANSWER.

BURLINGTON, VT., May 2, 1863.

MY DEAR SIRS: The pamphlet published in January, 1861, to which you have so kindly referred, is at your service, in its original form; as I have not found, in the numerous answers which it has drawn forth, any reason for changing my opinion. On the contrary, those answers have only strengthened my conviction as to the sanction which the Scriptures give to the principle of negro slavery, so long as it is administered in accordance with the precepts laid down by the Apostles. Such was the universal doctrine of Christian ministers, Christian lawyers, and Christian statesmen one hundred years ago, with a few exceptions which only proved the rule. The Constitution of the United States, as I firmly believe, made no concessions on the subject which were not warranted by the Bible. And therefore, while I should rejoice in the adoption of any plan of gradual abolition which could be accepted peacefully by general consent, I can not see that we have any right to interfere with the domestic institutions of the South, either by the law or by the Gospel. With this brief introduction, I proceed to the very serious question which your friendly application has submitted for discussion.

Your faithful servant in Christ,

JOHN H. HOPKINS,
Bishop of the Diocese of Vermont.

BIBLE VIEW OF SLAVERY.

THE word "slave" occurs but twice in our English Bible, but the term "servant," commonly employed by our translators, has the meaning of *slave* in the Hebrew and the Greek originals, as a general rule, where it stands alone. We read, however, in many places, of "hired servants," and of "bondmen and bondmaids." The first were not slaves, but the others were; the distinction being precisely the same which exists in our own day. Slavery, therefore, may be defined as *servitude for life, descending to the off-spring*. And this kind of bondage appears to have existed as an established institution in all the ages of our world, by the universal evidence of history, whether sacred or profane.

Thus understood, I shall not oppose the prevalent idea that slavery is an evil in itself. A *physical* evil it may be, but this does not satisfy the judgment of its more zealous adversaries, since they contend that it is a *moral* evil—a positive *sin* to hold a human being in bondage, under any circumstances whatever, unless as a punishment inflicted on crimes, for the safety of the community.

Here, therefore, lies the true aspect of the controversy, and it is evident that it can only be settled by the Bible. For every Christian is bound to assent to the rule of the inspired Apostle, that " sin is the transgression of the law," namely, the law laid down in the Scriptures by the authority of God—the supreme " Lawgiver, who is able to save and to destroy." From his Word there can be no appeal. No rebellion can be so atrocious in his sight as that which dares to rise against his government. No blasphemy can be more unpardonable than that which imputes sin or moral evil to the decrees of the eternal Judge, who is alone perfect in wisdom, in knowledge, and in love.

With entire correctness, therefore, your letter refers the question to the only infallible criterion—the Word of God. If it were a matter to be determined by my personal sympathies, tastes, or feelings, I should be as ready as any man to condemn the institution of slavery; for all my prejudices of education, habit, and social position stand entirely opposed to it. But as a Christian, I am solemnly warned not to be " wise in my own conceit," and not to " lean to my own understanding." As a Christian, I am compelled to submit my weak and erring intellect to the authority of the Almighty. For then only can I be safe in my conclusions, when I know that they are in accordance with the will of Him, before whose tribunal I must render a strict account in the last great day.

I proceed, accordingly, to the evidence of the sacred Scriptures, which, long ago, produced complete conviction in my own mind, and must, as I regard it, be equally conclusive to every candid and sincere inquirer. When the array of positive proof is exhibited, I shall consider the objections, and examine their validity with all the fairness in my power.

The first appearance of slavery in the Bible is the wonderful prediction of the patriarch Noah: "Cursed be Canaan, a *servant of servants* shall he be to his brethren. Blessed be the Lord God of Shem, and Canaan *shall be his servant.* God shall enlarge Japheth, and he shall dwell in the tents of Shem, and Canaan *shall be his servant.*" (Gen. 9 : 25.)

The heartless irreverence which Ham, the father of Canaan, displayed toward his eminent parent, whose piety had just saved him from the deluge, presented the immediate *occasion* for this remarkable prophecy ; but the actual *fulfilment* was reserved for his posterity, after they had lost the knowledge of God, and become utterly polluted by the abominations of heathen idolatry. The Almighty, foreseeing this total degradation of the race, ordained them to servitude or slavery under the descendants of Shem and Japheth, doubtless because *he judged it to be their fittest condition.* And all history proves how accurately the prediction has been accomplished, even to the present day.

We come next to the proof that slavery was sanctioned by the Deity in the case of Abraham, whose three hundred and eighteen bond-servants, born in his own house, (Gen. 14 : 14,) are mentioned along with those who were *bought with his money*, as proper subjects for circumcision. (Gen.

17 : 12.)   His wife Sarah had also an Egyptian slave, named
Hagar, who fled from her severity.   And " the angel of the
Lord " commanded the fugitive to *return to her mistress and
submit herself.*   (Gen. 16 : 9.)   If the philanthropists of our
age, who profess to believe the Bible, had been willing to
take the counsel of that angel for their guide, it would have
preserved the peace and welfare of the Union.

The third proof that slavery was authorized by the Almighty occurs in the last of the Ten Commandments, delivered from Mount Sinai, and universally acknowledged by
Jews and Christians as THE MORAL LAW : " Thou shalt not
covet thy neighbor's house, thou shalt not covet thy neighbor's wife, nor his *man-servant, nor his maid-servant,* nor
his ox, nor his ass, nor any thing that is thy neighbor's."
(Exod. 20 : 17.)   Here it is evident that the principle of
property—" any thing that is thy neighbor's "—runs through
the whole.   I am quite aware, indeed, of the prejudice which
many good people entertain against the idea of *property* in
a human being, and shall consider it, in due time, amongst
the objections.   I am equally aware that the wives of our
day may take umbrage at the law which places them in the
same sentence with the slave, and even with the house and
the cattle.   But the truth is none the less certain.   The
husband has a real *property* in the wife, because she is
bound, for life, to serve and to obey him.   The wife has a
real *property* in her husband, because he is bound, for life,
to cherish and maintain her.   The *character* of property is
doubtless modified by its design.   But whatever, whether
person or thing, the law *appropriates* to an individual, becomes of necessity his *property.*

The fourth proof, however, is yet more express, as it is derived from the direct rule established by the wisdom of God
for his chosen people, Israel, on the very point in question,
viz. :

" If thou buy a Hebrew servant, six years shall he serve,

and in the seventh year he shall go out free for nothing. If he came in by himself, he shall go out by himself. If he were married, then his wife shall go out with him. If his master have given him a wife, and she have borne him sons or daughters, *the wife and the children shall be her master's, and he shall go out by himself.*" (Exod. 21 : 2–4.) Here we see that the separation of husband and wife is positively directed by the divine command, in order to secure the property of the master in his bond-maid and her offspring. But the husband had an alternative, if he preferred slavery to separation. For thus the law of God proceeds : "If the servant shall plainly say, I love my master, my wife, and my children ; I will not go out free ; then his master shall bring him unto the judges ; he shall also bring him to the door or unto the door post ; and his master shall bore his ear through with an awl, and *he shall serve him forever.*" (Exod. 21 : 5, 6.) With this law before his eyes, what Christian can believe that the Almighty attached immorality or sin to the condition of slavery ?

The treatment of slaves, especially as it regarded the degree of correction which the master might administer, occurs in the same chapter, as follows : " If a man smite his servant or his maid with a rod, and he die under his hand, he shall be surely punished. Notwithstanding if he continue a day or two, *he shall not be punished ; for he is his money.*" (Exod. 21 : 20, 21.) And again : "If a man smite the eye of his servant or the eye of his maid, that it perish, he shall let him go free for his eye's sake. And if he smite out his man-servant's tooth, or his maid-servant's tooth, he shall let him go free for his tooth's sake." (Exod. 21 : 26, 27.) Here we see that the master was authorized to use corporal correction toward his slaves, within certain limits. When immediate death ensued, he was to be punished as the judges might determine. But for all that came short of this, the loss of his property was held to be a sufficient penalty.

1*

The next evidence furnished by the divine law appears in the peculiar and admirable appointment of the Jubilee. " Ye shall hallow the fiftieth year, and proclaim liberty throughout all the land to all the inhabitants thereof: it shall be a Jubilee unto you, and *ye shall return every man unto his possession, and ye shall return every man to his family.*" (Lev. 25 : 10.) This enactment, however, did not affect the slaves, because it only extended to the Israelites who had " a possession and a family," according to the original distribution of the land among the tribes. The distinction is plainly set forth in the same chapter, viz. :

" If thy brother that dwelleth by thee be waxen poor, and be sold unto thee, thou shalt not compel him to serve as a bond servant, but as a hired servant and as a sojourner he shall be with thee, and shall serve thee unto the year of Jubilee, and then shall he depart from thee, both he and his children with him, and shall return unto his own family, and unto the possession of his fathers shall he return. For they are my servants which I brought forth out of the land of Egypt, they shall not be sold as bondmen. *Both thy bondmen and bondmaids, which thou shalt have, shall be of the heathen that are round about you ; of them shall ye buy bondmen and bondmaids.* Moreover, of the children of the *strangers that do sojourn among you, of them shall ye buy, and of their families that are with you, which they begat in your land,* and they shall be your possession. And ye shall take them as an *inheritance for your children after you*, to inherit them for a possession ; THEY SHALL BE YOUR BONDMEN FOREVER ; but over your brethren, the children of Israel, ye shall not rule one over another with rigor. For unto me the children of Israel are servants; they are my servants whom I brought forth out of the land of Egypt : I am the Lord your God." (Lev. 39 : 40–46, with v. 55.)

The distinction here made, between the temporary servitude of the Israelite and the perpetual bondage of the heathen race, is too plain for controversy. And this express and positive law furnishes the true meaning of another passage which the ultra-abolitionist is very fond of repeating : " Thou shalt not deliver unto his master the servant which is escaped from his master unto thee : he shall dwell with thee, even among you, in that place which he shall choose, in one of thy gates where it liketh him best : thou shalt not oppress him." (Deut. 23 : 15, 16.) This evidently must be referred to the case of a slave who had escaped from a *foreign heathen master*, and can not, with any sound reason, be applied to the slaves of the Israelites themselves. For it is manifest that if it were so applied, it would nullify the other enactments of the divine Lawgiver, and it would have been an absurdity to tell the people that they should " buy bondmen and bondmaids of the heathen and the stranger, to be their possession and the inheritance of their children forever," while, nevertheless, the slaves should be at liberty to run away and become freemen when they pleased. It is the well-known maxim, in the interpretation of all laws, that each sentence shall be so construed as to give a consistent meaning to the whole. And assuredly, if we are bound to follow this rule in the legislation of earth, we can not be less bound to follow it in the legislation of the Almighty. The meaning that I have adopted is the only one which agrees with the established principle of legal construction, and it has invariably been sanctioned by the doctors of the Jewish law, and every respectable Christian commentator.

Such, then, is the institution of slavery, laid down by the Lord God of Israel for his chosen people, and continued for fifteen centuries, until the new dispensation of the Gospel. What change did this produce ? I grant, of course, that we, as Christians, are bound by the precepts and example of the Saviour and his apostles. Let us now, therefore, proceed to the all-important inquiry, whether we are authorized by these to presume that the Mosaic system was done away.

First, then, we ask what the divine Redeemer said in reference to slavery. And the answer is perfectly undeniable: HE DID NOT ALLUDE TO IT AT ALL. Not one word of censure upon the subject is recorded by the Evangelists who gave His life and doctrines to the world. Yet slavery was in full existence at the time, throughout Judea; and the Roman empire, according to the historian Gibbon, contained sixty millions of slaves, on the lowest probable computation! How prosperous and united would our glorious republic be at this hour, if the eloquent and pertinacious declaimers against slavery had been willing to follow their Saviour's example!

But did not our Lord substantially repeal the old law, by the mere fact that he established a new dispensation? Certainly not, unless they were incompatible. And that he did not consider them incompatible is clearly proved by his own express declaration. "Think not," saith he, "that I am come to destroy the law or the prophets. I am not come to destroy, but to fulfil." (Matt. 5:17.) On that point, therefore, this single passage is perfectly conclusive.

It is said by some, however, that the great principle of the Gospel, love to God and love to man, necessarily involved the condemnation of slavery. Yet how should it have any such result, when we remember that this was no new principle, but, on the contrary, was laid down by the Deity to his own chosen people, and was quoted from the Old Testament by the Saviour himself? And why should slavery be thought inconsistent with it? In the relation of master and slave, we are assured by our Southern brethren that there is incomparably more mutual love than can ever be found between the employer and the hireling. And I can readily believe it, for the very reason that it is a relation for life; and the parties, when rightly disposed, must therefore feel a far stronger and deeper interest in each other.

The next evidence, which proves that the Mosaic law was not held to be inconsistent with the Gospel, occurs in the statement of the apostles to St. Paul, made some twenty years, at least, after the establishment of the first Christian church in Jerusalem. "Thou seest, brother," said they, "how many thousands of Jews there are who believe, *and they are all zealous of the law.*" (Acts 21 : 20.) How could this have been possible, if the law was supposed to be abolished by the new dispensation?

But the precepts and the conduct of St. Paul himself, the great apostle of the Gentiles, are all-sufficient, because he meets the very point, and settles the whole question. Thus he saith to the Ephesians : "Servants," (in the original Greek, *bond servants* or slaves,) "be obedient to them that are your masters, according to the flesh, with fear and trembling, in singleness of your hearts, as unto Christ. Not with eye-service, as men-pleasers, but as the servants of Christ, doing the will of God from the heart, with good will doing service, as to the Lord, and not unto men, knowing that whatsoever good thing any man doeth, the same shall he receive of the Lord, whether he be bond or free. And ye masters, do the same things unto them, forbearing threatening, knowing that your Master also is in heaven, neither is there any respect of persons with him." (Eph. 6 : 5–9.)

Again, to the Colossians, St. Paul repeats the same commandments. "Servants," (that is, *bond servants* or slaves,) "obey in all things your masters according to the flesh, not with eye-service, as men-pleasers, but in singleness of heart, fearing God." (Col. 3 : 22.) "Masters, give unto your servants that which is just and equal, knowing that ye also have a master in heaven." (Col. 4 : 1.)

Again, the same inspired teacher lays down the law in very strong terms, to Timothy, the first Bishop of Ephesus ;

"Let as many servants as are under the yoke," (that is, the yoke of bondage,) "count their own masters worthy of all honor, that the name of God and his doctrine be not blasphemed. And they that have believing masters, let them not despise them because they are brethren, but rather do them service because they are faithful and beloved, partakers of the benefit. These things teach and exhort. *If any man teach otherwise, and consent not to wholesome words, even the words of our Lord Jesus Christ, and to the doctrine which is according to godliness, he is proud, knowing nothing, but doting about questions and strifes of words, whereof cometh envy, strife, railings, evil surmisings, perverse disputings of men of corrupt minds and destitute of the truth, supposing that gain is godliness.* From such withdraw thyself. But godliness with contentment is great gain. For we brought nothing into this world, and it is certain we can carry nothing out. And having food and raiment, let us be therewith content." (1 Tim. 6 : 1–8.)

Lastly, St. Paul, in his Epistle to Philemon, informs him that he had sent back his fugitive slave, whom the Apostle had converted to the Christian faith during his imprisonment, asking the master to forgive and receive his penitent disciple. "I beseech thee for my son Onesimus," saith he, "whom I have begotten in my bonds, which in time past was to thee unprofitable, but now profitable to thee and to me, whom I have sent again : thou therefore receive him that is mine own bowels, whom I would have retained with me, that in thy stead he might have ministered unto me in the bonds of the gospel. But without thy mind would I do nothing, that thy benefit should not be as it were of necessity, but willingly. For perhaps he therefore departed for a season, that thou shouldst receive him forever, not now as a servant, but above a servant, a brother beloved, specially to me, but how much more to thee, both in the flesh and in the Lord? If thou countest me therefore a partner, receive him as myself. If he hath wronged thee or oweth thee aught, put that on mine account. I Paul have written it with mine own hand, I will repay it; albeit I do not say to thee how thou owest unto me thine own soul besides." (Ep. to Philemon 5, 10, 19.)

The evidence of the New Testament is thus complete, plainly proving that the institution of slavery was not abolished by the Gospel. Compare now the course of the ultra-abolitionist, with that of Christ and his inspired apostle. The divine Redeemer openly rebukes the sanctimonious Pharisees, " who made void the law of God by their traditions." He spares not the wealthy, infidel Sadducees. He denounces the hypocritical Scribes, who " loved the uppermost rooms at feasts and to be called of men, Rabbi, Rabbi." He calls the royal Herod " that fox," entirely regardless of the king's displeasure. He censures severely the Jewish practice of divorcing their wives for the slightest cause, and vindicates the original sanctity of marriage. He tells the deluded crowd of his enemies that they are " the children of the devil, and that the lusts of their fathers they would do." He makes a scourge of small cords, and drives the buyers and sellers out of the temple. And while he thus rebukes the sins of all around him, and speaks with divine authority, he proclaims himself the special friend and patron of the poor—preaches to them his blessed doctrine, on the mountain, by the sea-side, or in the public streets, under the open canopy of heaven—heals their diseases, partakes of their humble fare, and, passing by the rich and the great, chooses his apostles from the ranks of the publicans and the fishermen of Galilee. Yet he lived in the midst of slavery, maintained over the old heathen races, in accordance with the Mosaic law, and uttered not one word against it! What proof can be stronger than this, that he did not regard it as a sin or a moral evil? And what contrast can be more manifest than this example of Christ on the one hand, and

the loud and bitter denunciations of our anti-slavery preachers and politicians, *calling themselves Christians*, on the
other? For they not only set themselves against the Word
of God in this matter, condemning slavery as the "monster
sin," the "sum of all villainies," but—strange to say—they
do it in the very name of that Saviour whose whole line of
conduct was the very opposite of their own!

Look next at the contrast afforded by the inspired Apostle of the Gentiles. He preaches to the slave, and tells him
to be obedient to his master for Christ's sake, faithful and
submissive, as a main branch of religious duty. He preaches
to the master, and tells him to be just and equal to his slave,
knowing that *his* Master is in heaven. He finds a fugitive
slave, and converts him to the Gospel, and then sends him
back again to his old home with a letter of kind recom-
mendation. Why does St. Paul act thus? Why does he
not counsel the fugitive to claim his right to freedom, and
defend that right, if necessary, by the strong hand of violence, even unto death? Why does he not write to his disciple, Philemon, and rebuke him for the awful sin of holding
a fellow-man in bondage, and charge it upon him, as a solemn
duty, to emancipate his slaves, at the peril of his soul?

The answer is very plain. *St. Paul was inspired, and knew
the will of the Lord Jesus Christ, and was only intent on
obeying it.* And who are we, that in our modern wisdom
presume to set aside the Word of God, and scorn the example of the divine Redeemer, and spurn the preaching and
the conduct of the apostles, and invent for ourselves a
"higher law" than those holy Scriptures which are given
to us as "a light to our feet and a lamp to our paths," in the
darkness of a sinful and a polluted world? Who are we
that virtually blot out the language of the sacred record,
and dictate to the majesty of heaven what HE shall regard
as sin and reward as duty? Who are we that are ready to
trample on the doctrine of the Bible, and tear to shreds the

Constitution of our country, and even plunge the land into the untold horrors of civil war, and yet boldly pray to the God of Israel to bless our very acts of rebellion against his own sovereign authority? Woe to our Union when the blind become the leaders of the blind! Woe to the man who dares to " strive against his Maker !"

Yet I do not mean to charge the numerous and respectable friends of this popular delusion with a willful or conscious opposition to the truth. They are seduced, doubtless, in the great majority of cases, by the feelings of a false philanthropy, which palliates, if it can not excuse, their dangerous error. Living far away from the Southern States, with no practical experience of the institution, and accustomed from their childhood to attach an inordinate value to their personal liberty, they are naturally disposed to compassionate the negro race, and to believe that the slave must be supremely wretched in his bondage. They are under no special inducement to " search the Scriptures " on this particular subject, nor are they in general, I am sorry to say, accustomed to study the Bible half as much as they read the newspapers, the novel, and the magazine. There they find many revolting pictures of slavery, and they do not pause to ask the question whether they are just and faithful. Perhaps a fugitive comes along, who has fled from his master, and who, in justification of himself, will usually give a very distorted statement of the facts, even if he does not invent them altogether. And these good and kind-hearted people believe it all implicitly, without ever remembering the rule about *hearing both sides* before we form our opinion. Of course, they sympathize warmly with the poor oppressed African, and are generously excited to hate the system of slavery with all their heart. Then the eloquent preacher chooses it for the favorite topic of his oratory. The theme is well adapted to rouse the feelings, and it is usually by no means difficult to interest and gratify the audience, when the supposed sins of

others, which they are under no temptation to commit, are
made the object of censure. In due time, when the public
mind is sufficiently heated, the politician lays hold of the
subject, and makes the anti-slavery movement the watch-
word of party. And finally the Press follows in the wake
of the leaders, and the fire is industriously fanned until it
becomes a perfect blaze; while the admiring throng sur-
round it with exultation, and fancy its lurid light to be
from heaven, until the flames begin to threaten their own
security.

Such has been the perilous course of our Northern sentiment on the subject of slavery. The great majority, in
every community, are the creatures of habit, of association,
and of impulse; and every allowance should be made for
those errors which are committed in ignorance, under a generous sympathy for what they suppose to be the rights of
man. I can not, however, make the same apology for those
who are professionally pledged to understand and inculcate
the doctrines of the Bible. On that class of our public instructors, the present perilous crisis of the nation casts a
fearful responsibility. Solemnly bound by their sacred office
to preach the Word of God, and to follow Christ and his
apostles, as the heralds of "peace and good will to men,"
they seem to me strangely regardless, on this important subject, of their highest obligations. But it is not for me to
judge them. To their own Master, let them stand or fall.

I have promised, however, to notice the various objections
which have been raised in the popular mind to the institution
of Southern slavery, and to these I shall now proceed.

First on this list stand the propositions of the far-famed
Declaration of Independence, "that all men are created
equal; that they are endowed by their Creator with certain
unalienable rights; that among these are life, liberty, and
the pursuit of happiness." These statements are here called
"self-evident truths." But with due respect to the cele-

*the expression was ill chosen, but
the meaning is true — "equal" before the law, (it should have read)*

brated names which are appended to this document, I have
never been able to comprehend that they are "truths" at all.
In what respect are men "created equal," when every
thoughtful person must be sensible that they are brought
into the world with all imaginable difference in body, in
mind, and in every characteristic of their social position?
Notwithstanding mankind have all descended from one common parent, yet we see them divided into distinct races, so
strongly marked, that infidel philosophers insist on the im-
possibility of their having the same ancestry. Where is the
equality in *body* between the child born with the hereditary
taint of scrofula or consumption, and the infant filled with
health and vigor? Where is the equality *in mind* between
one who is endowed with talent and genius, and another
whose intellect borders on idiocy? Where is the equality
in *social position* between the son of the Esquimaux or Hot-
tentot, and the heir of the American statesman or British
peer?

Neither am I able to admit that all men are endowed with
the *unalienable* right to life, liberty, and the pursuit of happiness, because it is manifest that since "sin entered into the
world, and death by sin," they are all *alienated*, forfeited
and lost through the consequences of transgression. Life is
alienated not only by the sentence of the law, but by in-
numerable forms of violence and accident. Liberty is *alienated* not only by imprisonment, but by the irresistible restraints of social bondage to the will, the temper, the prejudices, the customs, or the interests of others, so that there
is hardly an individual to be found, even in the most favored
community, who has really the liberty of word and action so
confidently asserted as the *unalienable* right of all men. And
as regards the "pursuit of happiness," alas! what multitudes
alienate their right to it, beyond recovery, not only in the
cells of the penitentiary, but in the reckless indulgence of
their appetites and passions, in the disgust arising from ill-

chosen conjugal relations, in their associations with the pro-
fligate and the vile, in the pain and suffering of sickness and
poverty as the results of vice, in the ruin of the gambler, the
delirium of the drunkard, the despair of the suicide, and in
every other form of moral contamination !

If it be said, however, that the equality and unalienable
rights of all men, so strongly asserted by this famous Declaration, are only to be taken in a *political* sense, I am willing to concede that this may be the proper interpretation of
its intended meaning, but I can not see how it removes the
difficulty. The statement is that "all men are *created equal*,"
and that "the CREATOR has endowed them with these *unalienable* rights." Certainly if the authors of this celebrated
document designed to speak only of *political* rights and *political* equality, they should not have thus referred them to
the act of creation ; because it is perfectly obvious that since
the beginning of human government, men have been created
with all imaginable inequality, under slavery, under despotism, under aristocracy, under limited monarchy, under every
imaginable form of political strife and political oppression.
In no respect whatever, that I can discover, has the Almighty sent our race into the world with these imaginary
rights and this fanciful equality. In his sight the whole
world is sinful, rebellious, and lying under the just condemnation of his violated laws. Our original rights, whatever
they might have been, are all forfeited and gone. And since
the fall, mankind have no *rights* to claim at the hands of the
Creator. Our whole dependence is on his *mercy and compassion*. And he dispenses these according to his sovereign
will and pleasure, on no system of equality that any human
eye can discover, and yet, as every Christian must believe,
on the eternal principles of perfect benevolence, in union
with impartial justice, and boundless knowledge, and wisdom that can not err.

Where, then, I ask, did the authors of the Declaration of

Independence find their warrant for such a statement? It was probably judicious enough to call these propositions "self-evident truths," because it seems manifest that no man can prove them. To estimate aright the vast diversity among the races of mankind, we may begin with our own, the highly privileged Anglo-Saxon, which now stands at the head, although our ancestors were heathen barbarians only two thousand years ago. From this we may go down the descending scale through the Turks, the Chinese, the Tartars, the Japanese, the Egyptians, the Hindoos, the Indian tribes, the Laplanders, the Abyssinians, the Africans, and how is it possible to imagine that God has made them all equal! As truly might it be said that all the trees of the forest are equal—that all the mountains, and seas, and rivers are equal—that all the beasts of the field are equal—that all the birds of the air are equal. The facts rather establish the very contrary. The Deity seems to take pleasure in exhibiting a marvelous wealth of power through the rich variety of all his works, so that no two individuals of any species can be found in all respects alike. And hence we behold a grand system of ORDER and GRADATION, from the thrones, dominions, principalities, and powers in heavenly places, rank below rank, to man. And then we see the same system throughout our earth displayed in the variety of races, some higher, some lower in the scale—in the variety of governments, from pure despotism to pure democracy—in the variety of privilege and power among the subjects of each government, some being born to commanding authority and influence, while others are destined to submit and obey. Again, we behold the system continued in the animal creation, from the lordly lion down to the timid mole, from the eagle to the humming bird, from the monsters of the deep to the sea-star in its shell. The same plan meets us in the insect tribes. Some swift and powerful, others slow and weak, some marshaled into a regular government—monarchy in the bee-hive, aristocracy in the ant-hill, while others, like the flies, have no government at all. And in perfect harmony with this divine arrangement, the inanimate creation presents us with the same vast variety. The canopy of heaven is studded with orbs of light, all differing in magnitude, all differing in radiance, and all yielding to the sovereign splendor of the sun. The earth is clothed with the most profuse diversity of vegetation, from the lofty palm down to the humble moss. The mineral kingdom shines with gold, silver, iron, copper, and precious stones, in all conceivable forms and colors. From the mammoth cave down to the minutest crystal— from mountains of granite down to the sand upon the shore,— all is varied, multiform, unequal : yet each element has its specific use and beauty, and the grand aggregate unites in the sublime hymn of praise to the wisdom, the goodness, and the stupendous resources of that ineffable power which produced the whole.

This brief and most inadequate sketch of the order of creation may serve at least to show that the manifest inequality in the condition of mankind is no exception to the rule, but is sustained by all analogy. It is the will of God that it should be so, and no human sagacity or effort can prevent it. And the same principle exists in our political relations. We may talk as we please of our equality in political rights and privileges, but in point of fact, there is no such thing. Amongst the other civilized nations it is not even pretended. None of the great galaxy of European governments can have a better title to it than England, yet who would be so absurd as to claim political equality in a land of monarchy, of hereditary nobles, of time-honored aristocracy ? The best approach to political equality is confessedly here, and here only. Yet even here, amidst the glories of our universal suffrage, where is it to be found ? Political equality, if it means any thing, must mean that every man enjoys the same right to political office and honor ; because the *polity* of any government consists in its *system of administration*, and hence it results, of necessity, that those who can not possibly be admitted to share in this administration, have no *political equality* with those who can. We do, indeed, say that the *people are sovereign*. But every one knows full well that the comparative few who are qualified to take the lead, by talent, by education, by natural tact, and by a conjunction of favoring circumstances, are practically *sovereigns over the people*. The man who carries a hod gives his vote for the candidate. The candidate himself can do no more, so far as it concerns the mere form of election. Are they therefore politically equal? Who formed the party to which the candidate belongs? Who ruled the convention by which his name was put upon the list? Who arranged the orators for the occasion? Who subsidized the Press? Had the poor hodman any share in the operation, any influence, any voice whatever? No more than the hod which he carries. Can any human power ever manufacture a candidate out of *him?* The notion would be preposterous. Where, then, is his political equality? Even here, in our happy land of universal suffrage, how does it appear that " *all men are born equal*"? The proposition is a sheer absurdity. All men are born *unequal*, in body, in mind, and social privileges. Their intellectual faculties are unequal. Their education is unequal. Their associations are unequal. Their opportunities are unequal. And their freedom is as unreal as their equality. The poor are compelled to serve the rich, and the rich are compelled to serve the poor by paying for their services. The political party is compelled to serve the leaders, and the leaders are compelled to scheme and toil in order to serve the party. The multitude are dependent on the few who are endowed with talents to govern. And the few are dependent on the multitude for the power, without which all government is impossible. From the top to the bottom of the social fabric, the whole is thus seen to be *inequality* and *mutual dependence.* And hence, although they are free from that special kind of slavery which the Southern States maintain over the posterity of Ham, yet they are all, from the highest to the lowest, in bondage quite as real, from which they can not escape — the *slavery of circumstances,* called, in the ordinary language of the world, NECESSITY.

I have been, I fear, unreasonably tedious in thus endeavoring to show why I utterly discard these famous propositions of the Declaration of Independence. It is because I am aware of the strong hold which they have gained over the ordinary mind of the nation. They are assumed by thousands upon thousands, as if they were the very doctrines of divine truth. And they are made the basis of the hostile feeling against the slavery of the South, notwithstanding their total want of rationality. Yet I do not wonder that such maxims should be popular. They are admirably calculated to gratify the pride and ambition so natural to the human heart, and are therefore powerful incentives in the work of political revolution. It was for this purpose, I presume, that they were introduced in that famous document, which publicly cast off the allegiance of the colonies to the British crown. And the same doctrines were proclaimed a few years later, in a similar service, by the French Directory, in the midst of a far more terrible revolution. *Liberty, equality, and fraternity*—THE RIGHTS OF MAN—were then the watchwords of the excited populace, while their insane leaders published the decree of Atheism, and a notorious courtesan was enthroned as the goddess of reason, and the guillotine daily massacred the victims of democratic fury, till the streets of Paris ran with blood.

I do not state this fact because I desire to place the revolutions in the Colonies and in France on the same foundation, with respect to the *spirit* or the *mode* in which they were conducted. God forbid that I should forget the marked features of contrast between them! On the one side there was religious reverence, strong piety, and pure disinterested patriotism. On the other, there was the madness of Atheism, the brutality of ruffianism, and the "reign of terror" to all that was good and true. In no one mark or character, indeed, could I deem that there was any comparison between them, save in this: that the same false assumption of human equality and human rights was adopted in both. Yet how widely different was their result on the question of negro slavery! The American revolution produced no effect whatever on that institution; while the French revolution roused the slaves of their colony in St. Domingo to a general insurrection, and a scene of barbarous and cruel butchery succeeded, to which the history of the world contains no parallel.

This brings me to the last remarks which I have to present on this famous Declaration. And I respectfully ask my readers to consider them maturely.

First, then, it seems manifest, that when the signers of this document assumed that "*all men* were born equal," they did not take the negro race into account at all. It is unquestionable that the author, Mr. Jefferson, was a slaveholder at the time, and continued so to his life's end. It is certain that the great majority of the other signers of the Declaration were slaveholders likewise. No one can be ignorant of the fact that slavery had been introduced into all the colonies long before, and continued to exist long after, in every State save one. Surely, then, it can not be presumed that these able and sagacious men intended to stultify themselves by declaring that the negro race had rights, which nevertheless they were not ready to give them. And yet it is evident that we must either impute this crying injustice to our revolutionary patriots, or suppose that the case of the slaves was not contemplated.

Nor is this a solitary example, for we have a complete parallel to it in the preamble to the Constitution, where the

important phrase, "We, the people of the United States,"
must be understood with the very same limitation. Who
were the people? Undoubtedly the free citizens who voted
for the Constitution. Were the slaves counted as a part of
that people? By no means. The negro race had no voice,
no vote, no influence whatever in the matter. Thus, therefore, it seems perfectly plain that both these instruments
must be understood according to the same rule of interpretation. The slaves were not included in the Declaration of
Independence, for the same reason precisely that they were
not included amongst the "people" who adopted the Constitution of the United States.

Now it is the established maxim of the law, that every
written document must be understood according to the *true
intent* of the parties when it was executed. The language
employed may be such that it admits of a different sense;
but there can be only one *just* interpretation, and that is
fixed unalterably by the apparent meaning of its authors at
the time. On this ground alone, therefore, I respectfully
contend that the Declaration of Independence has no claim
whatever to be considered in the controversy of our day. I
have stated, at some length, my reasons for rejecting its
famous propositions, as being totally fallacious and untenable. But even if they were ever so "self-evident," or
capable of the most rigid demonstration, the rule of law
utterly forbids us to appeal to them in a sense which they
were not designed to bear.

In the second place, however, it should be remembered
that the Declaration of Independence, whether true or false,
whether it be interpreted legally or illegally, *forms no part
of our present system*. As a great historical document, it
stands, and must ever stand, prominent before the nations
of the world. But it was put forth more than seven years
anterior to the Constitution. Its language was not adopted
in that Constitution, and it has no place whatever in the

all this is true, The Bishops doctrine would make the proud more proud the rich more rich to

obligatory law of the United States. When our orators, our preachers, and our politicians, therefore, take its propositions about human rights and human equality, and set them up as the supreme law, overruling the Constitution and the acts of Congress, which are the *real law* of the land, I can not wonder enough at the absurdity of the proceeding. And I doubt whether the annals of civilized mankind can furnish a stronger instance of unmitigated perversity.

Thirdly, and lastly, I am utterly opposed to those popular propositions, not only because I hold them to be altogether fallacious and untrue, for the reasons already given, but further, because their *tendency* is in direct contrariety to the precepts of the Gospel, and the highest interests of the individual man. For what is the unavoidable effect of this doctrine of human equality? Is it not to nourish the spirit of pride, envy, and contention? to set the servant against the master, the poor against the rich, the weak against the strong, the ignorant against the educated? to loosen all the bonds and relations of society, and reduce the whole duty of subordination to the selfish cupidity of pecuniary interest, without an atom of respect for age, for office, for law, for government, for Providence, or for the Word of God?

I do not deny, indeed, that this doctrine of equality is a doctrine of immense power to urge men forward in a constant struggle for advancement. Its natural operation is to force the vast majority into a ceaseless contest with their circumstances, each discontented with his lot, so long as he sees any one else above him, and toiling with unceasing effort to rise upon the social scale of wealth and importance, as fast and as far as he can. There is no principle of stronger impulse to stimulate ambition in every department. And hence arises its manifold influence on the business, the enterprise, the commerce, the manufactures, the agriculture, the amusements, the fashions, and the political strifes of our *[handwritten margin notes:] four — or a portion of personal duty to love + help our neighbor — to visit those in prison (or slavery) &c, &c,*

Northern people, making them all restless, all aspiring, and all determined, if possible, to pass their rivals in the race of selfish emulation.

But how does it operate on the order, the stability, and the ultimate prosperity of the nation? How does it work on the steadfast administration of justice, the honor and purity of our public officers, the quiet subordination of the various classes in the community, the fidelity and submission of domestics, the obedience of children, and the relations of family and home? Above all, how does it harmonize with the great doctrines of the Bible, that the Almighty Ruler appoints to every man his lot on earth, and commands him to be satisfied and thankful for his portion—that we must submit ourselves to those who have the rule over us—that we should obey the laws and honor the magistrates—that the powers that be are ordained of God, and he that resist-eth the power shall receive condemnation—that we may not covet the property of others—that having food and raiment, we should be therewith content—that we must avoid strife, contention, and railing accusations, and follow peace, char-ity, and good will, remembering that the service of Christ is the only perfect freedom, and that our true happiness de-pends not on the measure of our earthly wealth, on social equality, on honor, or on our relative position in the com-munity, but on the fulfilment of our personal duty according to our lot, in reliance on his blessing?

I have no more to add with respect to this most popular dogma of human equality, and shall therefore dismiss it, as fallacious in itself, and only mischievous in its tendency. As it is the stronghold of the ultra-abolitionist, I have devoted a large space to its examination, and trust that the conclu-sion is sufficiently plain. Happily it forms no part of our Constitution or our laws. It never was intended to apply to the question of negro slavery. And it never can be so applied without a total perversion of its historical meaning, and an absolute contrariety to all the facts of humanity, and the clear instruction of the Word of God.

The next objection to the Slavery of the Southern States is its presumed *cruelty*, because the refractory slave is punished with corporal correction. But our Northern law allows the same in the case of children and apprentices. Such was the established system in the army and the navy until very lately. The whipping-post was a fixed institution in England and Massachusetts, and its discipline was administered even to free citizens during the last century. Stripes, not exceeding forty, were appointed to offenders in Israel by divine authority. The Saviour himself used a scourge of small cords when he drove the money-changers from the temple. Are our modern philanthropists more merciful than Christ, and wiser than the Almighty?

But it is said that the poor slaves are treated with *barbarity*, and doubtless it may sometimes be true, just as soldiers and sailors, and even wives and children, are shamefully abused amongst ourselves, in many instances. It is evident, however, that the system of slavery can not be specially liable to reproach on this score, because every motive of interest as well as moral duty must be opposed to it. The owner of the horse and the ox rarely treats his brutes with severity. Why should he? The animals are his property, and he knows that they must be kindly and carefully used if he would derive advantage from their labor. Much more must the master of the slave be expected to treat him with all fairness and affection, because here there are human feelings to be influenced, and if the servant be not contented and attached, not only will he work unwillingly, but he may be converted into an enemy and an avenger. When the master is a Christian, the principles of the Gospel, as laid down by St. Paul, will operate, of course, in favor of the slave. But even when these are wanting, the motives of interest and prudence remain. And hence I can not doubt that the examples of barbarity must be exceedingly few, and ought to be regarded, not as the general rule, but as the rare exceptions. On the whole, indeed, I see no reason to deny the statement of our Southern friends, that their slaves are the happiest laborers in the world. Their wants are all provided for by their master. Their families are sure of a home and maintenance for life. In sickness they are kindly nursed. In old age they are affectionately supported. They are relieved from all anxiety for the future. Their religious privileges are generously accorded to them. Their work is light. Their holidays are numerous. And hence the strong affection which they usually manifest toward their master, and the earnest longing which many, who were persuaded to become fugitives, have been known to express, that they might be able to return.

The third objection is, that slavery must be a *sin* because it leads to *immorality*. But where is the evidence of this? I dispute not against the probability and even the certainty that there are instances of licentiousness enough among slaveholders, just as there are amongst those who vilify them. It would be a difficult, if not an impossible task, however, to prove that there is more immorality amongst the slaves themselves, than exists amongst the lower class of freemen. In Sabbath-breaking, profane cursing and swearing, gambling, drunkenness, and quarreling—in brutal abuse of wives and children, in rowdyism and obscenity, in the vilest excesses of shameless prostitution—to say nothing of organized bands of counterfeiters, thieves and burglars— I doubt whether there are not more offenses against Christian morality committed in the single city of New-York than can be found amongst the slave population of all the fifteen States together. The fact would rather seem to be that the wholesome restraints of slavery, as a general rule, must be, to a great extent, an effectual check upon the worst kinds of immorality. And therefore this charge, so often brought against it, stands entirely unsupported either by positive proof or by rational probability.

The fourth objection is advanced by a multitude of excellent people, who are shocked at the institution of slavery because it involves the principle of *property in man*. Yet I have never been able to understand what it is that so disgusts them. No slaveholder pretends that this property extends any further than the *right to the labor of the slave*. It is obvious to the slightest reflection that slavery can not bind the intellect or the soul. These, which properly constitute the MAN, are free, in their own nature, from all human restraint. But to have a *property in human labor*, under some form, is an essential element in all the work of civilized society. The toil of one is pledged for the service of another in every rank of life ; and to the extent thus pledged, both parties have a *property* in each other. The parent especially has an established *property* in the labor of his child to the age of twenty-one, and has the further power of transferring this property to another by articles of apprenticeship. But this, it may be said, ends when the child is of age. True ; because the law presumes him to be then fitted for freedom. Suppose, however, that he belonged to an inferior race which the *law did not presume to be fitted for freedom at any age*, what good reason could be assigned against the continuance of the property ? Such, under the rule of the Scriptures and the Constitution of the United States, is the case of the negro. God, in his wisdom and providence, caused the patriarch Noah to predict that he should be the *servant of servants* to the posterity of Japheth. And the same almighty Ruler, who alone possesses the power, has wonderfully adapted the race to their condition. For every candid observer agrees that the negro is happier and better as a slave than as a free man, and no individual belonging to the Anglo-Saxon stock would acknowledge that the intellect of the negro is equal to his own.

There have been philosophers and physiologists who contended that the African race were not strictly entitled to be called *men* at all, but were a sort of intermediate link between the baboon and the human being. And this notion is still maintained by some at the present day. For myself, however, I can only say that I repudiate the doctrine with my whole heart. The Scriptures show me that the negro, like all other races, descends from Noah, and I hold him to be a MAN AND A BROTHER. But though he be my *brother*, it does not follow that he is my *equal*. Equality can not be found on earth between the brothers even in one little family. In the same house, one brother usually obtains a mastery over the rest, and sometimes rules them with a perfect despotism. In England, the elder brother inherits the estate, and the younger brothers take a lower rank by the *slavery of circumstances*. The eldest son of the royal family is in due time the king, and his brothers forthwith become his subjects. Why should not the same principle obtain in the races of mankind, if the Almighty has so willed it? The Anglo-Saxon race is king; why should not the African race be subject, and subject in that way for which it is best adapted, and in which it may be more safe, more useful, and more happy than in any other which has yet been opened to it, in the annals of the world?

I know that there may be exceptions, now and then, to this intellectual inferiority of the negro race, though I belive it would be very difficult to find one, unless the intermixture of superior blood has operated to change the mental constitution of the individual. For all such cases the master may provide by voluntary emancipation, and it is notorious that this emancipation has been cheerfully given in thousands upon thousands of instances, in the majority of which the gift of liberty has failed to benefit the negro, and has, on the contrary, sunk him far lower in his social position. But no reflecting man can believe that the great mass of the slaves, amounting to nearly four millions, are qualified for freedom. And therefore it is incomparably better for them to remain under the government of their masters, who are likely to provide for them so much more beneficially than they could provide for themselves.

The difference then, between the power of the Northern parent and the Southern slaveholder, is reduced to this, namely, that the master has a *property in the labor of his slave for life*, instead of having it only to the age of twenty-one, because the law regards the negro as being always a child in understanding, requiring a superior mind to govern and direct him. But, on the other hand, the slave has just as really a *property for life in his master's support and protection*, and this property is secured to him by the same law, in sickness and in health, in the helplessness of old age, as well as in the days of youthful vigor, including, besides, a comfortable maintenance for his wife and family. Can any rational judgment devise a fairer equivalent?

The fifth objection which often meets the Northern ear, proceeds from the overweening value attached, in our age and country, to the name of liberty, since it is common to call it the dearest right of man, and to esteem its loss as the greatest possible calamity. Hence we frequently find persons who imagine that the whole argument is triumphantly settled by the question: *"How would you like to be a slave?"*

In answer to this very puerile interrogatory, I should say that whether any condition in life is to be regarded as a loss or an advantage, depends entirely on circumstances. Suppose, for example, that the Mayor of New-York should ask one of its merchant-princes: "How would you like to be a policeman?" I doubt whether the question might not be taken for an insult, and some words of indignation would probably be uttered in reply. But suppose that the same question were addressed to an Irish laborer, with what feelings would he receive it? Assuredly with those of gratitude and pleasure. The reason of the difference is obvious, because the employment which would be a degradation to the one, offers promotion and dignity to the other. In like manner, slavery, to an individual of the Anglo-Saxon race, which occupies so high a rank in human estimation, would be a debasement not to be thought of with patience for a moment. And yet, to the Guinea negro, sunk in heathen barbarism, it would be a happy change to place him in the hands of a Southern master. Even now, though the slaves have no idea of the pagan abominations from which their forefathers were taken, it is said that they usually value their privileges as being far superior to the condition of the free negroes around them, and prefer the certainty of protection and support for life, to the hazards of the liberty on which the abolitionist advises them to venture. How much more would they prize their present lot, if they understood that, were it not for this very institution of slavery, they would be existing in the darkest idolatry and licentiousness among the savages of Africa, under the despotic King of Dahomey, destitute of every security for earthly comfort, and deprived of all religious hope for the world to come!

If men would reflect maturely on the subject, they would soon be convinced that liberty is a blessing to those, and only those, who are *able to use it wisely*. There are thousands in our land, free according to law, but so enslaved to vice and the misery consequent on vice, that it would be a mercy to place them, supposing it were possible, under the rule of some other will, stronger and better than their own. As it is, they are in bondage to Satan, notwithstanding their imaginary freedom; and they do his bidding, not merely in the work of the body, but in the far worse slavery of the soul. Strictly speaking, however, the freest man on earth has no *absolute liberty*, for this belongs alone to God, and is not given to any creature. And hence it is the glory of the Christian to be the *bond servant* of the divine Redeemer

He has just said that the Soul cannot be enslaved

who " bought us to himself with his own precious blood."
The *service of* CHRIST, as saith the Apostle, is " the only
perfect freedom." All who refuse that service, are slaves
of necessity to other masters ; slaves to Mammon ; slaves to
ambition; slaves to lust; slaves to intemperance; slaves to
a thousand forms of anxious care and perplexity ; slaves at
best to pride and worldly decorum, and slaves to circumstances over which they have no control. And they are
compelled to labor without ceasing under some or all of
these despotic rulers, at the secret will of that spiritual task-
master, whose bondage does not end at death, but continues
to eternity.

The sixth objection arises from the fact that slavery sepa-
rates the husband from the wife and the parents from the
children. Undoubtedly it sometimes does so from necessity.
Before we adopt this fact, however, as an argument against
slavery, it is only fair to inquire whether the same separation do not take place, perhaps quite as frequently, amongst
those who call themselves free. The laboring man who has
a large family is always obliged to separate from his children, because it is impossible to support them in his humble
home. They are sent to service, therefore, one to this master and another to that, or bound as apprentices, as the case
may be, and thus the domestic relations are superseded by
strangers, for the most part beyond recovery. So among
the lower orders, the husbands are separated from their
wives by the same necessity. How many, even of the
better classes, have left their homes to seek their fortune
in the gold regions! How many in Europe have abandoned their families for Australia, or the United States, or
the Canadas ! How many desert them from pure wickedness — a crime which can hardly happen under the Southern system ! But above all, how constantly does this separation take place amongst our soldiers and sailors, so that
neither war nor foreign commerce could be carried on at

all without it! All these are borne by *freemen*, under the *slavery of circumstances*. Is it wise to declaim against this necessity in one form, when we are forced to submit to it in so many other kinds of the same infliction ?

There is only one other argument which occurs to me, requiring notice, and that is based upon the erroneous notion that the laws of God under the Mosaic dispensation allowed polygamy as well as slavery ; and, therefore, it is inferred that the legislation of the Old Testament is of no authority upon the subject, but as the Gospel did away the first, so also it should do away the other.

The facts here are misunderstood, and the inference is without any real foundation. Let us look at the matter as it is explained by the Saviour himself. "The Pharisees came to him, tempting him, and saying unto him : Is it lawful for a man to put away his wife for every cause ? And he answered and said unto them : Have ye not read that he which made them at the beginning made them male and female ; and said, For this cause shall a man leave father and mother, and shall cleave to his wife, and they twain shall be one flesh ? Wherefore they are no more twain, but one flesh. What, therefore, God hath joined together, let no man put asunder. They say unto him : Why did Moses then command to give a writing of divorcement, and put her away ? He saith unto them : Moses, because of the hardness of your hearts, suffered you to put away your wives, but from the beginning it was not so. And I say unto you, Whosoever shall put away his wife, except it be for fornication, and shall marry another, committeth adultery, and whoso marrieth her that is put away doth commit adultery." (Matt. 19 : 3–9.)

Now here our Lord plainly lays down the original law of marriage, referring expressly to Adam and Eve, one man and one woman, declared to be *one flesh*, and adding the command, *What God hath joined together, let no man put asunder.* But it is evident that polygamy must, of necessity, interfere with this divine union. The *twain* can no longer be *one flesh,* when another wife is brought between them, because the new wife must deprive the former one of her exclusive rights and privileges, and the husband destroys the very unity which God designed in joining them together. The doctrine of our Saviour, therefore, restores the law of marriage to its original sanctity; and the apostles, accordingly, always speak of the wife in the singular number, in no instance appearing to contemplate the possibility of the Christian having more wives than one, while, in the case of a bishop, St. Paul specifies it as an essential condition that he shall be " the husband of one wife." (1 Tim. 3 : 2.)

But how had the chosen people been allowed for so many centuries to practice polygamy, and divorce their wives for the slightest cause? Our Lord explains it by saying that *Moses* suffered them to put away their wives " because of the hardness of their hearts." The special questions addressed to him by the Pharisees did not, indeed, refer to polygamy, but only to the liberty of divorce, for at that time it should seem that the practice of polygamy had wellnigh ceased in *Judea,* and it is certainly not countenanced by the Jewish laws at this day. The principle, however, is precisely the same in the two cases. Dissatisfaction with the present wife and desire for another were the cause of action in both; and when the husband did not wish to be burdened by the murmurs or the support of his old companion, he would naturally prefer to send her away, in order to make room for her successor. We see, then, how readily this facility of divorce became the mode in which the Jews of that day sought for the gratification of their capricious attachments, instead of the more expensive and troublesome system of polygamy. And hence our Lord applied the remedy, where it was specially required, by forbidding divorces unless for the weightiest cause, such as adultery.

Yet this was no change in the divine arrangement, which had been the same from the beginning. He expressly declares, on the contrary, that the latitude assumed by the Israelites was an *indulgence granted by Moses,* on account of "the hardness of their hearts." And this is a very different thing from an authoritative decree of the Almighty.

It is surely therefore manifest, from this language of our Saviour, that God had never given any direct sanction to polygamy. Doubtless, as we must infer from many parts of the Old Testament, it had become common among the Israelites, who, supposing themselves justified by the case of Jacob, had probably adopted it in so many instances that Moses did not think it safe or prudent to put it down, lest worse evils might follow, unless he was constrained to do so by the positive command of the Almighty. All that can be truly stated, therefore, is, that *no such positive command* was given, and the Deity left the human law-giver to use his own discretion in the matter.

Such is the aspect of this question, according to the statement of our Lord, which must be conclusive to every Christian. And hence we may perceive, at once, that the case is in no respect parallel to that of slavery. For here the Almighty caused his favored servant Noah to predict that the posterity of Ham should be the servants of servants, under the descendants of Shem and Japheth. He recognized the bondman and the bondmaid in the Ten Commandments. He laid down the positive law to Israel, that they should buy the children of the heathen that were round about them, and of the strangers who dwelt in their land, to serve them and their families forever. The Saviour, when he appeared, made no allusion to the subject, but plainly declared that he had not come to destroy the law. The first church of believers in Jerusalem were all "zealous" for the law. And St. Paul preached obedience to the slaves among the Gentile churches, and sent a converted slave back to his Christian master.

Where, then, is the resemblance between these cases? In the matter of divorce and polygamy, the Deity is silent, leaving them to the discretion of Moses, until the Messiah should come. But in regard to the slavery of Ham's posterity, he issues his commands distinctly. And the Saviour disclaims the intention to repeal the laws of his heavenly Father, while he asserts the original design of marriage, and his inspired Apostle gives express sanction to slavery, and speaks of the one husband and the one wife, in direct accordance with the word of his divine Master. Here, therefore, it is plain that the cases are altogether unlike, and present a contrast, rather than a comparison.

We know that the doctrine of the primitive church was in harmony with this, for polygamy was never permitted, nor divorces for trifling causes; while slavery was allowed, as being perfectly lawful, so long as the slave was treated with justice and kindness. The ancient canons sometimes advert to the mode in which slaves might be corrected. Bishops and clergy held slaves. In later times, bondmen and bondmaids were in the service of convents and monasteries. And no scruple was entertained upon the subject until the close of the last century, when the new light burst forth which now dazzles the eyes of so many worthy people, and blinds them not only to the plain statements of Scriptures, but to the interests of national unity and peace.

Thus, then, I have examined the various topics embraced in your inquiry, and the conclusion which I have been compelled to adopt must be sufficiently manifest. The slavery of the negro race, as maintained in the Southern States, appears to me fully authorized, both in the Old and the New Testament, which, as the written Word of God, afford the only infallible standard of moral rights and obligations. That very slavery, in my humble judgment, has raised the negro incomparably higher in the scale of humanity, and seems, in fact, to be the only instrumentality through which

the heathen posterity of Ham have been raised at all. Out
of that slavery has arisen the interesting colony of Liberia,
planted by slaveholders, to be a place of refuge for their
emancipated bondmen, and destined, as I hope, to be a rich
benefit, in its future growth and influence, to Africa and to
the world. I do not forget, and I trust that I do not under-
value, the missionary work of England and our own land,
in that benighted continent. But I believe that the number
of negroes Christianized and civilized at the South, through
the system of slavery, exceeds the product of those missionary labors, in a proportion of thousands to one. And thus
the wisdom and goodness of God are vindicated in the sanction which his Word has given, and the sentence originally
pronounced on Canaan as a curse has been converted into a
blessing.

I have now gone over the whole ground covered by your
kind application, and would only here repeat that, on the
question of slavery, which lies at the root of all our present
difficulties, I have obeyed the rule of conscience and of duty,
in opposition to my habits, my prejudices, and my sympathies, all of which would tend strongly to the other side. I
need hardly say that I am no politician. More than forty
years have elapsed since I ceased even to attend the polls.
But as a Christian, I am bound to accept the doctrine of the
apostles for my guide. And as a citizen, I am bound to
sustain the Constitution of the United States, and defend
those principles of law, and order, and friendly comity,
which every State should faithfully regard in its relations to
the rest. Nor is this the first time that I have expressed
my opinions. In a lecture at Buffalo, published in 1850, and
again in a volume entitled *The American Citizen*, printed
by Pudney and Russell, in 1857, I set forth the same views
on the subject of slavery; adding, however, a plan for its
gradual abolition, whenever the South should consent, and
the whole strength of the Government could aid in its ac-

complishment. Sooner or later, I believe that some measure of that character must be adopted. But it belongs to the Slave States themselves to take the lead in such a movement. And meanwhile their legal rights and their natural feelings must be respected, if we would hope for unity and peace.

In conclusion, I would only say, that I am perfectly aware how distasteful my sentiments must be, on this very serious question, to the great majority of my respected fellow-citizens, in the region where divine Providence has cast my lot. It would assuredly be far more agreeable if I could conscientiously conform to the opinions of my friends, to whose ability, sincerity, and zeal, I am ready to give all just commendation. But it would be mere moral cowardice in me to suppress what I believe to be the truth, for the sake of popularity. It can not be long before I shall stand at the tribunal of that Almighty and unerring Judge, who has given us the inspired Scriptures to be our supreme directory in every moral and religious duty. My gray hairs admonish me that I may soon be called to give an account of my stewardship. And I have no fear of the sentence which He will pronounce upon an honest though humble effort to sustain the authority of HIS WORD, in just alliance with the Constitution, the peace, and the public welfare of my country.

With the fervent prayer that the Spirit of wisdom, unity, and fraternal kindness may guide our National Congress, the Legislatures of the several States, and the sovereign will of our whole people, to a happy accommodation of every existing difficulty,

I remain, with great regard,

Your faithful servant in Christ,

JOHN H. HOPKINS,
Bishop of the Diocese of Vermont.

I had anticipated the probability that the republication of the foregoing pamphlet would bring down upon me a liberal share of abuse and contumely from the abolition Press, and I was prepared to submit to it with quiet resignation. But I was not prepared for the extraordinary sentence of "indignant reprobation" which the Bishop of Pennsylvania, and a majority of his clergy, thought fit to fulminate against my course, in the following form, viz. :

PROTEST

OF THE BISHOP AND CLERGY OF THE DIOCESE OF PENNSYLVANIA, ETC.

"The subscribers deeply regret that the fact of the extensive circulation through this Diocese of a letter by John Henry Hopkins, Bishop of the Diocese of Vermont, in defense of Southern Slavery, compels them to make this public protest. It is not their province to mix in any political canvas. But as ministers of Christ, in the Protestant Episcopal Church, it becomes them to deny any complicity or sympathy with such a defense."

"This attempt not only to apologize for slavery in the abstract, but to advocate it as it exists in the cotton States, and in States which sell men and women in the open market as their staple product, is, in their judgment, unworthy of any servant of Jesus Christ. As an effort to sustain, on Bible principles, the States in rebellion against the government, in the wicked attempt to establish by force of arms a tyranny under the name of a Republic, whose ' corner-stone ' shall be the perpetual bondage of the African, it challenges their indignant reprobation."

PHILADELPHIA, *September*, 1863.

"Alonzo Potter,	John A. Vaughan,	W. H. D. Hatton,
John Rodney,	Charles D. Cooper,	Thomas W. Martin,
E. A. Washburne,	Wilbur F. Paddock,	Alfred Elwin,
Peter Van Pelt,	Thomas Crumpton,	James W. Robins,

H. W. Ducachet,
John S. Stone,
George Leeds,
Richard D. Hall,
Joseph D. Newlin,
B. Wistar Morris,
Daniel S. Miller,
Kingston Goddard,
Phillips Brooks,
Addison B. Atkins,
Herman Hooker,
Benjamin Watson,
Edward L. Lycett,
Lewis W. Gibson,
R. W. Oliver,
Henry Brown,
W. R. Stockton,
Edward A. Foggo,
J. Isador Mombert,
Joel Rudderow,
Archibald Beatty,
C. A. L. Richards,
George A. Strong,
Gustavus M. Murray,
George W. Shinn,
Samuel Hall,
George G. Field,
Reese C. Evans,
Robert G. Chase,
Samuel Hazlehurst,
Edwin N. Lightner,
David C. Page,
John Cromlish,
William Preston,
George Slattery,
Francis J. Clerc,
Robert J. Parvin,
Thomas S. Yocom,
Benjamin Dorr,
Jehu C. Clay,
William Suddards,

George D. Miles,
B. B. Killikelly,
Alexander McLeod,
Leighton Coleman,
Richard Smith,
Thomas H. Cullen,
J. McAlpin Harding,
William Ely,
Marison Byllesby,
J. Livingston Reese,
Augustus A. Marple,
B. T. Noakes,
D. Otis Kellogg,
Daniel Washburn,
Samuel E. Smith,
Treadwell Walden,
Herman L. Duhring,
Charles M. Dupuy,
John H. Babcock,
Anson B. Hard,
George A. Latimer,
R. Heber Newton,
John G. Furey,
Charles A. Maison,
R. H. Brown,
Richard Newton,
G. Emlen Hare,
W. W. Spear,
H. J. Morton,
Jacob M. Douglass,
R. A. Carden,
R. C. Matlack,
L. Ward Smith,
Samuel E. Appleton,
William J. Alston,
John Adams Jerome,
Joseph A. Stone,
Albra Wadleigh,
W. S. Perkins,
Francis E. Arnold,
George H. Jenks,

George Bringhurst,
Charles W. Duane,
George B. Allinson,
Joseph N. Mulford,
James DeW. Perry,
Thomas G. Clemson,
Francis D. Hoskins,
William P. Lewis,
J. L. Heysinger,
John Long,
Ormes B. Keith,
William N. Diehl,
Charles W. Quick,
H. T. Wells,
D. C. Millett,
J. W. Leadenham,
Frederick W. Beasley,
John P. Lundy,
George A. Crooke,
Richardson Graham,
E. S. Watson,
Samuel Edwards,
George A. Durborow,
Joseph R Moore,
Thomas B. Barker,
S. Tweedale,
Marcus A. Tolman,
John H. Drumm,
J. Newton Spear,
Louis C. Newman,
Edward C. Jones,
E. W. Hening,
Samuel Durburow,
C. C. Parker,
Henry Purdon,
Benjamin H. Abbott,
John H. Marsden,
Samuel B. Dalrymple,
William V. Feltwell,
John Leithead,
George C. Drake,

D. R. Goodwin,	William S. Heaton,	Peter Russell,
M. A. DeW. Howe,	John Reynolds,	George Kirke,
Henry S. Spackman,	William Hilton,	Henry B. Bartow,
James May,	Washington B. Erben,	John K. Murphy,
John A. Childs,	John Ireland,	J. F. Ohl,
Thomas C. Yarnall,	Benjamin J. Douglass,	John Tetlow,
Edward Lounsbery,	D. C. James,	J. C. Laverty,
Henry M. Stuart,	E. N. Potter,	Charles Higbee,
J. Gordon Maxwell,	Roberts Paul,	S. T. Lord.
Robert B. Peet,	William Wright,	

The answer to this strange assault was the following:

To the Right Rev. Alonzo Potter, of the Diocese of Pennsylvania :

I have seen, with great amazement, a protest against my letter on the "Bible View of Slavery," signed by you and a long list of your clergy, in which you condemn it as "*unworthy of any servant of Jesus Christ,*" as "an effort to sustain, on Bible principles, the States in rebellion against the government in the wicked attempt to establish, by force of arms, a tyranny in the name of a Republic, whose cornerstone shall be the perpetual bondage of the African," and as such you say that it challenges your "*indignant reprobation.*"

Now, my Right Reverend brother, I am sorry to be obliged to charge you, not only with a gross insult against your senior, but with the more serious offense of a false accusation. My letter was first published in January, 1861, more than three months before the war began, at a time when no one could anticipate the form of Government which the Southern States should adopt, or the course which Congress might take in reference to their secession. And when I consented to its publication, I did not suppose that it would be used in the service of any political party, although I had no right to complain, if it were so used, because the letter, once published, became public property. But in its present form there is nothing whatever in it which bears on the question of "rebellion," or of "the perpetual bondage of the African," or of "tyranny under the name of a Republic," of which slavery should be the "corner-stone." On the contrary, I referred, on the last page, to my lecture published in Buffalo in 1850, and to my book called *The American Citizen*, published in New York in 1857, where "I set forth the same views on the subject of slavery, adding, however, a plan for its *gradual abolition*, whenever the South should consent, and the whole strength of the Government could aid in its accomplishment." "Sooner or later," I added, "I believe that some measure of that character must be adopted. But it belongs to the Slave States themselves to take the lead in such a movement. And meanwhile their legal rights and their natural feelings must be respected, if we would hope for unity and peace."

With these facts before your eyes, I am totally at a loss to imagine how even the extravagance of party zeal could frame against me so bitter a denunciation. The whole object of my letter was to prove, *from the Bible*, that in the *relation* of master and slave there was necessarily no sin whatever. The sin, if there were any, lay in the *treatment* of the slave, and not in the relation itself. Of course, it was liable to abuse, as all human relations must be. But while it was certain that thousands of our Christian brethren who held slaves were treating them with kindness and justice, according to the Apostle's rule, and earnestly laboring to improve the comforts and ameliorate the hardships of the institution, I held it to be a cruel and absurd charge to accuse them as *sinners* against the Divine law, when they were only doing what the Word of God allowed, under the Constitution and established code of their country.

I do not know whether your band of indignant reprobationists ever saw my book published in 1857, but *you read it*, because I sent you a copy, and have your letter of acknowledgment, in which, while you dissented from some of my conclusions, you did it with the courtesy of a Christian gentleman. In that letter there is nothing said about my opinions being " unworthy of any minister of Jesus Christ," and nothing of " indignant reprobation." But *tempora mutantur, et nos mutamur in illis.*

Yes; the times are indeed sadly changed, and you have changed accordingly. For many years you have met in brotherly council with these same Southern slaveholders. You invited them to the hospitalities of your house, and paid them special deference. The new light of Eastern Abolitionism had not yet risen within our Church, and if you then thought as you now think, you took excellent care that no man amongst your Southern friends should know it. Moreover, your favorite Theological Seminary, only three years ago, was the Virginia school at Alexandria, raised to great prosperity by Bishop Meade—*a slaveholder;* and I am very sure that nothing at variance with my view of slavery was ever taught in *that* institution. Yes; we may well say of you, as of many others, *quantum mutatus ab illo!* How changed is the Bishop of Pennsylvania in three years from his former course of conservatism, peace, and Scriptural consistency!

But the Word of God has not changed; the doctrine of the Apostles has not changed; the Constitution of our country has not changed; the great standards of religious truth and real civic loyalty remain just as they were; and I remain along with them, notwithstanding this bitter and unjust assault from you and your clergy. I do not intend to imitate your late style of vituperation, for I trust that I have learned, even when I am reviled, not to revile again. I respect the good opinion of your clergy, and am not aware that I have done any thing to forfeit it. I respect your office, your talents, your personal character, and the wisdom and success with which, for many years, your Episcopate has been conducted. But I do not respect your departure from the old and well-settled rule of the Church, and from the Apostolic law of Christian fairness and courtesy. I do not believe in the modern discovery of those Eastern philanthropists who deny the divinity of our Redeemer, and attach no importance to the Bible except as it may suit themselves. I do not believe that the venerated founders of our American Church were ignorant of the Scriptures, and blind to the principles of Gospel morality. I do not believe that Washington and his compatriots, who framed our Constitution with such express provisions for the rights of slaveholders, were tyrants and despots—sinners against the law of God and the feelings of humanity. But I do believe in the teaching of the inspired Apostles, and in the Holy Catholic (or universal) Church, which you and your clergy also profess to believe. I *know* that the doctrine of that Church was clear and unanimous on the *lawfulness* of slavery for eighteen centuries together; and on that point I regard your "protest" and "indignant reprobation" as the idle wind that passes by.

I wish you, therefore, to be advertised that I shall publish, within a few months, if a gracious Providence should spare my life and faculties, a full demonstration of the truth "wherein I stand." And I shall prove in that book, by the most unquestionable authorities, that slaves and slaveholders were in the Church from the beginning; that slavery was held to be consistent with Christian principle by the fathers and councils, and by all Protestant divines and commentators, up to the very close of the last century, and that this fact was universal among all churches and sects throughout the Christian world. I shall contend that our Church, which maintains the primitive rule of catholic consent and abjures all novelties, is bound, by her constitution, to hold fast that only safe and enduring rule, or abandon her apostolic claims, and descend to the level of those who are "driven about by every wind of doctrine." And I shall print your " indignant reprobation," with its long list of names, in the Introduction, so that if I can not give you fame, I may, at least, do my part to give you notoriety.

That the nineteenth century is a period of vast improvement and wonderful discovery in the arts and sciences, I grant as willingly as any man. But in religious truth or reverence for the Bible, the age in which we live is prolific in daring and impious innovation. We have seen professedly Christian communities divided and subdivided on every side. We have seen the rise and spread of Universalism, Millerism, Pantheism, Mormonism, and Spiritualism. We have seen our venerable mother Church of England sorely agitated by the contagious fever of change, on the one hand toward superstition, and on the other toward infidel rationalism. And we have heard the increasing clamor against the Bible, sometimes from the devotees of geological speculation, sometimes from the bold deniers of miracles and prophecy, and, not least upon the list, from the loud-tongued apostles of anti-slavery. We have marked the orators which cry : " Down with the Bible if it maintains the lawfulness of slavery." We have marveled at the senatorial eloquence which proclaimed that " It was high time to have an anti-slavery God and an anti-slavery Bible." We have heard the Constitution of our country denounced as "A covenant with death and hell." We have heard the boasted determination that the Union shall never be restored, until its provision for the protection of slavery is utterly abolished. And what is the result of all this philanthropy ? The fearful judgment of God has descended to chastise these multiplied acts of rebellion against His divine Government, and what the final catastrophe shall be is only known to Him who seeth the end from the beginning.

After forty years spent in the ministry, more than thirty of which have been passed in the office of a bishop, I can look back with humble thankfulness to the Giver of all good for

[handwritten annotation: "Contrary — to your interpretation of the Scriptures. Although the Scriptures are infallible, you are not so, Bishop Hopkins"]

this, at least, that all my best labors have been directed to the preservation of the Church from the inroads of doctrinal innovation. At my ordination I promised "so to minister the DOCTRINE and sacraments and discipline of Christ, as the Lord hath commanded, and as this Church hath received the same," and certain it is that "this Church" had not received the modern doctrine of ultra-abolitionism at that time, as I trust she never will receive it, because it is contrary to the sacred Scriptures. I also promised "with all faithful diligence to banish and drive away from the Church all erroneous and strange doctrines contrary to God's word," and I made those promises in the true sense which the venerable Bishop White, my ordainer, attached to them. I believed then as he believed, that our Southern brethren committed no sin in having slaves, and that they were men of as much piety as any ministers in our communion. I believed as he believed, that the plain precepts and practice of the Apostles sanctioned the institution, although, as a matter of *expediency* the time might come when the South would prefer, as the North had done, to employ free labor. These promises I have kept faithfully to the present day : and if, when I am drawing near to the end of my career, I am to be condemned and vilified by you and your clergy, because I still maintain them to the utmost of my slender ability, be assured, my Right Reverend Brother, that I shall regret the fact much more on your account than on my own.

In conclusion, I have only to say that I feel no resentment for the grossly insulting style of your manifesto. The stability and unity of the Church of God are the only interests which I desire to secure, and I am too old in experience to be much moved by the occasional excesses of human infirmity.	JOHN H. HOPKINS,
Bishop of the Diocese of Vermont.

BURLINGTON, VT., Oct. 5, 1863.

3

My readers are now in possession of all the facts which led to the publication of the present volume. What I promised in my reply to my clerical assailants, I have fulfilled, as I trust will be manifest from the numerous testimonies which I have adduced upon the subject. Knowing, as I do, that I stand upon the ground which the Church of God has occupied from the beginning, I have no fears for the result of the conflict. It may be, indeed, that the subtlety of Satan, clothed like an angel of light, may succeed in dividing the Church to which I belong, as he has already divided so many Christian communities. It may be that the authority of the Bible, the writings of the fathers, the decrees of councils, the concurrent judgment of Protestant divines, and the Constitution, which is the supreme law of the land, may all be unable to resist the combined assaults of mistaken philanthropy, in union with infidelity, fanaticism, and political expediency. It may be that we are in "the last days when perilous times shall come," and that the predicted reign of the great Antichrist is impending. But however this may be, I desire that my lot may be found with the old martyrs and confessors of the primitive Church, and with their true successors. I believe that even though the enemy may come in like a flood, the Spirit of the Lord will lift up a standard against him. And I trust that the divine Redeemer, who has promised to be with the Church to the end of the world, will guard His heritage from the irruption of "all erroneous and strange doctrines," and preserve His faithful people in unity and peace.

CHAPTER I.

To the Right Rev. Alonzo Potter, D.D.,
> Bishop of the Diocese of Pennsylvania:

Right Reverend Brother: Before I enter on the main subject of this volume, I must take the liberty of premising a brief statement of my own position in relation to the controversy. I am no lover of slavery, and no advocate for its perpetuity any longer than circumstances may seem to require. It would be strange if I were. Born in Ireland, educated from my ninth year, partly in Trenton and Bordentown, but chiefly in Philadelphia, resident in Pittsburgh during my practice of the law, and the first eight years of my ministry; removed from thence to Boston, and then, after my election to the episcopal office, becoming a citizen of Vermont, where I have lived for more than thirty years—all my habits, sympathies, and associations are opposed to slavery, and in favor of abolition. But I hold that abolition can only be lawfully accomplished on the grounds of a just and wise *expediency*, with a sacred regard to the Holy Scriptures, which are the standard of the Christian faith, in accordance with the real welfare of the colored race, in harmony with the wishes as well as the best interests of the Southern States, and with a full recognition of the rights intended to be secured to them by the Federal Constitution.

My views on this subject, as I have stated in the introduction, were first published in a lecture delivered at Buffalo and Lockport in 1850, and afterwards in a volume entitled, *The American Citizen*, printed in 1857, a copy of which was sent to you and to the other Bishops of our Church, according to my general custom. In both of these I devoted a large space to a plan of *gradual and thorough abolition*, in connection with the planting of the emancipated negroes on the slave coast of Africa, under the fostering care of commissioners, so that a belt of colored republics should eventually be established in connection with Liberia, to regenerate that heathen and benighted continent; while the Southern masters should be paid the full value, and be enabled to replace their former slaves with free laborers. But this I proposed to have effected with the cordial assent of the Southern States and the coöperation of the Federal Government, devoting to it the whole avails of the public lands, and, if necessary, aiding it by direct taxation. And meanwhile I maintained the *rights* of the South to the peaceable enjoyment of their domestic institution, on the authority of the Scriptures and the Constitution of our country; while I earnestly urged the high *expediency* of the course which I recommended, to themselves, to the Union, to Africa, and ultimately to the whole civilized world.

The lecture published in 1850 was sent to the lamented Henry Clay, then on his sick-bed, and I have his answer in a long letter, written by another hand at his dictation, but signed by himself, in which he expressed his approbation in strong terms, and wished that the pamphlet could be read by every intelligent man throughout the country. The plan presented by the President of the United States in his Message to the Congress of 1862, was substantially the same, and my suggestions were further developed by the lectures delivered in many places by Mr. Elihu Burritt. I do not know that either the President or Mr. Burritt derived their views from me, but I believe that I was the first writer who published them, although I have since seen it stated that Mr. King, of New-York, and General Harrison had proposed a similar scheme. My own conclusions, however, were derived from a combination of the act of the British Parliament, when they emancipated the slaves in Jamaica, with the principles of the American Colonization Society. The main difficulty was to show that the measure was *practicable* as well as expedient. And certain it is, that if our leading statesmen had been willing, it might have been successfully inaugurated and ultimately accomplished at less than half the sum which our mournful war has already cost the nation.

I mention these facts here more fully than in my late letter, not for the purpose of telling *you* what you knew before, but in order to inform my friends that I have not changed my former opinions—that I am, and always shall be, in favor of a gradual, just, and kindly abolition of slavery, whenever it may please Divine Providence to incline the minds of Southern statesmen to adopt it. But then, as now, I stood forth as an honest and conscientious advocate for their rights. Then, as now, I contended that the fair admission of those rights was essential to the peace and welfare of the Union. Then, as now, I opposed the extravagance of ultra-abolitionism, because I believed it to be hostile to the divine authority of the Bible, hostile to the Church of God, hostile to the best interests of the slaves themselves, and hostile to the safety and prosperity of our country.

Having thus stated the kind of abolitionism which I have always advocated in my humble sphere, I proceed to set forth the ultra-abolition doctrine which I am bound to condemn, in order that the line may be distinctly drawn between them. This doctrine rests upon the wild and unscriptural assumption that it is a SIN in the sight of heaven to hold a human being in bondage under any circumstances—that the relation of master and slave is utterly abhorrent to the principles of Christianity—that the Constitution of the United States, which gives protection to the slaveholder and grants a right of suffrage based on the slave population of the South, is "a covenant with death and an agreement with hell"—that there is a "higher law" of humanity which justifies the citizen in rebelling against the " supreme law of the land" with respect to fugitives—that slaveholding is equivalent to *man-stealing*, which the Jewish code pronounced to be worthy of death—that the Union can not and ought not to be restored until slavery is entirely abolished—that it is, finally, the " sum of all villainies," or, to use the language of Dr. Adam Clarke, the Methodist commentator, that " although in heathen countries slavery was in some sort excusable, yet among Christians it is an ENORMITY AND A CRIME, for which *perdition has scarcely an adequate state of punishment.*"[*]

Now the whole of this modern and monstrous doctrine I utterly repudiate, as at war with the laws of God and man. You know as well as I do, that it is a pure novelty, unheard of while you were the Rector of St. Paul's Church, Boston. You know that, when it was first broached, it met with the general disapprobation of all intelligent men, as a weak delusion. Unhappily it is no longer a weak delusion. On the contrary, it has become a strong one—too strong in the minds of many, for the old system of Christian faith and practice—too strong for the conservative maxims of the Church—too strong for constitutional law, for the oath of office, and for the political bond

* Com. on Ephesians, ch. 6, v. 5.

of Union. But I hold it to be no less a delusion. As such I have opposed it again and again. And because I have done this, in the service of truth and peace—because I have presumed to stand fast upon the rock of faith in the Word of God, as it was interpreted by the whole Church from the beginning up to our own day, and thus reässerted what all men acknowledged at the time when you were ordained, you, and a majority of your clergy, have publicly stigmatized my work as "unworthy of any servant of Christ," and condemned it by your sentence of "indignant reprobation."

To myself, this extraordinary fulmination is a very small matter. To the cause of truth, it may prove to be a great one. Manifest, indeed, it is, that it destroys all the old fellowship between you and me. It is an act of such plain disorder, nay, such gross and wanton insult, that I hold myself bound, by the precept of the Apostle, to withdraw from your "company," though I am also bound not to "count you as an enemy, but to admonish you as a brother."* I address this volume to you, therefore, as a brotherly admonition. I do it in this public form, because your libellous act of censure was public, printed for public use, and scattered over the land in large placards to attract universal observation. I do it at considerable length, because I shall be obliged to maintain my course by the quotation of many authorities, which neither you nor any other man can justly impeach, and I do it in humble confidence that if it fails to bring you back to the truth which you once professed as I did, it may nevertheless be of service to the Church, and keep candid and intelligent minds from the infection of this mischievous and growing error.

I trust, however, that in thus vindicating my own course, I shall say nothing which can intimate that I "count you as an enemy." You have done me a grievous wrong. You and your clergy have laid yourselves open to a prosecution for a libel. It was certainly competent for you to publish the fact that you did not approve my little tract on the Bible View of Slavery, and were not to be held accountable for it. But you had no right to accuse me of an "effort to sustain, on Bible principles, the States in rebellion against the Government in the wicked attempt to establish, by force of arms, a tyranny in the name of a republic, whose 'corner stone' shall be the *perpetual bondage of the African.*" Not one word had I written to

Bishop P. was right

* 2 Thes. ch. 3, v. 14-5.

justify this false and baseless imputation. On the contrary, I had published more than you and all your clergy put together, against the idea of the "*perpetual bondage* of the African," and in favor of a *gradual abolition* of slavery, as soon as it could be done, in peace and good will, with due regard to the best interests of the parties. And as to *rebellion*, I have always been opposed to every thing which deserves the name, in the family, in the Church, in the State, or in any other relation of society.   The apostles commanded obedience, not only to the slave, but to the child, to the wife, and to every subject of earthly government.   "Submit yourselves to every ordinance of man, for the Lord's sake," * saith the Apostle Peter.   "Let every soul be subject to the higher powers," † saith St. Paul.   And on this very ground I abjured the doctrine of the ultra-abolitionist, who tramples "the supreme law of the land" under his feet, in pursuance of a "higher law" which merely exists in his own imagination, and therefore not only sins against the Word of God, but rebels, both in word and act, against the Constitution of his country.

In publicly branding my name with this utterly groundless charge, in condemning my course as "unworthy of any servant of Jesus Christ," and in affixing to it the sentence of your "indignant reprobation," you have, I repeat, done me a grievous wrong, and have yourself "rebelled" against the precepts of justice, fairness, and Christian courtesy.   Nevertheless, I do not "count you as an enemy," though you have done the work of one.   I believe that you acted mainly under the strong influence of *political expediency*. For it so happened that my pamphlet, though never written or intended by me for such a purpose, was largely circulated by the Democratic party on the eve of your late election in Pennsylvania, and you thought it necessary to put it down. You did not pause to inquire how far I was accountable. Yet the fact is, that I have never meddled, directly or indirectly, with party politics, never gave a party vote in my life, never made a speech at a party political meeting, never wrote a line for party purposes, and never attended the polls at all since I entered the ministry, forty years ago. But if gentlemen of any party saw fit to attach importance to that pamphlet, and to circulate it, they were at full liberty to do so, because it was public property, not subject to copyright, and I could not have objected,

---

* 1 Pet. 2 : 13.   † Rom. 13 : 1, 2.

with any consistency. There was nothing in it bearing upon party politics, unless it be supposed that your Union party in Pennsylvania are ultra-abolitionists, which they do not profess to be. My only object in writing it was to show the error of those mistaken philanthropists, by exhibiting the Bible view of slavery, in vindication of that Federal Constitution which is binding alike on clergymen and politicians, and to which, therefore, I owed my allegiance in common with every other citizen. And hence it was not only unjust, but utterly preposterous, to make me accountable for the management of a *party* movement, and that, not in my own State of Vermont, but in Pennsylvania, four hundred miles away.

But you paid no regard to these considerations. The pamphlet was there. It was circulated. It was read. Some of your wise men thought it was *politically expedient* to kill it, if possible. The best way to kill it was to brand and calumniate the author. And the most effectual mode of doing that was to induce the Bishop and clergy of Philadelphia to take the lead in the patriotic work of personal defamation.

I acquit you, in my own mind, of originating this remarkable specimen of party tactics. I doubt not that the suggestion came from the sagacious brain of some experienced politician, that it was embraced by a few of your astute clergy, and that you were persuaded, by the arguments of *political expediency*, to place your name and official influence at the head of the extraordinary manifesto. What signified the injury to the Bishop of Vermont? A man of little importance, set over a small diocese, on the border of Canada! Pennsylvania contains nine times as many people as Vermont. Therefore, her bishop was nine times the greater bishop. The influence which he might secure to the Church, by contributing to a grand political success, was worth the sacrifice of nine small bishops at any time. True, it would be necessary to indorse a calumny, but in the game of politics, all calumny is lawful, and slander itself becomes a duty, when clergymen can persuade themselves to think that they are governed by devotion to the best interests of the Church and of their country. It was only an adoption of the Jesuitical maxim, that "the end sanctifies the means."

But I must go a little farther, before I have done with your act of denunciation. For while I utterly deny that I either wrote my pamphlet for the service of any political party, or gave my consent to the publication of the *Bible View of Slavery* under an expectation, at the time, that it would be used by any such party, yet I do not mean to admit that it is wrong in a bishop or clergyman to publish a *political tract*, if he sees occasion. We have, indeed, no justification for bringing politics into the sanctuary of God, or the conventions of the Church, because *there* our duty is to preach the Gospel, and attend to the work of that spiritual kingdom of Christ, which is "not of this world." But we do not cease to be citizens when we become clergymen. We have still as much right to think, to speak, and to publish our opinions upon all other subjects, as any educated class in the community. No one presumes to doubt that a bishop has a right to *vote*, as your venerated predecessor, Bishop White, always did, at every party election. And it is absurd to say that a man shall have a right to *vote*, and yet not have a right to proclaim *his reasons for voting*, which reasons never can be proclaimed without more or less of political discussion.

In England, as you know, bishops sit in the House of Lords ; and although they usually decline acting in matters of war, yet they take a part in all other political questions. They do this, too, *as bishops*, clothed in their episcopal robes; and if an American were to denounce their conduct as "unworthy of any servant of Jesus Christ," he would be thought strangely deficient in wisdom and discretion. Nevertheless, while they act as politicians in the proper place, they would utterly condemn, as I do, the introduction of politics in the Church or the Convocation.

In our country, the Church and the State are entirely disconnected, and we have no official rank in the legislatures of the land. But we belong none the less to the *Sovereign People*, and no act which would be morally right in the layman can be morally wrong in the bishop. Hence I contend that so long as a bishop does nothing but what it is lawful for every one else to do, his conduct can not be condemned as "unworthy of any servant of Jesus Christ," and deserving of "indignant reprobation."

I say, therefore, distinctly, that I have not lost, by reason of my office as bishop, my right as a citizen, not merely to permit a political party to circulate one of my pamphlets, but to join that party, to write for that party, and to vote as a member of that party if I please, because every other Christian man has those rights, and my rights, as a citizen, are precisely the same. Dignity, delicacy, and propriety, may stand in the way of certain modes and customs, with regard to the exercise of those rights, and a judicious clergyman will always pay respect to those considerations, lest his character as a minister might be injured by too free a use of his political liberty as a citizen. "All things are *lawful* for me," saith the Apostle, "but all things are *not expedient*." But a deviation from the rules of expediency would not justify any one in denouncing such departure as "*unworthy of any servant of Jesus Christ*," and challenging "*indignant reprobation*." Such language can only be justly applied to offenses of a deep dye, against the moral law; and hence you stand chargeable not only with injustice, but with absurdity, in affixing it, as you have done, to my pamphlet against ultra-abolitionism.

If you meant what you say, in condemning my conduct as "unworthy of any servant of Jesus Christ," consistency would require you to regard me as utterly unworthy to be a bishop, and therefore it would become your solemn duty to proceed, according to the canons, to have me regularly presented for trial, and deposed as soon as possible. But this, I presume, you will hardly undertake. The gross libel which you have published, with your long array of clerical indorsements, was for *political effect*, and you have probably no desire to carry it any farther. You are mistaken, nevertheless, if you suppose that you can stand excused for this insulting aggression by the calm and sober judgment of any Christian community. And the time will come, if I do not greatly err, when you and your clergy will feel ashamed of your false and violent accusation, and wish that the record could be blotted out forever.

There is one petty cavil, however, which is urged by some of your apologists, namely, that I signed my name to the *Bible View of Slavery*, with my title as Bishop of Vermont attached, and therefore it is said that in consenting to its circulation in your diocese, I was at once invading your jurisdiction, and undertaking to represent the opinions of the Church at large, without authority.

To this I reply that the course which I pursued was no invasion of your diocese, because it was not an act of episcopal authority. It is true, indeed, that the letter of request was *addressed to me as a bishop*, and that I *replied to it* as a bishop. But the same inquiry might have been made of any one else, and the same answer might have been given by a presbyter or a layman, for it only involved the expression of individual opinion. Nothing is better understood than the rule that an official *title* does not imply an official *act*, unless the *act* be of an *official character*. Thus I have before me the *Treatise on the Records of Creation*, written by the Rev. John Bird Sumner, and published some time *before* he was elevated to the episcopate. Yet in the title-page to the fifth edition the author is stated to be " John Bird Sumner, D.D., *Lord Bishop of Chester*." So I find that a work on topics which were purely secular, viz. "*On Secondary Punishments, on Transportation to New South-Wales, and on Colonization,* was published by "Richard Whately, D.D., *Archbishop of Dublin.*" Did any man ever suppose that this addition of the title gave any *official character* to the books themselves ? Nay, so far is this practice carried in England, that the title is never dropped even in private correspondence. You know as well as I do that John *Cantuar.* signifies John, Archbishop of Canterbury, and Richard, *Dublin.* signifies Richard, Archbishop of Dublin, and Henry, *Exon.* signifies Henry, Archbishop of Exeter, etc., precisely equivalent to my signature of J. H. Hopkins, Bishop of Vermont. And yet the English and colonial bishops use this official title in all their notes and letters, without exception. But does this stamp them with the assumption of any *official* authority ? The notion is a pure absurdity. In all such cases the title is used merely to *designate the individual.* And the attempt to make any thing more of it, in the present instance, is only a proof that the cause must be weak indeed, which seeks support from such a trifling cavil.

Independently of this, however, there is a strange degree of folly in supposing that the writings of a bishop are to be confined to his own diocese, while those of every other author are free to be circulated wherever they can find readers. The laity of the Church in Pennsylvania are, to a certain extent, under your jurisdiction, while I am not. Would you tell them that they must *ask your leave,* before they seek for instruction from any other quarter ? And must I obtain your *imprimatur* before I exercise the right of the humblest citizen, to publish what I believe to be the truth, and send it forth for general information ?

With respect to the other part of the accusation, viz. that by signing my name as a bishop, I undertook to represent the Church at large, I reply that no individual bishop can represent the Church at large in any other sense than that which attaches to every presbyter, deacon, and even layman, namely, that we are all bound to speak and to write nothing but what agrees with, or at least what does not stand opposed to, the doctrine of the Church to which we belong. But beyond this general obligation to be faithful to the Church, which rests on all her officers and members, my pamphlet assumed nothing. I asserted in it that the Church at large had always held the same doctrine on the lawfulness of slavery, considered in itself, and that the *sin*, if there were any, consisted not in the *relation* of master and slave, but in the *treatment*. And this assertion I now undertake to prove by indisputable authority.

But resuming my hypothesis in accounting for your extraordinary manifesto, I would merely add that I can not conceive any better way of explaining my conclusion. I regard you, therefore, not as a *personal enemy* so much as an able performer, brought upon the stage to give due effect to the designs of the politicians. I can not justify, but I shall do my utmost to palliate your error. I confess all the superiority which you may claim over myself in talents, influence, reputation, management, and tact. I am perfectly conscious, also, of your superiority in *position*, and I am well aware that the world at large pays more regard to that fact than to any other, in estimating the comparative importance of human opinion. It has been always, and I suppose it will always be, that the multitude bow down to official eminence, and would gladly render to Silenus on a pedestal, the honor which they would refuse to Apollo in the dust. I take, therefore, the most favorable view of the probable circumstances. Doubtless you were beset with importunity. Doubtless the importance of your influence in Church and State was urged adroitly, and you yielded to the pressure. Your motive was not specially to act as *my* enemy, but to follow what you deemed to be the rule of *political expediency*. The wrong is done. And it is a grievous wrong, excuse it as we may. May God forgive it, as I most freely do, notwithstanding the personal results which I presume to be irreparable.

This abusive chapter is from a meekly forgiving injured man, who declares that he feels no "resentment"

+ The Bishop had no "resentment" — He thanks god, no doubt, that he is not as other men — like Bishop Potter.

CHAPTER II.

RIGHT REVEREND BROTHER : I do not know precisely where you stand on the field of this very serious controversy ; for while you have assaulted my position with unexampled severity, you have thus far preferred, for yourself, the policy of *non-committal.* That is a kind of policy, however, which I have not worldly wisdom enough to admire, in questions of religious truth and duty, I have always regarded it as a solemn obligation to " contend for the faith once delivered to the saints," and to do what I could, in my humble sphere, to " drive away from the Church all erroneous and false doctrine, contrary to the Word of God." Whether " in honor or in dishonor, through evil report or good report," I have held my duty to be the same. For I know, and you know, that this was the rule laid down to the Apostles by their Divine Lord and Master, and faithfully pursued by them, in despite of danger and suffering, till they finished their glorious course by gaining the crown of martyrdom. If they had adopted the time-serving policy of the present day, the Church of Christ could never have been planted in the face of heathen and Jewish opposition. This is the reason, and the only reason, why I have always been ready to bear my part in every controversy which involved religious principle. In worldly matters, where my own personal interest was alone concerned, I have willingly yielded my rights sooner than contend in the service of Mammon. But in the service of Christ and his Church I have considered myself a " soldier," enlisted for life in His warfare " against sin, the world, and the devil." And this, which the baptismal office makes the duty of every Christian, becomes ten-fold the duty of a bishop, whose office calls him to be one of the chief leaders in the host of God's elect, to defend with honest boldness the sacred cause of religious truth against every assault of opposing error.

I am quite aware that this was not the way to popularity. If I could conscientiously have held my peace on all disputed questions,

He is an apostle.
Perhaps Bishop Potter has no very high opinion of controversy or of controvertialists

I should have been deemed a far wiser man in the general opinion. But I thank our divine Redeemer for making me willing to be called a fool, when I abandoned my prosperous profession of the law for the poor vocation of the ministry. I thank Him who has enabled me to defend His truth without regard to odium and abuse. I thank Him who taught me to follow, in my weakness, that eminent Apostle who was also called a fool, and to adopt his noble declaration : " With me it is a small thing to be judged of you, or of man's judgment—He that judgeth me is the Lord." I thank Him who showed me that it was *not* my duty to be popular, but that it *was* my duty to be faithful, and to prove, on all occasions of religious controversy, that I did not " love the praise of men more than the praise of God."

If I should be accused of "boasting" in this, which I doubt not that I shall be, I must shelter myself under the example of the same Apostle by saying that "you have compelled me" by your bitter and groundless accusation. Your *theory* of Christian duty is of course the same as mine. Your *practice* is very different, for notwithstanding your acknowledged literary talents, you have carefully abstained from taking the smallest public share in any religious controversy to this day ; although you have undertaken to sit in judgment on myself because I presumed to repeat my former argument at a time which did not suit your views of political expediency. But I have not denounced your course of worldly wisdom. I have not murmured at your success and popularity. I wish, on the contrary, to give you all the praise to which, in many respects, you are so justly entitled. Nevertheless, I would not adopt your prudent abstinence from controversy as a rule for myself, if the homage of the whole world were offered as the inducement. Rather would I endeavor, in the words of the Apostle, to "take pleasure in reproaches for Christ's sake,"* so long as I provoke them only by an honest though humble effort to discharge what I esteem to be my duty.

The life of our divine Redeemer, from the time when He commenced His public ministry, was an open and constant controversy against all existing error. The life of His apostles was a life of controversy, like that of their Lord and Master. And therefore I claim the highest authority for my poor efforts to obey the rule which commands me to follow their example. It is not that I esteem my trifling labors as worthy to be named in comparison with the stupendous task

* 2 Cor. 12 : 10.

committed to the inspired messengers of Christ. God forbid! Yet the obligation to imitate them is none the less imperative, and, however humble the performance, the spirit which animates it should be the same.

I should be altogether wanting, however, in justice to myself, if I failed to state the fact, that I have only been induced to engage in the present controversy by a sense of duty to religious truth, unity, and peace, in the communion of the Church of which I am a member. That Church was extended South as well as North. Its union, as well as the Union of the States, was deeply involved in the question of slavery. The views of ultra-abolitionists, if they prevailed, must break that union asunder, and therefore I held myself bound to raise my feeble voice against a doctrine which I regarded as not only false in itself, but perilous to the Church and to the nation. Alas! the result which I dreaded has come to pass. The unity of the Church is lost. The unity of the States is invaded. And slavery still stands as the cardinal point of separation. If ever the union of the Church is restored—if ever the Union of the States is reëstablished, it can only be, in my humble judgment, by a return to the old and Scriptural doctrine, once held alike by the whole Christian community, that slavery, *in itself*, involves no sin. That the Gospel does not require its abolition, but commands the slave to be obedient to the master, and commands the master to treat the slave with justice and kindness. That, nevertheless, it is *expedient and desirable* that slavery should be done away, as soon as it can be peaceably, by common consent. That until it pleases Providence to open the way to this happy consummation, the rights of the South must be respected according to the Constitution. That meanwhile it is our religious as well as our civil duty to treat those rights with a fair and just allowance, and avoid all language and all acts which can only tend to excite ill-will, and provoke hostility and alienation.

These were the views of all our Christian teachers and all our eminent statesmen, during the first forty years of our existence under the Federal Constitution. They continued to be the views of almost all, for twenty years more. They were held by our own Church, without any known exceptions, up to October, 1859, when our General Convention met at Richmond under the Presidency of Bishop Meade, himself a slaveholder. As to my own position, I retain the same views still, with a stronger conviction than ever, because I re-

*This man bears no resentment"
— the hypocrite, with his clumsy
attempts at Sarcasm —*

gard the deplorable events of the last three years to be an awful
confirmation of their truth. And if you have ceased to hold them,
since you have not yet favored us with your reasons for the change,
the best hypothesis by which I can account for it, in all Christian
charity, must be derived from your favorite maxims of *political
expediency.*

And I do not mean to deny that this political expediency is a principle of vast practical importance, although, not being a politician, I
can not pretend to understand its mysteries. But I know enough
about it to be perfectly aware that it is like charity in one respect,
because it " covers a multitude of sins." In the tactics of the State,
the newspapers on all sides bear witness that political expediency
employs bribery, oppression, partiality, fraud, force, falsehood, and
calumny. Individual freedom lies down in willing slavery at the
feet of party dictation. Conscience shuts her eyes, and goes to sleep.
The idol of power is invoked to divide the spoils, and the mantle of
official honor is expected to hide the body of foulness and corruption.

And when this political expediency is admitted into the Church,
though its garment is changed and its aspect is modified, to suit its
new associations, yet its acting spirit is the same selfish love of dominion, working by the same unscrupulous management of party,
and descending to employ the same instruments of false accusation,
unfair influence, bitter writing, and abusive tongue. But in one important respect there is a difference. The politicians in the State
work in the name of the people, and are always aware that they
must be governed by the public will. The politicians in the Church
work in the name of Christ, while his precepts of truth and righteousness and brotherly love are ignored and forgotten.

And therefore it is that I have always been opposed to party spirit
in the Church, because it is one of the most dangerous foes to Christian peace and unity. Therefore it is, that in the Church I would
have no place granted to *political expediency.* I deny not that in
the affairs of worldly government, there must be parties. I deny
not that the object of those parties is often right and true. I deny
not that the leaders of party may be honest, patriotic men, who are
only bent on maintaining the real and abiding principles of the public welfare. Neither do I deny that in the Church the leaders of
party may be sincere and upright in their intentions, as I presume
yourself to be, however I may think that you are grievously misled

in your recent action. But I dread the introduction of political expediency into the Church, because I dread the effects of party spirit, which must tend, in times like these, to produce the bitterest strife and the most perilous contention. You have placed yourself at the head of a novel movement, which, if it succeeds, will probably divide the Church, as it has divided so many Christian denominations. You have not been content with an answer to my pamphlet, in your own name, which would have been perfectly allowable; but you have brought forward a small army of your clergy to unite in the condemnation of a brother bishop : and thus you have inaugurated a new party on the one side, which is directly calculated to produce the formation of a party on the other. The shape into which you have chosen to put the subject, therefore, is but too likely to inflame our whole communion. And if the mercy of God, and the good sense of the majority do not control the storm, the disunion of the Church may add another trophy to the victories of ultra-abolitionism, and another testimony to the dangers which lurk in the ecclesiastical adoption of POLITICAL EXPEDIENCY.

CHAPTER III.

RIGHT REVEREND BROTHER : I have already said that I do not know precisely where you stand, in this very serious controversy, but I have been favored with a number of anonymous pamphlets, some of which claim the authorship of ministers in the Protestant Episcopal Church, in which my *Bible View of Slavery* is attacked with abundance of zeal, not always accompanied either by Christian courtesy or knowledge. It may be well, therefore, to occupy a little space in the examination of some of their arguments, although it is not my custom to pay any attention to anonymous opponents. Through my whole course, I have made it a matter of principle to publish nothing without my name; because I have always held anonymous attacks on individuals to be a sort of stabbing in the dark, belonging, of right, to the art of assassination. The individual assailed has a just claim to know who it is that assails him. The public has a just claim to be informed who it is that undertakes the office of censor. And there is a lack of Christian manliness and honesty in this too common kind of cowardly warfare, which wears a mask when it strikes the blow, and dares to incur the responsibility of the act, while it shrinks from the responsibility of detection.

Passing over, as quite unworthy of notice, the bitterness and sarcasm of those writers, I shall state their arguments fairly and candidly, and give them what I deem a satisfactory reply.

The first point which I shall notice is the assault made against the application of the prophecy of Noah to the posterity of Ham, on the ground that it was limited to the offspring of Canaan, who were not negroes, and who are now *probably extinct*. Moreover, it is said that Canaan was not in Africa, and that the negroes are not descended from Canaan, but from Cush, on whom there is no curse recorded. And we have a quotation given from Josephus, to prove the correctness of these positions.

In reply to this, I have only to observe that none of these writers pretend to deny what I asserted, namely, that "the Almighty, fore-seeing the *total degradation* of the race, ordained them to servitude under the descendants of Shem and Japheth."

Now the whole question in dispute is, whether the Bible author-izes slavery *at all*, under any circumstances. The ultra-abolitionist denies it, insisting that slaveholding is a sin *per se*, and pronouncing absolute condemnation upon the act of keeping a man in bondage. I contend, on the contrary, that the Deity pronounced the curse of slavery on the posterity of Ham, "foreseeing their *total degrada-tion*," and whether that curse included the whole of his posterity or a portion of them only, does not make the slightest difference in the main fact, which remains uncontroverted, namely, that God *did* au-thorize slavery for a race, whom he foresaw would be *utterly de-graded.*

The old maxim is a sound one : " *Ubi eadem ratio, ibi eadem lex.*" Where there is the same *reason*, there is the same *law*. It is not and it can not be denied, that the reason why the Canaanites were to be enslaved, was the foresight of their *total degradation.* Let us look, therefore, at the condition of the African race in our own days, as it is described by Malte Brun, one of the most reliable of our modern geographers ; and then we shall be enabled to judge whether the same reason which justified the slavery of the one, does not equally justify the slavery of the other.

"The slave coast of Africa," saith this writer, " consists of several petty states, which are all under the despotic sway of the King of Dahomey. This barbarian monarch chooses to have women for his body-guard, and his palace is surrounded by one thousand of these Amazons, armed with javelins and muskets, from whom he selects his special military aids and messengers. His ministers, when they come into the royal presence, are obliged to leave their silk robes at the gate of the palace, and approach the throne, walking on all fours, and rolling their heads in the dust. The ferocity of this African des-pot almost surpasses conception. The road to his residence is strew-ed with human skulls, and the walls are adorned and almost covered with jaw-bones. On public occasions, the sable monarch walks in solemn pomp, over the bloody heads of vanquished princes, or dis-graced ministers. At the festivals of the tribes, to which all the people bring presents for the king, he drenches the tombs of his fore-fathers with human blood. Fifty dead bodies are thrown around the royal sepulchre, and fifty heads displayed on poles. The blood of these victims is presented to the king, who dips his fingers into it, and licks them. Human blood is mixed with clay, to build temples in honor of deceased monarchs. The royal widows kill one another, till it pleases the new sovereign to put an end to the slaughter. And the crowd assembled at their most joyous festivals applaud such scenes of horror, and delight in tearing the unhappy victims to pieces." *

The people, as might be expected, are sunk into the most degraded habits, in all the social relations of life, and especially in all their notions of religion. "They eat the carcass of the elephant," saith our author, "even when full of vermin. The musky eggs and flesh of the crocodile are welcome to their appetite. Monkeys are generally used for food. Animals found dead and putrid give no disgust, and at their greatest feasts, a roasted dog is counted a luxury. Their dwellings are rude huts, consisting of a few trunks of trees, covered with straw or palm leaves. Their furniture is usually confined to a few calabashes. The rich have some fire-arms, obtained from the Europeans; and the sovereigns, who adorn their residence with human skulls and jaw-bones, have stone-ware and carpets of English manufacture. But the mass look for nothing beyond the supply of the simplest wants of nature. Twenty days in the year are enough, in that luxuriant climate, for their labors in husbandry. Their clothing is woven by the women from wild cotton. And their time is given up, for the most part, to dancing at night to the sound of horns and drums, and their days to gaming, of which they are passionately fond. Polygamy is practiced to a greater degree than is found among any other people. As to their religion, it is the lowest kind of idolatry. They adore, and in time of difficulty consult, any object that strikes their fancy—a tree, a rock, a fish-bone, an egg, a horn, a date-stone, or a blade of grass. In Whidah, a serpent is regarded as the god of war, of trade, of agriculture, and of fertility. It is kept in a kind of temple, and attended by an order of priests. A company of young women are consecrated to it, whose business it is to please their deity with wanton dances, and a life of systematic licentiousness. In Benin, a lizard is the object of public worship, and a leopard in Dahomey."†

* Malte Brun's *System of Universal Geography.* Vol. ii. p. 77. Boston ed. of 1864.
† Ib. p. 88–9.

Of course, neither liberty nor social comfort can exist, where laws and manners so barbarous prevail. "*Two thirds* of the negro population," continues our author, "*lead lives of hereditary bondage in their own country*, and those who are free, are *liable to be reduced to slavery* at any moment, by the order of their despots. As an instance of the awful tyranny under which they groan, it is related that, on the death of Freempoong, king of the Akims, the people sacrificed his slaves upon his tomb, to the number of several thousands, together with his prime-minister, and three hundred and sixteen of his women. All these victims were buried alive, their bones having been previously broken. And for several days the crowd performed dances, accompanied with songs, round the spot, where these unfortunate beings suffered lingering and horrible agonies."*

Here, then, we have the best testimony, with which every subsequent writer agrees,† as to the awful debasement, the groveling idolatry, the flagitious immorality, the *total degradation* of the posterity of Ham, in the slave-region of Africa. And this testimony is given by the first geographer of the age, who was, himself, a friend to abolition. If my antagonists can show that the Canaanites were in a worse condition than this, I should like to see the evidence. In the Providence of God, the negro slavery of the South has been the means of saving millions of those poor creatures from the horrible state in which they must otherwise have lived and died. It has raised them on the scale of humanity, and brought them toward civilization under the light of religious truth, until a portion of them were enabled to establish, through Southern direction, the Colony of Liberia, and we have reason to hope that many of the rest may be qualified to emulate them, in due time. If any man can seriously contemplate the awful debasement of the native Africans, and candidly compare it with the present condition of the Southern slaves, and then *denounce, as a sin*, the means which divine Providence has chosen to save them from their former state of wretched barbarism, and deliberately prefer that they should rather have remained in that dark sink of heathen cruelty and abomination, in honor of PHILANTHROPY, I can only say that I am at a loss whether I should be most astonished at the waywardness of his heart, or the blindness of his understanding.

But my censors think that they have settled the whole application

---

* Malte Brun's *System of Universal Geography.* Vol. ii, p. 90.
† See the Appendix, for some later authorities.

of Noah's prophecy by confining it to the posterity of Canaan, and
exclaim against my supposed error in extending it to the posterity of
Ham, or the African generally.   Let me therefore recall to the memory
of my antagonists the language of Bishop Newton, whose well-known
work upon the Prophecies is on the list selected by the Church for
students in Theology, and must therefore, as I suppose, have been
once regarded, by some of themselves, as a safe guide of ministerial
opinion,

" Ham, the father of Canaan, is mentioned," saith Bishop Newton,
" in the preceding part of the story, and how then came the person
of a sudden to be changed into *Canaan ?* The Arabic version in
these three verses hath *the father of Canaan*, instead of *Canaan*.
Some copies of the Septuagint likewise have *Ham* instead of *Canaan*,
as if Canaan was a corruption of the text. Vatablus and others, by
Canaan, understand *the father of Canaan*, which was expressed
twice before. And if we regard the metre, this line, *Cursed be Canaan*, is much shorter than the rest, as if something was deficient.
May we not suppose, therefore, that the copyist, by mistake, wrote
only *Canaan* instead of *Ham the father of Canaan*, and that the
whole passage was originally thus ? 'Cursed be Ham the father of
Canaan, a servant of servants shall he be to his brethren.'

" By this reading," continues Bishop Newton, " all the three sons of
Noah are included in the prophecy, whereas otherwise Ham, who was
the offender, is excluded, or is only punished in one of his children.
Ham is characterized as the father of Canaan particularly, for the
greater encouragement of the Israelites, who were going to invade the
land of Canaan ; and when it is said, 'Cursed be Ham, the father of
Canaan, a servant of servants shall he be to his brethren,' it is im-
plied that his *whole race* was devoted to servitude, but particularly
the Canaanites. Not that this was to take effect immediately, but
was to be fulfilled in process of time, when they should forfeit their
liberties by their wickedness. Ham at first subdued some of the
posterity of Shem, as Canaan sometimes conquered Japheth. The
Carthaginians, who were originally Canaanites, did particularly so in
Spain and Italy ; but in time they were to be subdued, and to become
servants to them and Japheth ; and the change of their fortune from
good to ·bad would render the curse still more visible. Egypt was
the land of Ham, as it is often called in Scripture, and for many years
it was a great and flourishing kingdom ; but it was subdued by the

Persians, who descended from Shem, and afterward by the Grecians, who descended from Japheth, and from that time to this, it hath constantly been subject to some or other of the posterity of Shem or Japheth.   The whole continent of Africa was peopled principally by the children of Ham, and for how many ages have the better parts of that country lain under the dominion of the Romans, and then of the Saracens, and now of the Turks ?   In what wickedness, ignorance, barbarity, slavery, and misery, lie most of the inhabitants ?   In fine," concludes our author, "nothing can be more complete than the execution of the sentence upon *Ham* as well as upon *Canaan*."*

These extracts from the work which, amongst Episcopalians, has been held as the best authority, may suffice, I trust, as a satisfactory answer to my adversaries.   As to the notion that the race of Canaan is probably extinct, they have only stumbled a second time against Bishop Newton.   "The Greeks and Romans," saith this author expressly, "who were the descendants of Japheth, not only subdued Syria and Palestine, but also pursued and conquered *such of the Canaanites as were anywhere remaining*, as, for instance, the *Tyrians and Carthaginians*, the former of whom were ruined by Alexander and the Grecians, and the latter by Scipio and the Romans.   And ever since, the *miserable remainder of this people* have been slaves to a foreign yoke, first to the Saracens, who descended from Shem, and afterwards to the Turks, who descended from Japheth, and *they groan under their dominion at this day*."†

But some of these modern theologians have discovered that Ham was blessed along with the other sons of Noah, because it is said (Gen. 9 : 1) that " God blessed Noah and his sons," while, in the twenty-fifth verse, it is said that Noah cursed Canaan, not *Ham ;* "*God's blessing remaining untouched*.   So reads the record."

Truly this is a precious piece of Biblical criticism.   God " blessed Noah and his sons" when they issued from the ark ; but this was several years before Canaan was born, for it is unquestionable that only eight souls were saved from the deluge—Noah, his three sons, and their wives.   And Canaan was the fourth son of Ham, because Cush, Mizraim, and Phut had preceded him.   If then, during those years, Ham became disrespectful and irreverent toward his father,

* *Dissertation on the Prophecies*, by Bishop Newton.   Vol. i. pp.32–4.   Phil. ed. 1818.
         † Ib. p. 31.

) Here we see that Josephus was included in the curse,— did he to be called upon as a witness against the Canaanites

and trained his children in a course which, of all others, is most hateful in the eyes of that God, who commands that HONOR must be given to the father and the mother, on what principle is the Almighty to be restrained from predicting a curse to his posterity, instead of the original blessing? Were not Adam and Eve blessed in their state of innocence, and yet did not a curse follow their disobedience? Were not the Israelites blessed repeatedly, and yet does not the prophet Malachi say: "Ye are cursed with a curse, even this whole nation"? Does not every tyro in Christianity know that blessings and curses are conditional, so that the commission of sin can change the blessing to a curse, and the repentance and reformation of the sinner can change the curse into a blessing? If these anonymous clergymen did not know all this—if they were capable of preaching to their people that a blessing once given must remain "untouched," even when a malediction is deserved by subsequent transgression, I should be alarmed for their own state of mind, and sorry for their congregations. But this is impossible. Such doctrine is only admissible on special occasions and for a special purpose; as, for example, in an assault upon my humble work, under the new stimulus of *political expediency.*

As to the quotation from Josephus, it does not agree with the statement of my antagonists, but rather with that of Bishop Newton. "Noah is described," saith this historian, "as praying for prosperity to his other sons, *but for Ham, he did not curse him by reason of his nearness of blood, but cursed his posterity*, and when the rest of them *escaped* that curse, God inflicted it on Canaan." Here Josephus plainly asserts that although Noah did not curse Ham personally by reason of his nearness of blood, yet he *did curse his posterity*. True, he adds that "when the rest of them *escaped* that curse, God inflicted it on Canaan," evidently alluding to the fact that although Egypt, which was preëminently called the land of Ham, had become great, and thus seemed to have escaped the curse for a considerable period, yet it still continued to operate in the line of Canaan. Josephus was born A.D. 37, and if he had lived in our day, he would have seen abundant proof that the *rest* of Ham's posterity had *not escaped* at all, but had been sunk for centuries into the lowest state of social and moral degradation.

For myself, however, the question has little interest, because I am perfectly satisfied that the posterity of Canaan still exists in Africa, to a vast extent; and that the curse pronounced by Noah was not fulfilled, nor intended to be fulfilled, by the conquest of the Israelites over the seven nations which occupied the promised land. Those seven nations were not the whole of Canaan's progeny, for we read of his having *eleven* sons, whose families were "spread abroad." (Gen. 10 : 18.) Nor have we any authority for supposing that the whole of even those seven tribes abandoned Africa for the land of Canaan, nor for doubting that large numbers returned from Canaan to Africa, in order to escape the conquering sword of Joshua. A part only of Canaan's posterity was doomed to be exterminated by the divine command, while a far greater portion were to be slaves according to the prophecy. This will be made evident, however, in a future chapter

4

+ "the servant" is the servant of Sin and man as a sinner is a slave or in "bondage." but his master is not another man who may also be in bondage; but the true master is truth and virtue

CHAPTER IV.

Right Reverend Brother: Proceeding to the cases of Abraham, Hagar, and Ishmael, my anonymous assailants do not pretend to deny that Abraham had slaves, but require me to show that the Deity sanctions the *kind of slavery* in which negroes are held at the South, and boldly assert that the case of Ishmael proves the children of a slave to be free, and their mother, under the circumstances of Hagar, to be entitled to an *open acknowledgment as the wife of the master*.

In my pamphlet I defined slavery to be "servitude for life, descending to the offspring." This constitutes the *relation* between the master and the slave, and must be considered independently of the *mode of treatment*, which may be good, bad, or indifferent, according to circumstances. It is the constant error of the ultra-abolitionist to confound these things together, like the *Free-love* disorganizers, who rake up all the cases of tyrannical abuse in the relation of married life, and then modestly recommend mankind to abolish matrimony on account of its liability to those abuses. But I have nothing to do, in my argument, with the abuses of slavery. I condemn them as heartily as any one. What I insist on is that the Almighty sanctions the *relation* of master and slave. And I am equally ready to insist that while, in the language of the Apostle, the slave is commanded to "obey his master," the master is also commanded to "render to the slave what is just and equal, remembering that he also has a Master in heaven."

"The Hebrews," saith Cruden in his Concordance, a work in universal use by all Protestant clergymen, "had two sorts of servants or slaves. Some were *strangers*, either bought or taken in the wars, and their masters *kept them, exchanged them, sold them, or disposed of them as their own goods*. (Lev. 25, 44, 45, etc.) The others were Hebrew slaves, who being poor, sold themselves or were sold to pay their debts, or were delivered up for slaves by their parents, in case of necessity. This sort of Hebrew slaves continued in slavery but *[handwritten annotation at top: "Six years — corresponding to the number of the days (Symbolical) of the creation (of the moral man"]*

six years, then they might return to liberty again, and their masters could not retain them against their wills. If they would continue voluntarily with their masters, they were brought before the judges; there they made a declaration that for this time they disclaimed the privilege of the law, had their ears bored with an awl by applying to the door-posts of their master, and after that they had no longer any power of recovering their liberty except at the next year of Jubilee."

These were the only *kinds of slavery* known to the people of Israel, and it can not be pretended that Hagar was a slave in any other sense than that of a " stranger," because she was an Egyptian, one of the race of Ham. But it may be well to quote the whole of the Scriptural narrative, for my reader's satisfaction: "And Sarai said unto Abram, Behold now, the Lord hath restrained me from bearing: I pray thee go in unto my maid, it may be that *I may obtain children by her.* And Abram hearkened to the voice of Sarai." (Gen. 16 : 2.) Here it is perfectly manifest that the offspring was intended to be accounted as Sarai's, and not Hagar's, the right of the mistress over the slave continuing precisely as it was before. It appears, however, that Hagar became proud and insolent under her new dignity. And then we read that " Abram said unto Sarai, Behold, *thy maid is in thy hand, do to her as it pleaseth thee.* And when Sarai *dealt hardly* with her, she fled from her face. And the angel of the Lord found her by a fountain of water in the wilderness—and he said, Hagar, *Sarai's maid*, Whence comest thou, and whither wilt thou go? And she said, I flee from the face of *my mistress* Sarai. And the angel of the Lord said unto her, *Return to thy mistress, and submit thyself under her hands.*" (Gen. 16 : 6–9.)

We read next that after Hagar had borne Ishmael, God changed the name of Abram to Abraham, and the name of Sarai to Sarah, promising that she should bear Isaac, with whose seed the covenant of grace should be made to all generations. Isaac was born accordingly, and " Abraham made a great feast the same day that Isaac was weaned. And Sarah saw the son of Hagar the Egyptian, which she had borne unto Abraham, mocking. Wherefore she said unto Abraham, Cast out *this bondwoman and her son*, for the son of this bondwoman shall not be heir with my son, even with Isaac. And the thing was very grievous in Abraham's sight, because of his son. And God said unto Abraham, Let it not be grievous in thy sight, because of the lad, and because of thy *bondwoman :* in all that Sarah

Vide the comment of St. Paul
Gal. 4. 21 – 30. "These things
are an 'allegory'"

hath said, hearken unto her voice; for in Isaac shall thy seed be called. And also of the son of the *bondwoman* will I make a nation, because he is thy seed. And Abraham rose up early in the morning, and took bread and a bottle of water, and gave it unto Hagar, and the child, and sent her away, and she departed." (Gen. 21: 8–14.)

Here is the whole of the sacred narrative, and it is plain that Hagar, from first to last, continued to be a slave, until she was *sent away*, or manumitted. The word "wife" is indeed applied to her *once*, where it is said that Sarai gave her to her husband *to be his wife*," (Gen. 16 : 3 ;) but everywhere else she is called a *bondwoman*, and specially is she so called by the angel, and by the Lord. It is not true, therefore, as my learned antagonists assert, that she was ever " openly acknowledged" as the wife of Abraham. She was only a concubine, and that merely by the will of her mistress. The Deity everywhere limits the name of wife to Sarah. " Sarah, *thy wife*," and " Hagar thy *bondwoman*," are the phrases constantly employed. Neither is it true that this example proves the right of the children of slaves to be free; because it is evident that Sarah did as she pleased both with the mother and the son, expressly declaring, from the first, that Ishmael should be accounted as her own, because she was barren, yet finally casting him off, along with Hagar, when she saw that the envious feelings of the boy were likely to endanger the peace of the family.

The whole of this sacred narrative is a peculiar and exceptional case, having no point which is fairly applicable to the question under consideration save the *principle* of slavery, for which I quoted it. The conduct of Sarah in giving her bondmaid to Abraham, in order that the offspring might be counted for her own, was afterwards imitated by Rachel and Leah, the wives of Jacob. But that has no connection with the subject before us. The only facts which *do* bear upon the controversy are these: that Hagar was insubordinate to her mistress, that Sarah *dealt hardly* with her bondwoman, that Hagar ran away, and that the angel reproved her, and commanded that she should "*return to her mistress and submit herself to her hands*." We see, therefore, that even under circumstances where Hagar seemed entitled to more than ordinary indulgence, the *rights* of the mistress and the *submission* of the slave are recognized and affirmed by " the angel of the Lord." Sarah is not rebuked for her

If the plain statement justifies
slavery – the equally plain statements justifies other matters.

hard dealing with the bondmaid, which was probably no more than her disobedient demeanor had deserved; but Hagar is *sent back again*, with a wholesome exhortation to keep her proper place, and do her duty.

Some of my sagacious adversaries inform their readers that "Rebekah called Abraham's servant, 'my lord.' She watered his camels. And Bethuel received that 'lord' and the men that were with him, into his house, and treated them as honored visitors at his own table." Here, again, we have that constant absurdity which confounds the occasional *treatment* of a slave with the *relation itself.* Suppose the slaves of Abraham were received with generous hospitality by the family, to whom they were sent, loaded with rich presents, to propose a marriage for their master. What then? Did that change their relation as slaves to Abraham? Did it affect their bounden duty of submission to Isaac and Rebekah, after they returned home? Or is it an example which my learned antagonists are themselves ready to follow even with regard to the free negroes of their own city? Will they call them "lords," water their horses, and admit them as "honored visitors" at their table? Such puerile stuff as this may be called 'argument' by these writers, but how any man of common sense can so regard it, is a mystery quite too deep for my humble comprehension.

CHAPTER V.

RIGHT REVEREND BROTHER: One of the most virulent among my adversaries, who calls himself a Presbyter of the Church, endeavoring to evade the argument which I derived from the Ten Commandments, is compelled to admit that the fourth and the tenth of these Commandments " do, undoubtedly, apply to voluntary service, and *also to that kind of servitude authorized by the Jewish law*."

He then proceeds to say that if the Ten Commandments sanction the slavery of negroes, they must also sanction the slavery of the white race, both Jew and Gentile. Because "justice holds an even balance, and God hath made of one blood all the nations of men."

That the condition of slavery was not confined to the negro, but was extended to all the various races of mankind, is a fact to which the history of the world bears ample testimony, as we shall see by and by. The question in controversy, however, is whether the relation of master and slave involves sin ; and the admission of the author that it was sanctioned by two of the Ten Commandments, ought, of itself, to have been decisive to any believer in the Word of God. Yet he pays no regard whatever to this divine authority, preferring to place his faith in the assumed *equality* of men, proclaimed by the Declaration of Independence. He does not, indeed, attempt to meet the argument on the subject, but contents himself, like the other writers and orators of his school, with repeating the language of the Declaration, as if *that* was conclusive and incontrovertible. But however such arguers may talk or write, they know and feel that there are enormous distinctions in the conditions of the human race, which they can not account for, save by referring them to the will of the All-wise and Supreme Disposer. It is not in their power to equalize them even in a single village. And if, in the order of divine Providence, they have themselves been placed in any of the higher ranks, either by education, property, or social position, I run no risk in saying that they are quite as tenacious of their privileges, and quite as averse to see them invaded by their inferiors, as any of those who maintain the lawfulness of the Southern institution.

This writer, however, does not pretend to deny the Mosaic law which I adduced, proving that the Almighty expressly directed his chosen people to buy slaves of the heathen nations round them, as well as of the alien races that dwelt within the coasts of Israel.

But he objects, first, That this relates only to Jewish servants, and not to heathen slavery.

Secondly. That this law was given to the Jews, and not to us Gentiles.

And, thirdly, That the relation of master and slave is equivalent to man-stealing.

Now this is merely a poor attempt to evade the real question, namely, whether slavery, in the ordinary legal sense of *servitude for life descending to the offspring*, involves a sin *per se*. The ultra-abolitionist asserts that it *does*, and on that ground, insists on the immediate emancipation of all the Southern slaves, and abuses the Constitution as a *covenant with death and an agreement with hell*. I insist, on the contrary, that the relation of master and slave, when authorized by the law of the land, involves no sin, but is justified by the Word of God, as well as by the Constitution. I appeal to the Old Testament for the proof, and I am told that this law was given to the Jews, and not to the Gentiles, as if the Almighty authorized the Jew to do what would be a sin in the Christian ! And this is done by a writer who calls himself a clergyman of the Protestant Episcopal Church, and who, therefore, has solemnly assented to the thirty-nine articles, in the seventh of which we read that " The Old Testament is *not contrary to the New*—that although the Law given from God by Moses, as touching ceremonies and rights, do not bind Christian men, nor the civil precepts thereof ought of necessity to be received in any commonwealth, yet notwithstanding, *no Christian man whatever is free from the obedience of the commandments which are called moral.*" He had been compelled to admit that the fourth and the tenth commandments of the Decalogue did " undoubtedly apply to that kind of servitude authorized by the Jewish law." He can not deny that the Ten Commandments are, preëminently, regarded by all men as " the moral law." And yet, in the face of the

Article, and of his own admission, he insists that this part of the law does not concern Christians !

But he contends that the Mosaic system did not refer to *heathen slavery*. And here I would ask, What does he mean by *heathen* slavery ? Is it that the *masters* were heathen, or that the *slaves* must be taken from a heathen race ? If the term *heathen* refers to the masters, there is an end at once to his whole objection ; because the masters of our Southern slaves are not heathen, but as good Christians, in general, as any of their defamers. If the word *heathen* refers to the *race* which the Jews were allowed to hold in bondage, then the Jewish system *was heathen slavery*, that is, the slavery of a *heathen race ;* and such precisely was the fact with respect to the negro race, imported from Africa.

His third objection is, that " the Jewish law forbids ' *man-stealing*,' which is part and parcel of the heathen code of slavery." " He that stealeth a man and selleth him, or if he be found in his hand, he shall surely be put to death." And here I can not but admire the beautiful consistency which, just after telling us that the law was given to the Jews, and not to us Gentiles, goes back to that law most gladly, when he thinks it in his favor. But he ought to have quoted it as it stands in the very place to which he refers. Deut. 24 : 7. " If a man be found stealing *any of his brethren of the children of Israel*, and maketh merchandise of him, or selleth him, . . then that thief shall die." My assailant omits, in this verse, the whole limitation which gave the law its proper character. For the Almighty had repeatedly commanded that the children of Israel should not be sold as bondsmen. "Both thy bondmen and bondmaids which thou shalt have," saith the Deity, " shall be of the heathen that are round about you, of them shall ye buy bondmen and bondmaids. Moreover of the children of the strangers that do sojourn among you, of them shall ye buy, and of their families that are with you *which they begat in your land*, and they shall be your possession. And ye shall take them for an inheritance *for your children after you*, to inherit them for a possession. They shall be your *bondmen forever*, but over your brethren the children of Israel, ye shall not rule over one another with rigor. *For unto me the children of Israel are servants* whom I brought out of the land of Egypt. I am the Lord your God." (Lev. 25 : 40–46, with v. 55.)

The law is here given, therefore, with the reason of it. If the

Israelite were stolen, the man that stole him was a thief, because he stole the *property of the Lord*, who counted all the Israelites as *his bondservants*. But this only applied to the children of Israel. There is another application of the principle, which the ultra-abolitionist does not consider, as when a slave, lawfully belonging to a Jewish or a Christian master, is stolen from that master. For it is impossible to *steal* that which has no owner. The very crime of stealing consists in a *felonious taking* of the lawful property of another. And it is not the subsequent *use* of that property, but the felonious *taking* which constitutes the theft, for a man may be quite as much a thief by taking from the owner what he can not use himself, as if he intended to make a profit of it. On this plain ground of law and justice, it is worthy of very serious reflection whether the abolitionist, who secretly entices the negro slave to abscond from his lawful owner, and thus *deprives the master of his legal property*, is not, on principle, liable to this very charge of *man-stealing ;* and therefore subject to the condemnation of the divine law.

The next point made by this writer is derived from the Mosaic precept which commanded that "a slave, escaping from a *heathen* master, and coming under the authority of the Jewish law, should should not be delivered up, but should be free in Israel." And here my antagonist thanks me for having said that "this evidently must be referred to the case of a slave who had escaped from a *foreign* heathen master, and can not, with any sound reason, be applied to the slaves of the Israelites themselves."

It is certainly amusing to read the conclusion which my ingenious critic draws from this statement, viz. : "That by the Jewish law no person could be held in heathen slavery, and therefore *if that law was in force at the South, it would free every slave by an authority higher than that of man.*"

I shall not undertake to decide whether the author of this sentence thought that his readers had lost their understanding, or that the effervescence of his zeal had deprived him of his own. But in all the nonsense that I have read upon the subject, I have never seen a more puerile absurdity. The law in question is admitted by himself, and rightly admitted, to apply to a slave who had escaped into Judea "from a *foreign heathen master*," so that "it can not with any sound reason, be applied to the slaves of the Israelites themselves." If,

4*

then, it could not be applied to the slaves belonging to the Jews,
how, in the name of common-sense, can it be applied to the slaves
belonging to the Southerners?

His last effort, however, is to get rid of the whole testimony of the
Mosaic law, by the bold declaration that " between the Hebrew bondman and the Southern slave there is *no point of resemblance,* so that
we can not use the first to justify the second," and he quotes from
the respectable Jewish Rabbi, Dr. Raphall, as follows, viz. : " The
slave under the Jewish law, though a Gentile or a heathen, is a
person in whom the dignity of human nature is to be respected; *he
has rights.* Whereas the heathen view of slavery which prevailed
at Rome, and which, I am sorry to say, is adopted at the South, re-
duces the slave to a thing, (a chattel,) and *a thing can have no
rights.*"

Now here, while I readily admit that the heathen law of slavery
which prevailed at Rome, differed in some particulars from the Jewish system, yet I shall prove that the slave in the South is more
nearly like the Jewish slave than like the Roman. I shall also show
that, granting the Southern slave to be in some respects a *chattel,*
the Jewish slave was also a chattel in the same respects, precisely.
But I shall contend that in every other aspect of his condition, the
Southern slave is considered *a person :* for his life is protected, his
maintenance is secured, and he is the subject of *lawful manumission,*
from which has proceeded a result which neither Judea nor Rome
ever accomplished, in the new State of Liberia.

1. The Jewish law confined slavery to the races of the heathen.
And in this it resembled the Roman law, by comprehending all the
nations "round about" Judea, without reference to their barbarism,
or savage degradation. It was sufficient that they were "strangers"
to the Jewish stock, and I have proved, by the express quotation
from Leviticus, (ch. 25 : 40, etc.,) that the rule extended to the families of strangers, resident among them, and "begotten in the land."

Such, precisely, is the Southern system, confining slavery to a
heathen race, but *limiting* it, as the Jewish law did *not,* to the posterity of Ham, the negroes who, in their native state, are confessedly
the most degraded and brutalized people known to history. In this
respect, therefore, the slave-system of the South has the advantage
over the law of Moses.

2. The Jewish institution was like the Roman law, in regarding

the slaves as *chattel property*, because, in the words of Cruden, already quoted, "they were either *bought* or *taken in the wars*, and their masters kept them, exchanged them, *sold them*, or disposed of them *as their own goods*." That they were liable to be beaten at the master's pleasure, short of maiming or death, is perfectly proved in Exod. 21 : 20-1, and the only difference between the Jewish and the Roman law in this respect was, that prior to the reign of the Emperor Antonine, the Roman master was allowed to kill his slave. The Jewish master, on the contrary, was punished if the slave died under his correction, but suffered no penalty unless the death occurred within "a day or two" after the blows had been given ; for if the slave died on the third day, the loss of his labor and of the "money" which he had cost, was held to be a sufficient infliction.

Such, substantially, is the *chattel property* of slavery in the South. The slaves may be kept, bought and sold, or punished at the master's pleasure, provided death does not ensue. In one respect, however, the Jewish law had an advantage by enacting, that if the master struck out the eye or the tooth of his slave, he should let him go free. But this is quite balanced by the superior guardianship of life according to the Southern law, which does not measure the responsibility of the master by the fact that the slave survived his punishment for "a day or two," but holds him liable for causing the death of his slave, after any interval.

3. But although the slave was *chattel property*, alike by the Jewish, the Roman, and the Southern law, in which point there is no real difference between them, yet I insist upon the unquestionable fact, that in all of them "the dignity of human nature was respected," whatever may be said or thought by any man to the contrary. Because, in all of them, the slave was acknowledged to be *a man*, to be maintained and supported, with his family, to have access to religious privileges, and to be *set free by manumission*, if the master were willing. These are privileges which belong to PERSONS, not *things*. And therefore the notion that because slaves are *chattel property*, they are regarded as *nothing else but chattels*, is a manifest error. The truth is, that they partake of both these characters. As CHATTELS, they can be bought and sold. As PERSONS, they must be maintained and supported, in sickness and in old age, as well as in their helpless infancy. By the Jewish and the Southern law their lives are protected. By all the laws of Judea, Rome, and the South, they

are entitled to a share in religious privileges, and they may be manumitted, or set free, if the master thought them worthy.

4. With respect to the marriages of slaves, the law of the South is
silent. So was the ancient law of Rome. But so, likewise, is the
law of Moses. There is, however, one remarkable passage, already
quoted in the *Bible View*, which bears, on this subject, a very plain
testimony : "If thou buy a Hebrew servant, six years shall he serve,
and in the seventh year he shall go out free, for nothing. If he came
in by himself, he shall go out by himself. If he were married, then
his wife shall go with him. *If his master have given him a wife,
and she have borne him sons or daughters, the wife and the children
shall be her master's, and he shall go out by himself.*" (Exod.
21 : 2–4.) This is a plain proof that, *in the case of slaves*, marriage was
not allowed to interfere with the master's right of property. The
husband had no remedy allowed, except to become himself a slave
for life, if he wished to remain with his wife and children.

There is no doubt that this feature in the Southern institution is
liable to much occasional hardship, and it is greatly to be desired
that it might be regulated, as I presume it will be, in time, by a better system. But meanwhile we have no right to censure it as inexcusable, so long as the same difficulty presents itself in the Mosaic
system. Nor ought we to doubt that the Christian slaveholders and
clergy of the South do all that they can to bring the marriages of the
slaves under the rule of religious obligation ; and that the negro race
there are elevated in their marriage state immeasurably above the
polygamy and licentiousness which prevail in their parent land of
Africa.

5. The last topic which I shall notice here, respects the exclusion
of slaves from giving testimony before a court of justice, which has
been the subject of an immense amount of objurgation from the eloquent adversaries of the Southern system. Of course it is allowed
that the same rule is found in the Roman law, and in the law of
every other land in which slavery existed, which comprehended, until lately, the whole civilized world. But as the Mosaic system lays
down no special rule upon the subject, I shall have recourse to the
historian Josephus, to whom one of my antagonists displayed so
much partiality, on a different subject, that he tried to make him
contradict the statements of Bishop Newton, though happily in vain.

Here, then, is the passage, taken from the same translation, vol. 1,

p. 264 : "Let not a single witness be credited, but three, or two at the least, and those such whose testimony is confirmed by their good lives. But let not the testimony of women be admitted, on account of the levity and boldness of their sex. *Nor let servants be admitted to give testimony*, on account of the ignobility of their soul ; since it is probable that they may not speak truth, either out of the hope of gain, or fear of punishment."

Thus we have, again, another instance of agreement with the Jewish law of slavery. And on the whole survey the reader can readily perceive how much confidence may be placed in the reckless assertion of my adversaries, that "*between the Hebrew bondman and the Southern slave,* THERE IS NO POINT OF RESEMBLANCE."

CHAPTER VI.

RIGHT REVEREND BROTHER : Having gone through the principal objections of the anonymous pamphleteers, which relate to the Mosaic law of slavery, the next question presented is the all-important one, viz. What aspect did slavery bear in the judgment of the Church of Christ ? I have promised you, in my reply to your protest and denunciation, that I should demonstrate the "truth wherein I stand," by proving from the most unquestionable authorities, that "slaves and slaveholders were in the Church from the beginning—that slavery was held to be consistent with Christian principle by fathers and councils, and by all Protestant divines and commentators, up to the very close of the last century, and that this fact was universal among all churches and sects throughout the Christian world." This promise I shall now proceed to fulfil, and then I shall notice the few points which may have been left untouched in the course of the argument.

The system of slavery, according to the Old Testament, disappeared of course, when Israel ceased to be a nation ; which event took place at the destruction of Jerusalem by the army of Titus, A.D. 76, although I presume that the Jews, dispersed throughout the world, observe the law of Moses so far as circumstances render it practicable, to this day. The Roman code, therefore, is that which we have now to consider, because it was under this code that the Gentile churches were all gathered by the Apostles : and the authoritative repository of it is well known to be the civil law, as laid down in the " Institutes " of the Christian Emperor, Justinian. To this, then, as the foundation of my argument, I shall first direct your attention, and afterwards to the fathers, councils, historians, lawyers, divines, and commentators. And I shall prove from the whole, that Christianity never undertook to *abolish* slavery, even when it extended over all races and all varieties of men—that religion operated to *ameliorate*, but not to do it away—that its extinction in Europe was not the result of any direct

So then — the Bishop peers atheist above christianity in the work of humanity —

assault, but a gradual dying out through the changes of society—that the first positive attack upon it was not from the Church, nor from Christians, but from the Atheists of the French Revolution; and that it was never supposed to be a *sin* to hold a slave, where the laws of the country authorized it, until our own age assumed the novel work of ultra-abolitionism.

You must be prepared, therefore, for a large amount of testimony. And if *you* can no longer do me that justice, my other readers, I trust, will bear in mind that I undertake the task in defense of the Bible, in defense of the Church through all former times, in defense of their own forefathers, in defense of the heroes and sages of the Revolution, in defense of the Constitution, and in defense of what I believe to be a most important truth for the future welfare of our country. There is this difference, however, between my publications in 1850 and 1857 and my present labor; viz., that *then* I wrote as a volunteer, foreseeing the approaching danger; but *now* I write under the new compulsion of self-defense, against the gross and insulting denunciation of my own brethren.

The evidence which I shall adduce is gathered from many sources, and it will be found entire in the original extracts which are arranged in the Appendix. The substance will be stated in my argument, but all who desire to see the very words of my authorities can satisfy themselves by turning to the notes, which are regularly numbered, and occasionally accompanied by explanatory observations.

Commencing, according to the order prescribed, with the testimony of that most celebrated code of civil law, which bears the name of the Institutes of Justinian, we find the slave system largely set forth in the very commencement, under the title of THE RIGHTS OF PERSONS. And I pray you to mark this title, because it proves that this much-abused code regarded slaves as *persons* and not as *things*.

"The chief division in the rights of persons," saith this code, " is this: that all men are either free or slaves. Liberty is the natural faculty of him who does as he pleases, unless when forbidden by force or by law. But slavery is the constitution of the law of nations, by which the individual, contrary to nature, is subject to the mastery of another. Slaves are called (in Latin) *servi*, from *servare*, (to save,) because the generals were accustomed to sell their captives instead of killing them, and so saved them. They are also called *mancipia*, because they were *manu capti*, taken by hand from the enemy."

"Slaves are either born in that condition, or they are made so. They are born slaves from our bond-maids. They are made slaves either by the law of nations, (*Jure gentium*,) that is, by captivity, or by the civil law, as when a freeman of twenty years allows himself to be sold, in order to share in the price. In the condition of slaves there is no difference ; in that of freemen there are many differences, for they are either free by birth or freed from slavery." (3)

"Those are freedmen who are manumitted from lawful slavery. Which thing (manumission) takes its origin *from the law of nations.* For by the LAW OF NATURE all were born free, and *there could be no manumission when slavery was unknown.* But after slavery became established by the *law of nations*, the benefits of manumission followed. Hence, by the law of nations there are three kinds of men— the freemen, the slaves, and the freedmen, or those who have been manumitted from slavery. And manumission may be granted in many ways, either by the sacred canons in the holy churches, or by letter or by will," etc. (4)

"Slaves are in the power of their masters by *the law of nations.* For in almost all nations the power of life and death was exercised by the masters over their slaves, and whatsoever was acquired by the slave belonged to the master. But at this time, no men under our government are allowed to rage against their slaves without restriction. For, by the edict of the Emperor Antonine, whoever, without cause, should kill his own slave, is to be punished no less than if he had killed the slave of a stranger. And the same Antonine also decreed that if the slave were treated with intolerable cruelty by his master, he should be sold for a just price to another, and the master should receive the money." (5)

"By the law of nations, those things which we take from an enemy become ours. And therefore freemen are reduced to slavery, who, nevertheless, if they escape from our power and return to their own people, are restored to their first condition." (6)

"Slaves are not entitled to maintain an action in their own persons, but their masters may maintain it, in case of any atrocious injury, as if a stranger should beat a slave with great severity, his master may have an action. But if any one reviles a slave or only strikes him with his fist, the master can have no action." (7)

"We utterly prohibit slaves to be admitted among the clergy, even if their masters consent and desire it, because they may first set them free, and thus open to them the honors of the ministry, if they will." (8)

"If a slave, with the knowledge of his master, who does not oppose it, be ordained by the bishop, he shall be held as one born free. But if he be ordained without the knowledge of his master, it shall be lawful for the master, within one year, to prove that he was his slave, and to claim him again as such. And if a slave, whether with or without the knowledge of his master, being made free by ordination, shall leave his ecclesiastical ministry and return to a secular life, he may be delivered again in slavery to his former master." (9)

"With respect to fugitive slaves entering monastic life, it was decreed that if within three years it became manifest that any such were a fugitive, he should be stripped of his monastic habit, and his master might reclaim him; but that if he were not detected until three years had expired, even though he were afterwards discovered, he should be free against his master's will. But since we see that many slaves have taken advantage of this law to flee from their masters, and abuse the honest monastic profession by making it a cloak for their malice, we command that however long a slave who has thus become a monk may lie hid, if at any time his master discover him, he shall be deprived of the habit which he assumed with an evil purpose, and be subject again to his master's power." (10)

"Concerning those slaves who, without their master's knowledge, have ascended to the honors of the Episcopal office, we decree that they shall be degraded and returned to their servile condition." (11)

"As the giving of testimony is an act of great importance, it should not be allowed to every one, but only to those who are free from ignominy. But the laws formerly admitted slaves to testify in certain cases. Now, however, the law of the new Constitution must be enforced, that in all cases none but free men shall be allowed to give testimony." (12)

"If any one is so demented as to exchange liberty for slavery by selling himself, the contract shall not be binding, but on the contrary shall be annulled, and both he who is the betrayer of his own liberty, and he who was a party to the crime, shall be chastised by scourging, and the intended slave shall remain a freeman." (13.)

These copious extracts from the civil law show distinctly the general aspect of slavery as it existed in quiet union with the primitive Church, saving only the last four clauses, which were not introduced until the ninth century, under the Emperor Leo. And I ask your candid attention to a few remarks, which may aid in the proper application of this highest kind of testimony, to the points under consideration.

First, then, we see the law of the Roman empire recognizing and regulating slavery in the reign of the Christian Emperor Justinian, more than two hundred years after the Gospel had become established. For you know that the Emperor Constantine was converted to the faith in A.D. 312, and the famous code which was compiled by Tribonian and his colleagues by order of Justinian, and which bears his name, was not published until the middle of the sixth century.

Secondly, we see that slavery is here said to subsist by the LAW OF NATIONS—not by local law, confined to this or that territory, but by the universal law which extended throughout the whole of the then known world.

Thirdly, we see that its origin is ascribed to war. The captives taken in battle, were liable to death. From this death, slavery saved them, and therefore the Romans called them *servi*, as persons *saved*, or *mancipia*, as *taken by hand* from the enemy.

Fourthly, we see that the law of NATURE is distinguished from the law of *nations* in this: that "by the law of NATURE all men *were born free*, and there could be no manumission *when slavery was unknown*." Here the civil law differs from the Declaration of Independence, for this informs us that all men *are* created equal, whereas the civil law only states that they *were* born free *when slavery was unknown*, that is to say, during the period before wars arose amongst the posterity of Noah. Doubtless it was so, because war is the parent of slavery. But after war was introduced, through the progress of iniquity, it became the universal practice; and slavery which followed in its train as an act of comparative mercy to the captive, became universal likewise, both existing by the same law—"the law of nations."

Fifthly, we see that this universal system of slavery, throughout the Roman empire, was not confined to the race of Ham, but included all the nations with which the Romans had ever been in conflict. And the necessary result was that a considerable portion of the slaves were quite equal to their masters in race, in knowledge, in talent, and in mental energy.

Sixthly, we see that, until the reign of the Emperor Antonine, the master had the power of life and death over his slaves. But this emperor did not ascend the throne until A.D. 161. So that at the time when St. Paul taught slaves to be obedient to their masters, and sent back the fugitive Onesimus, the system of Roman slavery included this very power.

Seventhly, we see that the Church, notwithstanding it existed, from the fourth century, in the highest dignity and honor, could not emancipate the slave, even when he had been ordained to the office of a bishop, against the will of the master; but he was liable to be reclaimed at any time as a fugitive, and reduced to slavery again.

Eighthly, we see that although slavery, in the first instance, was the result of captivity in war, yet afterwards it continued to be propagated to the posterity, and that this was the result even when the father was a freeman, provided the mother were a slave.

And lastly, we see that nothing could liberate the slave but the will of his master. In case of excessive cruelty, indeed, the Emperor Antonine, in the second century, decreed that the slave should be sold to another, but still he remained a slave, and his first master received the price of the transfer.

On the whole, therefore, it is manifest that the slavery of the old Roman empire was more severe than Southern slavery in some respects, and superior in none, save in this last particular, which was not enacted until a hundred years after the martyrdom of St. Paul. The greater hardships of the Roman Code consisted in these particulars: that all prisoners of war became slaves, no matter how elevated they might be in race, in education, or in mental capacity, whereas the Southern institution is confined to the negro race, which is confessedly inferior: that prior to the reign of the Emperor Antonine, A.D. 161, the master had the power of life and death over his slave, which never was allowed in the Southern system; and that any freeman at the age of twenty, was authorized to sell himself into slavery, until the Emperor Leo took that abuse away, in the ninth century.

And no one can deny that this system of slavery, in its most extreme form, existed from the earliest ages. It was in full force, when the spirit of liberty expelled Tarquin, and established the consular government by election. It was in full force when the same spirit of liberty roused contest after contest, between the patricians and the plebeians. It was in full force when the spirit of liberty sacrificed the famous Julius Cesar, on the mere suspicion that he sought to be a king. It was in full force in all the states of Greece, and in every other country known to history. In a word, it was universal, sustained everywhere, notwithstanding the indisputable fact that the world has never produced more energetic struggles for liberty, and has never heard more eloquent declamations in its praise, than those which have come down to us from the poets, the orators and the sages of antiquity. But this ardent love of liberty had no effect on the condition of the slaves. That remained as it had been from the remotest periods of history. And we have just seen what it was, long after the Roman empire had absorbed the Grecian states, when heathenism had sunk prostrate before the Cross of Christ, and the Church was established in all the power of its pristine energy and devotion.

If this shows anything it shows how little christianity has had to do in humanizing the world and that still, after more that 1864 years much good is left for the atheists to accomplish — page 87.

[handwritten marginalia at top: Let "interest" then govern in the matter, but do not let an arbitrary [...] say who shall be master + who shall do the work. Service of some kind must be performed but let no the arbitrary decrees of power say by whom.]

CHAPTER VII.

RIGHT REVEREND BROTHER: Before I enter upon the opinions of the Fathers, I deem it only just to the *philosophy* of my subject, to present a copious extract from the *Politics* of the famous Aristotle, who was the chosen preceptor of Alexander the Great, and whose influence had not only so large a field among the ancients, but continued to operate, during many ages, upon the Church itself. I quote from Bohn's London edition:

"By nature," saith Aristotle, "some beings command, and others obey, for the sake of mutual safety; for a being endowed with discernment and forethought is by nature the superior and governor, whereas he who is merely able to execute by bodily labor, is the inferior and a *natural slave:* and hence the *interest of master and slave is identical.*" *

Again: "He then is *by nature formed a slave*, who is *fitted to become the chattel of another person,* and on that account is so, and who has just reason enough to perceive that there is such a faculty as reason, without being endued with the use of it. Now it is the intention of nature to make the bodies of slaves and freemen different from each other, that the one should be robust for their necessary purposes, but the others erect; useless indeed for such servile labors, but fit for civil life, which is divided between the duties of war and peace; though the contrary often takes place, namely, that the one have the bodies, but the other have the souls, of free citizens. For this at all events is evident, that if they excelled others as much as the statues of the gods excel the human form, every one would allow that the inferiors ought to be slaves to the others. And since this is true with respect to the body, it is still more just to determine in the same manner, when we consider the soul, though it is not so easy to perceive the beauty of the soul as it is of the body. It is clear then that some men *are free by nature,* and *others are slaves,*

* *The Politics and Economics of Aristotle.* Book 1, ch. ii. p. 4.

and that in *the case of the latter, the lot of slavery is both advanta-geous and just.*" *

Proceeding in the argument, our philosopher next takes into consideration the opinions of Plato and others, who held the lawfulness of enslaving prisoners taken in war, and therein differed from him.

"It is not difficult," saith Aristotle, "to perceive that those who maintain the contrary opinion have some reason on their side, for slavery and a slave have each two different senses, (significations;) for there is such a thing as a slave by custom; and this custom is a sort of compact by which whatsoever is taken in battle, is said to be the property of the conqueror. But many persons call in question this right, and say that it would be hard that whoever is compelled by violence should become the slave and subject of another, who has the power to compel him, and is his superior in strength; and even of those who are wise, some think one way, and some another on this subject. But the source of this doubt and that which makes this conflict of opinions is the fact that ability, when accompanied with proper means, in a certain way, is able to commit the greatest violence, for victory is always owing to some superior advantage; so that it seems that violence does not prevail without ability, and so the dispute is only concerning what is just. For on this account some persons think that justice consists in benevolence, while others think it just that the superior should govern, since in the midst of these contrary opinions, the opposite argument has nothing weighty enough to persuade us that the superior on the score of ability ought not to rule and govern. But nevertheless, some persons, (the Platonists,) clinging, as they think, to a certain plea of right, (for custom is a kind of right,) insist that slavery in war is just, but at the same time they contradict themselves. For it may happen that the principle upon which the wars were commenced is unjust; and no one will say that the man who is undeservedly enslaved is therefore a slave, for if so, men of the noblest families might happen to be slaves, and the descendants of slaves, if they chance to be taken prisoners in war, and sold. And on this account they do not choose to give the name of slaves to such persons, *but only to barbarians*. But when they say this, they do nothing more than inquire *who is a slave by nature*, as we said at the first, for we must

* *Aristotle's Politics.*   Book 2, ch. v. p. 13.

acknowledge that *some persons, wherever they may be, are of neces-sity slaves, but that others can in no case be slaves.* Thus it is also with those of noble descent; it is not only in their own country but everywhere, that men esteem them as such, while barbarians are respected at home only; as if nobility and freedom were of two sorts, the one universal, the other not so. Those who express these senti-ments show that they distinguish the slave and the freeman, the noble and the ignoble, from each other, by no other test save that of their virtues and their vices; for they think it reasonable, that as a man begets a man, and a beast a beast, so from a good man, a good man should be descended; and this is what nature desires to bring about, but oftentimes can not accomplish it. *It is evident then that this doubt has no reason in it, and that some persons are slaves and others freemen by the appointment of nature ;* and also that in some instances there are two distinct classes, for the one of whom *it is ex-pedient to be a slave,* and for the other to *be a master,* and *that it is right and just that some should be governed, and that others should exercise that government for which they are fitted by nature.* And if so, then the rule of the master over the slave *is just also.* But to govern ill is disadvantageous to both; for the same thing is useful to the part and to the whole, to the body and to the soul; but the slave is, as it were, a part of the master, as though he were an animated part of his body, though separate. For which reason a *mutual util-ity and friendship may subsist between the master and the slave.* I mean when they are placed by nature in that relation to each other; for the contrary is the case with those who are reduced to slavery by custom or by conquest." *

One passage more will close my extracts from Aristotle: "The art of war," saith he, "is, in some sense, a part of the art of acquisi-tion; for hunting is a part of it, which it is necessary for us to em-ploy against wild beasts, and *against those of mankind who, being intended by nature for slavery, are unwilling to submit to it, and on this occasion, such a war is by nature just."* †

To these copious selections from the prince of philosophers I add the remarks of Dr. Gillies, who thus sums up this part of the system of Aristotle in the introduction, page xxxviii. etc. :

"In the relation of master and servant, the good of the master may be the primary object, but the benefit of the servant or slave is also a necessary result, since he only is naturally and justly a slave, whose powers are competent to mere bodily labor, who is capable of listening to reason, but incapable of exercising that sovereign faculty, and whose weakness and short-sightedness are so great, that it is safer for him to be guided or governed through life by the prudence of another. But let it always be remembered that 'one class of men ought to have the qualifications requisite for masters, before another can either fitly or usefully be employed as slaves.' Government, then, not only civil but domestic, is a most serious duty—a most sacred trust: a trust the very nature of which is totally incompatible with the *supposed inalienable rights of all men to be self-governed.* Those rights and those only, are inalienable, which it is impossible for one person to exercise for another, and *to maintain those to be natural and inalienable rights, which the persons supposed to be invested with them can never possibly exercise, consistently either with their own safety, or with the good of the community,* is to CONFOUND ALL NOTIONS OF THINGS, and to INVERT THE WHOLE ORDER OF NATURE, of which it is the primary and unalterable law that forecast should direct improvidence, reason control passion, and wisdom command folly."

Here, then, we have a perfect demonstration of the principle on which the advocates of negro slavery, *in perpetuity,* rest their argument. We have seen that the civil law held men to be *free by nature,* meaning by *nature* the condition of humanity *before war was known,* or during that golden age of the poets, when all was supposed to be peace and affection. We know, from divine revelation, that since the expulsion of Adam from paradise, no such age has ever existed. The murder of Abel by his brother Cain, and the shameful irreverence of Ham towards his father Noah, prove distinctly that sin was ever at work, from the period of the fall. War, indeed, in its common acceptation, could not exist, until the multiplication of mankind had gone on for a considerable period. But the spirit of war, which is the spirit of selfish contention, is always active in the human heart, until it has experienced that mighty change from heaven which makes it "a new creature."

Referring the word, *nature,* therefore, to this supposed original condition of humanity, the civil law rested slavery upon the *law of nations,* or, in other words, upon the universal custom of the world. In the philosophy of Aristotle, however, the word *nature* signifies, not the imaginary condition of men before war was introduced, but

*) The question is, — Has fallible man
the right to determine who shall
labor 9 — instead of leaving
to law of nature to &c &c

SOUTHERN ARGUMENT. 97

the constitution of the mind and temperament which is inherent from his birth in every individual, and stamps its character upon his future life, under every modification of circumstances. It needs no argument to prove that the great philosopher is right, in this use of the word, *nature*, because it is in the same sense that all men use it in our own day.

When, in this strictly proper application of the term, Aristotle saith that some men are slaves *by nature*, and others freemen by nature, he merely declares a fact which all human experience demonstrates, namely, that the natural constitution of mind and temperament qualifies the individual either to govern, or to be governed. And freedom is therefore the best condition for the one, and slavery is the best condition for the other. Hence he deduces the rule that the man who is, by nature, fitted for freedom, can not, in justice, be made a slave. And the man who is, by nature, fitted for slavery, can not, in justice, be made a freeman. For justice requires that every man should occupy that condition for which nature has designed him. To force him into any other, is to contradict and oppose the order of nature, and can not be beneficial either to the individual himself, or to the community.

Thus, then, the Southern slaveholder insists that the sound philosophy of Aristotle is altogether on his side, in the bondage of the African. For, if ever there was a race of men, fitted, by nature, for slavery, the African race must be admitted to be in that condition. Hence the negro, when set free, rarely fails to grow worse, instead of better. He is happier, safer, more contented, and more useful, as a slave, than in any other position. That there are occasional exceptions, the Southern arguer admits; and for these, emancipation is allowed, and the colony of Liberia was planted expressly for their accommodation. But for the great mass of the negro race, he contends that slavery is their proper state, on the very ground laid down by Aristotle; and claims the experience of the world, as a demonstration in his favor.

In the view of the Southern slaveholders, therefore, the general emancipation of their negroes would not only be ruinous to the masters, but cruel, to the last degree, towards the slaves themselves; because it would thrust into the dangers and difficulties of freemen, millions of human beings who are entirely unfitted by nature for freedom, and who need the protection and government of their masters, even more than the masters need their labor. And therefore

5

they resist the policy of abolition, on the very ground of humanity and affection towards their slaves, and regard it as an act of Christian duty not to cast them off, into a condition of suffering, peril and degradation, but to continue their government and guardianship as a trust committed to their hands by divine Providence, which they can not give up without making themselves accessory to the fearful consequences.

Of course, my Right Reverend brother, you and I would not be likely to view the subject in the same light. Men are usually the creatures of circumstances, and rarely reason upon any subject except in accordance with the habits and prejudices which have formed the greater part of their own training. If we had been born and educated at the South, it is at least probable that we might have taken the most extreme ground on the subject of negro slavery. And even as it is, though all my notions and feelings lead me towards abolitionism, yet I can not deny that there is great force and apparently great truth in the argument of these Southern gentlemen. At all events I must admit that they become attached to their slaves, and the slaves to them, in a manner which I am not in a position to appreciate ; and that, in the words of Aristotle, "*a mutual utility and friendship may subsist between the master and the slave*, when they are placed, by nature, in that relation to each other." I must also admit that the subject is one with which they are perfectly familiar, in all its bearings, of necessity ; while, to me, it is a mere matter of abstract speculation, and therefore, supposing that they have as much intellect and Christian principle as I have, they ought to understand it much better than any one, who, like myself, is a stranger to the system. Am I justified in assuming that I have a vast deal more of intellect and Christian principle, than the Southern clergy, who defend their domestic institution on these grounds, of Scripture, of law, and of sound philosophy ? Can I say to them : "Stand by, for I am holier than you ? Stand by, for I am more intellectual than you ! Stand by, for I have more philanthropy than you ! Stand by, for I have the *master mind* by nature, and your minds ought to be, in justice, the *slaves of mine*, by reason of my superiority !"

You, my Right Reverend brother, may think and say thus, if you can prove your right to such preëminence ; but I must be excused if I dare not occupy a position which seems to me the very reverse of common-sense, of sound argument, and of Christian moderation.

CHAPTER VIII.

RIGHT REVEREND BROTHER: I come, now, to the statements of the ancient authors on the subject of slavery, and shall commence with Philo Judæus, a learned Jew of Alexandria, who lived in the first century of the Christian era, when slavery existed according to the old Roman law.

"There is one kind of slavery," saith Philo, "of the mind, and another of the body. Men are the masters over the bodies, and the appetites and vices over the minds." (14)

"The divine law accommodates the rules of right, not to fortune but to nature. Therefore masters ought not to abuse their power over their domestic servants, but should beware of insolence, contempt, and cruelty. For these are not the signs of a serene mind, but of tyrannical weakness; exercising arbitrary licentiousness instead of judgment." (15)

Near the latter end of the second century we have the works of the famous Tertullian, a presbyter of Carthage, whose writings were held in such esteem by the martyr Cyprian, that when he called for them he was accustomed to say: "Give me the master." Amongst the numerous treatises of Tertullian there are some against the heretic Marcion. And here we meet with a passage which shows with what abhorrence Tertullian regarded the attempt to draw away the slave from the service of his master.

"For what," saith this celebrated father, "can be more unjust, what more iniquitous, what more shameful than an attempt to benefit the slave in such way that he shall be snatched from his master, that he shall be delivered to another, that he shall be suborned against the life of his master, while he is yet in his house, living on his granary and trembling under his correction? Such a rescuer would be condemned in the world no less than a man-stealer." (16)

The fourth century beheld the Church freed from persecution, and her bishops and clergy held in high reverence and honor. Let us next turn to the testimony of those eminent Christian fathers, whose authority has been universally respected to this day.

Thus Jerome, one of the oracles of the ancient Church, gives his comment on St. Paul's first Epistle to Timothy, ch. 6, v. 1, "*Let as many servants as are under the yoke count their masters worthy of all honor,*" etc.

"Not only the good," saith Jerome, "but even the infidels, lest the slaves might seem to have been made worse by their religion. Neither let them despise their master as only equal to themselves. If they formerly served unbelievers with a hateful fear, how much more should they serve the faithful, of whose kindness they participate." (17)

The same father remarks as follows on 1 Cor. 7 : 21 :

"The condition of a slave can not be opposed to the Christian religion. Say not, therefore, How can I please God, who am a slave? For God does not regard the condition, but He seeks the will and the mind. Therefore neither does liberty profit nor slavery hurt. Whoever is the slave of man is free with God, and he who is free from men is the slave of Christ. Therefore both are one." (18)

Again, commenting on Eph. 6 : 5–9, Jerome saith :

"The Apostle here provides that the doctrine of God may not be blasphemed in any thing; if believing slaves become useless to their masters. For he who is about to permit his other slaves to become Christians, may begin to repent of his intention through those who have already become so. But if he sees that these have been improved, and from being unfaithful have become faithful servants, not only will he wish that his other slaves may believe, but even he himself may perhaps be a partaker of salvation." (19)

An ancient writer, formerly confounded with Ambrose, the Bishop of Milan, gives this commentary on the Epistle to the Colosians.

"Through the iniquity of the world this occurred, that while one invaded the territory of another, freemen were taken into captivity, from whence they were called *manu capti*, and then *mancipia*. The same condition of things continues now. Some are redeemed, others remain slaves. But with God, he is esteemed a slave who sins. For it was by reason of sin that Ham heard the sentence : 'Cursed be Canaan, a servant of servants shall he be to his brethren.'" (20)

The same author furnishes this comment on 1 Tim. 6 : 1–2 :

"He" (the Apostle) "desires masters to return thanks to God for the services of their slaves, since when, through the doctrine of God, they rendered such faithful services, it might be that the masters would subject themselves to the same doctrine. If he commands profane masters to be served with entire diligence, how much more the faithful ? For then the slave proves himself subject to the fear of God, if he devotes himself to his faithful and earthly master with his whole mind." (21)

The celebrated Augustine, as you know, was the Bishop of Hippo, in Africa. He flourished in the fourth century, and as he is commonly esteemed. the prince of the fathers, I shall give you a liberal specimen of his teaching upon the subject. Repetition is unavoidable, because I am bound to justify my position by many witnesses, in order that the opposers of the truth shall have no possible escape from the conclusion.

Addressing himself to the holy Catholic Church, this eminent father uses the following language :

"Thou" (the Catholic Church) "teachest slaves to adhere to their masters, not so much from the necessity of their condition as from the pleasure of their office. Thou, in consideration of that supreme God who is their common Lord, makest the masters to be placable to their slaves, and more inclined to consult than to coërce them." (22)

But Augustine had no intention to weaken or destroy the corrective discipline, which the refractory or rebellious slave might sometimes require. Therefore he lays down this plain statement.

"The slave fears to offend his master, lest he may order him to be beaten, or to be put into the stocks, or to be shut up in prison, or committed to the workhouse. Fearing these things, the slave does not sin." (23)

Again, presenting his views on the origin and principle of servitude, Augustine adds his authority to what we have already seen, in these words, viz. :

"That one man should be the slave of another is the result either of adversity or of iniquity. Of iniquity, as it is written : *Cursed be Canaan, he shall be the slave of his brethren ;* but of adversity, as it happened to Joseph, when, being sold by his brethren, he became a slave to a foreigner. Therefore, the wars made the first slaves, as is indicated by their name in the Latin tongue. For the man who was conquered by another, might be killed according to the law of war ; and because he was saved (*servatus*) he was called a slave, (*servus*,) and from thence they were also called *mancipia*, because *manu capti*, taken by hand. It is also the *natural order* amongst men that the women should serve their husbands, and sons their parents, because in this there is justice, that the weaker should serve the stronger. This, therefore, in servitudes and masterships, is clear justice, that those who excel in reason, should excel in domination also." (24)

Another extract from Augustine clearly proves his opinion concerning the *permanent* character of bondage.

"It was ordered," saith he, "that the Hebrew slave should serve six years, and then be dismissed free. But lest Christian slaves should exact this from their masters, the Apostolic authority commands that slaves should be subject to their masters, that the name of God and his doctrine be not blasphemed. And the precept is sufficiently apparent, in a symbol, from this: that God commands the man who had refused his liberty to have his ear bored with an awl to the door-post." (25)

One interesting extract more will close the testimony of this eminent teacher.

"The first and daily power of man over man," saith he, "is that of the master over the slave. Almost every house has this sort of power. There are masters, there are also slaves—those names are different, but men and men are equal names. And what saith the Apostle, teaching slaves to be subject to their masters? "Ye bond-servants, be obedient to your masters according to the flesh, because there is a Master according to the Spirit." He is the true Master and Eternal, but these are temporal, according to the time. While thou art walking in the way, while thou art living in this world, Christ is not willing to make thee proud. This happens to thee that thou mayest be made a Christian, and having a man for thy master, thou art not made a Christian that thou shouldst disdain to serve. Yet since thou servest man, by the order of Christ, thou dost not serve the man, but Him who has so ordered thee. And therefore he (the Apostle) saith: 'Obey your masters according to the flesh, with fear and trembling, in simplicity of heart, not as eye-servants, or as men pleasers, but as the servants of Christ, doing the will of God from the mind, with good will.' Behold, therefore, he *does not make free men* of servants, but he makes *good* servants of *bad* servants. How much do the wealthy owe to Christ, who thus regulates their home"! (26)

From this witness to the doctrine of the primitive Church, I pass on to another, little less distinguished—Basil, surnamed the Great, who was the Bishop of Cesarea in the fourth century, and held in high honor by all the Oriental Christians, as one of their most illustrious saints. Laying down rules for the monastic order, of which he was an authoritative guide, Basil writes as follows :

" Moreover let slaves detained under the yoke, if they fly to the convent of the brethren, be first admonished and made better, and then be returned to their masters ; in which the blessed Paul is to be imitated, who, when he had brought forth Onesimus, through the Gospel, sent him back to Philemon." (27)

In those rules of Basil we also find a collection of Scriptural texts, under this expressive title, viz. :

" RULE LXXV.

" That it is fitting for slaves, with all good-will to the glory of God, to be obedient to their masters according to the flesh, certainly in those things wherein the law of God is not violated."

" Servants, obey your masters in the flesh with fear and trembling, in simplicity of heart, as unto Christ, not as eye-servants, or as men-pleasers, but as the servants of Christ, doing the will of God from the heart, with good-will doing service, as to the Lord and not to men, knowing that whatever good thing any man doeth, he shall receive from the Lord, whether he be a slave or free. Let as many servants as are under the yoke hold their masters worthy of all honor, lest the name of God and his doctrine be blasphemed. And those who have believing masters, let them not despise them because they are brethren, but serve them the more, because they are faithful and beloved, partakers of the benefit. Let the slaves be subject to their masters, pleasing them in all things, not contradicting, not defrauding, but showing all good fidelity, that they may adorn the doctrine of God our Saviour in all things." (28)

Another passage will suffice from the testimony of this distinguished witness. Speaking of the state of subjection or servitude in which men were placed by divine Providence, Basil saith that " they are either oppressed by power, and brought under the yoke of slavery, as captives in war, or reduced to servitude by reason of poverty, as the Egyptians under Pharaoh, or, according to a certain wise and mysterious dispensation, those who are unworthy among sons, are made servants to the wiser and the better, by the parental voice; which, nevertheless, a just estimator of things would by no means consider as a condemnation, but rather as a benefit. For to him who, on account of the poverty of sense, has not in himself what nature demands, *it is more useful to be made the slave of another man.*" (29)

Thus far, my Right Reverend brother, we see the most perfect unity of doctrine on the subject of slavery, in the primitive Church, in those purest ages which came next after the Apostles; and when the system which prevailed was that of the Roman law, embracing slaves of every nation, instead of being confined, as it is at the South, to the most degraded of all races, the barbarous tribes of Africa. And I must take the liberty of reminding you and my other clerical brethren, that no Protestant Episcopalian can set such authorities aside, without being false to the first principles of his own Church; whose great Reformers constantly referred to them, whose Homilies argue every question of religious truth by the language of the fathers, whose ordination services recognize these "ancient authors" as the witnesses to our form of government, and whose Articles cite two of them, Jerome and Augustine, by name. But I have not yet done with their testimony, and shall proceed with the list in the next chapter.

Bah — Mr Chrysostom — Would you preserve the System of ashes?

CHAPTER IX.

RIGHT REVEREND BROTHER : After Tertullian, Jerome, Augustine, and Basil, the order of chronology brings me to the great Chrysostom, the Bishop of Constantinople, that orator of the "golden mouth," whose praise was so preëminent, and one of whose supplications is still retained in our own Liturgy. And I shall present to your consideration a very long extract from one of his famous Homilies, of which you will find the original in the notes, according to the Latin version. That version I have preferred in the case of all the Greek writers, because I take it for granted that even my scholastic readers will generally peruse it with greater ease and satisfaction. Commenting on the text in 1 Cor. 7 : 21, Chrysostom speaks as follows :

"Let every one of you remain in that vocation wherein you are called. Art thou called, having an unbelieving wife ? Remain with her, and do not put her away on account of the faith. Art thou called, being a slave ? Care not for it ; continue serving. Art thou called, being uncircumcised ? Remain uncircumcised. Hast thou believed, being circumcised ? Remain circumcised. For even as circumcision profiteth nothing, and uncircumcision hurteth nothing, so neither does slavery or liberty. And in order that he (the Apostle) might teach this yet more plainly, he saith : 'But if thou mayest be made free, use it rather.' That is, *serve rather.* But why does he command him that might be free, to remain a slave ? Because he desires to show that slavery does not hurt, but even profits. We are not ignorant, indeed, that some interpret the words, '*use it rather*,' as referring to liberty, saying : 'If thou mayest be freed, Be free.' But this is very contrary to the meaning of Paul. For his design being to console the slave by showing that his condition was no injury, he would not have ordered him to become free. For some, perhaps, might say, If I can not (be free) I suffer injury, and have received damage. He does not therefore say this, but as I have said, desiring to show that he who is made free gains no advantage, he

5*

saith: 'Although it may be in thy power to be manumitted and
made free, remain rather in servitude.' And then he adds the reason:
' For he who is called in the Lord, being a bondman, is the freedman
of Christ. In like manner also, he who is called, being free, is the
bondman of Christ.' For in those things which are according to
Christ, both are equal. But how is it that he who is a bondman is
free ? Because He has freed thee not only from sin, but even from
external slavery, though remaining a slave. And how is it that he
who is a slave is free, remaining a slave ? When he has been freed
from the passions and afflictions of the mind. When he has learned
to despise money, anger, and the other perturbations of the soul.
' You are bought with a price, be not the servants of men.' This is
said not only to slaves but also to freemen. For it is possible that
while he is a slave, he is not a slave, and while he is free, he may be
a slave notwithstanding. But how, when he is a slave, can it be
true that he is not a slave ? When he does every thing for the sake
of God, when he is neither a deceiver, nor a hypocrite, nor an eye-
servant: this is to be the slave of men, and yet free. And how,
again, does any freeman become a slave ? When he performs any
action which works evil to men, or works in the service of gluttony,
or covetousness, or ambition. For he who is of this sort, is a worse
slave than all others, although he be a freeman. But consider these
things. Joseph was a slave, but not the servant of men, for even in
his slavery he was freer than they all. He certainly did not yield to
the mistress who owned him, in those acts which she desired. Again,
she was free, yet she was a greater slave than all, because she besought her slave, and implored and provoked him, but did not persuade the freeman to do what she desired. Here therefore (on Joseph's
part) was not slavery, but the highest liberty. What hindrance,
then, was slavery to his virtue ? Let both slaves and freemen hear.
This truly is what the Apostle tacitly signifies by saying: 'Be not
the servants of men.' But if it be otherwise—if he orders them to
leave their masters, and contend that they should be made free, how
could he say, 'Let every man remain in the condition in which he
was called ;' and again, 'Whoever are under the yoke of slavery, let
them esteem their masters worthy of all honor.' To the Ephesians
and the Colossians also he writes, ordering and commanding the
same things. From all which it is evident, that he does not take
away *this* slavery, but *that which is from vice*, in which respect,
slaves themselves are free." (30)

This passage has no reference whatev[er]
to Slavery. — "good servitude" mean[s]
simply duty to God

PROSPER AND GREGORY.   107

This long and most interesting specimen of true Christian doctrine, from the illustrious Chrysostom, is, of itself, enough to satisfy a candid mind on the subject before us; proving distinctly that the primitive Church had no idea of regarding slavery as involving sin, in the relation of the master and the slave, but on the contrary esteeming the condition of servitude as better than freedom for the slave, while the bondage to sin, whether in the master or the servant, was the worst kind of slavery; and the only kind which God requires all men to cast aside, whether they be bond or free.

From Chrysostom, I proceed to his disciple, Prosper of Aquitaine, who flourished in the fifth century, and a short sentence will suffice to show that he held the same sentiments as his eminent teacher.

"It was transgression and not nature," saith Prosper, "that produced the name and condition of slavery, and the first cause of this subjection was sin; as it is written, every one that committeth sin is the slave of sin. Hence the condition of him who is a bond-servant to man, is better than that of him who is a slave to his own cupidity." (31)

There is no name in the sixth century which shines with greater lustre than that of Gregory the Great, the Bishop of Rome, and from his writings I shall take my next testimony.

"It is well known," saith Gregory, "that there are two kinds of good servitude, one of fear, the other of affection; one, the service of bondmaids and bondmen, who dread their master; the other, of children who love and please their parent. The bondmaid fears, lest she should be punished; the wife fears, lest she should offend her husband." (32)

Again, in his book concerning the "Pastoral Care," we have this rule laid down to the clergy:

"Slaves should be admonished in one way, and the masters in another. The slaves, to wit, that they should always, in themselves, regard the humility of their condition; but the masters, that the memory of their nature, in which they are created equally with their slaves, must not be forgotten. Slaves should be admonished, lest they should despise their masters, lest they offend God by proudly contradicting his ordinance; the masters are also to be admonished, that they do not grow proud of his gift, against God, (the Giver,) by refusing to acknowledge that those who are by condition their subjects, are their equals by nature. These are to be admonished that they may know themselves to be the slaves of their masters: those are to be admonished, that they may confess themselves to be the fellow-servants of their slaves. For to these it is said: *Servants, obey your masters according to the flesh.* And again: *Let those who are under the yoke of bondage, esteem their masters to be worthy of all honor.* But to those it is said: *And you, masters, do the same things unto them, forbearing threats, knowing that their Master and yours is in heaven.*" (33)

There is another evidence of the doctrine maintained by Gregory the Great, which is not only conclusive in itself, but is also interesting as a specimen of the ancient forms observed in such matters. And this is the deed of gift conveying one of his own slaves to the Bishop of Porto, which was a small suburban diocese, in the vicinity of Rome. It is as follows:

"Gregory, to Felix, the Bishop of Porto.

" Moved by favor of your charity, lest we should seem unfruitful to you, and chiefly because we know you to have few servants, therefore we give and grant unto you, our brother, by direct right, John, a servant of the church law, by nation a Sabine, of the Flavian property, aged about eighteen years, whom you have had in your possession, by our will, for a long while, so that you may have and hold him, and preserve and maintain your right to him, and defend him as your property, and do, by the free right of this donation as his master, whatsoever you will concerning him. Against which charter of our munificence, you may know that neither we nor our successors are ever to come. And this donation, written by our notary, we have read and subscribed, granting also, your profession not being expected, our license of recording it, whenever you will, with the legitimate stipulation and security. Done at Rome." (34)

To these clear and decisive testimonies of the famous Gregory the Great, I shall add one witness more, a saint likewise in the Roman Catholic calendar, Isidore, who was Bishop of Seville, in A.D. 601, and died A.D. 636. This will bring us to the seventh century. A single extract from his valuable writings will suffice to prove his unity of doctrine with all that were before him:

" On account of the sin of the first man," saith Isidore, " the punishment of slavery was brought upon the human race, by the Deity, so that to those for whom he sees liberty to be incongruous, he may mercifully appoint servitude.   And although original sin is remitted to all the faithful by the grace of baptism, nevertheless God has equitably put this difference of life in men, making some to be slaves, and others masters ; that the licentiousness of evil-doing on the part of servants, might be restrained by the power of their lords. For if all men were without fear, who could prohibit any one from evil ?   Hence also, princes and kings are chosen over the nations, that they may coërce the people to abstain from evil by terror, and oblige them to live rightly according to the laws.   Better is slavery in subjection than liberty in pride.   For many are found freely serving God under wicked masters, who, although they are inferior to them in body, are far above them in mind." (35)

Here, my Right Reverend brother, I shall close the testimony of the fathers, only reminding you that all these writers lived before the unity of the Church was broken by the separation of the East from the West, that they were the lights and ornaments of their day, that they are held to the present hour, throughout the whole Christian world, in the highest veneration, and that our own reformers had constant recourse to them in every controversy, as the most authoritative guides to the sense of the Holy Scriptures.   The Bible was the unquestionable rule of faith.   The Church was the interpreter.   And as it is the undoubted maxim of the courts, in every construction of written law, to take the earliest decisions as the most binding, so it has been among all sound theologians, that the oldest voices of the Church are heard with the greatest reverence.

But although I have closed the testimony of the individual fathers, I have not done with the testimony of the primitive Church, presented in a still more solemn form by the Councils of her bishops.   To these, therefore, I invite your attention, in the following chapter.

whatever may be thought of this principle on this particular subject it is against all rule in every other subject; for it would compel enlightened advanced ages to deny its knowledge and advantages and to derive its rules of life from

CHAPTER X.

RIGHT REVEREND BROTHER : The first place in the list of the Councils of the Church is due to the very ancient code called "The Canons of the Apostles." In the eighty-first of these we read as follows:

"We do not allow slaves to be advanced to the order of the clergy without the will of their masters, to the injury of those who possess them ; for such things produce the overthrow of houses. But when a slave is seen to be worthy, who may be chosen for that degree, as also our Onesimus was, and the masters shall have consented, and given liberty, and dismissed them from their houses, it may be done." (36.)

The Clementine Constitutions may be reckoned next, being an old compilation, supposed formerly to have been arranged by Clement, who was the companion of the apostles, and became, by their authority, Bishop of Rome. By many critics, however, amongst the Roman Catholics themselves, the work is assigned to the third or fourth century. But be this as it may, these Constitutions, contained in eight books, are full of very admirable matter, expressed with great force and beauty, and held, especially by the eastern Churches, in the highest veneration.

From the fourth book, chapter second, I quote the following passage : "Concerning slaves, what more can we say than that the servant should have benevolence towards his master, with the fear of God, though he should be impious, though he should be immoral, even though he should not accord with him in religion ? So likewise let the master love his slave, and though he is above him, let him notwithstanding acknowledge equality inasmuch as he is a man. And let him who has a Christian master, the authority being secured, love him not only as his master, but as a companion in the faith and as a father ; not serving with eye-service, but as loving his master, knowing that the reward of his service will be rendered to him by God. In like manner let him who has a Christian slave, his subjection *being* secure, love him as a son, and as a brother, for the sake of the communion of faith." (37.)

From these, I pass on to a number of Councils, extending from A.D. 341, to the seventh century :

COUNCIL OF GANGRA, A.D. 341.

"If any one, under pretext of religion, shall teach a slave to despise his own master, that he should depart from his service, and no longer submit to him with benevolence and honor, let him be accursed," (*anathema*.) (38.)

COUNCIL OF AGDE, A.D. 506.

"If the bishop shall have granted liberty to any slaves belonging to the Church, who have been well-deserving in his judgment, let the liberty thus granted be preserved to them by his successors, with whatever property their manumittor bestowed." (39.)

COUNCIL OF ORLEANS, A.D 511.

"The slave who has taken refuge in the Church for any transgression, if he has received the sacrament after the admission of his fault, shall be compelled to return immediately to the service of his master." (40.)

COUNCIL OF EPONE, A.D. 517.

"If any one shall kill his own slave without judicial authority, he shall expiate the effusion of blood by excommunication during two years." (41.)

COUNCIL OF ORLEANS, A.D. 541.

"It shall not be allowed to the slaves of the Church or of the priests, to take spoils or captives, for it is unjust that while their masters are sustaining the benefit of redemption, the discipline of the Church should be stained by the excesses of the slaves." (42.)

COUNCIL OF ORLEANS, A.D. 549.

"No bishop shall presume to ordain any slave who has not received liberty from his own master, nor even one who is already free, without the consent of him to whom he is either a slave, or who is known to have enfranchised him." (43.)

COUNCIL OF MAÇON, A.D. 581.

"Therefore, in this present Council, God being the author, we decree that no Christian from henceforth shall serve a Jew, but that any Christian may have license to redeem him, either for freedom or for slavery, twelve shillings being given for a good slave. For it is an impiety that those, whom Christ our Lord has redeemed with the shedding of His blood, should remain bound with the chains of his persecutors. And if any Jew be unwilling to consent to our decree, it shall be lawful for the slave to dwell with Christians, wherever he chooses, so long as his Jewish master delays to come for his money." (44.)

COUNCIL OF TOLEDO, A.D. 589.

"Since we are informed that in many cities the slaves of the churches, and of the bishops, or of all the clergy, are wearied out with various vexatious burdens by the judges or the public functionaries, this whole Council asks of the piety of our lord (the king) that he will prohibit such presumptuous doings from henceforth: so that the slaves of the aforesaid officers shall labor for their use, or for the Church." (45.)

COUNCIL OF NARBONNE, A.D. 589.

"Every man, whether free, or bound, Goth, Roman, Syrian, Greek, or Jew, shall abstain from work on the Lord's day, neither shall he yoke the oxen, except necessity compels in harvest. And if any presume to act contrary, if he be a free man, he shall pay six shillings, as a fine to the treasurer of the city, and if he be a slave he shall receive one hundred stripes." (46.)

COUNCIL OF BERGHAMSTEAD, A.D. 697.

"If any one shall manumit his slave at the altar, let him be free, and capable to enjoy heirship and weregild, and it shall be lawful for him to go wherever he will, without restraint." (47.)

COUNCIL OF AIX-LA-CHAPELLE, A.D. 816.

"On account of the sin of the first man, the punishment of servitude was divinely appointed to the human race: so that to those whom He (the Almighty) saw to be unfit for freedom, he mercifully ordained slavery. And although original sin is remitted to all the faithful by the grace of baptism, nevertheless God, in equity, distributed life to men, constituting some slaves, and others masters, in order that the license of evil-doing by the slaves might be restrained by the power of their lords. There is no accepting of persons with God. For our only Lord sets forth His ordinance equally to the masters and to the slaves. Better is a *subject* servitude than a proud liberty. For many are found freely serving God under flagitious masters, who, although they are subject to them in body, are far above them in mind." (48.)

The next extract is from the capitulary of the Emperor Louis, which, though not in the usual form of a Council, is of equal authority as bearing testimony to the doctrine and practice of the Church.

"Concerning the ordination of slaves who are everywhere promoted to the ecclesiastical degrees with indiscretion, it is agreed by all that regard should be had to the sacred canons; and it is therefore decreed that henceforth none of the bishops shall presume to advance them to Holy Orders, unless they have first received their freedom from their own masters. And if any slave is a fugitive from his master, or lies hid, or brings forward witnesses influenced by a gift or corrupted, or receives the ecclesiastical degrees by any fraud or knavery, it is decreed that he shall be deposed, and his master shall again receive him." (49.)

COUNCIL OF WORMS, A.D. 868.

"If any one shall kill his slave, whatever he may have committed worthy of death, without the knowledge of the judges, he shall cleanse away the guilt of blood by a penance of two years, or by excommunication." (50)

The same Council enacted another canon, with which I shall close this portion of the evidence:

"If any slave, during the absence, or without the knowledge of his master, the bishop being aware that he was a slave, shall be ordained a deacon or a presbyter, let him remain in the office of the clergy, but the bishop shall pay to the master a double price. But if the bishop did not know that he was a slave, those persons who gave their testimony concerning him, or demanded that he should be ordained, shall be held liable to pay the same recompense." (51)

This may be the best place, however, for the consideration of another Council, held at London, A.D. 1111, in which the selling of Englishmen appears to have been forbidden, in the following words:

"Let no one by any means presume, henceforward, to engage in that nefarious traffic, by which, hitherto, men have been accustomed to be sold, like brute beasts, in England." (52)

The distinguished Bishop of Oxford, son of the celebrated Mr.

Here is a general overthrow of
all that. Other Councils ("God
being the author" p. 111.) had done

Wilberforce, wrote, when a presbyter, an able and interesting History of the American Church, in which, toward the end, his sympathies with abolitionism are stated very strongly, as might be naturally expected. And he quotes the supposed canon above mentioned, saying, that "this must be the *Church's rule*, on the banks of the Mississippi, as it was on those of the Thames." From his book, some of our American Churchmen have taken this Council of London as an authority of great importance; and as I was not a little surprised to find an English council of that age contradicting so strongly the whole course of ecclesiastical legislation on this subject, throughout the rest of Christendom, I took the pains to look into the real state of the matter, and discovered that the statement was founded upon a mistake.

It is true that such a council was holden, under Anselm, the Archbishop of Canterbury, and the canon, as quoted, appears as if it were a part of its doings. But on the following page, we have a letter from the Archbishop himself, which deprives it of all its supposed authority. This letter I shall proceed to set before you:

"Anselm, Archbishop, to William, his beloved Archdeacon, health and benediction:"

"I am not willing to send to you, or to any one, at present, the resolutions of the chapters of the Council as set forth; because, although they were brought before the Council, they could not be fully and perfectly stated, by reason of their being proposed suddenly, without the premeditation and competent examination which were meet. Hence, it appears that some things are to be added, and perhaps some things must be changed, which I am not willing to do, unless by the common consent of our episcopal colleagues. I intend therefore to suggest and show those matters to those bishops, when we next come together, before the acts set forth are sent to the churches of England. The titles, nevertheless, of the matters, concerning which we there conferred, we send to you; that according to what you may be able to remember, you may consider us to have decreed concerning these." Then the Archbishop sets down a list of subjects, in which nothing whatever is said about the selling of slaves, so that this topic is entirely omitted from the real deliberations of the Council. (53)

This positive statement from Anselm, who was the official head or president, must be conclusive to prove that there was no definitive action on the subject, but only what we should call a proposition, recorded by the secretary, without any discussion, or any vote, and therefore not in any sense the act of the Council. The matter does not appear again, in any form. And hence this supposed decree of the Council of London really amounts to nothing.

And yet, even if this imaginary canon had been actually passed, it would only prove that "the nefarious business of selling men *like brute beasts*," was to be done away ; and therefore it might have been intended to abolish the *public slave-market*, without affecting the institution of Villenage, which we know, from history, continued to exist in England for several centuries after this time. This, you will perceive at once, on consulting the original Latin, because the words *slave, slavery*, or any term equivalent to them, is not to be found there. We shall see, in the progress of my work, that there was no change on this subject in the thirteenth century ; for, if there had been, it is impossible that the lawyers and the historians, whom I shall quote by and by, should have failed to notice it.

Setting aside, then, this supposed action of the Council of London, we have the testimony of the other parts of the Church throughout the world, clear and unanimous, in support of the doctrine of the fathers. Beginning with the Apostolic Canons, and the Clementine Constitutions, which governed the East, we have the Council of Gangra, in Asia Minor, the Councils of Agde, Narbonne, and Orleans, in France ; the Council of Epone or Epanum, and Maçon, in Burgundy ; the Council of Toledo, in Spain ; the Council of Berghamstead, near Canterbury, in England ; the Councils of Aix-la-Chapelle and Worms in Germany—all distinctly proving the institution as it was acknowledged by the Church for the first nine hundred years of the Christian era, providing for the return of fugitive slaves to their masters, repeating the duty of the slave to be faithful to his lord, and the duty of the master to be kind to the servant, while not one suggestion can be found imputing *sin* to the relation between the master and the slave, nor regarding it as a matter that ought to be abolished, nor treating it as inconsistent, in the slightest degree, with the purest principles of Christian piety. Nor is this the whole. For these councils further prove that slaves belonged to the churches, the monasteries, the bishops, and the clergy, during all these ages. So that thus far, no fact of ecclesiastical history admits of a fuller and more decisive demonstration. Yet I shall give you still more evidence, so that you shall say, *satis, superque.*

Of course — they stood out for their property

CHAPTER XI.

RIGHT REVEREND BROTHER : Some extracts from Fleury's Ecclesiastical History will now be set before you, in further confirmation of the fact that the Church attached no sin to the relation of master and slave. In the *treatment*, there might be sin enough, as there may be in any other relation. But the institution was not to be blamed for that ; and hence, while it was the duty of the Church to *ameliorate*, she made no movement to *abolish it*. Such, from the beginning under the Apostles, was the universally accepted Christian doctrine.

To the examples already given I shall add the following, viz. :

" We have still," saith Fleury, " the testament of St. Gregory, of Nazianzum, dated the last day of December, A.D. 381. He there takes the title of Bishop of Constantinople. He continues to a virgin, named Russina, the pension which he had allowed for her support, with a house at her discretion, and he gives her two girls as slaves, such as she shall choose, to live with her all her lifetime ; he also gives her power to emancipate them, which if she fails to do, they shall belong to the Church of Nazianzum." (54)

St. Perpetuus was another of these primitive Christian slaveholders. He " lived," saith Fleury, " until A.D. 491, and we have his testament made about May first, A.D. 475, in which he liberates several slaves, remits all the debts due to him, and bequeaths to his church several lots of land and his books." (55)

Alcuin, as you know, was an English prelate of the eighth century, educated by the Venerable Bede. Being sent on an embassy from Offa to Charlemagne, he became the instructor of that famous monarch in rhetoric, logic, and divinity. He also was an extensive slaveholder. For " Alcuin," saith our historian, " had the control of the revenue of his abbeys, and as the lands belonging to them were inhabited by serfs, Elipand of Toledo reproaches him with having of those bondmen no less than twenty thousand." (56)

" In the Council of Soissons," saith the same author, " holden A.D.

853, the bishops invoked the king to use his authority—that he would forbid the seigneurs to hinder the bishops from having the peasants, who were serfs under those seigneurs, scourged with rods, when they deserved it for their crimes." (57)

One quotation more from Fleury will suffice for his testimony. He gives us the decree of Pope Benedict VIII. A.D. 1022, just eleven years later than the supposed Canon of the Council of London, on which the Bishop of Oxford laid so much stress. And in this decree the Pontiff " declares," saith our historian, " that the children of the clergy are serfs to the Church in which their fathers officiated, even if their mothers were free, and he pronounces an anathema against the judges who should decide the contrary. And no serf of the Church, clerk or layman, should acquire any property under the name of a freeman, without incurring the punishment of the whip or the prison, until the Church should have withdrawn all the titles of the property." (58)

The tender sensibilities so fashionable at the present day, will probably be shocked to find the bishops in the ninth, and the Pope in the thirteenth century, authorizing the punishment of the whip and the prison, but I hope that they will remember how the pious Puritans of New-England, when their system was in its glory, and their preachers proclaimed that it was the most admirable manifestation of Christianity which had ever been known, scourged the Baptists at the public whipping-post, fined and imprisoned the Episcopalians, banished the Roman Catholics and Quakers, and when these last dared to return, actually hung them on the gallows ! those punishments being inflicted, not for any crimes, but merely because the Episcopalians, Baptists, and Quakers insisted on following their own religion ! Since those days, indeed, the posterity of these worthy Puritans have become exceedingly tolerant in matters of faith, so far as faith concerns the doctrines of the Bible or the ancient creeds. But they are far from being tolerant on their modern dogma about the *sin* of slaveholding. If the Apostle Paul himself should come again, and preach the language of his own epistles, and presume to send back a fugitive slave to his Southern master, they would think no language too bitter, and punishment too severe for his transgression.

But I must not anticipate nor wander too far from the order of my witnesses. The next which I shall summon is one belonging to our mother Church, and worthy of all acceptation.

CHAPTER XII.

Right Reverend Brother : The work of the learned Bingham, entitled, *The Antiquities of the Christian Church*, is well known to you and your clergy, and from this I shall next take a few corroborative testimonies.

"Another state of life," saith this author, "which debarred men from the privilege of ordination, was that of slaves or vassals in the Roman empire, who, being *originally tied by birth or purchase to their patron's or master's service*, could not legally be ordained, because the service of the Church was incompatible with their other duties, and no man was to be *defrauded of his right* under pretense of an ordination. In this case, therefore, the patron was always to be consulted before the servant was ordained. Thus, in one of those called the Apostolical Canons, we find a decree that no servants should be admitted among the clergy without the consent of their masters, to the grievance of the owners and subversion of their families. But if a servant be found worthy of an ecclesiastical promotion, as Onesimus was, and his master gave his consent and granted him his freedom and let him go forth from his house, he may be ordained. The Council of Toledo has a canon to the same purpose."[*]

"The imperial laws," saith the same author, "also made provision in this case, that no persons under such obligations should be admitted to any office of the clergy, or, if they were admitted merely to evade their obligations, their masters should have power to recall them to their service, unless they were bishops or presbyters, or had continued thirty years in some other office of the Church. By which it appears that the ordination of such persons was prohibited only on a civil account ; *not because that state of life was sinful*, or that it was any undervaluing or disgrace to the function to have such persons ordained, but because the duties of the civil and ecclesiastical state could not well consist together."[†]

---

[*] *Bingham's Origines Ecclesiasticæ.* Vol. i. p. 487. London ed. of 1843.

[†] Ib. vol i. p. 488.

Again, saith our author: "By one of the laws of the Theodosian Code, no slave is allowed to have sanctuary or entertainment in any church above one day, when *notice was to be given to his master, from whom he fled* for fear of punishment, that he might *reclaim him and carry him back to his own possession*, only giving promise of indemnity and pardon for his faults, if they were not very great and heinous." *

And again: "A slave," saith Bingham, "was not allowed to enter himself into a monastery, or take orders, without the consent of the master, as has been showed in other places, because this was to *deprive his master of his legal right of service, which, by the original state and condition of slaves, was his due: and the Church would not be accessory to such frauds and injustice, but rather discouraged them, by prohibitions and suitable penalties laid upon them.*" †

This learned author died, as you know, in A.D. 1723, a hundred years before the rise, in England, of the modern abolition fever. He regarded the subject, therefore, in the old and familiar light of the Scriptures and the Church, and had no idea that, in the course of a century and a half, the maintenance of those views would be condemned as "unworthy of any servant of Jesus Christ," by a bishop and a long train of clergy, and branded with their sentence of "indignant reprobation."

* Ib. vol. ii. p. 576.   † Ib. vol. vi. p. 197-8.

This only shows how backward the Church was in being reformed from ancient savage practices by the ameliorating spirit of christianity. No wonder not Christianity has been slow growth in the world when its ministers have opposed it

[Handwritten annotation at top of page: "+ all we have to do, then, is to change the laws and abolish Slavery and the church should be obedient to the change."]

CHAPTER XIII.

RIGHT REVEREND BROTHER: It is now time to adduce the next class of witnesses, namely, the divines and commentators since the Reformation in the sixteenth century, who will all demonstrate the same truth on which I stand, and thus, as I trust, condemn your act of condemnation.

Beginning with Melancthon, the famous colleague of Luther, and one of the wisest and best men of his age, I shall present to you his comment on the sixth chapter of St. Paul's first epistle to Timothy, "Let as many servants as are under the yoke count their own masters worthy of all honor," etc.

"In the beginning of the sixth chapter," saith Melancthon, "he gives a command to slaves, where the young should remember that the common rule is confirmed which is so often repeated, that *the Gospel does not abolish the established order and polity*, but preaches of other things, namely, of eternal good, eternal justice, and eternal life, which God produces in the hearts of men, whom, nevertheless, He wills, in this mortal life, to be subject to that order which, according to the will of God, is suitable to corporal life. He wills us to be sustained with meat and drink, He wills lawful marriage and progeny, He wills the ordinary consociation of the human race, the distinction of dominions, the defense of imperial government, contracts, laws, judgments, punishments. So here we see that *slavery is approved, such as was then laid down in the laws*. For it is profitable both to consciences and to peace that we should understand this doctrine concerning the *approbation of political order*." (59)

From this sound and conservative sentence of Melancthon, I proceed to his no less celebrated contemporary, Calvin, whose opinions were for a long while regarded as of the highest human authority, not only by the reformed Christians on the continent of Europe, generally, but specially by the Church of England herself. This is his comment on the same passage, viz.:

"As every man is disposed, with a false estimate, to arrogate superiority to himself, there is no one who bears with equanimity that others should govern him. Those who can not avoid the necessity, do indeed unwillingly obey their superiors: but inwardly they fret and feel indignant, as if they thought some injury was done to them. All such disputations, however, the Apostle cuts off with one word, when he *exacts a willing subjection from all who are under the yoke.* For he shows that *they were not to inquire whether they were worthy of such fortune, or of a better one ; because it was enough that they were bound in that condition.*" (60)

In his commentary on the latter part of the verse, "that the name of God be not blasphemed," this eminent reformer and divine proceeds as follows:

"We are always more ingenious than is fit, in defense of our own accommodation. Thus, when the slaves had unbelieving masters, the objection was at hand, that it was shameful for those who served the devil to have dominion over the children of God. But Paul, on the contrary, returns the argument that even unbelieving masters must be obeyed, lest the name of God and His Gospel should be blasphemed, *as if the Gospel made those to be contumacious and stubborn who ought to be subject to others.*" (61)

And in his introduction to the Epistle of Paul to Philemon, he gives this passage:

"How great was the elevation of Paul's spirit, although it may be better perceived in his more weighty writings, is also witnessed in this epistle, in which, treating an argument otherwise humble and abject, he raises it sublimely to God. *Sending back again to his master a slave who was a fugitive and a thief,* he asks that he may be forgiven." (62)

I invite your attention next to the commentary on this same epistle to Philemon, which we have in Pool's *Synopsis Criticorum.* I need not inform you that this belongs to the Presbyterian school, as it is extracted from the continental writers who had no episcopacy.

In the introduction to the commentary, we read the following:

"This epistle is written by Paul in a new style, and alone deserves to be called, truly and properly, a letter. Its utility is manifold. It admonishes us, first, that no one is to be despised, however abject his condition ; second, that we should not despair of the capacity of slaves ; third, *that slaves, believing in Christ, are not on that ac-*

count to be made free, or taken away from unwilling masters;
fourth, what is the office of a bishop, as well towards inferiors as
towards the more noble. The motive of writing this letter was that
the Apostle might reconcile the slave to his master. Which, as it
seemed difficult, the master having the most just cause to be of-
fended—since the slave had fled, as it is believed, with stolen property—he (St. Paul) approaches him (Philemon) with all the art of
oratory. If there is any thing to be admired in the line of per-
suasiveness, certainly it is this epistle." (63)

From the same work I take another and very precise comment on
the Epistle to the Ephesians, 6 : 5, "Servants, be obedient to your
masters," etc.

"The Apostle does not take away the custom then established of
using slaves, for it has its advantages, and it is lawful to use it
rightly. He teaches that *Christian liberty is consistent with political slavery*, and that *political arrangements are neither taken away
nor changed by Christ.*" (64)

Another important comment occurs in Pool's Synopsis on 1 Cor.
7 : 21 : "Art thou called, being a servant? care not for it, but if
thou mayest be made free, use it rather." That is, saith the commentator, "Use *servitude:* rather serve, for the sake of greater good,
namely, for thine own exercise, and the salvation of thy master.
Syrus thus renders this text: 'But even if thou art able to become
free, (meaning, by thine own arts and fraud,) *choose rather to remain
in slavery.*' To this sense the following consolatory reason is most
accordant: '*For he who is called, being a slave, is the Lord's freeman.*' Nevertheless he does not will this, that they should prefer
slavery to freedom when freedom is spontaneously offered by the
master, but that they should prefer it to an illegitimate freedom, by
flight or fraud." (65)

CHAPTER XIV.

Right Reverend Brother : It would be less laborious to myself, and probably more agreeable to you, if I should limit my quotations to a few of the more important passages of the Commentators. But I am pledged to make thorough work of my undertaking, as I have to deal with a widely spread and popular error. And therefore I shall here commence with all the texts cited in the *Bible View of Slavery*, and prove, beyond the possibility of any honest doubt, that I have given them the settled and established interpretation, by which you were bound, as well as myself, when you were admitted to the ministry.

The list of commentators embraces Pool's Synopsis, Patrick, Lowth and Whitby, Gill, Henry, Scott, the Comprehensive Commentary, D'Oyley and Mant, Clark, and on the New Testament, Davenant, Hammond, Doddridge, McKnight, Wordsworth, and Alford. Reckoning Melancthon for the Lutherans, the others will represent the Presbyterians, the Baptists, the Methodists, and the Congregationalists, as well as the Protestant Episcopalians. The *Letters on Slavery* by the late learned Bishop England, will next be cited for the Church of Rome. And no one pretends to doubt the opinions of the Church of Russia and the Oriental Christians. Thus you will have the whole of Christendom, up to the time of your ordination, and beyond it, in support of Scriptural truth, which I trust will be quite enough for my justification. The voice of the entire Catholic (or universal) Church, on the one side, and the Bishop of Pennsylvania with his hundred and sixty-four clergymen on the other, will then present a contrast which should convert the most zealous ultra-abolitionist, unless he be determined to scorn alike the plain sense of the Bible, and the unanimous consent of all its chief expounders, for eighteen hundred years together.

Beginning with the prophecy of Noah, let us look at the commentary in Pool's *Synopsis*, Gen. 9 : 25 : *"Cursed be Canaan,"* etc.

"Some read here אֲבִי the father of Canaan. So is the Arabic version, as it is twice expressed a little before. Others accept *Canaan*. That this people was cursed is shown by the event. Hence it is inferred with probability that he was the companion of his father's iniquity. But Ham was not exempt from the curse, because his son was named, as Shem was blessed in the next verse, although God is named, and Jacob is said to have blessed Joseph, Gen. 48 : 15, when he blessed his children, v. 16. For the parent is punished in his children, being conscious of the sin, and perhaps both its author and exhibitor, as the Hebrew doctors and Theodoret explain the subject. Some writers remark that Noah cursed the posterity of Ham, but that Moses, omitting the other sons of Ham, specified Canaan individually, because he wished only to record those things which might strengthen the Israelites and make them more ready to take possession of the promised land of Canaan." (66)

Here we have the result of Pool's authorities, which substantially agrees with the opinion of Bishop Newton, already set forth in the third chapter.

The phrase "servant of servants" in the malediction of Noah, is rendered "slave of slaves" by Pool, that is, the lowest and most vile of slaves. (67)

On the text in Gen. 17 : 12, where Abraham is commanded to circumcise those who were born in the house, and also *those who were bought with money* of any stranger, the same work gives us the following opinions, viz. :

"The uncircumcised man could live in the land of the Hebrews, under good laws, but not in the house of an Israelite, lest his example might corrupt the people. And the question arises whether the servants bought with money could be compelled to submit to circumcision. Many, from this text, affirm that they could. For, first, *the slave is the property of the master*. Second. The language is that of *command*, which would be destroyed if you understand it as depending on the will of the slave. Third. If it were otherwise, there would be no distinction between the hireling and the slave, for the hireling was permitted (not commanded) to be circumcised. (Exod. 12 : 44.) Others, however, deny these conclusions. They think that no adult slave was obliged to be circumcised, nor his children, unless he willingly consented. For otherwise he would be placed under a necessity of sinning, and ordered to be a hypocrite. Nor would such a circumcision have been a sacrament of the divine covenant, which can only be embraced by the willing. Moreover, true religion ought to persuade rather than compel. Maimonides thus explains it, when, treating of circumcision, ch. 1, sect. 6, he saith, '*If any one bought an adult slave from the Cushites who refused to be circumcised, he ought to be sold to the Cushites again.*" (68)

I have quoted this passage mainly in order to prove that the Israelites, according to Maimonides, the highest Jewish authority, did not confine their purchases of slaves to the posterity of Canaan, but included the other progeny of Ham, viz., the Cushites, even as Abraham held Hagar, the Egyptian, descended from Mizraim, another son of Ham, as a slave to his wife, Sarah. These facts give additional force to the opinion of Bishop Newton, showing how the Jews themselves understood the prophecy of Noah.

In the commentary of Pool on the Ten Commandments, which contain, by preëminence, the moral law, bound by our own Seventh Article upon all Christians, there are two passages, one on the fourth and the other on the tenth, which are worth your notice.

Exodus 20 : 10, where the Almighty commands the Sabbath-day to be kept holy, our author translates "thy man-servant," by the proper term, "thy *slave*," and adds this comment, "Nor shalt thou enjoin any labors to them," (the slaves,) "nor suffer them to work. This is to be understood of those who were *not Jews*, for the Jews were prohibited from work by the words preceding." (69)

The same chapter, v. 17, contains the Tenth Commandment, which forbids coveting the "man-servant and the maid-servant." And here our commentator gives this interpretation, viz. : "By these words of the law the *dominion* and *property* of those things which it is not permitted to covet are *thoroughly established*, as also *slavery* and the *power of the master*." (70)

If it pleased the All-Wise and Supreme Lawgiver to sanction the institution of slavery in two of the commands issued from Mount Sinai, and engraved on the tables of stone by the hand of God, that fact alone should be conclusive, to every man who professes to believe the Bible, that there was no *sin* necessarily involved in it.

I turn next to the commentary of Pool, on that famous verse, Deut. 23 : 15, which the ultra-abolitionist is never weary of quoting, "Thou shalt not deliver unto his master the servant which is escaped from

his master unto thee," etc.   "He speaks," saith Pool, "of a *foreign*
master.   Thus the land of Israel becomes an asylum.   Understand
it as referring to those slaves who fled to the Israelites from *heathen
masters*, on account of their tyranny, *for the sake of embracing Judaism*." (71)   This, which is the only rational interpretation, would
evidently give no warrant for refusing obedience to the Constitution
and the law of Congress, in the case of fugitive slaves, unless two
facts could first be clearly established, first, that they had escaped
from a *foreign* land, and secondly, that their masters *were heathen*.

The text in Exodus, 21 : 16, which forbids man-stealing, is interpreted to apply to Israelites only.   "*He that stealeth a man*," "namely," saith Pool, "an *Israelite*, as appears from Deut. 24 : 7, whom
any Jew, by force or by fraud, should *bring into slavery, and sell to
the Gentiles*." (72)   You will find, before I conclude my labor, that
this law of Moses, so constantly perverted by the school of ultra-
abolitionism, has no reference whatever to the case of the Jewish
slaves, but was designed to protect the liberty of the chosen people,
lest any should imitate the sons of Jacob who sold their brother
Joseph to the Midianites.

I shall only add one quotation more from Pool, where the book of
Ezra states the numbers of the Israelites, who returned from their
captivity under the decree of Cyrus, at forty-two thousand three
hundred and sixty, "besides their servants and their maids, of whom
there were seven thousand three hundred and thirty-seven." *Ezra*,
2 : 64–5.   On this passage, our commentator saith : "Behold the
poor fortune of the captives, when so many thousands had no more
slaves than these." (73)

But I doubt not that you have had enough of Pool's *Synopsis*,
though it gives the cream of the best European commentators up to
the middle of the seventeenth century, and has been the main guide
of all who have succeeded him.   I shall therefore pass on to another
work of the highest reputation, especially among Episcopalians, which
will furnish further evidence to confirm the truth.

× The vagabond has no sympathy
for the Slaves themselves!

CHAPTER XV.

RIGHT REVEREND BROTHER: I need not inform you that the Commentary of Patrick, Lowth, and Whitby stands in the front rank of authority, in our mother Church of England, and in our own. Simon Patrick, Bishop of Chichester, and afterwards of Ely, was distinguished for learning, piety, and talent. Robert Lowth, successively Bishop of St. David's, Oxford, and London, was little less eminent. And Dr. Whitby, for erudition and judgment, had few equals in his day. Let us next, therefore, attend to their testimony on the texts to which I have referred.

On the prophecy of Noah, Gen. 9 : 22–7, this Commentary states it as the opinion of the Hebrew doctors, "that Canaan first saw Noah in this indecent posture, and made sport of it to his father, who was so far from reproving him, as he ought to have done, that he also did the same." "In the street, publicly before the people, he proclaimed his father's shame and mocked at it. For Ham is generally thought to have been an impious man, and some take him to have been the first inventor of idols after the flood."

Verse 25: *Cursed be Canaan*, etc. "If what I have said," continues Bishop Patrick, "be allowed, it makes it easy to give an account why Canaan is cursed rather than Ham, because he was first guilty. Ham, indeed, was punished in him; but he had other sons, on whom the punishment did not fall, but only on this. For which I can find no other reason so probable as that before named. Which, if it be not allowed, we must have recourse to a harsh interpretation; *and by Canaan, understand Canaan's father, as some do.*"

And Canaan shall be his servant. "As the blessing promised to Abraham was not fulfilled in his own person, but in his posterity many ages after his death; so this *curse upon Cham* did not take place till the same time; the execution of God's curse upon the one being his conferring a blessing on the other."

"It is observed by Campanella that 'none are descended from Cham but slaves, and tyrants, who are indeed slaves.' But Mr. Mede's observation is more pertinent. 'There hath never yet been a son of Cham that hath shaken a sceptre over the head of Japhet. Shem hath subdued Japhet, and Japhet subdued Shem, but Cham never subdued either.''

Here we have a different opinion, in some respects, from that which is preferred by Bishop Newton and others. But the commentator gives the worst character to Ham; and refers to the other interpretation as adopted by some, while he proposes his own with great modesty, and does not mention the Arabic version. Taking the whole, indeed, together, there is no serious conflict between these commentators.

We come next to Abraham's history, Gen. 12 : 5 : where Bishop Patrick interprets "*all the souls they had gotten,*" to mean, "All the *slaves* born in their house or bought with their money." And he refers to this in his comment upon Gen. 14 : 14, where we read that Abraham "*armed his trained servants,*" in these words: "Abram drew forth a select number of his servants, whom he had instructed to handle arms in case of any assault by robbers or injurious neighbors. We read before (12 : 5) of the servants (slaves) they brought with them from Haran; and now they were more increased, so that he might well make a little army out of them." It is plain, therefore, that these three hundred and eighteen servants were home-born *slaves*, according to this commentator.

In his remarks on Gen. 17 : 13, he is still more express, as follows: Verse 13. *He that is born in thy house, or bought with money, must needs be circumcised.* "Not whether they would or no, for men were not to be compelled to religion, which had been a profanation of this covenant. But Abraham was to persuade them to it; and if they consented not, to keep them no longer in his house, but *to sell them to some other people.* So Maimonides expounds it, in his book of Circumcision, chap. 1, which is true both of servants born in the house, and bought with money; but as for the children of these slaves, they were to be circumcised whether their parents would or no; *because they were the possession of their masters, not of their parents.* For which cause, *when the parents were set free, their children were left behind, as their master's goods.* Exod. 21 : 4."

Turning next to Bishop Patrick's Comment on the Tenth Commandment, Exodus 20 : 17, *Thou shalt not covet*, we find these words, *so,—god's commandment is cruel and needs Bishop Patrick's nursing to help it along.*

"*nor his man servant nor his maid servant,* etc., which are his PRIN-CIPAL GOODS."

On Exodus 21 : 4 : *If his master have given him a wife,* this learned commentator saith as follows: "Unto such a servant as this, who was sold by the Court of Judgment, his master might give a Gentile maid to wife (and no other Hebrew but such as he might marry a Gentile) that he might beget children of her, *who were to be the master's servants or slaves forever.*"

"*The wife and children shall be his master's.* For the wife was a slave as well as himself when he married her. And she was given to wife, merely that he might beget slaves of her, who therefore *continued with the master, as well as their mother, when the man had his liberty, for they were not so much his, as his master's goods;* who had such a power over them, that he might circumcise them, as he did his own children, without their consent."

Here we see that the separation of the family was not considered so awful a thing under the Jewish system of slavery. Nor, indeed, can one help wondering at the indignant reproaches of many philanthropic persons, on account of the same difficulty in the Southern institution. For we all know that our free families separate of their own accord every day, on the slightest inducements of advantage; and the bonds of parental and filial attachment are so weak, that any personal inclination or interest suffices to break them. So general is this fact that I doubt whether there is half as much of this very separation amongst the slaves by the act of their masters, as there is amongst freemen, by the force of discontent, the love of change, cupidity, and ambition.

But let us not digress too much from our commentary, where the case of the slave, killed by his master, next invites attention.

Exod. 21 : 20 : *If a man smite his servant.* "A slave," saith Bishop Patrick, "who was not an Israelite, but a Gentile."

He shall surely be punished. "With death, say the Hebrew doctors, (in Selden, lib. iv.,) if the servant died while he was beating him; for that is meant by dying *under his hand.* But it seems more likely to me that he was to be punished for his cruelty, as the judge who examined this fact thought meet. For his smiting *with a rod,* not with a sword, was a sign that he intended only to correct him, not to kill him. And besides, no man could be thought to be willing to lose his own goods, as such servants were.

4*

Verse 21 : *Notwithstanding if he continue a day or two.* "A day and a night, as the Hebrew doctors interpret it."

He shall not be punished. "Because it might be presumed he did not die of these strokes."

He is his money. "His death was a loss to his master, who therefore might well be judged not to have any intention to kill him, and was sufficiently punished by losing the benefit of his service."

We come now to the Jubilee, which the ultra-abolitionist always quotes as a proof that every fiftieth year set free not only those Hebrews who were held in temporary bondage, but also the slaves, without any exception. No error could be more grossly inexcusable than this. But let us look at the judgment of Bishop Patrick upon the question.

Leviticus 25 : 10. *And ye shall hallow the fiftieth year, and proclaim liberty throughout all the land unto all the inhabitants thereof.* "That is," saith our commentator, to all *the children of Israel* who were servants ; or so poor that they had sold their estates."

And ye shall return every man to his possession. "Unto his field or his house, which his poverty had forced him to sell, but now was restored to him without any price, because they were not sold absolutely but only to this year. By which means the estates of the Israelites were so fixed, that no family could ruin itself or grow too rich. For this law provided against such changes, revoking once in fifty years all alienations, and setting every one in the same condition wherein he was at the first."

V. 39. *And if thy brother that dwelleth by thee be waxen poor, and be sold unto thee.* "Some were sold by the court of judgment when they had committed theft, and were not able to make satisfaction. Others were sold by their parents, (Exod. 21 : 7, 8.) But others sold themselves, being reduced to great poverty, notwithstanding the alms that had been bestowed upon them. And of such the Hebrew doctors understand these words."

Thou shalt not compel him to serve as a bond-servant. "As a *slave*, which they bought of other nations or took in their wars ; over whom they had an *absolute dominion*, (as they had over their goods and cattle,) and might *bequeath them and their children to their sons and posterity forever* (v. 45–6) *or sell them and their children at their pleasure.*"

Verse 40. *But as a hired servant and as a sojourner.* "They were to treat him gently, as they did those who let out their service for wages, for a certain time, and then were at their own disposal again."

And shall serve thee unto the year of Jubilee. "Beyond which time it was not lawful to keep him in service; for in the very beginning of this year, all such servants were dismissed."

Verse 41. *And then shall he depart from thee, both he and his children with him.* "His master to whom he was sold might keep him till the Jubilee, whereas he that was sold by the court of judgment might go free, if he pleased, in the *seventh* year of release." (Exod. 21 : 2.)

Verse 42. *For they are my servants which I brought forth out of the land of Egypt.* "A good reason why they should not be treated like slaves, because they were all redeemed by God out of the slavery of Egypt into a state of perfect liberty."

Verse 44. *Both thy bondmen and thy bondmaids which thou shalt have, shall be of the heathen.* "If they would have any slaves, they were to be such of other nations as were sold to them or were taken by them in their wars. Whence the very name of *mancipia* came, as the Roman lawyers tell us, *quasi manu capti*, and the name of *servus* also, which signifies one who was saved when he might have been killed."

Verse 45. *Moreover of the children of the strangers that do sojourn among you, of them shall ye buy.* "Whether they were perfect proselytes by circumcision or only proselytes of the gate, their children were not exempted from being made slaves, if they sold them to the Hebrews."

And of the families that are with you, which they begat in your land. "If any of their family or kindred, as the Seventy translate it, had begat children in Judea, and would sell them, the Jews might make a purchase of them."

They shall be your possession. "Become your proper goods and continue with you, as your lands do, unless they have their liberty granted to them. And the first sort of proselytes obtained it three ways; either by purchasing it themselves or by their friends; or by being dismissed by their master, by a writing under his hand; or in the case mentioned in Exod. 21 : 26, when the loss of an eye or a tooth by the master's severity serve only for examples of other maims, which procured such a servant his liberty. But the second sort of proselytes did not obtain their liberty, if we may believe the Hebrew doctors, by this last means, but only by the two first. *And the year of Jubilee gave no servants of either sort their liberty.*

Verse 46. *And ye shall take them as an inheritance for your children after you.* "To whom they might bequeath the very bodies of them and their children."

To inherit them for a possession. "That they might have the same power and dominion over them that they had over their lands, goods, or cattle."

They shall be your bondmen forever. "*Not have the benefit of the year of Jubilee,* but be your slaves as long as they live; unless they, by any of the means before mentioned, obtain their liberty."

I have thus shown, clearly and distinctly, that according to this learned commentator, who was particularly conversant with the writings of the Jews, the slaves of the heathen races, notwithstanding they were proselytes, were *not set free* in the year of Jubilee, that privilege being entirely confined to the posterity of Jacob, the chosen people. And next I shall set before you the judgment of Bishop Patrick upon that other text, which is equally misrepresented by the teachers of ultra-abolitionism.

Deut. 23 : 15. *Thou shalt not deliver unto his master the servant which is escaped from his master unto thee.* "The Hebrew doctors understand this of a servant of another nation who was become a Jew; whom his master, if he went to dwell out of Judea, might not carry along with him against his will; and if he fled from him when he had carried him, he might not be delivered to him, but suffered to dwell in the land of Israel. *Which they understand also of a servant that fled from his master out of any of the countries of the Gentiles into the land of Israel, which was to be a safe refuge to him.*" (See Selden, lib. vi.)

The latter part of the above is the explanation given in the *Bible View of Slavery*, where it is shown that the distorted interpretation of the ultra-abolitionist is a sheer absurdity.

And now I come to the other favorite text about man-stealing. Deut. 24 : 7. *If any man be found stealing any of his brethren the children of Israel, and maketh merchandise of him or selleth him, then that thief shall die.*

The comment of Bishop Patrick refers to a similar law in ancient Athens, by which if any one stole a man, "*death should be his punishment,* as Xenophon reports it. And he was accounted a *man-*

stealer, who, not only by force or by fraud, carried away a freeman and sold him for a slave, or suppressed him ; but *he who inveigled away another man's servant, and persuaded him to run away, or concealed such a fugitive.* (As Sam. Petitus observes, out of Pollux and others, lib. vii. Leges Atticas, tit. 5. p. 533.) Which makes me think," continues our commentator, " not only he that stole *one of his brethren of the children of Israel,* but he that stole *a proselyte of any sort, or the servant of a stranger,* was liable to the punishment mentioned in this law of Moses."

I commend this passage, my Right Reverend Brother, to your special attention, because it has a double application against the doctrine of the ultra-abolitionist. By that doctrine we are told that, according to the Mosaic law, the deadly sin of man-stealing was committed by those who first brought the savage negro from the slave-coast of Africa, and continues to attach to the slave-owner of the present day, whose title is no better than the original. And by the same doctrine we are assured, that it is laudable and virtuous to induce a slave to run away from his master, and to conceal the fugitive, if necessary to insure his escape. But Bishop Patrick repudiates both these assumptions, showing, with respect to the first, that the law of Moses forbade the stealing of *an Israelite,* and said nothing of the heathen barbarian ; and, with respect to the second, that he who inveigled a proselyte, being a bond-servant, and " persuaded him to run away from his master, or concealed such a fugitive," was so far from the performance of a meritorious action, that he was " liable to the punishment" mentioned in this very law. If Bishop Patrick had foreseen the reckless style in which our ultra-abolitionists pervert this text at the present day, he could hardly have written a more apposite condemnation.

Let us now pass on to the texts in the New Testament, and examine what the same commentary pronounces concerning them. And here we have it arranged in the manner of a paraphrase.

Eph. 6 : 5 : " Servants be obedient to them that are your masters, (though they be only so,) according to the flesh, (the spirit being immediately subject to God alone,) with fear (of displeasing them) and trembling (lest you should justly incur their anger, serving them) in singleness of your heart, as (knowing that in thus serving them you do service) unto Christ, (who requires this of you, whose Gospel you will credit by your sincere obedience to your masters for his sake,

Tit. 2 : 2, and whose doctrine you will blaspheme by your disobedience, under pretense of any Christian liberty, from the observance of
your duty to them. 1 Tim. 6 : 1, 2.   9. "And, ye masters, do the
same things to them, (show the like good-will to and concern for
them,) forbearing threatening, (remitting oft the evils which you
threaten to them,) knowing that your Master also is in heaven."

Colos. 2 : 22 : "Servants, obey in all (lawful) things (those who are)
your masters according to the flesh." Verse 25. But he (of you)
that doeth wrong (to his master) shall receive (of the Lord, punishment) for the wrong which he hath done, and there is no respect of
persons with him."

Ch. 3 : 1 : "Masters, give unto your servants that which is just
and equal, knowing that you also have a Master in heaven, (who,
with what measure ye mete to others, will mete to you again, Matt.
7 : 2, and deal with you, his servants, as you deal with yours.) "

In the annotation on verse 25 of the second chapter, the commentator saith as follows, viz. :

Verse 25, *Respect of persons.* "Christ, in judging men at the last
day, will have no respect to the quality or external condition of any
man's person ; but whether he be bond or free, he shall receive recompense *for the good that he hath done*, in obedience to him, whether he be master or servant, he shall be punished for the *wrong that
he did* in those relations. It being certain, from the second chapter,
that the Judaizers were got into the Church of Colosse, and that
many of them denied that the Jews ought to be servants to any, and
the Essenes judging all servitude unlawful, this might be the reason
why here, and Titus 2, the Apostle is so large in charging this duty
on servants."

In the preface to the Epistle of St. Paul to Philemon, the commentator proceeds as follows :

"First, no Christian, though of the meanest sort, is to be contemn-
ed. Christianity makes the vilest servant both profitable and worthy
to be highly loved and honored by persons in the highest dignity,
Onesimus being by the Apostle styled his son, and his bowels."

"Secondly. Christianity *doth not impair the power of masters
over their servants,* or give any authority to them who convert them
to use them as their servants, without leave granted from their masters."

"Thirdly. Servants ought to make satisfaction for any wrong or injury they have done to their masters."

"Fourthly. There is an affection due from the master to a profitable servant."

These extracts are abundantly sufficient to prove the substantial accordance of Patrick, Lowth, and Whitby, with all that has gone before.

CHAPTER XVI.

Right Reverend Brother: The commentary of the Rev. Dr. Matthew Henry, which is a favorite with very many, may next be cited, and I shall make several extracts from it, bearing on our subject.

On Levit. 25 : 39, etc., this author writes as follows : "We have here the laws concerning servitude. First. That a native Israelite should never be made a bondman for perpetuity. If he was sold for debt, or for a crime, by the house of judgment, he was to serve but six years, and to go out the seventh. That was appointed, Exod. 21 : 2. But if he sold himself, through extreme poverty, having nothing at all left him to preserve his life, and if it was to one of his own nation that he sold himself, in such case it is here provided, first, that he should not serve as a *bond-servant*, nor be *sold with the sale of a bondman*, that is, it must not be looked upon that his master that bought him had as *absolute a property in him as in a captive taken in war, that might be used, sold, and bequeathed, at pleasure*, as much as a man's cattle; no, he shall serve thee as a hired servant. Second. That he should not be ruled with rigor, and his work and usage must be such as were fitting for a son of Abraham. Third. That at the year of jubilee he should go out free, he and his children, and should return to his own family and possession."

"But the Jews might *purchase bondmen of the heathen nations that were round about them*, or of those strangers that sojourned among them, and might claim a dominion over them, and entail them upon their families as an inheritance, *for the year of jubilee should give no discharge to them.*"

I turn next to the comment on Deut. 23 : 15, where the precept occurs : "Thou shalt not deliver unto his master the servant which is escaped from his master unto thee." And here we find Matthew Henry adopting the same interpretation which we have already seen in the other commentaries—the only one which could be adopted with any sense or reason, viz. :

"First. The land of Israel," saith he, "is here made a sanctuary, or city of refuge, for servants that were wronged by their masters, and fled thither for shelter, *from the neighboring countries*, v. 15–16. We can not suppose that they were hereby obliged to give shelter to all the unprincipled men that ran from service; Israel needed not (as Rome at first did) to be thus peopled. But, first, they must not deliver up the trembling servant to his enraged master, *till upon trial it appeared that the servant had wronged his master, and was justly liable to punishment*. Note, it is an honorable thing to shelter and protect the weak, provided they be not wicked. God allows his people to patronize the oppressed. The angel bid Hagar return to her mistress, and St. Paul sent Onesimus back to his master, Philemon, because they had neither of them any cause to go away, nor were either of them exposed to any danger in returning. But the servant here is *supposed to escape, that is, to run for his life* to the people of Israel, of whom he had heard that they were a merciful people, to *save himself from the fury of a tyrant*, and in that case, to deliver him up, is to *throw a lamb into the mouth of a lion*."

"Second. If it appeared that the servant was abused, they must not only protect him, but, supposing him willing to embrace their religion, they must give him all the encouragement that might be, to settle among them. Thus would he soon find a comfortable difference *between the land of Israel and other lands*, and would choose it to be his rest forever."

Here we see, 1st, That this commentator properly limits the precept to the case of fugitive slaves "from the neighboring countries," namely, *foreigners*, and therefore it could have no application to the slaves who abscond from the Southern States, because those States were bound with the rest under the same Constitution, which specially provided for them.

2. We see that, even in the case of foreign fugitives, Henry would have the Israelites *hear the master*, and judge whether the slave had any cause to justify his running away. And if, on a hearing, it appeared that he had wronged his master, and was justly liable to punishment, he should be delivered up again.

3. We see that the commentator refers to Hagar, whom the angel sent back to her mistress, and to Onesimus, whom St. Paul sent back to his master Philemon, because "neither of them had any cause to run away, nor ere either of them exposed to any danger in return-

ing." And the kind of danger to which Henry refers is perfectly manifest when he tells us, that the servant is "supposed to *run for his life*," to save himself from "the *fury of a tyrant*," in which case, "to deliver him up is to *throw a lamb into the mouth of a lion.*"

4. We see, lastly, that the Israelites, on hearing the facts, as well on the part of the master as on the part of the fugitive, would be likely to decide according to the established laws of servitude, because they likewise were slaveholders, and would therefore be sufficiently careful to pronounce no judgment unfavorable to the rights of the master, or likely to encourage the rebellion of slaves against themselves.

Thus reasonably interpreted, it needs no argument to show that this precept, so constantly cited by the ultra-abolitionists as an excuse for violating the fugitive slave law, has not the slightest application to the subject. And the popular perversion of it to such a purpose is only a specimen of the "wresting of Scripture," which is unhappily so common at this day.

The text in Deut. 24 : 7, which forbids man-stealing, is commented on very briefly by Dr. Henry, but he does not differ from the rest. These are his words, viz. :

"This was a very heinous offense, for, first, it was robbing the public of one of its members; second, it was taking away a man's liberty, the liberty of a *free-born Israelite*, which was next in value to his life; third, it was driving a man out from the *inheritance of the land* (Israel) to the privileges of which he was entitled, and bidding him *go serve other gods*, as David complains against Saul. 1 Sam. 26 : 19."

This is the whole; but brief as it is, we see that Henry considers the law as only applicable to the case of stealing and selling *an Israelite to a heathen people*.

The remarks of Cruden, in his *Concordance*, under the word "steal," are very fair, viz. : "Though there was no penalty annexed to the law forbidding theft," saith he, "except restitution, yet to steal away a freeman, or an Hebrew, and to reduce him to the state of servitude, was punished with death. Exod. 21 : 16. The Jews do not think that the stealing of a man of any other nation deserves death, but only the theft of a free Hebrew. If it be a stranger that is stole, they were only condemned to restitution. They found this distinction upon a law in Deut. 24 : 7, which limits this law concerning man-stealing : *If a man be found stealing any of his brethren of the children of Israel ;* which exception the Septuagint and Onkelos have inserted in the text of Exod. 21 : 16."

On the passages which I have cited from the New Testament, the commentary of Dr. Henry confirms what we have seen in the others. Thus, on 1 Cor. 7 : 21, "*Art thou called, being a servant? care not for it, but if thou mayest be made free, use it rather,*" he saith : " It was common in that age of the world, for many to be in a state of slavery, bought and sold for money, and so the property of those who purchased them. 'Now,' says the Apostle, '*art thou called, being a servant? care not for it.*' Be not over-solicitous about it. It is not inconsistent with thy duty, profession, or hopes, as a Christian. *Yet, if thou mayest be made free, use it rather.* (21) There are many conveniences in a state of freedom, above that of servitude ; therefore, liberty is the more eligible state. But men's outward condition does not let nor further their acceptance with God. For he that is called, *being a servant, is the Lord's freeman, as he that is called, being free, is the Lord's servant.* Though he be not discharged from his master's service, he is freed from the dominion and vassalage of sin. He who is a slave may yet be a Christian freeman; he who is a freeman may yet be Christ's servant. He is bought with a price, and should not therefore be the servant of man. *Not that he must quit the service of his master, or not take all proper measures to please him, (this were to contradict the whole scope of the Apostle's discourse,)* but he must not be so the servant of men, but that Christ's will must be obeyed and regarded, more than his master's. He has paid a much dearer purchase for him, and has a much fuller property in him."

V. 24. *Let every man wherein he is called, abide therein with God.* "This," continues our commentator, " is to be understood of the state wherein a man is converted to Christianity. *No man should make his faith or religion an argument to break through any natural or civil obligations.* He should quietly and comfortably abide in the condition in which he is, and this he may well do, when he may abide therein with God. Note, the special presence and favor of God are not limited to any outward condition or performance. He may enjoy it who is circumcised. And so may he who is uncircumcised. He who is bound may have it, as well as he who is free.

In this respect, *there is neither Greek nor Jew, circumcision nor un-circumcision, barbarian nor Scythian, bond nor free.* (Col. 3 : 2.)"

Again, in the comment on Eph. 6 : 5 : *Servants, be obedient,* etc., we read as follows, viz. : "The duty of servants is summed up in one word, which is obedience. *These servants were generally slaves : civil servitude is not inconsistent with Christian liberty.*"

V. 9. *And ye masters, do the same thing unto them.*   "Observe," saith our commentator, "masters are under as strict obligations to discharge their duty to their servants, as servants are to be obedient and dutiful to them."

The same doctrine occurs, in yet stronger terms, in the comment on 1 Tim. 6 : 1 : *Let as many servants as are under the yoke, count their own masters worthy of all honor,* etc. Thus the author writes, viz. :

" If Christianity finds servants under the yoke, *it continues them under it, for the Gospel does not cancel the obligations any lie under,* either by the law of nature or by mutual consent."—"Suppose the master were a Christian and a believer, and the servant a believer too, would not that excuse him, because, *in Christ there is neither bond nor free?* No, by no means, *for Jesus Christ did not come to dissolve the bond of civil relation,* BUT TO STRENGTHEN IT."

We now come to the epistle of St. Paul to Philemon.   " The occasion of it," saith our commentator, "was this: Philemon, one of note, and probably a minister in the church of Colosse, a city of Phrygia, had a servant named Onesimus, who, having purloined his goods, ran away from him, and in his rambles came to Rome, where Paul was then a prisoner for the Gospel; and providentially coming under his preaching there, was, by the blessing of God, converted by him: after which, he ministered awhile to the Apostle in bonds, and might have been further useful to him ; but understanding him to be another man's servant, he would not, without his consent, detain him, but sends him back with this letter commendatory. With what earnestness does he concern himself for this poor slave ! Being now, through his preaching, reconciled to God, he labors for reconciliation between him and his master."

V. 16. *Not now as a servant, but above a servant, a brother beloved,* etc.   "That is," saith our commentator, "not *merely* or so much, but above a servant in a spiritual respect, to be owned as a brother in Christ, and to be loved as such, upon account of the holy change wrought in him, and who will therefore *be useful to thee on better principles and in a better manner than before.*"

I shall add but one extract more, from this esteemed commentary, and that is on 1 Pet. 2 : 18 : *Servants, be subject to your masters with all fear, not only to the good and gentle, but also to the froward.* Thus saith our author, viz. :

"The case of servants wanted an apostolical determination as well as that of subjects, for they imagined that their Christian liberty set them free from their unbelieving and cruel *masters.* To this the Apostle answers: *Servants, be subject.* By *servants,* he means those who were strictly such, whether hired, or bought with money, or taken in the wars, or born in the house, or those who served by contract for a limited time, as apprentices; these he orders to be *subject,* to do their business faithfully and honestly, to conduct themselves, as inferiors ought, with reverence and affection, and to submit patiently to hardships and inconveniences. This subjection they owe to their *masters,* who have a right to their service; and that *not only to the good and gentle,* such as use them well, but even to the crooked and perverse, who are scarcely to be pleased at all."

Here, then, we have a number of clear and distinct statements on the subject of slavery, as well under the Mosaic law as under the apostles, from the favorite commentary of our Presbyterian brethren, which not only occupied the first rank during the eighteenth century, but was republished in A.D. 1829, by the eminent Dr. Archibald Alexander, with the warmest commendations, as worthy of all regard and confidence. The Rev. Edward Bickersteth gave it his high praise. The judicious Charles Buck, author of the *Theological Dictionary,* said : "In my opinion, Henry takes the lead for common utility." And the pious William Romaine declared that there was "no comment on the Bible, either ancient or modern, in all respects equal to Mr. Henry's." Distinguished as it is by our Presbyterian brethren, and by the evangelical party in our own Church, I trust that you will be ready to adopt its doctrine as a safe guide, notwithstanding the temptation to favor the very contrary assumptions of ultra abolitionism.

CHAPTER XVII.

RIGHT REVEREND BROTHER: I proceed, in the order laid down, to the commentary of Rev. Thomas Scott, republished in Philadelphia in 1862, from the London edition of 1822. It belongs therefore, properly, to the present century, and has been, I presume, the most extensively patronized in our own country. The same ground must be again gone over, notwithstanding the repetition, because I have promised to make thorough work of my labor. And we shall see that as Scott wrote his commentary, after the great abolition movement in England, commenced by Wilberforce and others, he shows the influence of the times very strongly, in many places, and was evidently disposed to sympathize with the popular sentiment, as far as possible, without too glaring a contradiction to the sacred text.

Thus, on Gen. 9 : 24–7, containing the prophecy of Noah, this commentator saith that the posterity of Canaan "were no doubt *principally* though *not exclusively* intended." And he quotes from Bishop Newton: "The whole continent of Africa was peopled principally by the descendants of Ham, and for how many ages have the better parts of this country lain under the dominion of the Romans, and then of the Saracens, and now of the Turks. In what wickedness, ignorance, barbarity, slavery, misery, live most of the inhabitants! And of the poor negroes, how many hundreds every year are sold and bought, like beasts in the market, and conveyed from one quarter of the world to do the work of beasts in another." "This, however," saith Scott, "in no measure vindicates the covetous and barbarous oppression of those who thus enrich themselves with the products of their sweat and blood. God has not commanded us to enslave negroes, as he did Israel to extirpate the Canaanites, and therefore, without doubt, he will severely punish this cruel injustice." He then proceeds to say that "true religion has hitherto flourished very little among Ham's descendants. They remain to this day almost entire strangers to Christianity, and *their condition in every age has remarkably coincided with this prediction.*"

Here we have the key-note of Rev. Thomas Scott's commentary on the subject. And yet, notwithstanding his evident bias towards abolitionism, he is obliged to acknowledge, first, that the prophecy of Noah did not *exclusively* refer to Canaan's descendants. If not, then it must have included the other descendants of Ham. And secondly, he admits that the *condition of Ham's descendants* in every age, *coincided remarkably* with the prophecy. Thus we have a reluctant admission of the same substantial truth stated by the previous commentators.

As to his statement about the negroes, and the judgment of God upon their oppressors, there is no question about the truth that the Almighty will punish all oppression and injustice, whether towards slaves or hirelings, whether it be exhibited under the law of bondage, or by the power of Mammon, grinding the face of the poor. But it must be remembered that in all remarks like these, he is not performing the work of a commentator on the Bible, whose duty it is to explain the Word of God, and not to set his personal notions or feelings in opposition to it. I shall have occasion to pass the same censure on this author on other occasions, as I proceed. Meanwhile his admissions, on this very account, are the more valuable, because they are extorted from him, in spite of his prejudices, by the force of truth.

The change of sentiment which had now taken place is plainly manifested in his note on Exodus 21. Thus he saith, that "Slavery was almost universal in the world, and though, like war, it always proceeded of evil, and was generally evil in itself, yet *the wisdom of God deemed it better to regulate them to prohibit it.* We should not, however, judge of the practice itself by these *judicial* regulations, but by the *law of love.* Slavery, like war, may in some cases in the present state of things be lawful; for the crime which forfeits life no doubt forfeits liberty; and it is not inconsistent even with the moral law for a criminal to be sold and treated as a slave, during a term of time proportioned to his offense. In most other cases, if not in all, it must be *inconsistent with the law of love.*"

And again, in his comment on verse 16 of the same chapter, we have another example. *He that stealeth a man and selleth him, or if he be found in his hand, he shall surely be put to death.* "The Jewish writers assert," saith he, "that it was not a capital crime to steal one of another nation, but only when the person stolen was a

Hebrew. Yet this is by no means consistent with the text, which certainly implies that he who stole any one of the human species, in order to make a slave of him, should be punished with death."

Now in the first of these extracts the commentator entirely disregards the fact that the law of love was laid down to the Jew as well as to the Christian, and yet in the Ten Commandments, which are the *moral law* by eminence, we find the bondman and the bondmaid distinctly specified as property not to be coveted. In the second extract he ignores the text in Deut. 24 : 7, where the same law respecting man-stealing is stated more fully, with the very limitation on which the Jewish doctors insist, viz. :

"*If a man be found stealing any of his brethren of the children of Israel, and maketh merchandise of him or selleth him, then that man shall die.*" And when we come to his commentary on this text we read as follows, viz. :

"Christianity has *annihilated that distinction of nations*, which, for typical and political reasons, was during a time established, and in this respect *every man is now our brother*, whatever be his nation, complexion, or creed. How, then, can the merchandise of men and women be carried on without transgressing this commandment, or abetting those who do ?"

Here this author asserts a downright absurdity. Christianity has not annihilated the distinction of nations, nor was it intended, as all the previous commentaries plainly declare, to change the laws of earthly governments, or do away with the social relations established among mankind. The brotherhood which the Gospel sets forth is not carnal but spiritual. The kingdom of Christ is not of this world. True, indeed, God hath made of one blood all the nations upon earth, and therefore, by reason of our common parentage, all men may be called brethren in a certain sense. But Christian brotherhood is created by our adoption into the family of Christ, through faith and baptism, by which we are entitled to call God our Father in heaven. And nothing can be more false than the assertion that Christianity has made the heathen savage any more *our* brother than he was the brother of the Jew under the Mosaic dispensation.

Dr. Scott gives a notable comment also upon Lev. 25 : 44, etc. "Both thy bondmen and thy bondmaids which thou shalt have, shall be of the heathen that are round about you ; of them shall ye buy bondmen and bondmaids. Moreover of the children of the strangers that do sojourn among you, of them shall ye buy, and of their families that are with you, and they shall be your possession. And ye shall take them as an inheritance for your children after you, to inherit them for a possession ; they shall be your bondmen forever; but over your brethren, the children of Israel, ye shall not rule one over another with rigor."

Now here is his commentary : " The Israelites were *permitted* to keep slaves of other nations ; perhaps in order to typify that none but the true Israel of God participate of that liberty with which Christ hath made his people free. *But it was also allowed in order that the Gentiles might become acquainted with true religion :* and when the Israelites copied the example of their pious progenitors, there can be no reasonable doubt that it was *overruled to the eternal salvation of many souls.* It does not, however, appear from the subsequent history that the people availed themselves of this allowance to any great extent, for we read but little of slaves from among the Gentiles possessed by them."

It seems passing strange to me that this good man could see so clearly the reason of the Almighty in directing the slavery of the heathen nations round about Judea, viz., in *order that the Gentiles might become acquainted with true religion,* so that it was *overruled to the eternal salvation of many souls,* and yet could not see that the slavery of the negro race admits of the very same justification. For certain it is that they were by that means redeemed from the slavery of Guinea, where two thirds of the whole people are in that condition, and redeemed besides from the awful barbarism and idolatry described by Malte Brun. And it is equally certain that millions of their posterity have found the way to eternal salvation, under the Southern institution, who must otherwise have lived and died in utter darkness and misery.

But Dr. Scott was not in the mood to discern this application of his argument. Neither does he inform his readers that the Jubilee, of which he had been writing at great length, did not operate on the condition of the slaves, though that fact was stated plainly by the previous commentators. He fancies, however, that the Israelites did not avail themselves of the divine allowance to any great extent, although he knew that Abraham had three hundred and eighteen servants born in his own house, which were but a portion of the whole. He knew, moreover, that when the Jews returned from the captivity

7

in Babylon, the free population amounted to forty-two thousand three hundred and sixty, and the slaves to seven thousand three hundred and thirty-seven, (Ezra 2 : 64–5,) that is, about one slave to every six persons, women and children included. And he also knew that when David ordered Joab to number Israel, it was found that the men who were fit for war amounted to one million three hundred thousand, which, computing that these could not have been more than one fourth of the whole population, reckoning both sexes and all ages, would bring the sum total to five million two hundred thousand souls. Now, if we allow only the moderate proportion of one sixth, which was the actual number of the slaves when the Jews returned from Babylon, we shall have eight hundred and sixty-six thousand six hundred and sixty-six slaves as the aggregate in the reign of David. And as the tribe of Levi was not numbered, we can not seriously err if we compute the number of slaves to nearly a million. But our commentator saith that we read *but little* concerning them. Do we read any more, or even as much, of the hired servants? How plainly do we see here the strong bias of his mind, which could not allow him to deal fairly by the positive text of the sacred Scriptures when slavery was in question!

But we shall find this commentator more faithful in the Epistolary portions of the New Testament. Thus, Eph. 6 : 5 : "*Servants, be obedient to your masters*," etc. "The Apostle," saith our commentator, "next exhorts servants who had embraced Christianity to be obedient to their masters, according to the flesh, that is, to whom they were subjected in temporal matters. In general, the servants at that time were slaves, the property of their masters, and were often treated with great severity, though *seldom with that systematic cruelty which commonly attends slavery in these days*." (Where did Dr. Scott find his authority for this statement? The testimony of history is altogether against him.) "But the apostles were ministers of religion," continues he, "not politicians; they had not that influence among rulers and legislators which would have been necessary for the abolition of slavery. Indeed, in that state of society as to other things, this would not have been expedient: God did not please miraculously to interpose in the case, and they were not required to exasperate their persecutors by expressly contending against the lawfulness of slavery. Yet both the law of love and the Gospel of grace tend to its abolition as far as they are known and regarded; and the universal prevalence of Christianity must annihilate slavery, with many other evils, which, in the present state of things, can not wholly be avoided. In the wisdom of God the apostles were left to take such matters as they found them, and to teach servants and masters their respective duties, in the performance of which the evil would be mitigated, till in due time it should be extirpated by Christian legislators."

On 1 Tim. 6 : 1 : *Let as many servants as are under the yoke count their own masters worthy of all honor,* etc. "The Apostle next," saith our commentator, "directed, that Christians, who were under the yoke of slavery, should quietly attend to the duties of their lowly situation, counting their own masters entitled to all the respect, fidelity, and obedience, which that superior relation demanded; and not supposing that their religious knowledge, privileges, or liberty, gave them a right to despise their heathen masters, to speak or act disrespectfully to them, to disobey their lawful commands, or to expose their faults to their neighbors. And such of them as enjoyed the privilege of believing masters, ought by no means to despise them, or withhold from them due respect and obedience, because they were brethren in Christ, and so upon a level in respect of religious privileges; but rather do them service, with double diligence and cheerfulness, because of their faith in Christ, and their interest in his love, as partakers of the inestimable benefit of his salvation. This shows that *Christian masters were not required to set their slaves at liberty,* though they were instructed to behave towards them in such a manner as would greatly lessen and nearly annihilate the evils of slavery. It would have excited much confusion, awakened the jealousy of the civil powers, and greatly retarded the progress of Christianity, had the liberation of slaves by their converts been expressly required by the Apostles : [though the principles of both the law and the Gospel, when carried to their consequences, will infallibly abolish slavery.] These things Timothy was directed to teach and enforce as matters of the greatest importance, and if any persons taught otherwise, and consented not to such salutary words, which were indeed the words of Christ 'speaking by him,' and an essential part of the doctrine according to godliness, he must be considered as a self-conceited ignorant man, who, being puffed up with an opinion of his own abilities, was ambitious of distinction and applause, though entirely unacquainted with the real nature and tendency of the Gospel."

"It is not absolutely certain," continues Dr. Scott, "to what set of men the Apostle referred; but as many of the Jews deemed it unlawful to submit to heathen governors, it is probable some of the Judaizing teachers inculcated that the worshipers of God ought not to obey heathen masters, and so paid their court to servants, by persuading them that they ought to assert their liberty. But there might be others also who disregarded and despised those practical instructions, while their attention was taken up with curious and nice speculations and distinctions. Such persons, however, were to be considered as doting or talking wildly, like sick and delirious persons, about hard questions and disputes of words, names, forms, or notions, which had no connection with the power of godliness. Indeed, these questions and disputes tended to excite envy and competition between one and another, angry contests for victory and preëminence, mutual reviling and calumnies, injurious suspicions and jealousies, and absurd, obstinate, and violent controversies, betwixt men of corrupt and carnal minds, who were destitute of the real knowledge of the truth and its sanctifying efficacy, and who only sought their own secular advantage; supposing religion to be valuable, in proportion as it tended to enrich them, as if *gain* and *godliness* had been but two names for the same thing. Thus they wanted to persuade the Christian servants that the recovery of their liberty was to be considered as a Christian privilege of great value, which they ought to claim, whatever the consequence might be. From such men, Timothy was exhorted to *withdraw himself*, and neither have acquaintance with them, nor spend his time in disputing with them."

Now so far as these extracts are *commentaries*, they are just and true, agreeing with the previous authors whose language I have quoted. The fault is that Dr. Scott interlards them with what is not a commentary on Scripture, but his own notions about the *reasons* which influenced the divine mind to have nothing said which could excite commotion, provoke the civil government, or hinder the progress of the Gospel. But while I object to the error of confounding the notions of Dr. Scott with the real authority of an inspired Apostle, I am willing to accept them so far as this, viz.: that they apply with all their force to the attacks of ultra-abolitionism upon the Constitution and the laws of the Union at the present day. It is sufficient for my purpose, however, to have the testimony of this commentator to the fact, that Christian masters *were not required to emancipate their slaves by the Gospel, as St. Paul expounded it.* Of course, the Apostle could not have supposed that slaveholding was a *sin*, and I contend that until it pleases God to send us a new revelation, by inspired men, able, like the Apostles, to prove their divine commission by miracles, the Church is solemnly *bound* to set forth the *same doctrine that St. Paul commanded Timothy to teach;* and if she dares to authorize the contrary doctrine, she becomes, so far, an apostate, and a rebel against the Word of the Almighty.

In the preface to the Epistle to Philemon, Dr. Scott pursues the same track with the other commentators, and in his note on verses 12–16, he saith as follows:

"Onesimus was Philemon's legal property, and St. Paul had required and prevailed with Onesimus to return to him, having made sufficient trial of his sincerity; and he requested Philemon to receive him with the same kindness as he would the aged Apostle's own son according to the flesh, being equally dear to him as his spiritual child. He would gladly have kept him at Rome, to minister to him in his confinement; but he would not do any thing of this kind without his master's consent, lest he should seem to extort the benefit, and Philemon should appear to act from 'necessity,' rather than 'from a willing mind.' He had, indeed, hopes of deriving benefit from Onesimus's faithful service, at some future period, by Philemon's free consent, yet he was not sure that this was the Lord's purpose respecting him, for perhaps he permitted him to leave his master for a season in so improper a manner, in order that, being converted, he might be received on his return with such affection, and might abide with Philemon with such faithfulness and diligence, that they should choose to live together the rest of their lives, as fellow-heirs of eternal felicity. In this case he knew that Philemon would no longer consider Onesimus *merely as a slave*, but view him as 'above a slave, even as a brother beloved.' This he was become to Paul in an especial manner, who had before been entirely a stranger to him: how much more, then, might it be supposed that he would be endeared to Philemon, when he became well acquainted with his excellency, seeing he would be near to him, both in the flesh, *as one of his*

domestics, and in the Lord, being one with him in Christ, as a believer!"

Now, my Right Reverend Brother, while I can not close my eyes
to the manifest bias in favor of abolition which is so apparent in many
parts of Scott's Commentary, I have shown that he does not differ,
substantially, from any of the rest. He tells us indeed, frequently,
that the law of love will eventually annihilate slavery. But this law
of love was proclaimed by Moses, and our Lord recognizes the fact,
(Luke 10 : 26–7) when He said to one of his tempters : "What is written in the law? how readest thou?" And he answering said : "Thou
shalt love the Lord thy God with all thy heart, and with all thy soul,
and with all thy strength, and with all thy mind, and thy neighbor
as thyself." The Gospel added nothing to this law of love, because
any enlargement of it was impossible. But He alone fulfilled it to
perfection, and gave us a glorious example, and a new motive for our
obedience, according to the declaration of the Apostle, (1 John
3 : 16 :) "Hereby we perceive the love of God, because he laid down
his life for us, and we ought to lay down our lives for the brethren."
If, then, the law of love was set forth by the Almighty from the beginning, and the sanction of slavery was also given, both under the
law and under the Gospel, how shall it be believed that there is any
thing in the relation of master and slave which is inconsistent with
love?

For what is this relation? That one man shall belong to another,
and serve him as his master. Is this hostile to love? Suppose the
slave to be free, and he would be a hireling to his employer. Does
that relation secure love? Is it not manifest that my love for any
thing becomes increased by making it belong to me, since now it is a
part of myself, and my attachment to it is insured by that very reason?

Why do I love my children better than all others? Simply because they belong to me. Why do I love my wife better than all
other women? Because she belongs to me. Why do I love my house
better than any other habitation? Because it belongs to me. So far
is ownership from preventing love, that it secures and increases love
beyond any other principle of human action. And if so, why should
not the same law operate in the relation of servitude? For while
the servant is only my hireling, and may depart from me at any moment, I am not disposed to look upon him with any stronger affec-

tion than I have for others. But let him be my own, and I can not help regarding him with a new sense of attachment. My sympathy, my responsibility, my solicitude, are all engaged as they could not be without the bond that now unites us, and I have a love for him, of necessity, which I could not have had before.

And therefore it is that the highest love in the universe, the love of Christ, is manifested in the language of servitude. "Let this mind be in you," saith the Apostle, (Phil. 2 : 5–8) "which was also in Christ Jesus, who, being in the form of God, thought it not robbery to be equal with God, but made himself of no reputation, and took upon him the form of a servant," (μορφὴν δδυλου, literally the *form of a slave*,) "and was made in the likeness of men, and being found in fashion as a man, he humbled himself, and became obedient unto death, even the death of the Cross."

That principle runs throughout His whole course. As God, He was the Lord of life and glory, receiving the worship and homage of all that approached Him. But as man, He was the servant of all, attending to every call for His labors, Himself so poor that He had not where to lay His head, and not shrinking from reproaches, blows, and scourgings, the treatment too often given to slaves. He washed His disciples' feet, the office performed by slaves. He died upon the Cross, the punishment of the slave according to the Roman law. And after He had thus fulfilled His wondrous work, "in the form of a slave," and risen to His throne of glory, He presents the same principle to us. "Ye are not your own," saith St. Paul, (1 Cor. 6 : 19–20,) "for ye are bought with a price." And "ye know," saith St. Peter, (1 Pet. 1 : 18,) "that ye were not redeemed with corruptible things, as silver and gold; but with the precious blood of Christ, as of a lamb without blemish and without spot." And hence the law of love is inseparable from the law of servitude, and the service of Christ is our only "perfect freedom."

The relations of this mortal life are all regarded in the Bible as typical of our relations to God, and to the divine Redeemer. Thus the matrimonial relation is a type of the union between Christ and the Church, and hence, as the Church is obedient to Christ, so, saith the Apostle, let the wife be to her husband. Thus the filial relation is a type of our relation, as the children of God, to our Father in heaven. Thus, too, the relation of bond-servants, or slaves, is the type of our relation to our glorious Lord and Master.   And the principle of love runs throughout the whole.

It is no answer to this, that slaves are liable to be treated with cruelty or barbarity.   So are men, in all the relations of society. Such treatment is a sin, because it is in direct contrariety to the commands of God, who lays down the plainest rules upon the duties of husbands, fathers, and masters, as well as those which belong to wives, and children, and servants or slaves.   The *relation* itself is not to be censured, because the *treatment* may be wrong.   And therefore the Bible says nothing about *abolishing* slavery, but only *regulates* it according to the will of God.   Therefore, too, we have seen that the Church never made any effort to abolish it.   Therefore we shall find, in examining the subject, that the causes which led to its extinction in Europe were secular, and not religious, arising from changes gradually taking place amongst each particular people.   But this must be reserved for another place, and I shall now proceed to our next commentary.

CHAPTER XVIII.

RIGHT REVEREND BROTHER: The name of Adam Clarke is of high reputation amongst our Methodist brethren, and his influence has doubtless been very great in producing the controversy about the slave question which ended in the separation, North and South, of that very numerous and powerful denomination. Of course, as his commentary appeared after the English Parliament had emancipated the slaves in Jamaica, he belongs to the modern school of abolitionists. Yet we shall find that, notwithstanding his sweeping denunciation, he does not, as a commentator, give any authority for the ultra doctrine to which I stand opposed.

Thus, on Gen. 9 : 22- 4, *And Ham, the father of Canaan*, etc., he writes as follows : "Ham, and very probably, his son Canaan, had treated their father on this occasion with contempt or reprehensible levity. Had Noah not been innocent, as my exposition supposes him, God would not have endowed him with the spirit of prophecy."

This, by the way, is stated too strongly, for God endowed Balaam with the spirit of prophecy, notwithstanding he was a wicked man, and Caiaphas prophesied, though he was the enemy of our Saviour. The power of prophecy is not a personal privilege to the man, but a gift to the Church, for whose sake it is delivered.

" The conduct of Shem and Japheth," continues Dr. Clarke, " was such as became pious and affectionate children, who appear to have been in the habit of treating their father with decency, reverence, and obedient respect. On the one, the spirit of prophecy (not the incensed father) pronounces a curse : on the others, the same spirit (not parental tenderness) pronounces a blessing. These things would have been just as they afterward occurred, had Noah never spoken. God had wise and powerful reasons to induce him to sentence the one to *perpetual servitude*, and to allot to the others prosperity and dominion. Besides, the curse pronounced on Canaan neither fell immediately upon himself nor on his worthless father, but upon

7*

the Canaanites, and from the history we have of this people, in Lev. 18 : 20, and Deut. 9 : 4, 12 : 31, we may ask, could the curse of God fall more deservedly on any people than on these ? Their profligacy was great, but *it was not the effect of the curse*, but being foreseen by the Lord, the curse was the effect of their conduct. But even this curse does not exclude them from the possibility of obtaining salvation : it extends not to the *soul* and to *eternity*, but merely to their bodies and to time. How many, even of these, repented, we can not tell."

I would only remark here : First. That Dr. Clarke clearly regards *perpetual servitude* as the decree of God upon the Canaanites ; and, secondly, that he confines the operation of this decree to their *bodies*, with perfect propriety. It may be well, however, now to consider whether the execution of this decree does not of necessity require the continuance of the race of Canaan. For the land of Canaan was to be given to Israel, and the inhabitants thereof included *seven nations*, all of whom were commanded to be *cut off ;* not enslaved, but *exterminated*. If there were no Canaanites anywhere else but in Canaan, how could the decree of *extermination* and the decree of *perpetual servitude* be made to agree together ?

Now we know that the Canaanites were not exterminated completely, even in Canaan ; and we find them still existing in our Saviour's days, because "a woman of Canaan" came from the coasts of Tyre and Sidon, to ask relief for her daughter at the hand of our Lord, (Matt. 15 : 22.) Moreover, we read, that "Canaan begat Sidon and Heth, and the Jebusite, and the Amorite, and the Girgasite, and the Hivite, and the Arkite, and the Sinite, and the Arvadite, and the Zemarite, and the Hamathite ; and *afterward were the families of the Canaanites spread abroad*," (Gen. 10 : 15–18.) Dr. Clarke, in his note on this passage, saith, that the Jebusite, Amorite, etc., " are well known as being the ancient inhabitants of Canaan, *expelled* by the children of Israel." And this, to a considerable extent, must have been the case. A large number were slain in the wars of Israel. Another probably large number continued to dwell in the land, and could not be driven out, because the Israelites were faithless and disobedient. But it is obvious that when they found it impossible to resist the victorious sword of Joshua, a considerable proportion of the wealthier classes, who were able to emigrate, would fly from the conqueror, and seek a refuge in other lands.

Here, then, we have to inquire, where did they go? We have *eleven* names of the heads of tribes set forth as the posterity of Canaan in Genesis 10: 15–18, of whom only *seven* were involved in the invasion of the Israelites. What became of the other four? We have, besides, the emigrating portion of those seven nations to place somewhere. We have also to allow room for the families of the Canaanites which, long before the investment of Canaan, are said to have been "*spread abroad.*" We can trace some of the Canaanites to Tyre and Sidon, Phœnicia and Carthage, but there can not be any reasonable doubt that the other nations of the race occupied a far more extensive range. And as we know nothing about the locality in which these families of the Canaanites were "spread abroad," nor where a portion of the seven nations "expelled" from Canaan betook themselves, what is to prevent our supposing that they settled in various parts of Ethiopia and Guinea, and that the descendants of Canaan are there to this day?

The argument for this conclusion seems to my mind unanswerable. For, in the first place, Africa is acknowledged by all to be the *land of Ham,* peopled by his posterity. 2d. The progeny of Canaan, which would seem, from the names recorded in Gen. 10, to have been far more numerous than that of his other sons, would naturally be found on the same continent with their brethren of the same race, with whom, in language, in idolatry, and in general licentiousness, they must have been most nearly associated. 3d. We can find no traces elsewhere of the posterity of four of these sons of Canaan, which were not concerned in the wars of Israel. And, 4th, the account given by Malte Brun, and all other writers, concerning the present state of Guinea, agrees with the Scriptural statement of the immorality and corruption of the Canaanites. It is true, indeed, that the portion of those which had settled in the promised land appear to have been farther advanced in the arts than the people of Dahomey. But this only proves that idolatry and wickedness tend to barbarism. We know that our continent was peopled once by a race superior to the Indians. We know that vast portions of Asia and Africa were more civilized two thousand years ago than they are at this day. The result, on the whole, would therefore seem most probable, that the African race at the South are a portion of the posterity of Ham, *through the line of Canaan.* And hence, the most limited interpretation of Noah's prophecy would agree with the historical facts of their degradation and their slavery.

Dr. Clarke, in his note on Gen. 9 : 25, *Cursed be Canaan*, recognizes the same fact which is stated by Bishop Newton and others, viz., that "the Arabic version has *Ham, the father of Canaan ;*" but "this," saith he, "is acknowledged by none of the other versions, and seems to be merely a gloss." It has not been so regarded, as we have seen, by others, but I care nothing about the choice between the versions, as either will suffice to vindicate the consistency of the Deity, when properly applied, and save us from the common mistake of supposing that the Lord decreed the *servitude* of the very same people at one time, whom he ordered to be *exterminated* at another. As soon as we understand that the portion of the Canaanites who were to be exterminated by Israel was *only a part* of the whole, this difficulty vanishes. The subject, however, will be more fully considered in a subsequent chapter.

Our commentator gives a clearer statement on the case of Hagar, Gen. 16 : 2, than some others. " It must not be forgotten," saith he, " that female slaves constituted a part of the private patrimony or possession of a wife; and that she had a right, according to the usage of those times, to dispose of them as she pleased. *The slave being the absolute property of the mistress*, not only her person, but the fruits of her labor, *with all her children, were her owner's property also*. The children, therefore, that were born of the slave were considered as the children of the mistress. It was on this ground that Sarai gave her maid to Abram."

The text in Exodus, ch. 21, v. 16, *He that stealeth a man*, etc., affords an example of Dr. Clarke's bias towards modern ultra-abolitionism. " By this law," saith he, " every man-stealer, and every receiver of the stolen person, should lose his life; no matter whether the latter stole the man himself, or gave money to a *slave-captain*, or *negro-dealer*, to steal it for him."

In this he manifests a great degree of disingenuousness, because he passes by, in total silence, the language in Deuteronomy 24 : 7, where the same law is laid down in more precise terms, limiting the offense to the stealing of *an Israelite*, to make merchandise of him. The maxim of all courts of justice is, that laws *in pari materia*—i.e., on the same subject—must be construed together, but Dr. Clarke disregards this, and gives a false construction to the briefer text, while he ignores the longer and more complete one. Moreover, he contradicts the exposition of the Jewish doctors, who have the best right to be heard, in the interpretation of their own law.

On Lev. 25, where the express direction is given by the Almighty that the Israelites should buy bondmen and bondmaids of the *heathen*, who should serve them and their children forever, Dr. Clarke is *entirely silent*. He also passes over, without remark, the fact that the Jubilee only freed the Jewish servant, and had no application to the slaves. In both of these I should consider him unfaithful to his duty as a commentator, unless he supposed that the texts were so plain as to make comment quite unnecessary.

But he gives a correct note on the text, Deut. 23 : 15, *Thou shalt not deliver unto his master the servant which is escaped from his master unto thee*—a text which the ultra-abolitionist is so fond of using as a warrant for refusing to obey the Constitution and the Fugitive Slave law. On this, however, Dr. Clarke is very clear: "That is," saith he, "a servant who left an *idolatrous master*, that he might join himself to God and to his people. *In any other case it would have been injustice to have harbored the runaway*." A most true and righteous exposition !

And in his comments on the leading texts of the New Testament, Dr. Clarke is usually fair, with one very marked exception. Thus, on 1 Cor. 7 : 21, "*Art thou called being a servant? Care not for it*," etc., he gives the following note, viz. : "Art thou converted to Christ, while thou art a slave? the property of another person and bought with his money? *Care not for it :* this will not injure thy Christian condition ; but if thou canst obtain thy liberty, *use it rather :* prefer this state for the sake of *freedom*, and the temporal advantages connected with it."

V. 22. *For he that is called*, etc. "The man who, being a *slave*, is converted to the Christian faith, is the Lord's freeman ; his condition as a slave does not vitiate any of the privileges to which he is entitled as a Christian ; on the other hand, all freemen who receive the grace of Christ, must consider themselves the *slaves of the Lord*, *i. e.*, his real property, to be employed and disposed of according to his godly wisdom, who, notwithstanding their state of subjection, will find the service of their Master to be perfect freedom."

V. 23. *Ye are bought with a price.* "As truly as your bodies have become the property of your master, in consequence of his paying down a price for you, so surely you are now the Lord's property, in consequence of your being purchased by the blood of Christ."

"Some render this verse interrogatively: *Are ye bought with a price* from your Slavery? *Do not* again become *slaves of men*. Never *sell yourselves;* prefer and retain your liberty, now that ye have acquired it."

"In these verses the Apostle shows that the Christian religion *does not abolish our civil* connections—in reference to *them*, where it finds us, there it leaves us. In whatever relation we stood before our embracing Christianity, there we stand still: our secular condition being no further changed, than as it may be affected by the amelioration of our moral character."

This is sound doctrine, in agreement with Scripture and with reason. But in his comment on the next text which I have quoted, his ultra-abolitionism blazes forth in a sentence which stands at the head of all others for its virulence; plainly proving how the spirit of fanaticism may carry away the best men into the most extravagant inconsistency. Thus it reads:

Eph. 6 : 5 : *Servants be obedient.* "Though δουλος frequently signifies a *slave* or *bondman*, yet it often implies a *servant* in general, or any one bound to another, either for a limited term or for life. Even a slave, if a Christian, was bound to serve him faithfully, by whose money he was bought, however illegal the traffic may be considered. *In heathen countries slavery was in some sort excusable.* AMONG CHRISTIANS, IT IS AN ENORMITY AND A CRIME FOR WHICH PERDITION ITSELF HAS SCARCELY AN ADEQUATE STATE OF PUNISHMENT!"

And yet, in his comment on the following verses, the same Dr. Clarke writes these words, viz. :

V. 7 : *With good will.* "Μετ' εννοιας, with *cheerfulness;* do not take up your service as a cross, or bear it as a burden ; but *take it as coming in the order of God's Providence, and a thing that is pleasing to him !*"

I shall only observe, here, that the proper duty of a commentator on the Bible is to give the meaning of the text. So far as Dr. Clarke does this, we find him generally correct in the New Testament. But the declaration about slavery being *an enormity and a crime among Christians* has no relation whatever to the text of the Apostle. It is simply the feeling of Dr. Adam Clarke, under the stimulus of the new-born spirit of English abolitionism. And therefore, although he has placed it in his Commentary, it is entirely destitute of the character which every real commentary should possess. Instead of explaining the Scripture, it actually opposes it, making God to sanction for his chosen Israel, and afterwards for His Church of Christ, under the government of his inspired Apostles, *a crime and an enormity for which perdition itself has scarcely an adequate punishment!* To my mind, such language is nothing better than blasphemy, and I should consider it an enormity and a crime to indorse it. It is found, indeed, in a commentary, just as a toad has sometimes been found in a rock. Yet no one could be so foolish as to suppose that between the toad and the rock there was any natural affinity. But as the subject will recur again, I need not enlarge upon it now, and shall proceed to the remaining extracts from this author.

1 Tim. 6 : 1: *Let as many servants as are under the yoke,* etc. "The word δουλος here," saith Dr. Clarke, "means *slaves* converted to the Christian faith, and the ζυγον or yoke, is the *state of slavery.* Even these, in such circumstances, and under such domination, are commanded to treat their masters with all honor and respect, that the name of God, by which they were called, and the doctrine of God, Christianity, which they had professed, might not be blasphemed, might not be evil spoken of, in consequence of their improper conduct. CIVIL RIGHTS ARE NEVER ABOLISHED BY ANY COMMUNICATIONS FROM GOD'S SPIRIT. The civil state in which man was before his conversion is not altered by that conversion, nor does the grace of God absolve him from any claims which either the state or his neighbor may have upon him. All these outward things *continue unaltered.*" Here is sound doctrine again, entirely free from abolitionism.

Lastly, in his note on the Epistle to Philemon, (v. 12 : *Whom I have sent again,*) Dr. Clarke gives this correct comment : "The Christian religion," saith he, "*never cancels any civil relations: a slave,* on being converted, and becoming a free man of Christ, has *no right to claim, on that ground, emancipation from the service of his master.* JUSTICE, therefore, required St. Paul to send back Onesimus to his master, and CONSCIENCE obliged Onesimus to agree in the propriety of the measure."

I have now given a full exhibition of the course pursued by this eminent Methodist commentator. In the main, he is sound and correct. I shall leave it to you or any other advocate to reconcile his occasional inconsistency, which I acknowledge to be a task quite beyond my power. There is still, however, one of those works belonging to the nineteenth century, which I have placed upon my list, and to that I shall next invite your attention.

CHAPTER XIX.

RIGHT REVEREND BROTHER : The Comprehensive Commentary which professes to contain nearly all that is valuable in Henry, Scott, and Doddridge, may be considered as the book of the Orthodox Congregationalists, and will not require much space to be given to it, because I have already quoted largely from Henry and Scott, and shall by and by quote from Doddridge, all of whom will speak for themselves. A respectful attention, however, is due to this work, and I shall make some extracts from it accordingly.

Lev. 25 : 39–55.   The Israelites "might purchase bondmen," saith this commentary, "of the heathen nations round about them, (except of the seven nations to be destroyed,) and might claim a dominion over them, and entail them on their families, as an inheritance, *for the year of Jubilee should give no discharge to them.*   Thus *negroes* only are used as slaves, how much to the credit of Christianity I shall not say."

Exod. 21 : 16.   "Here is a law," saith the commentator, "against man-stealing.   *He that steals a man,* woman, or child, *with a design to sell them to the Gentiles,* (for no Israelite would buy them,) was adjudged to death by this statute."   This writer is in better agreement with the other law on the same subject, in Deut. 24 : 7, than either Scott or Clarke, and his note on this last is not unfair, as it quotes the words of Henry, who belonged to the eighteenth century.

On Deut. 23 : 15: *Thou shalt not deliver unto his master the servant which is escaped from his master unto thee,* the interpretation is taken from Henry and Scott, and both of these are substantially in accordance with my own in the *Bible View of Slavery*, but entirely inconsistent with the misapprehension of the ultra-abolitionist, who sets it against the other laws of God, as well as against the Constitution of his country.

But in 1 Cor. 7 : 21, *Art thou called being a servant, care not for it, but if thou mayest be made free, use it rather* this commentary not only gives the notes of Henry and Scott, but also an original one from Dr. Jenks, which is worth transcribing.

"The sense," saith he, "is not clear. Chrysostom and all the old comtrs. (commentators) understand, 'You need care so little, that even if you can gain your freedom, prefer your servitude as a greater trial of Christian patience!' (So a religion of despotism counsels, contrary to the precept, 'Do not evil that good may come,' and to the prayer, 'Lead us not into temptation.' By what right can any man imbrute God's *image*, which Christ atoned for, to a mindless, will-less, soulless, rightless *chattel!* Yet) so Camer, Schmidt, Sparck, Estius, De Dieu, and the Syr. And this sense, they think, is confirmed by the following consolatory words, 'For he,' etc. It is also ably defended by *De Dieu* and Wolf. But there is a certain harshness about it to which necessity alone would reconcile me. What is detrimental to human happiness can not be promotive of virtue. The true intent seems that of Beza, Grot., Ham., and most recent comtrs. 'Do not feel a too great trouble on that account, as if it could materially affect your acceptance with God, and as if that were a condition unworthy of a Christian.' 'Grace knows no distinctions of freedom or servitude, therefore bear it patiently.' Grotius adds: 'And above all, let it not drive you to seek your freedom by unjustifiable means.' And he remarks that a misunderstanding of the nature of Christian liberty had made many Christian slaves not only murmur at their situation, but seek to throw off all bondage. O just yet merciful God! enlighten the slave and his master in these United States, at once and always to do Thy will!"

Now this is a fair specimen of the rhetoric which has become so common, of late years, on the subject of slavery, taking it for granted that the slave must be made a brute, without mind, soul, will, or right, a mere *chattel;* although these gentlemen must know that among the ancients the slaves were often highly educated to be instructors of youth, that Esop was a slave, and Terence was a slave, and Epictetus was a slave, while amongst the slave population of the South, enough of their negroes have been taught and emancipated to plant the new State of Liberia, and of those who still remain with their masters, nearly five hundred thousand are reported as members of Christian societies, in good standing. These facts being perfectly notorious, one can hardly read such a display of our commentator's anti-slavery prejudice without desiring that he might study the Ninth Commandment, "Thou shalt not bear false witness against thy neighbor," with a wholesome regard to personal application.

On the text quoted from Eph. 6 : 5–9, *Servants, be obedient to your masters, etc.*, the notes of Henry and Scott are repeated in this commentary, as I have already given them, and so are they likewise in the corresponding passage, Col. 3 : 22: *Servants, obey in all things your masters according to the flesh, etc.*

And in that strong and most important precept delivered by St. Paul to the first bishop of Ephesus, 1 Tim. 6 : 1–5, *Let as many servants as are under the yoke count their own masters worthy of all honor, etc.*, Henry and Scott are again employed in the Comprehensive Commentary. And the same authors meet us again, in the preface and notes to the Epistle to Philemon. Thus, in the preface we read as follows : " Philemon, one of note, and probably a minister in the Church of Colosse, had a servant named Onesimus, who, having purloined his goods, ran away from him and came to Rome, where Paul was then a prisoner for the Gospel, and providentially coming under his preaching there, was, by the blessing of God, converted by him ; after which he ministered awhile to the Apostle in bonds, and might have been further useful to him ; but he, understanding him to be *another man's servant*, would not, without his consent, detain him, but *sends him back* with this letter commendatory, wherein he earnestly sues for his pardon and kind reception."

V. 16. *Not now as a servant*, "that is," saith this commentary, "not *merely* or so much, but above a servant, in a spiritual respect, a *brother beloved*, one to be owned as a brother in Christ," etc.

" But why such concern and earnestness for a *servant, a slave*, and such a one as had misbehaved ? *Answer.* Onesimus being now penitent, it was doubtless to encourage him, and to support him in returning to his master."

V. 18. *Put that on my account.* " Paul here engages for satisfaction. Whence observe, first, The communion of saints *does not destroy distinction of property.* Onesimus, now converted and become a *brother beloved, is yet Philemon's servant still*, and indebted to him for wrongs he had done, and not to be discharged but by free and voluntary remission," etc.

Here, my Right Reverend Brother, I shall close for the present my extracts from the commentators of the nineteenth century, having proved that notwithstanding their occasional exhibitions of anti-slavery prejudice, yet their explanations of the Bible are usually the same with the rest, the exceptions being very few, and those, as I shall show by and by, being of no importance to the general argument. Dr. Clarke rages most wildly indeed in one place against the institution of slavery, and Dr. Scott is very zealous for the abolition of the *slave-trade*, in which we all agree. But none of them can be found denying the main facts, or imputing it as *a sin* in any Christian man to own a slave, provided it be in accordance with the law of the land, and the slave be treated with kindness and with justice, in obedience to the precepts of the Gospel. None of them denounces the *right of property* in the master, nor the duty of obedience and fidelity on the part of the slave. None of them maintains the doctrine of the ultra-abolitionist, that the slave ought to run away, and that if his master should reclaim him, he may be justified in forcible resistance even unto death, in the pursuit of his liberty.

I shall now, however, revert to the commentators of the eighteenth century, by whom I maintained that the original doctrine of the Church was still preserved in its primitive integrity; and after I shall have gone through this list, the way will be clear for the remaining portions of my undertaking.

CHAPTER XX.

RIGHT REVEREND BROTHER: The Exposition of the Old and New Testaments, by Dr. Gill, is one of the most learned and highly esteemed works of modern times, in the judgment of very many, and holds the first rank in the Baptist denomination. I shall next take up this, and quote its authority on the texts in question.

On the prophecy of Noah, Gen. 9 : 22, our commentator saith : " It may seem strange that *Canaan* should be cursed, and not *Ham*, who seems to be the only transgressor by what is said in the context ; hence one copy of the Septuagint, as Ainsworth observes, reads *Ham*, and the Arabic writers, the *father of Canaan*, and so, as *Aben Ezra* relates, *Saadiah Gaon* supplies it, and the same supplement is made by others. But as *both* were guilty, and *Canaan* particularly was first in the transgression, it seems most wise and just that he should be expressly named, since hereby *Ham is not excluded* from a share in the punishment of the crime he had a concern in, being punished in his son—Canaan only, and not any of the other sons of *Ham*, were guilty : he, and not *Ham* by name, is cursed, lest it should be thought that the curse would fall on *Ham* and all his posterity, wheras the curse *descends on him*, and very justly *proceeds in the line of Canaan*—the father of the accursed race of the Canaanites, whom God abhorred, and for their wickedness, was about to drive out of their land, and give it to his people for an inheritance," etc.

According to this learned author, therefore, the curse *descended on Ham*, and *proceeds in the line of Canaan*. And in his notes upon the line of Canaan, whose children are named in the fifteenth verse, he saith that as the families of the Canaanites increased, "they spread themselves farther every way," although his elaborate attempt to trace their course, like all similar efforts, amounts to nothing, because there is no history to guide us, beyond the outline given by Scripture, and all that can be done must be limited to probable conjecture.

With respect to Abraham's servants, Gen. 14 : 14, Dr. Gill saith that they were "*born in his own house,* of his servants, and *so were his property, and at his disposal and command;* their number was three hundred and eighteen—a large number for servants, which showed how great a man Abraham was, what possessions he must have to employ so many," etc.

On Gen. 16 : 3, he saith, that Hagar was "the secondary wife or *concubine*" of Abraham. That this did not change her condition as a slave is plain, because, when she ran away, "she acknowledged Sarai to be her mistress," and the angel of the Lord commands her accordingly, "*Return to thy mistress and submit thyself to her hands;* go back to her, acknowledge thy fault, do her work, bear her corrections and chastisements, and *suffer thyself to be afflicted* by her, as the word may be rendered; take all patiently from her, which will be much more to thy profit and advantage than to pursue the course thou art in."

In his notes on Gen. 17 : 12, where circumcision is commanded for those who were *born in the house,* or *bought with money* of any stranger, not being of Abraham's seed, Dr. Gill quotes from Maimonides the following rules: "A servant born in the power of an Israelite, and another that is taken from heathens, the master is bound to circumcise them, but he that is born in the house is circumcised the eighth day, and he that is bought with money is circumcised on the day that he is received; even if he received him on the day he is born, he is circumcised on that day. If he receives a grown servant of heathens, and the servant is not willing to be circumcised, he bears with him a whole year; but more than that he is forbidden to keep him, seeing he is uncircumcised, *but he must send him again to the heathens.*"

On Exod. 20, our commentator saith, in his notes on the Fourth Commandment, *thy man-servant and thy maid-servant,* "this is to be understood, according to the Jews, *not of hired servants,* concerning whose rest from labor a man was not bound, *but of such as were born in the house and bought with their money,* and of such men-servants as were circumcised, and in all things professed to be proselytes to the Jewish religion."

And in his comment on the Tenth Commandment, *thou shalt not covet thy neighbor's house, nor his man-servant nor his maid-servant,* etc., he saith, this "serves to explain the Eighth Commandment, showing that we are not only forbid to take away *what is another man's property*, any of the *goods here mentioned*, or any other, but we are not secretly to desire them," etc.

On Exod. 21 : 4, *If his master have given him a wife*, Dr. Gill explains it as meaning: "One of his slaves, a *Canaanitish woman, on purpose to beget slaves on her, since all born in his house were his own.*"

The twenty-fifth chapter of Leviticus, verse 44, *Both thy bondmen and thy bondmaids which thou shalt have*, etc., is thus explained by our commentator: "Such it seems were allowed them—but they were not to be of the nation of Israel, but of other nations—they *shall be of the heathens that are round about thee*, of them *shall ye buy bondmen and bondmaids ;* that is, of the *Ammonites, Moabites, Edomites*, and *Syrians*, as *Aben Ezra* saith, that were their neighbors, OF ANY BUT THE SEVEN NATIONS WHICH THEY WERE ORDERED UTTERLY TO DESTROY ; whereupon *Jarchi* observes, It is said, that are *round about thee*, not in the midst of the border of your land, for them they were not to save alive." (Deut. 20 : 16.)

V. 45. *Moreover, of the children of the strangers that do sojourn among you*, etc. "The uncircumcised sojourners," saith Dr. Gill, "as they are called in the *Targums* of *Onkelos* and *Jonathan*, proselytes of the gate, such of the nations round about, who came and sojourned among them, being subject to the precepts given to the sons of Noah respecting idolatry, etc., but were not circumcised, and did not embrace the Jewish religion ; *of them shall ye buy* for bondmen and bondmaids, *and of their families that are with you, which they begat in your land*, but, as the *Targum* of *Jonathan* adds, are not of the Canaanites."

Here our learned commentator shows clearly the judgment of the highest Jewish authorities, proving that the decree of slavery did not apply to the seven nations who were ordered to be destroyed, when the land of Canaan was given to the Israelites for a possession, but to *the other idolatrous nations :* and therefore we see, first, that the Jews were authorized to buy slaves of any heathen people ; and secondly, that the prophecy of Noah was not to be limited to that portion of the race of Canaan which inhabited the promised land, but should be extended to all the rest of his posterity. For when we read that the sons of Canaan included *eleven* distinct names, and that their families were *spread abroad* many centuries before the time of

Moses, it is absurd to suppose that they were not to be found in many other parts of Africa, *the land of Ham*, besides that portion of them which had settled in Palestine.

V. 46. *And ye shall take them as an inheritance for your children after you*, etc. "Which," continues Dr. Gill, "they might leave them at their death to inherit, as they did their estates and lands; for such servants are, with the Jews, said to be like immovable goods, as fields, vineyards, etc., *to inherit them for a possession*, as their property, as any thing else that was bequeathed to them, *as negroes now are in our plantations abroad; they shall be your bondmen forever*, and NOT BE RELEASED AT THE YEAR OF JUBILEE, NOR BEFORE NOR AFTER; unless they obtained their liberty either by purchase or by a writing under their master's hand," etc.

On the favorite text of the ultra-abolitionist, "*Thou shalt not deliver unto his master the servant which is escaped from his master unto thee*, Deut. 23 : 15, Dr. Gill gives this commentary: "That is," saith he, "one that has been used ill by a cruel and tyrannical master, and was in danger of his life with him, and therefore obliged to make his escape from him on that account; such an one when he fell into the hands of an Israelite, was not to be taken and bound and sent back to his master again, but was to be retained till his master's anger subsided, or however, until inquiry could be made into the cause of the difference between him and his master, and matters made up between them to mutual satisfaction; for it can not be thought that this law was made to encourage every idle, disobedient, and fugitive servant, which would be very sinful and unjust. The Jewish writers generally understand it of the servants of idolaters, fleeing for the sake of religion. *Onkelos* renders it 'a servant of heathen people.' The *Targum of Jonathan* is: 'Thou shalt not deliver a stranger into the hands of those that worship idols, but he shall be delivered by you that he may be under the shadow of my *Shekinah*, because he hath fled from the worship of his idol.' *Aben Ezra* interprets it of a servant, not an Israelite, who, in time of war, flees from his master, not an Israelite also, unto the camp of Israel, and that for the glory of the divine name. Such an one, though a servant, might not be delivered to his master."

And on the text in Deut. 24 : 7, *If a man be found stealing any of his brethren of the children of Israel*, our commentator saith: "Whether grown up or little, male or female, an Israelite or a prose-

lyte, or a freed servant, all, as *Maimonides* says, are included in this
general word, brethren ; though *Aben Ezra* observes that it is added
of the children of Israel, for explanation, since an Edomite is called
a *brother*.   Now a man must be *found* committing this fact ; that is,
it must plainly appear; there must be full proof of it by witnesses, as
Jarchi explains this word," etc.

It is perfectly manifest, according to this and the other commentators, that the attempt of the ultra-abolitionist to press these texts into
his service is in utter contradiction of all the doctors among the Jews ;
as well as all the Christian writers anterior to Scott and Clarke,
who belong to the innovating school of the nineteenth century.   And
now I shall proceed to those texts in the New Testament, which are
the chief guides to the Church of Christ.

Beginning as before with 1 Cor. 7 : 21, *Art thou called being a
servant*, etc., Dr. Gill gives the following comment, viz., " That is,"
saith he, " art thou called by grace whilst in the condition of a servant, *care not for it*—be not anxiously solicitous to be otherwise ;
bear the yoke patiently, go through thy servitude cheerfully, and
serve thy master faithfully, *but if thou mayest be made free use it
rather*.   The Syriac version renders the last clause, *choose for thyself
rather to serve;* perfectly agreeable to the sense given of the words
by several great critics and excellent interpreters, who take the Apostle's meaning to be, that should a Christian servant have an opportunity of making his escape from his master, or could he by any art,
trick, and fraudulent method obtain his liberty, it would be much
more advisable *to continue a servant* than to become free by any such
means.   Yea, some carry the sense so far, that even if the servants
could be made free in a lawful way, yet *servitude was most eligible*,
both for their own and their masters' good ; for their own, to keep
them humble, and exercise their patience ; for their masters' not only
temporal but spiritual good, since by their good behavior they might
be a means of recommending the Gospel to them, and of gaining them
to Christ.   But one should rather think the more obvious sense is,
that when a Christian servant has his *freedom offered him by his
master*, or he can come at it *in a lawful and honorable way*, this being
preferable to servitude, he ought rather to make use of it, since he
would be in a better situation and more at leisure to serve Christ and
the interest of religion."

The comment of Dr. Gill on Eph. 6 : 5, *Servants, be obedient to them that are your masters*, etc., is very clear, and in perfect accordance with all the others, viz.: "The Apostle," saith he, "enlarges on the duty of servants, as well as frequently inculcates it in his epistles, because, generally speaking, they were more rude and ignorant, and less pains were taken with them to instruct them; they were apt to be impatient and weary of the yoke, and scandal was likely to arise from servants in the first ages of Christianity through some libertines, and the licentiousness of the *false teachers* who insinuated that *servitude was inconsistent with Christian freedom;* the persons exhorted are servants, bond-servants, and hired servants, who are to be subject to and obey their masters, of each sex, whether believers or unbelievers, good or bad-humored, gentle or froward—in things pertaining to the flesh, in things temporal, which concern the body and this temporal life, not in things spiritual and religious, that belong to conscience. And obedience is to be yielded to them with *fear and trembling*, with great humility and respect, with submission to their reproofs and corrections, and with fear of punishment, but more especially with the fear of God, *in singleness of heart*, without hypocrisy and dissimulation, and with all integrity and faithfulness *as unto Christ*, it being *agreeable to His will*, and what makes for His glory, and serves to adorn the doctrine of God our Saviour in all things."

On 1 Tim. 6 : 1, *Let as many servants as are under the yoke*, etc., the same commentator writes as follows : "*Under the yoke of government*, as the Arabic version renders it, that is, under the yoke of men, in a state of servitude, under the government of masters and in their service, being either apprentices to them or *bought with their money*, or hired by them, let them *count their own masters worthy of all honor*, and give it them, which includes subjection to them, obedience to all their lawful commands," etc.

Verse 3. *If any man teach otherwise*, etc., or "*another doctrine*, as the Syriac version renders it, a doctrine different from what the Apostle had now taught *concerning the duty of servants to their masters, as did the false teachers* who despised government or dominion," etc.

Verse 4. *He is proud, knowing nothing*, etc. "Or swelled up," continues Dr. Gill, "with a vain conceit of himself and his own notions, and treats with a haughty air the faithful ministers of the Word, *knowing nothing* as he ought to know, not any thing substantial, *but doting about questions and strifes of words*, or his mind is distempered, his head is light and wild, his fancy is roving, and he talks of things he knows not what, the ill effects of which are as follow, *whereof cometh envy* and *strife*, contention, quarreling, the peace and comfort of particular persons, and even of *whole communities are broken and destroyed thereby ;* yea, these also produce *railings* at one another, and especially at the faithful ministers of the Gospel : for when the false teachers can not overcome them by Scripture and argument, they fall to *railing and reviling of them*," etc. " Wherefore the Apostle gives the following advice to Timothy, and through him to *all ministers and churches. From such withdraw thyself ;* do not come near them, have nothing to do with them, have no communion with them, either in a civil or religious way ; avoid all conversation with them," etc.

As to the Epistle of St. Paul to Philemon, Dr. Gill agrees with all the other commentators. " The design of the epistle," saith he, " was this : Philemon's servant, Onesimus, having either embezzled his master's goods or robbed him, ran way from him and fled to Rome, where the Apostle was a prisoner, in chains, in his own hired house, under the custody of a soldier, and where he received all that came, and preached the Gospel to them. Among those that went to hear him this fugitive servant was one, and was converted under his ministry. Now the design of this epistle is to reconcile Philemon to his servant, and to entreat him to receive him again, *not only* as a servant, but as a brother in Christ ; and the most proper and prudent methods and arguments are used to engage him in it. The epistle, though it is a familiar one and short, is very instructive ; it shows great humility in the Apostle, and that he did not think it below him to be concerned in doing such an office as to reconcile a master to his servant, and which is worthy of imitation ; as also it teaches the *right that masters have over their servants*, which is *not lost by their becoming Christians*," etc.

I shall only add one extract more from this learned commentator, viz., on 1 Pet. 2 : 18, *Servants, be subject to your masters*, etc. " This," saith Dr. Gill, " was another notion of the Jews, that because they were the seed of Abraham, they ought not to be the servants of any ; and particularly such as were believers in Christ, thought they ought not to serve unbelieving masters, nor indeed believing ones, because they were equally brethren in Christ with them. Hence the Apostle Peter here, as the Apostle Paul frequently elsewhere, inculcates this duty of servants to their masters: the manner in which they are to be subject to them is *with all fear*, with reverence to their persons, strict regard to their commands, faithfulness in any trust reposed in them, diligence in the discharge of their duty, and all this not only to *the good and gentle, but also to the froward*, the ill-natured, morose, and rigorous," etc.

I have been thus copious in my extracts from the exposition of Dr. Gill, not only in consideration of his acknowledged learning, but because the various societies of the Baptist denomination, of which he was the most eminent oracle for a very long period, form the largest Christian body on our continent, and deserve a proportionate measure of respectful attention. But now I shall hasten onward to my remaining authorities, which can be satisfactorily dispatched with greater brevity.

CHAPTER XXI.

RIGHT REVEREND BROTHER: Before I return to the Episcopalian commentators, there is one name deservedly high in the estimation of our Presbyterian brethren, and of many amongst ourselves, whom I may not pass by—that of the Rev. Dr. Doddridge. From his well-known and greatly esteemed Paraphrase, therefore, I quote the following passage on Eph. 6 : 5.

"There is yet another relation between masters and servants, concerning which I shall proceed to advise you. I would exhort you who are servants, whether of the meanest rank, such as *bondmen* and *slaves*, or in the station only of hired servants, that ye be *subject* and *obedient* to those who are your masters and proprietors, though they be only so according to the flesh."

And to this I shall add his Introduction to the Epistle of St. Paul to Philemon, which agrees with the preceding commentators precisely:

"Philemon," saith Dr. Doddridge, "was an inhabitant of Colosse. He seems, from several hints given in the Epistle, to have been a person of distinction, particularly from the mention made of the Church in his house, (v. 2,) and his liberal contributions to the relief of the saints, (v. 5, 7,) and the general strain of the letter shows that the Apostle held him in very high esteem, and looked upon him as one of the great supports of religion in that society."

"The occasion of the letter was this: Onesimus, Philemon's slave, had robbed his master, and fled to Rome, where, happily for him, he met with the Apostle, and by his instructions and admonitions was converted to Christianity, and reclaimed to a sense of his duty."

"St. Paul seems to have kept him for some considerable time under his eye, that he might be satisfied of the reality of the change, and when he had made a sufficient trial of him, and found that his behavior was entirely agreeable to his profession, he would not detain him any longer for his own private convenience, but sent him back to his master. And as Philemon might well be supposed to be strongly prejudiced against one who had left his service in so infamous a manner, he sends him this letter, in which he employs all his influence to remove his suspicions, and reconcile him to the thoughts of taking Onesimus into his family again."

The next commentary, and one of much reputation amongst Episcopalians, is that which is known as *Hammond's Paraphrase and Annotations on the New Testament.* And here we have the same doctrine repeated in plain terms. Thus the paraphrase on 1 Tim. 6 : 1 is as follows, viz. :

"Those Christians that are bondmen to heathens must perform all service and obedience to them which belong to them by the *law of servants among the heathens;* that the profession of Christianity and the doctrine of the Gospel be not looked upon by the heathens as that which makes men worse livers than they were, neglecting their *moral duties* for being Christians."

"And those Christians that have Christian masters must not withdraw any of that obedience which is due to them upon the plea that they are Christians, and so their *equals* or *brethren ;* but think themselves the more obliged to serve them, because the faith and love that constitutes men Christians consist in helping to do good, and consequently the performing due service to them is a very Christian thing, and that which *Christianity doth not less but more oblige them to.* There are things of such a nature, so much *required by the Christian religion,* and the contrary at this time, so taught by the Gnostic heretics, that it is necessary for thee to give these admonitions to all."

The celebrated Locke, as you know, wrote a commentary on the Epistles of St. Paul, which obtained considerable reputation in our mother Church of England. And there is a note appended to his remarks concerning the text in 1. Cor. 7 : 28, worthy of your attention. It is in these words, viz. :

1 Cor. 7 : 23. *Ye are bought with a price.* "Slaves were bought and sold in the market, as cattle are, and so, by the price paid, there was a property acquired in them. This, therefore, is a reason for what he advised that they should not be slaves to men, because Christ had paid a price for them, and they belonged to Him. The slavery he speaks of is civil slavery, which he makes use of to convince the Corinthians that the civil ties of marriage were not dissolved by a man's becoming a Christian, *since slavery itself was not,* and in

general, in the next verse, he tells them, that *nothing in any man's civil estate or rights is altered by his becoming a Christian."*

I shall next proceed to quote some portions of the well-known work of Rev. George D'Oyly, B.D., and Rev. Richard Mant, D.D., domestic chaplains to the Archbishop of Canterbury, which was published under the direction of the Society for Promoting Christian Knowledge in England, and republished, with some additional notes, by the eminent Bishop Hobart, as being well adapted for our American Church, in A.D. 1818. It belongs, therefore, to the present century, though several years anterior to the emancipation of the slaves in Jamaica by the British Parliament.

I commence with a statement of the learned Dr. Hales, which is placed in the notes on Gen. 10 : 1 : "The following curious and valuable commentary," saith he, "which records the primitive settlements of the three families, is furnished by Abulfaragi, in his history of the Dynasties. 'In the one hundred and fortieth year of Phaleg the earth was divided, by a second division, among the sons of Noah. To the sons of Shem was allotted the middle of the earth, namely, *Palestine*, Syria, Assyria, Samarra, (a town of Babylonian or Chaldean Irac,) Babel, Persia, and Hegiaz, (or Arabian Petræa.) To the sons of Ham, Teman, (or Idumæa, Jer. 49 : 7,) Africa, Nigritia, Egypt, Nubia, Æthiopia, Scindia, and India, on both sides of the Indus. To the sons of Japheth also, Garbia, (the North,) Spain, France, the countries of the Greeks, Sclavonians, Bulgarians, Turks, and Armenians."

Now here the allotment gives a large range to Ham, but Palestine is expressly included as belonging to Shem, and therefore the portion of the Canaanites who obtained possession of it were not the original owners of the soil.

This fact would only add another reason for bestowing the land on the Israelites, who were of the posterity of Shem, and had the right to claim it, as belonging to them by express allotment.

This original distribution of the earth is regarded by learned and thoughtful men as of very high importance. For thus our commentary proceeds : "It was made," saith Joseph Mede, "in an orderly manner, and not by a confused, irregular dispersion, wherein every one went and seated himself where he thought good." And Bryant saith that "This distribution was by the *immediate appointment of God.* We have full evidence of this in that sublime and pathetic hymn of Moses, Deut. 32 : 7, 8, 9. From this we may see that the whole was by God's appointment, and that there was a reserve for the people who were to come after. St. Paul likewise speaks of it expressly as a divine ordinance, Acts 17 : 26. This is taken notice of by many of the fathers. Eusebius in particular mentions 'the distribution of the earth,' and adds that it happened in the two thousand six hundred and seventy-second year of the Creation, and in the nine hundred and thirtieth year of the patriarch's life. Thus it was that Noah, by *divine appointment*, divided the world between his three sons. It is remarkable that "the Grecians," saith Bryant, "had some traditions of this partition of the earth, which they supposed to have been by lot, and between Jupiter, Neptune, and Pluto."

It is further worthy of note, as "Sir William Jones has demonstrated, that *three* great branches of language are sufficient to account for all the varieties now extant." (*Calmet's Dictionary, Supplement.*)

That Melchizedek was a "Canaanitish prince" was the opinion of Dr. Hales, because he was the king of Salem, "the most ancient quarter of Jerusalem," and the name of Canaan is supposed, though erroneously, to have been given to that land in the time of Abraham, Gen. 12 : 5. But even if this supposition were correct, I could not conceive that Melchizedek belonged to the *race* of that Canaan, whose posterity had been doomed to a curse by the patriarch Noah. Nothing was more common at that time, and nothing is more common in our own day, than to find the same name given to *men* and to *places*. This coïncidence, of itself, would therefore be entirely insufficient to prove that Melchizedek was a Canaanite with *respect to his genealogy.* We read, indeed, in the next verse, that "the Canaanite was then in the land. But by this," as the commentator saith, "is meant, not *all the posterity of Canaan*, or *all the Canaanitish tribes, but only one particular tribe of them.*" This tribe may have been living there, and Sodom and Gomorrah may have been built by them, and become petty principalities long before, without interfering with the king of Salem, Melchizedek.

I consider it altogether more reasonable, therefore, to regard this priest and king as of the race of Shem, in whom the prophecy of Noah had placed the high prerogative of belonging specially to the Lord God, "Blessed be the Lord God of Shem." For to this "king

of righteousness and prince of peace" the chief rank of religious
privilege had been vouchsafed, in being the eminent type of the
Lord Jesus Christ, a priest of the Most High God, and set before all
others in this respect, that the divine Redeemer was to be "a priest
forever, after the order of Melchizedek."

The trifling extent of kingdoms, even five centuries later than the
time of Abraham, may be easily inferred from the fact that Joshua
smote thirty-one kings, although he did not conquer the whole land
of Canaan. Hence it is obvious, as saith Bishop Patrick, that "by
the term 'Kings' we are merely to understand petty princes or lords
perhaps of some single cities, with a few dependent villages, whose
inhabitants were their tenants." (Joshua 12 : 24.) One of these
kings was the king of Ai, the population of which is stated to have
been twelve thousand ; but this was much smaller than many of the
others.

With respect to Melchizedek, however, Pool, in the *Synopsis Criti-*
corum, saith that the oldest and best of the Hebrew doctors supposed him to be the patriarch Shem himself. "*Noah constituit Sem*
dominum terræ Canaan, speciali titulo. Huc ergo venit Sem, et
urbem Salem ædificavit, et hic regnavit," *i. e.,* Noah appointed Shem
to be lord of the land of Canaan, by special title. Here, therefore,
Shem came, and built the city of Salem, and reigned there. The
name *Melchizedek,* signifying the "king of righteousness," was given
to him, according to St. Augustin and others, as a title of honor, and
was not his proper name ; just as we see that names of the same sort
were given to many other persons in the Old Testament. And the
text might have been translated with perfect propriety, "*The king*
of righteousness, who was the king of Salem, brought forth bread
and wine," etc. (Gen. 14 : 18.) So, in the 110th Psalm, "*The Lord*
sware and will not repent, Thou art a priest forever, after the
order of Melchizedek," might have been rendered, "*after the order*
of the king of righteousness." St. Paul, referring to this name in his
epistle to the Hebrews, is careful to give its signification, as also that
of *Salem,* which is "Peace," so that on the whole there is a strong
probability that the Jewish doctors were right in their hypothesis,
and we may confidently say that no good reason can be brought
against it.

The argument, therefore, which I have already, in part, indicated,
will stand thus :

First, we have the prophecy of Noah, in which the name of Canaan, signifying *Humiliation*, is given to the son of Ham; and his posterity are doomed to servitude in its lowest form, slavery. (*Gen.* 9 : 25.)

Next, we have the sons and descendants of Canaan set forth, Sidon, Heth, the Jebusite, the Amorite, the Girgasite, the Hivite, the Arkite, the Sinite, the Arvadite, the Zemarite, and the Hamathite, eleven different names in all, and considerably exceeding the number set down to the brethren of Canaan. For the sons of Cush were Seba, Havilah, Sabtah, Ramah, and Sabtichah, only *five.* Mizraim begat Ludim, Anamim, Lehabim, Naphtuhim, Pathrusim, Casluhim, and Caphtorim, only *seven*, while the children of Phut are not named at all. Thus we have *eleven* names set down to Canaan, and *twelve* to Cush and Mizraim both together, plainly leading to the conclusion that the posterity of Ham, in the line of Canaan, was almost one half of the population to which Africa was to be assigned. (Gen. 10.)

In the third place, we have an intimation of the wide diffusion of Canaan's descendants, in the statement of the sacred historian, that "afterwards *were the families of the Canaanites spread abroad*" (Gen. 10 : 18)—a statement which is not made concerning any other part of Ham's posterity.

Fourthly, we have the fact, that in the days of Peleg *the earth was divided.* (Gen. 10 : 25.) And we have seen the tradition of the Jews, as stated by Abulfaragi, together with the extracts from Mede and Bryant, referring to Eusebius and many of the fathers, that this division was by *divine appointment*, under the authority of Noah, and in the nine hundred and thirtieth year of the patriarch's life. In this division, Africa fell to the lot of Ham's posterity, Asia to that of Shem, and Europe to that of Japheth, while *Palestine* is specially mentioned as belonging to Shem. But there is a statement in Gen. 10 : 19, which appears to be, at first sight, inconsistent with this arrangement. For there we read that "*the border of the Canaanites was from Sidon, as thou comest to Gerar, unto Gaza, as thou goest unto Sodom and Gomorrah*," which certainly looks like a location of the Canaanites in Palestine. This difficulty, however, arises only from the introduction of the definite article, which is not authorized by the original Hebrew. Instead of "*the border* of the Canaanites," it should be *a border* of the Canaanites, meaning that Palestine was *one* of the places into which their fami-

8*

lies had "*spread abroad.*" We have seen that eleven heads of tribes
proceeded from Canaan, and we know that only seven of them were
established in the promised land, five hundred years after Abraham
went there. And therefore it is reasonable to conclude that at this
time, namely, when Abraham became a resident, a small portion—
perhaps, as Bishop Patrick estimated it, part of one tribe of Canaan's
descendants—had emigrated from Africa, and made a settlement in
Sodom and Gomorrah, for " the Canaanite was then in the land,"
(Gen. 12 : 6,) while the far greater bulk of them still remained in the
land of Ham, namely, in Africa, their allotted heritage.

Fifthly, we read of Melchizedek, or " the King of righteousness,"
in Salem, the principal city in Palestine, whom we can not reasonably
suppose to be of the race of Canaan, but either Shem himself, or one
of his posterity. We also find that Abraham and Lot met with no
difficulty in settling where they pleased ; a plain proof that the land
was at that time unoccupied to a great extent, and open to any emigrants who chose to go there. This fact is a conclusive demonstration that the tribe of Canaanites had then established only a partial
and very limited possession, amounting to little more than Sodom
and Gomorrah. Now there can be no objection made to this, except
what may be predicated upon the single fact that the whole region,
elsewhere called Palestine, is here styled *Canaan,* as if it were the
proper and original seat of the Canaanites. And such, doubtless,
has been the general impression, although it appears to my mind to
be altogether a mistaken one.

For we read, before the full establishment of Abraham, that there
was a famine in the land, " and Abraham went down to sojourn in
Egypt." How long he remained there, we can not tell ; but after
his return, we find that an addition had been made to the strangers
from abroad, who came into Canaan. For whereas, before, we read
that the *Canaanite* was then in the land, we now read that " the
Canaanite and the Perizzite dwelled then in the land." (Gen.
13.) From this it is easy to perceive the growth of the Canaanitish
tribes, by accessions of their brethren. The country was delightful.
It was favorable to agriculture. It was open to the settler. And it
combined, with these advantages, a commodious position on the
Mediterranean Sea, admirably adapted to commerce. That the race
of Canaan, in those early ages, had a spirit of active enterprise and a
fondness for trade and speculation, must be inferred from the fact

that the word *Canaanite* became, in due time, synonymous with *merchant*, whereas the race of Shem was devoted to agricultural and pastoral life, as we see in the cases of Abraham, Isaac, Jacob and his sons in the land of Goshen, and yet more especially in the arrangement which the Almighty made for Israel in Canaan, where a farm was given to every family.

But in order to account for the name of Canaan being given to Palestine, in connection with the commencement of Abraham's residence, and while the patriarch Shem, or one of his immediate progeny, reigned as Melchizedek, or the king of righteousness, in Salem, I shall state my view at large, which I think will be found in perfect analogy with other historical facts, familiar to us all.

The most reasonable statement of the matter, in my opinion, is the following, viz. : That Moses, who wrote this narrative for the special instruction of the Israelites, some five hundred years after Abraham's sojourn, set down the names of the places, not as they were known *then*, but as they were known in his own time; because his narrative could not have been understood by any other method.   Thus in Gen. 10 : 19, the names of Sidon, Gerar, Gaza, Admah, etc., are not to be supposed as belonging to the places indicated, at that early day. Sodom and Gomorrah, indeed, must have been then planted by the Canaanite and the Perizzite, because they were destroyed during the life of Abraham and Lot; but the other places were probably not known under those names, until some centuries later.

Thus, for example, suppose an historian of our times, writing about the condition of the country two hundred years ago, should say, that the English and the Dutch were then in the land, but Massachusetts, Rhode Island, Connecticut, New-Hampshire, Vermont, New-York, and Pennsylvania were all a wilderness, trodden by the Indians, and the wild animals.   This language would be perfectly correct and intelligible ; but no one would infer from it that the region of country, now comprehended by those States, was then marked out and known by their present appellations.   And the historian would be justified in his mode of expression, because, even if these portions of the land had acquired any names at all in that early period, those names must have been given to them by the Indians, and the recital of them to us, would convey no clear idea of the locality.

It seems manifest, therefore, that when Moses speaks of Abraham coming, at the divine command, into the land of Canaan, we are authorized to suppose, *not* that it was *then* known by that name, but that this was its name *at the time when the sacred history was written;* and therefore he used it, according to the rule of common-sense, viz., in order to be perfectly understood by those to whom his history was addressed.

How it came afterwards to be known by that name is easily comprehended. The Canaanites began by a portion of one tribe; then their praises of the region brought others, and so, by degrees, the whole was settled by emigrants from the seven nations, whose commercial activity and enterprise gained them the distinction of being the *merchants, by excellence,* of the surrounding regions. Their great advancement, in numbers and in power, took place while the Israelites were in Egypt, a period longer than these United States have passed since the first settlement of the colonists from England. And their commercial success had made the word *Canaanite* almost synonymous with that of merchant, from which fact the *secondary* meaning of the word *Canaan* was derived, according to Taylor, and all our best Hebrew authorities.* So that, in common usage, the *land of Canaan* was understood to be the land of *the merchant,* or the *land of commerce,* as well as the land of the Canaanite. And their prosperity and wealth became manifested, as in all similar cases, by their splendid cities, walled round and fortified; and their pride and licentiousness increased with their idolatry. The curse of Noah had long been forgotten, or derided in their heathenism; and they boasted of their genealogy as the largest and most powerful race descended from the patriarch, whose families had thus *spread abroad;* until at length, "the iniquity of the Amorites" was full, and the decree of God commanded the Israelites to take possession of the land, and devote its flagitious inhabitants to destruction.

The land of Canaan now became, therefore, the land of Israel, and subsequently, Judea. The Canaanites, as a nation or nations, ap-

---

* In Taylor's Hebrew Concordance we have the following statement, viz.:

בנע hath two significations.

1. *Humiliare se, deprimere,* to bow down, to bring low. Applied to the subduing of a nation, to the humbling the proud, to a wicked person's being humbled for his sins, etc.

2. *Canaan, negotiator. Canaan,* the grandson of Noah, so called because he was depressed by his grandfather into the low condition of a servant of servants. Gen. 9 : 25. And because the Canaanites were much in the mercantile way of life, hence a *merchant.*

Of this latter meaning Taylor cites nine examples.

pear no more, under their former names. But nevertheless we know that the whole were not exterminated. A considerable portion remained whom the Israelites were not able to expel. Probably a much larger portion escaped from the sword of Joshua, and these may have been the founders of Tyre and Sidon, and Phœnicia and Carthage, which all agree to have been planted by the race of the Canaanites. The most natural course, however, for many of them, would be to betake themselves to Africa, for that was the *land of Ham*, and there they would have met with the most hospitable reception from their kindred and brethren. And therefore I think it the more probable hypothesis, that the greatest numbers of the fugitives from the land of Canaan became the inhabitants of that region which was designated for their abode by the division under Noah, so many centuries before; and with which they had doubtless kept up a friendly intercourse of old attachment and consanguinity, as descendants from their common progenitor.

We thus behold the same events in the early history of Palestine, which took place long afterwards among other nations. For example, England was originally inhabited by the Britons, and was known by the name of Britannia. But the Angles and the Saxons came in from the continent, first as friends, and then they resolved to establish themselves as conquerors. They succeeded, and the island was divided among seven independent powers, and they gave it the new name of Anglia. But these invaders were only a part of the whole, *the main body of their race remaining on the continent.*

So, in the case of our own country. It was in possession of the Indians. The English planted first one, and then another feeble colony. They multiplied, and finally gained full possession, calling the land by new and English names. But the great body of the English *remained at home*, and the numbers who emigrated made no serious inroad on the increase of the population, in the mother-country.

So in the settlement of our Western States. They received settlers from the old States, and grew rapidly ; but in no instance were the numbers withdrawn by emigration so great, as to prevent the growth of the population which they had left behind them.

Reasoning, then, from all historical analogy, there can be no doubt that the course of the Canaanites in Palestine was substantially the same. The land belonged to Shem, by virtue of the division made

by Noah under the divine direction. Melchizedek, the king of righteousness, was in possession at Salem, but the greater part of the region was uninhabited, and there was abundant room for strangers.
The Canaanites found their way into it from Africa, which had been
allotted to Ham and his posterity. They came at first in small numbers. The Perizzites, another tribe which descended from Canaan,
followed. They came as friends, and settled peaceably, and built
Sodom, and Gomorrah, and Zoar, before Abraham arrived at the
command of the Almighty. By degrees they increased, and when
we survey their condition, five centuries later, they had filled the
land, and no trace of the posterity of Shem appears amongst them.
Salem, which was once the territory of Melchizedek, had become the
seat of the Jebusites, who called it Jebus, and the name of their
common progenitor, Canaan, was given to the whole region. But
we are not to believe that the entire body of any of the seven nations
had left Africa. As in the other cases to which I have referred, we
must suppose that only a portion, and that the much smaller portion
of each, abandoned that continent, which was their allotted home.
And therefore we may fairly conclude that the bulk of the eleven
nations comprising the posterity of Canaan *remained in Africa*, and
multiplied there, notwithstanding a part of seven of those nations
had emigrated to Palestine, and, as in all such instances, had " called
the land after their own name."

The result would therefore be that the great body of the posterity
of Canaan, at the time of Israel's invasion, were not in Palestine, but
in Africa. We have seen that his descendants included *eleven* distinct names, while those of Cush were only *five*, and those of Mizraim
only *seven*. Four of the eleven appear not to have gone to Palestine,
as we only find seven nations enumerated there, whom the Israelites
were commissioned to destroy. And these four, along with the bulk
of the other seven who had remained in Africa, *the land of Ham*,
not only made up almost one half of the population, but must have
mingled their blood with all the rest, by the promiscuous intercourse
of the sexes, which has prevailed in that benighted continent for so
many centuries. And hence the strong probability is that the whole
negro race, for several ages, has been literally descended from Canaan,
and would therefore come within the terms of Noah's prophecy, that
they should be the *servants* of their brethren. We have seen how
this prophecy is actually fulfilled in the present state of Africa, from

the statement of Malte Brun, who saith that *two thirds* of the native negroes are *slaves*, under the most cruel and inhuman yoke of their savage and heathen masters.

It is supposed by some, however, that the Canaanites could not be negroes, 1, because they were not black, and 2: because they were builders of great cities, and active promoters of commerce—very different, in these respects, from the Africans of the present day.

To this, I think it easy to make a satisfactory reply. With respect to color, we all suppose that Noah and his sons were white men. But the posterity of Ham comprises a variety of shades, some of them being as black as ebony. Now the general opinion of physiologists is, that the color depends on the climate, the food, and the habits; but no one has ever discovered how many generations must pass before these will change the white man into a negro. Nor would it be possible to determine whether these causes are sufficient to account for the present differences, not only in color, but in the form, the countenance, and the very anatomy of the frame, amongst the races of the human family. For aught we know, it may require the special act of God, to adapt each race to its peculiar location and circumstances. And assuredly, when we see that the hand of Providence has established this adaptation in the insects, the birds, the animals, and the very trees and flowers of each climate on our globe, we can not with any reason deny that the same beneficent power has been as considerate and kind to the human family.

But at what time, and in what measure, the change of color was accomplished, it is impossible to ascertain. Three thousand eight hundred years have elapsed since the time of Abraham, and more than two thousand since the fall of Carthage. What color *then* marked the Canaanites no man can tell. How far the more temperate climate of Palestine, Tyre, Sidon, and Carthage, assisted by intermarriages with a fairer race, may have made a difference between that portion of them which had emigrated from Africa, and the bulk of the Canaanites who remained there, is a mere matter of conjecture. But certain it is that we can not assign any reason why the posterity of Canaan in Africa should be lighter in their hue, than the posterity of Cush. Certain it is, that Canaan was the son of Ham, and that the negroes are Ham's posterity. And if, as I have shown, the great body of the Canaanites must have lived and multiplied in Africa, they could not have been exempted from the general result which

Providence has produced in the form and the complexion of their brethren, whether that result was brought about in the course of ten or twenty centuries.

With respect to the second objection, viz., that the Canaanites were builders of great cities and active promoters of commerce, so that, as we have seen, the name of *Canaanite* became synonymous with the business of a merchant, there is no difficulty whatever. For I have never denied that the negro race is capable of attaining a high degree of skill in any of the ordinary departments of human knowledge, under proper circumstances. They differ, of course, as all men differ, in their mental capacity and energy. We know that, as a general rule, those persons who emigrate from their native country, in order to plant new settlements abroad, are the most enterprising, bold, and adventurous spirits in the community. The change of condition in which they place themselves calls forth the exertion of all their faculties, and whatever amount of intellect they possess becomes developed in the most available form, by the constant stimulus of necessity. Hence we may readily account for the difference between that portion of the Canaanites which left Africa for Palestine, and the great body of those who remained in their native land; where, as Malte Brun informs us, twenty days in the year suffices for the labor of their maintenance, and there is no room for any emulation in the arts of civilized life, because they have no standard of comparison. The contrast, indeed, may be easily imagined, when we regard the inhabitants of Liberia, advancing rapidly in commerce, in architecture, and even in literature; and then turn our eyes upon the millions of negroes still living in the Southern States. It is the same race, but under totally different circumstances. And therefore it is that I have always been the advocate of a *gradual abolition of slavery*, connected with the *transmission of the freedmen to African soil*, where the stimulus of their new location would develop their powers to the best advantage. While, on the contrary, I have opposed their immediate emancipation in the South, remaining there, under the overshadowing superiority of the white race; not only because such a state of society would be intolerable to their former masters, but also because it would be fatal to the advancement and final elevation of the negroes themselves.

Thus, then, I have shown, and, as it seems to me, satisfactorily, how the prophecy of Noah has been truly fulfilled, and is still in the progress of fulfillment, upon the posterity of Canaan, the negro race, according to the letter of Scripture. From that sentence there is no escape, until the time shall come, which I doubt not is appointed in the order of Providence. Like the sentence pronounced upon the race of Israel, the prophecy of Noah will have its allotted course, and no wisdom or power of man can defeat it. But the period is approaching when the designs of the Almighty will be accomplished. The Jews will again occupy their own land, and Mount Zion will be "a praise throughout the world," and "all nations shall flow unto Jerusalem." The race of Canaan also shall be relieved from the curse, "Ethiopia shall lift up her hands unto God," and "the knowledge of the Lord shall cover the earth, as the waters do the sea." How long a period may elapse before this glorious consummation, is only known to Him who seeth the end from the beginning. It may, for aught that we can tell, be at the close of the present dispensation, which so many suppose to be nigh at hand. It may be deferred for several centuries. But it *will come*, for "the mouth of the Lord hath spoken it."

And until it comes, it is our duty to submit with patient faith to our allotted condition. Not rebelliously warring against the will of the Most High, nor vainly opposing ourselves to the arrangements of His providence, nor accusing our brethren in Christ as *sinners* because they keep in slavery the race which God saw fit to doom to servitude ; but doing our best, in conjunction with the precepts of the apostles, the rules and practice of the Church, and the Constitution of our country, to ameliorate the condition of the slave by the kind and gracious influence of the Gospel.

Believing as I do, that a thorough examination of the subject will lead to the result to which I have arrived, namely, that the posterity of Canaan are existing at this day in the African race, and compose the greater part of it, I am nevertheless quite aware that many of my readers, as well as yourself, may think the conclusion untenable from the fact that we hear no more of the Canaanites after the conquest of Palestine by ancient Israel. But this, on reflection, will be seen to amount to nothing. Nations, as such, are liable to many changes. They rise, decline, and disappear from the page of history. And yet the *races of men* remain and form other combinations, and are known by new names, though the people are substantially the descendants of the same ancestry.

Thus, amongst the multitude of nations mentioned in the Penta-
teuch, nearly all have passed away, yet there is not one whose population can be said to be extinct. We can trace the Jews, because their
religion forbade them to commingle with any other people. We can
trace the Edomites, because their peculiarities are found among the
unconquered tribes of the Arabs to this day. We can trace the
Egyptians, because their kingdom, however debased, has continued
to exist. But the rest, though we can not trace them, and therefore
we talk as if they were annihilated, have in reality continued to exist
as individuals and families; and still form, by constant propagation,
their proportion of the world's inhabitants. The same remark may be
applied to all other cases. If we take, for example, the Commentaries
of Cæsar, we find a large number of nations specified as the communities in ancient Gaul, hardly any of which were known by the
same names five centuries later. Yet no reasonable man can doubt
that these were the ancestors of the Germans and the French, the
Swiss and the Belgians, of our own period. The various races may
intermingle, their old nationalities may undergo many mutations;
language, manners, and customs may change; but all this does not imply the *extinction of the people.* So far, therefore, as we have evidence to guide us, we have full authority for saying that no race
which existed since the time of Noah has ceased to exist in their posterity; although their former landmarks have been all obliterated, and
their old appellations have long passed away.

This being true universally, there can be no question about its
being more especially true in the continuance of the race of Ham,
through the line of Canaan, since it is the only race which it has
pleased God to mark by such strong characteristics. Their doom of
servitude in its lowest form, their location in Africa, in the climate
of which the races of Shem and Japheth can not long exist, their
wonderful adaptation to that climate, their still more wonderful
adaptation to the state of slavery, for which the mercy of Providence seems to have qualified them beyond any other race of people
in the known world, and, lastly, their peculiar color, which distin-
guishes them so manifestly from the rest of the human family—all
these must serve to identify them beyond the possibility of mistake.
And as it is an established rule among theologians that nothing proves
the true sense of prophecy so conclusively as its fulfillment, I may
claim the application of the maxim to these indisputable facts—that

up to this period of modern history no race but theirs has been subject to slavery, and *perfectly contented under it*, for thousands of years. No race but theirs has been so stationary and so degraded in their own land. And no race but theirs has shown such a disposition to look up to the posterity of Shem and Japheth with admiring love, and cling to them with such constancy and affection.

CHAPTER XXII.

RIGHT REVEREND BROTHER: Resuming my extracts from the commentary of D'Oyly and Mant, I shall commence this chapter with some instructive remarks on the color of the human species. (Gen. 10 : 32.)

"Man, though white in Europe, black in Africa, yellow in Asia, and red in America," saith the celebrated naturalist Buffon, "is still the same animal, tinged only with the color of the climate. Where the heat is excessive, as in Guinea and Senegal, the people are perfectly black; where less excessive, as in Abyssinia, the people are less black; where it is more temperate, as in Barbary and in Arabia, they are brown; and where mild, as in Europe and in Lesser Asia, they are fair."

"Shaw, in his travels through Barbary, found a tribe in the mountains of Auress, south of Algiers, who appeared to be of a different race from the Moors; far from swarthy, their complexion is fair and ruddy, and their hair a deep yellow, instead of being dark, as among the neighboring Moors. He conjectures that they are a remnant of the Vandals. And they probably retained their complexion from their high mountainous situation; as the natives of Armenia, in Western Asia, and Cashmere, in Eastern, are fair, owing to the great elevation of the soil in both places, and the temperature of the climate occasioned thereby."

"On the other hand, a colony of Jews settled at Cochin, on the Malabar coast, from a very remote period, of which they have lost the memory, though originally a fair people in Palestine, and from their customs preserving themselves unmixed, are grown as black as the other Malabarians, who are hardly a shade lighter than the negroes of Guinea. And at Ceylon, the Portuguese, who settled there only a few centuries ago, are degenerated and grown blacker than the original natives. They are in number about five thousand, still speak Portuguese, wear the European dress, and profess the Romish religion."

"Still there are anomalies or exceptions to the general conclusions of the influence of climate and customs, that must be ascribed to other, and perhaps, undiscovered causes, which baffle the pride of human sagacity to develop, and which, after all, must be resolved into the will and pleasure of the Creator, and deposited among the 'unsearchable riches' of His wisdom and providence in the *variety*, no less than in the *regularity* of His works."

On Exod. 21, *And he that stealeth a man and selleth him*, etc., the commentator saith : "As liberty is equally valuable with life, the Jewish law, with the strictest equity, ordained that if any man were convicted of attempting to reduce any *fellow-citizen* to slavery, he should be punished with death."

Here I would remark that the learned Dr. Graves, from whom this comment is taken, agrees with almost all the other commentators in restricting the law of Moses to the case of stealing a *fellow-citizen*, *i. e.* an Israelite. But he differs from the whole stream of human history, and, as I think, from common-sense, in the reason which he assigns for it, namely, that "liberty is equally valuable with life." This proposition seems to me quite untenable. Slavery, as we have seen, came in with war ; and it was universally held that it was a favor to the captive taken in battle that he should have his life spared, on condition of his becoming the slave of his conqueror. Hence the very name of *servus*, from *servatus*, viz. one *saved* from death, became the title of the slave, according to the Roman law and the judgment of the fathers. And no reasonable mind could hesitate as to the choice which the vast majority of men would make, if death or slavery were proffered to them.

On Lev. 25 : 13, *Ye shall return every man to his possessions*, etc., we have the following comments, in D'Oyly and Mant, viz. :

"By appointing that, on the year of jubilee, the owner of estates which had been sold should return to his possession, and that every *Israelitish slave* should be at perfect liberty to *return to his family*, God wisely provided for the suppression of luxury, cruelty, and ambition ; for the preservation of a perfect distinction of tribes, families, and genealogies ; and chiefly for ascertaining the descent of the future Messiah, whose more eminent deliverance, wrought for all mankind, was shadowed out by the privileges bestowed upon the Israelites, in the year of jubilee." And on v. 39, *If thy brother that dwelleth by thee be waxen poor, and be sold unto thee, thou shalt not compel him to serve as a bond-servant,* we read this comment from Bishop Patrick: "That is," saith he, "as a slave bought from other nations, over whom the *dominion of the Israelites was as complete as over their cattle.*"

On Deut. 23 : 15, "*Thou shalt not deliver unto his master the slave that is escaped unto thee,* we have the following: "That is, the servant *not* of a Hebrew, but of an alien and stranger."—*Bishop Kidder.* And again: "A heathen soldier or servant who deserted and came over to the Israelites, with intent of turning proselyte to the true religion."—*Pyle.*

Thus far we find a reasonable degree of harmony between the commentary of D'Oyly and Mant, indorsed by Bishop Hobart, and the great body of Biblical critics which had gone before, so far as the Old Testament is concerned. And when we turn to the same commentary on the New Testament, we shall have no reason to complain of any substantial variation.

Beginning with our Saviour's strong declaration in His sermon on the Mount, Matt. 5 : 17, "*Think not that I am come to destroy the law and the prophets,*" etc., we have the following comment from the learned Dr. S. Clarke: "Do not think that I am come to destroy or abrogate the law and the prophets: no, I am not come to dissolve any one natural or moral obligation; but, on the contrary, to fulfill what was typified, to explain what was obscure, and to complete what was imperfect."

And again, from Archbishop Tillotson: "I am not come to destroy but to fulfill, to carry on the same design which was intended by the Jewish religion, and to perfect and accomplish it."

On 1 Cor. 7 : 22, *He that is called in the Lord, being a servant,* etc., we have this comment, viz. : "Though he be a slave to man, yet, as a Christian, he is Christ's freeman, in the most honorable sense of true freedom ; and the Christian who is no man's slave is yet a servant, and owes an absolute obedience to Christ, our common Lord and Master."—*Pyle.*

The important text in 1 Tim. 6 : 1, *Let as many servants as are under the yoke,* has these comments, viz. : "*Under the yoke* signifies," saith *Dr. Whitby,* "the yoke of bondage to the heathens." And *Burkitt* is quoted in the following words: "The Apostle here particularly directs Timothy to instruct Christian servants in the performance of the duty of obedience to their masters, whether infidels or Christians. Hence it appears that *the Christian religion allows of an inequality amongst men*, and as it gives to superiors the power of commanding, so it lays inferiors under an obligation to obey."

And on the Epistle to Philemon, Bishop Tomline is cited for the following : " The Epistle to Philemon is a plain proof that Christianity was *not intended to make any alteration in the civil conditions of men*. St. Paul considered Onesimus, although converted to the Gospel, as *still belonging to his former master*, and by deprecating the anger of Philemon, he acknowledged that Onesimus continued liable to punishment for the misconduct of which he had been guilty, previous to his conversion."

The name of Bishop Davenant stands high among the worthies of our mother Church of England, and I shall occupy the remainder of this chapter with some valuable passages from his exposition of St. Paul's Epistle to the Colossians, translated by the Rev. Josiah Allport, who has added many valuable notes, and thus adorned a work of great merit and usefulness. The following passages embrace all that belongs to our subject :

Col. 3 : 22 : *Servants, obey in all things your masters according to the flesh*, etc. " The occasion of this precept," saith Bishop Davenant, " seems to spring from the circumstance, that servants converted to Christianity thought themselves to be exempt from the yoke of servitude. *Which opinion, full of error, the devil without doubt instilled into the minds of men*, that thence he might render the Christian religion odious among the heathen, as a disturber of order. This error perhaps had some color. If masters embraced the Christian religion together with their servants, it was unjust that they should still hold them as slaves whom they were bound to account as brethren. If masters still adhered to paganism, when their servants were converted, it seemed much more unjust that he who had been delivered and redeemed from the power of the devil should nevertheless remain in bondage to a pagan man who himself remained a slave to the devil. These things seemed to have an air of probability ; but, notwithstanding, the Apostle gives a contrary precept, in which every word hath its weight, to demonstrate the equity and even the necessity of the precept."

" *Servants*. He addresses Christians, and yet he still calls them servants, δουλοι. This word does not denote such domestics as we now employ, who are in reality free and free-born, although they serve others for hire; but it denotes such as the ancients used, who were either taken in war, or bought, and on that account were wholly in the power of their masters."

"Concerning the foundation of this servitude, whether it be just or violent, I shall not contend, yet it appears to have been allowed and established by the law of nations. Hence Aristotle asserts (Polit. 1, 3) that servants of this kind were nothing else than *certain animated instruments of their masters.* And even amongst the sacred writers, these servants are reckoned among the goods and possessions of their masters, (Job 1 : 3,) and the servant is called, in Exod. 21: 21, *the money* of his master. The Apostle, therefore, shows, by this very name, that they were bound to obedience, and on that account he adds his command, *Servants, obey in all things.*

"But that is to be restricted to things lawful and honest. Rightly, therefore, has Jerome put in this exception. *In all things*, namely, saith he, *in which the lord of the flesh doth not command contrary to the Lord of the spirit.*"

"The Christian religion," continues Bishop Davenant, "does *not subvert political order;* nay, it doth not deprive heathen masters of their legitimate authority over Christian servants. Therefore the Anabaptists err, who think all authority to be opposed to evangelical liberty, even of Christians over Christians."

"But the Christian religion frees from the yoke of human servitude that which is the best and most excellent thing in man, namely, the spirit and conscience. (See Gal. 5 : 1.) They therefore err who would rule the minds and consciences of men by virtue of any superiority and human lordship, for they are masters *according to the flesh, not according to the spirit.*"

"Christians may and ought to submit themselves according to the flesh, (*i.e.*, in things external, doubtful, and temporal,) even to the unjust commands of those who are *masters according to the flesh.* Thus Augustine, (in Expos. Epist. ad Rom. propos. 74:) *We must not resist masters, although they unjustly take from us temporal things.* And St. Peter, 1 Epist. 11 : 18 : *Be subject to your masters, not only to the good and gentle, but also to the froward.*"

Verse 23 : *And whatsoever ye do, do it heartily, as to the Lord, and not unto men.* "That is," saith Bishop Davenant, "to the Lord Christ, more than to men, because for the sake of Christ you serve them."

" But why," continues he, " in these lower and external observances, are they said to obey the Lord more than men, whose commands they serve, and whom alone they profit ?"

" First, because they who obey are more the servants of Christ than of earthly masters. For earthly masters buy their servants with silver and gold : Christ buys them with his precious blood ; they redeem the body alone, and that for another service : Christ redeems both soul and body for perpetual liberty. They must therefore especially serve Christ."

" Secondly, because they obey earthly masters only *at the appointment of Christ ;* therefore they rather obey Christ than them ; not unlike as inferior servants who obey a steward, yet are said more to obey their master, at whose will they yield to his steward ; he is opposed if he shall order the contrary to his master."

" Thirdly, because *Christ himself hath declared that he wishes his servants to obey their masters,* and this he strictly commands in his word ; and he himself also, in his wise governance and by his authority, *hath ordained some to service and others to dominion.* Whilst faithful servants have respect to all these things, they are rightly said *to serve the Lord and not men.*"

Ch. 4 : 1 : *Masters, give unto your servants that which is just and equal.* " That which is just," continues Bishop Davenant, " in this place, includes whatever is due to servants from legal obligation, or according to positive laws, and excludes whatever is contrary to the same. Aristotle (Œcon. 1 : 5) lays down three things as necessary and due to servants, *their work, their sustenance, their correction.* We shall add also a fourth, viz., *their wages,* which is due to our servants, because they are not slaves, as they were formerly among the ancients. It pertains, therefore, to the justice of masters to render all these things to their servants according to due measure ; it is the part of injustice, or at least of folly, if they deal otherwise with them. For instance, in enjoining work upon a servant, he observes justice who neither imposes immoderate labor, nor suffers him to grow stupid in ease and idleness. So in allowing them sustenance, he who neither withholds necessary or convenient food, nor suffers them to indulge gluttony or drunkenness. In applying correction, he who does not inflict punishment upon them with a cruelty exceeding the extent of the fault, nor yet allows them to commit any crime with impunity. In rewarding them, he who is neither so sparing

9

that they can not thereby procure for themselves necessaries, nor so lavish as to yield them matter for dissoluteness."

That which is equal. "In the Greek it is *equality* or *equability*, which word we must not take in that sense, as if it were incumbent upon masters to give to their servants the same honors, the same obedience, which they exact from them, for well spoke Plato : *To give equal things to unequals is inequality.*"

"This word *equal*, therefore, does not designate the labors themselves, or the duties of servants and masters, which are different and plainly the reverse : but it refers to the mind and manner of acting, which in each ought to be equal by a certain proportionate analogy. For instance, servants are commanded to obey their masters in singleness of heart and the fear of God : now masters give them *that which is equal* when they rule them piously and religiously. Servants are commanded to obey their masters from the heart and with good will : masters repay them for their services when they rule their servants with *mildness and a sort of parental affection.* Therefore, that we may bring the difference of these words *just* and *equal* in this place, under a brief view : that is called *just* which the law requires, or what is due to servants from legal obligation. That is called *equal* which charity and Christian lenity requires, or what is due to them from moral obligation."

The translator in a note saith : "The reader will bear in mind that the word servants is used here for *slaves, δουλοι*, in conformity with the authorized version of the Bible," p. 205. But in the Latin of Bishop Davenant the word *servus* should be rendered *slave* or *bondman* throughout, because this is its only proper signification. Nevertheless, as it stands, the meaning of the writer is perfectly clear, and I have cited the commentary at great length because it is well worth your attention ; for you are aware, of course, that the author was one of King James's envoys to the famous Synod of Dort, and a special favorite with that important branch of the clergy which are called *Evangelical* by the non-conformists of England, and their successors in our own land.

CHAPTER XXIII.

Right Reverend Brother : As I have every desire to deal frankly and fully with the question in controversy, I shall devote this chapter to a quotation from Dr. Jortin, which I find in the commentary of D'Oyly and Mant, republished by Bishop Hobart, because it looks favorably, like certain passages from Scott and Clarke, on the abolition side of the argument.

1 Peter 2 : 18. *Servants, be subject to your masters with all fear*, etc. "In the time when the Gospel was first preached," saith Dr. Jortin, "servants for the most part were slaves, and, as many of them were converted to Christianity with or without their masters, it was to be feared lest they should take too much upon them, and think too well of themselves, by entering into a religion which commanded all men to treat one another as brethren. This might have brought a discredit on the Gospel, and have been a hindrance to its progress. Therefore St. Peter and St. Paul earnestly exhort servants or slaves to obey their masters, and to be industrious and honest, and dutifully to serve, not only the just and gentle, but the harsh and froward. *The law of nature knows no such thing as slavery, for by nature all men are free and equal ;* but by the civil laws, and by the practice of nations, it was established and it still continues amongst those who know not the Gospel ; and *the more is the shame and the pity, it is to be found in some places where Christianity is professed.* The religion of Christ, when it first made its progress in the world, left the civil laws of nations in a great measure as it found them, *lest, by altering or repealing them, it should bring confusion and disturbance into human society ;* but as by its own genius and tendency it leads men gently back to the precepts of nature and equity, to kindness and to mercy, it put an end, by degrees, in most civilized places, to that excessive distance and difference between masters and slaves, which owed its origin to outrage and war, to violence and calamity ; so that in Christian countries the service which

is performed is usually, as it ought to be, voluntary and by agreement. But what the writers of the New Testament have said concerning slaves holds true concerning hired servants, and all those
who are employed in other denominations under a master; that they
discharge their office modestly, diligently, and willingly, and act with
faithfulness and integrity in every thing that is committed to them."

Now here, along with much that is true, this learned and excellent
divine has set forth some very common but not the less mischievous
errors, and these I shall proceed to consider.

" *The law of nature knows no such thing as slavery, for by nature
all men are free and equal.*" So declared Dr. Jortin some time previous to our celebrated Declaration of Independence, because he died
in 1770, six years anterior to our Revolutionary War. But in the
first place I would ask, what did he mean by the *law of nature?*
Was it the law of our creation, in Paradise, before the fall, when
there was but one man and one woman in existence? This would be
preposterous, and therefore can not be pretended for a moment. It
must then have been the *law of nature after the fall*, when sin had
corrupted it. And where, in the history of that fallen nature, can
we find that all men are *free and equal?* The earliest account of it
is in the third and fourth chapters of Genesis, where the Almighty
pronounced this sentence on Eve : " Thy desire shall be to thy husband, and *he shall rule over thee.*" (Gen. 3 : 16.) The same principle
meets us again in the case of Cain and Abel, for, speaking of the relation between the elder and the younger brother, the Lord said unto
Cain : "Unto thee shall be his desire, and *thou shalt rule over him.*"
(Gen. 4 : 7.) Already, in this first generation of mankind, we see
dominion and subjection, but where are the *freedom and equality?*

If, from this beginning, we go on in the sacred history, what do we
find ? Little else but contest, strife, and the struggle for dominion.
The earth becomes filled with violence and iniquity, and the deluge
sweeps away the flagitious race, leaving only the patriarch Noah and
his family. And in the prophecy of Noah we have a proclamation
of the Divine purpose, which is totally unlike this favorite hypothesis
of ultra-abolitionism. " Cursed be Canaan, a servant of servants
shall he be unto his brethren. Blessed be the Lord God of Shem,
and Canaan shall be his servant. God shall enlarge Japheth and he
shall dwell in the tents of Shem, and Canaan shall be his servant."
Superiority for Shem in religious privileges, dominion over Shem by

Japheth in temporal power, and subjection of Canaan to both, are here indicated.   Where, again, are the freedom and equality ?

The posterity of Noah multiplies, and the earth is divided among them.   But immediately we find the exhibition of *dominion and power.*   Nimrod, the mighty hunter, appears as the founder of the Assyrian empire ; the patriarchal authority, which was absolute, rules the tribes ; Abraham, the favorite of God, becomes a petty prince, having three hundred and eighteen servants born in his own house; and *bondmen* and *bondmaids* are reckoned amongst the property of his children and grand-children.   That slavery was generally prevalent appears further from the fact, that the sons of Jacob resolved to get rid of their own brother Joseph, by selling him to the Midianites. These Midianites sold him again to Potiphar.   And when, after the death of Jacob, the brethren of Joseph feared that he would use his power to be revenged of their cruel conduct, " they went and fell down before his face; and they said, Behold, we be *thy servants.*" (Gen. 50 : 18.)   Where are the *freedom* and *equality*, even among the sons of Israel ?

We read next that the descendants of Jacob multiplied in Egypt, where they were oppressed to the lowest point of human suffering, for their children " were cast out that they might not live," and the Almighty, in mercy, sent Moses and Aaron to deliver them, and make them a prosperous and independent nation in the promised land.   And lo ! for the first and only time in the history of the world, the Lord condescended to provide a complete code of laws for his chosen people, comprehending both their religious and their civil duties. But here, again, though it was confessedly the most perfect system which mankind had ever known, yet the whole was arranged according to the strictest subordination.   A chief ruler appointed by divine direction, an hereditary priesthood, a prince over every tribe, rulers over thousands, and hundreds, and fifties, and tens, slavery for six years as the result of debt or poverty, even to the free-born Israelite, and slavery for life, descending to the offspring, for the races of the surrounding heathen.

Where, then, are we to look for this *law of nature*, of which Dr. Jortin spake, as many others now speak, under the delusive idea that there is good proof of its existence ?   We have seen, indeed, that the civil law had recognized something very like it, but this was evidently in reference to the supposed golden age, which poets and philosophers among the ancients accepted as a fact, although it was nothing more than a fanciful amplification of the condition of man, either in Paradise, or in the age of the patriarch Noah, whom they converted into Saturn. We know, likewise, that the notion may be found in various writers, and that the infidel Rousseau set forth the superiority of the state of nature in eloquent terms, before the French Revolution. And we also know that the people proclaimed their platform of *liberty, equality, and fraternity,* in pursuance of his hypothesis; and acted upon it, in the midst of the most bloody and cruel carnage, until the sword of the first Napoleon forced them to submit to the hand of power. As to our own assertion of it in the Declaration of Independence, I have already treated the matter sufficiently, in the *Bible View of Slavery,* and do not mean to repeat that argument here. But it must be obvious to all candid and thoughtful minds, that this favorite theory has no foundation in the facts; and, judging by the existing constitution of all created things, could never have been consistent with the purposes of the Almighty.

The nearest approach on earth to what men call freedom and equality, consists in *subjection to good laws.* Hence, we have the best political condition made *dependent on subjection.* What compels this subjection ? *The Government.* What is the Government? It is the systematic organization of *force.* No law is of any efficacy among men, unless there be a *power able to execute it.* But the importance of government is seen in this, that the force which it exercises is regulated by the fixed principles of justice, and intended to operate on every class in the community, so as to protect their rights and privileges. And hence arises the duty of supporting it, as an obligation of indispensable necessity; because the law of force which, without government, would arm every man against his neighbor, and make society a constant scene of anarchy and violence, becomes, under the rule of a just government, the preserver of peace, and the guardian of order and security.

But there can be no *government,* without a certain amount of *subjection,* and this subjection demands the surrender, to the same extent, of individual freedom and equality. Hence it is manifest, that these are incompatible with government, because it is impossible that any should be able to govern, unless the rest are bound to obey. We may say, indeed, that it is the *law* which governs; but this is only a phrase which serves to mislead our personal pride of independence by an agreeable delusion. For the law is the decree of the legislature, and the legislature is composed of *men*, commissioned to establish their judgment, as a *rule of obligation* to the whole community. And when it is established, it can not fulfill the work of government, unless it be *administered ;* and the administrators are also men, set over the rest, in order to *enforce the law on every individual.* The administrators of the law are therefore, practically, the *rulers*—the *actual governors*—whom the community are *bound to obey.* And hence it is plainly impossible that human society should exist, without *dominion* and *subjection.*

Here, then, and not in this imaginary freedom and equality, is the real *law of nature,* because mankind have never existed, and never can exist, without government, and all government involves *dominion* and *subjection,* more or less complete. The principle is fixed by the Almighty Creator, and whatever be the *form* under which it is exhibited, the *substance* is the same. It begins in the family. The husband and the wife. The parent and the children. The master and the servant. The teacher and the pupil. The magistrate and the citizen. The captain and the sailor. The general and the army. The king or the viceroy, and the people. Every class and all departments demand a *power to govern and an obligation to obey,* and freedom and equality can be found nowhere.

When we come to consider the operation of this essential principle of dominion and subjection in the case of human government, we find that it commences with our birth, and involves *servitude for life, descending to the offspring,* which is the very definition of slavery. But slavery is an odious word, in modern ears; and therefore I use the more acceptable term of *subjection.* In its practical character, the government exercises dominion over the *labor, the liberty, and the life* of every individual under its control. The *labor* is involved in the right of taxation, and in this form we are compelled to work for the government, whether we like it or not, every day, or pay an equivalent in property. The *liberty* is taken away in prisons and penitentiaries. *The life* is involved not only by the punishment of crime, but also by our liability to be drafted into the army, willing or unwilling, or even to be forced, by a conscription, to stand before the cannon's mouth, at the command of our rulers. And this subjection belongs to the *duty of our allegiance.* It continues to

the end of our mortal existence, and *attaches to our children, in per-*
petuity.

But all this, you may say, is for the advantage of the people. Certainly it is ; for I have already said that society could not exist without it. The result, however, is, that *not* freedom and equality, but
DOMINION AND SUBJECTION, are essential to the best interests of mankind. And therefore this is the real *law of nature*—the law adapted
to our nature, and to which our nature is adapted, for we can nowhere find society constituted on any other principle, since the world
began.

And this is the reason why the Sacred Scriptures are so imperative
on the duty of subjection. "Let every soul," saith St. Paul, "*be
subject to the higher powers.* For there is no power but of God : the
powers that be are ordained of God. Whosoever therefore resisteth
the power, *resisteth the ordinance of God ;* and they that resist shall
receive to themselves damnation." (Rom. 13 : 1, 2.)

And, again, in his epistle to Titus, the Bishop of Crete, the same
Apostle commands as follows, viz. : "Put them in mind to be *subject
to principalities and powers*, to obey magistrates, to be ready to
every good work." (Tit. 3 : 1.)

And again, we have this most comprehensive precept from the
Apostle Peter : "*Submit yourselves to every ordinance of man*, for
the Lord's sake, whether it be to the *king as supreme*, or unto *governors*, as unto them that are sent by him, for the punishment of
evil-doers, and for the praise of them that do well." (1 Pet. 2 : 13–14.)

Now it is very true that in this country we have no "king as supreme," and yet we are none the less bound by the Apostle's injunc-
tion ; because we have a Constitution, the sixth article of which establishes the standard of our subjection in these words, viz. :

"This Constitution, and the laws of the United States which shall
be made in pursuance thereof, and all treaties which shall be made,
under the authority of the United States, shall be the *supreme law
of the land*, and the judges in every State shall be bound thereby,
any thing in the constitution or laws of any State to the contrary notwithstanding."

The President, before he enters on the execution of his office, is
bound to take an oath or affirmation, to "*preserve, protect, and defend*" this Constitution. (Art. 2, sec. 1.)

"The judicial power of the United States shall be vested in one

Supreme Court—and shall extend to all cases, in law and equity, arising under this Constitution." (Art. 3, sec. 1 and 2.)

" The senators and representatives, and the members of the several State legislatures, and all executive and judicial officers, both of the United States and of the several States, shall be bound by oath or affirmation to *support this Constitution.*" (Art. 6.)

And in this Constitution, slavery is recognized and regarded as a standing institution, first, in Article 1, Section 2, where three fifths of the slaves are taken as the basis for the elective franchise; and secondly, in Article 4, Section 2, where fugitives, escaping from one State to another, are directed to be "delivered up on claim of the party to whom their service or labor is due." Such is the settled interpretation of the Supreme Court, and of Congress in their legislation on the subject. And it admits of no dispute. Twelve out of the thirteen States which adopted the Constitution were Slave States at the time. And although Massachusetts had abolished slavery, yet her *delegation,* along with that of the other Eastern States, insisted on continuing the slave-trade for twenty years more, against the wishes of Virginia.

Here, therefore, in this Constitution of the United States, is the *supreme dominion* on all those subjects for which it was designed. And to this, accordingly, the command of the Apostle applies. To this, every naturalized foreigner is obliged to swear allegiance. To this, every native citizen is bound, by his birth, to be loyal. You are bound by it. I am bound by it. Every citizen in the land is bound by it, from the President down to the humblest laborer on the soil. And therefore with us, the Constitution is *the king,* and the President is the *prime minister.*

Is there any power in these United States which can absolve me from this obligation? Suppose the President were to desire it—which I should be very sorry to impute to him—could he do so? Clearly not; for how can he absolve the citizen from a duty which he was obliged, by oath, to take upon himself, before he could enter upon his eminent office? If he is sworn to "preserve, protect, and defend" the Constitution, by what imaginable right can he authorize me to violate it?

Can Congress absolve me from this obligation? I answer, No; for the same reason. The power of Congress, like the power of the President, is exercised only by virtue of the Constitution. The mem-

9*

bers of the Senate and the House of Representatives are all bound by the same oath. And it would be an absurdity, surpassing all other absurdities, to suppose that a subordinate authority, created by the Constitution, should have a right to nullify the provisions of the very law on which it depends for its only power to legislate at all.

But we have been told that there is a "higher law," above the Constitution. And this, to the Christian, is certainly true. The Almighty "Law-giver, who is able to save and to destroy" — the glorious God, whose government rules the universe, whose throne is the heavens, and the earth his footstool—the all-wise and absolute Ruler, on whose decree the destiny of nations and of individuals is alike dependent—He has given us his unerring commands to be our guide, and in His Word we have the plainest directions on this very question. For there, as I have just shown, His inspired apostles require us to be "*subject to the higher powers*," and declare, moreover, that " whosoever resisteth the power, resisteth the ordinance of God, and they who resist, shall receive to themselves damnation."

Yet this, as all men acknowledge, refers only to those matters in which the laws of earth do not contradict the laws of heaven; for no one doubts that in case of a conflict between those laws, " we must obey God rather than man." Happily, however, the only point on which the ultra-abolitionist desires to trample on the Constitution, namely, slavery, is specifically provided for in the Bible; and the same apostles who command us to be *subject to the higher powers*, command the slave to be obedient and faithful to his master, and the master to be kind to his slave, while one of them, St. Paul, adopts a fugitive slave-law for himself, and, of his own accord, sends Onesimus back again to his legal owner.

Thus Christianity itself enforces the *dominion* of the Constitution, and I am bound to be *subject* to it, " not only for wrath, but also for conscience' sake," (Rom. 13 : 5,) and hence loyalty to that Constitution becomes a dictate of my religion. How any man can consider it a part of *his* religion to oppose it—how any officer of the Government can suppose it consistent with conscience to *swear that he will support the Constitution*, and yet make it his business to break it down—how any minister of the Gospel can lend his influence to sustain such a course, and even to brand an honest effort to justify the Constitution, as "unworthy of any servant of Jesus Christ," and an act which "challenges indignant reprobation" — these are things which you may think yourself able to explain. But for my own part, I regard them as the most astounding facts in the modern history of human delusion and perversity.

But now I return to Dr. Jortin, in order to take a brief survey of his remaining statements about slavery. He saith that it "still continues among those that know not the Gospel, and *the more is the shame and the pity, it is to be found in some places where Christianity is professed.*"

Now as to the *shame*, why did he not extend it to the Apostles, whom he admits to have sanctioned its continuance? For he acknowledges that "St. Peter and St. Paul earnestly exhort servants or slaves to obey their masters, and to be industrious and honest, and dutifully to serve, not only the just and gentle, but the hard and froward." And he tells us that "the religion of Christ, when it first made its progress in the world, left the civil laws of nations in a great measure as it found them, *lest by altering or repealing them, it should bring confusion and disturbance into human society.*" Is it not manifest that the same reason ought to have influenced the Christian ministers of our day to follow the Apostle's example? Was it possible for any man in his sober senses to believe that the dogmas of our ultra-abolitionists could prevail without "bringing confusion and disturbance into human society"? Alas! what a commentary do we behold on their opposition to the course which Dr. Jortin, and all others, confess to have been adopted by St. Peter and St. Paul; when not merely "confusion and disturbance," but the sacrifice of half a million of valuable lives, and the ravages of the most awful desolation, and a multitude of torn and bleeding hearts, and the kindling of bitter hatred and deadly animosity between those who were once friends and brethren, have marked the results of their insane determination! Why could they not have been content with the guidance of the inspired Apostles, confirmed by the voice of the whole primitive Church? Why must they denounce, as "a covenant with death and an agreement with hell," the Constitution of their country? Why could they not be *subject* to that "supreme law of the land," which they were bound to support by every rule of religious and civil obligation, and suffer our noble Union to continue in harmony and peace?

With regard to the "pity" of Dr. Jortin, I shall only say that he ought to have known the condition of the negro slaves under the cruel and heathen yoke of African slavery, as *subjects to the king of Da-homey*, before he *pitied* their state in the hands of their Christian masters. If he had duly reflected upon this, he would perhaps have discovered that, instead of being pitied for the change, it was rather a subject for devout thankfulness to the mercy of God, who, in His Providence, had saved so many of that barbarous and wretched race, and given them a lot so much more elevated and hopeful.

His subsequent statement, that slavery was abolished through the *growing influence of the Gospel*, is one of the popular fallacies which I shall consider by and by, and prove it to be entirely inconsistent with the facts of history. And I shall close this long chapter by expressing my surprise that the excellent Bishop Hobart, when he republished the Commentary of D'Oyly and Mant, should have re-tained an extract, which, however it might agree with the constitu-tional safety of England, was plainly unsuited to the harmony and welfare of these United States; besides being in utter discordance with the teaching of the Apostles, and the voice of the universal Church, for eighteen centuries together.

CHAPTER XXIV.

RIGHT REVEREND BROTHER: As I consider freedom and equality to be the popular idols of the age, especially in our own country, I shall recur to them again, because the subject is by no means exhausted. But before I resume these topics, I must complete my extracts from the modern Protestant commentators, the next on the list being the learned and candid Presbyterian, Macknight, whose " New Translation, Paraphrase, and Notes on the Epistles" are held in just and universal estimation.

On the text in 1 Cor. 7 : 20, 24, *Let every man abide in the same calling wherein he was called. Art thou called being a servant ? Care not for it; but if thou mayest be made free, use it rather*, our author gives the following paraphrase :

"Since *the Gospel makes no alteration in men's political state*, let every Christian remain in the same political state in which he was called. Agreeably to this rule, wast thou called, being a bondman ? Be not thou solicitous to be made free, fancying that a bondman is less the object of God's favor than a freeman. Yet, if thou canst even be made free by any lawful method, rather obtain thy freedom."

And on v. 24, *Brethren, let every man, wherein he is called, therein abide with God*, he gives this interpretation : " Brethren, whether in a state of bondage or of freedom each one was called, in that let him remain, while he remains with God ; that is, while he remains a Christian." And in the notes, he states that " this exhortation, which is three times given in the compass of the discourse, was intended to correct the disorders among the Christian slaves at Corinth, who, agreeably to the doctrine of the *false teachers*, claimed their liberty, on pretense that as brethren in Christ, they were on an equality with their Christian masters."

On Eph. 6 : 5, 9, *Servants, be obedient to them that are your masters according to the flesh, with fear and trembling*, etc., Dr. Macknight presents this statement, viz. :

" As the Gospel *does not cancel the civil rights of mankind*, I say
to bond-servants, Obey your masters, who have the property of your
body, with fear and trembling, as liable to be punished by them for
disobedience; obey, also, from the integrity of your own disposition,
as obeying Christ, (v. 6.) Do this, not merely when their eye is
upon you, or they are to examine your works as those do whose
sole care it is to please men; but as bondmen of Christ, doing the
will of God in this matter from the Lord; that is, diligently, (v. 7.)
With cheerfulness do your duty to your earthly masters, as servants
to the Lord Christ : for *in serving them faithfully, ye serve him;*
and therefore do not consider yourselves as servants to men only."
(Verse 8.)   " And that ye may be supported under the hardships of
your lot, recollect what your religion teaches you, that whatever
good action any man does, though he should receive no reward from
men, he shall receive at the judgment a reward from Christ, whether
he be a slave or a freeman," (v. 9.)   " And masters, behave in the
same benevolent conscientious manner towards your slaves: give
them all things necessary with good will, not aggravating the miseries
of their condition by the terror of punishment, but moderating threatening; knowing that the Lord even of you yourselves is in heaven on
the throne of God, and that in judging his servants, respect of persons
is not with him : He will reward or punish every one according to
his real character."

In his notes on the Epistle to the Colossians, ch. 3, v. 22, *Servants,
obey in all things your masters*, etc., this learned commentator makes
the following remarks on our English version :

"Though the word δουλος properly signifies a *slave,* our English
translators, in all the places where the duties of slaves are inculcated,
have justly translated it *servant;* because anciently the Greeks and
Romans had scarce any servants but slaves, and because the duties
of the hired servant, during the time of his service, are the same
with those of the slave. So that what the Apostle said to the slave,
was in effect said to the hired servant.   In this," continues Dr. Macknight, " and the parallel passage, Ephes. 6 : 5, the Apostle is very
particular in his precepts to slaves and lords, because, in all the countries where slavery was established, many of the slaves were exceedingly addicted to fraud, lying, and stealing, and many of the masters
were tyrannical and cruel to their slaves.   Perhaps also he was thus
particular in his precepts to slaves, because the Jews held perpetual

slavery to be unlawful, and because the Judaizing teachers propagated that doctrine in the Church. But from the Apostle's precepts it may be inferred, that *if slaves are justly acquired, they may be lawfully retained; as the Gospel does not make void any of the political rights of mankind.*"

I proceed, next, to the 1st Epistle of St. Paul to Timothy, ch. 6, v. 1–4, *Let as many servants as are under the yoke,* etc., on which our commentator gives the following paraphrase, viz. :

"Let whatever Christian slaves are under the yoke of unbelievers, pay their own masters all respect and obedience, that the character of God whom we worship may not be calumniated, and the doctrine of the Gospel may not be evil spoken of, as tending to destroy the political rights of mankind."

(V. 2.) "And those Christian slaves who have believing masters, let them not despise them, fancying that they are their equals, because they are their brethren in Christ: for, though all Christians are equal as to religious privileges, slaves are inferior to their masters in station. Wherefore, let them serve their masters more diligently, because they who enjoy the benefit of their service are believers and beloved of God. These things teach and exhort the brethren to practice them."

(V. 3.) "If any one teach differently, *by affirming that, under the Gospel, slaves are not bound to serve their masters, but ought to be made free,* and does not consent to the wholesome commandments which are our Lord Jesus Christ's, and to the doctrine of the Gospel, which in all points is conformable to true morality," (v. 4,) "he is puffed up with pride, and knoweth nothing, either of the Jewish or the Christian revelation, although he pretends to have great knowledge of both. *From all such impious teachers withdraw thyself, and do not dispute with them.*"

And in the notes on the first and second verses, Dr. Macknight saith that, "By ordering Timothy to teach slaves to continue with and obey their masters, the Apostle hath showed that *the Christian religion neither alters men's rank in life, nor abolishes any right to which they are entitled, by the law of nature or by the law of the country wherein they live.*" "Instead of encouraging slaves to disobedience, *the Gospel makes them more faithful and conscientious.* And by sweetening the temper of masters, and inspiring them with benevolence, it renders the condition of slaves more tolerable than formerly. For in proportion as masters imbibe the true spirit of the Gospel, they will treat their slaves with humanity, and even give them their freedom when their services merit such a favor."

This is the language of truth, of justice, and of right reason; and it not only agrees with the teaching of the apostles, but it is also the doctrine of the Church from the beginning, combining the reverence due to established law and order, with "peace and good-will to men."

And now I come to this fair and judicious commentator's views of the Epistle to Philemon, which it has become the fashion of late, amongst a considerable portion of the professed ministers of Christ, to wrest entirely from its old and true meaning. These are his words, viz. :

"Onesimus, a slave, on some disgust, having run away from his master Philemon, came to Rome; and falling into want, as is supposed, he applied to the Apostle, of whose imprisonment he had heard, and with whose benevolent disposition he was well acquainted, having, as it seems, formerly seen him in his master's house. Or, the fame of the Apostle's preaching and miracles having drawn Onesimus to hear some of the many discourses, which he delivered in his own hired house in Rome, these made such an impression on him that he became a sincere convert to the Christian faith. For the Apostle calls him, (v. 9,) *his son whom he had begotten in his bonds.* After his conversion, Onesimus abode with the Apostle, and served him with the greatest assiduity and affection. But *being sensible of his fault in running away from his master, he wished to repair that injury by returning to him.* At the same time being afraid that on his return, his master would inflict on him the punishment which, by the law or custom of Phrygia, was due to a fugitive slave, and which, as Grotius says, he could inflict without applying to any magistrate, he besought the Apostle to write to Philemon, requesting him to forgive and receive him again into his family."

"To account for the solicitude which the Apostle showed in this affair, we must not, with some, suppose that Philemon was keen and obstinate in his resentments. But rather that *having a number of slaves, on whom the pardoning of Onesimus too easily might have had a bad effect,* he might judge scme punishment necessary as a warning to the rest. At least the Apostle could not have considered the pardoning of Onesimus as a matter which merited so much earnest

entreaty with a person of Philemon's piety, benevolence, and gratitude, unless he had suspected him to have entertained some such
apprehension."

"What the Apostle wrote to Philemon on this occasion is highly
worthy of our notice, namely, that although he had great need of an
affectionate honest servant to minister to him in his bonds, such as
Onesimus was, and although, if Onesimus had remained with him
he would only have discharged the duty which Philemon himself
owed to his spiritual father; yet the Apostle would by no means detain Onesimus without Philemon's leave, because it *belonged to him
to dispose of his own slave in the way he thought proper*. Such was
the Apostle's regard to *justice* and *to the rights of mankind*."

This language is clear and conclusive. But I shall make one
extract more to sum up the whole.

"Chrysostom," saith Dr. Macknight, "hath showed several excellent uses which may be made of this epistle, to which I add some
others, namely, that although no article of faith is professedly hand-
led in this epistle, and no precepts for the regulation of our conduct
be directly delivered in it, yet the allusions to the doctrines and precepts of the Gospel found in it may be improved in various respects
for regulating our conduct. For it is therein insinuated, 1. That all
Christians are on a level. Onesimus, the slave, on becoming a Christian, is the Apostle's son and Philemon's brother. 2. That *Christianity makes no alteration in men's political state*. Onesimus, *the
slave*, did not become a freeman by embracing Christianity, but was
still obliged to be Philemon's *slave forever*, unless his master gave
him his freedom. 3. That slaves *should not be taken nor detained
from their masters without their master's consent*. 4. That we
should not contemn persons of low estate, nor disdain to help the
meanest when it is in our power to assist them, but should love and
do good to all men," etc.

The fifteenth and sixteenth verses are so frequently wrested from
their proper meaning by ultra-abolitionists, that it may be well to
quote them with our author's paraphrase.

(V. 15.) *For perhaps he therefore departed for a season, that thou
shouldest receive him forever.*

(V. 16.) *Not now as a servant, but above a servant, a brother beloved, specially to me, but how much more to thee, both in the flesh
and in the Lord.*

The paraphrase is as follows, viz. :

(V. 15.) " To mitigate thy resentment, consider that perhaps also for this reason he was separated from thee for a little while, that thou mightest have him *thy slave for life*."

(V. 16.) " No longer as a slave *only*, but above a slave, even a beloved Christian brother, especially to me who know his worth, and have been indebted to him for his services : how much more to thee as a brother, both by nation and by religion, *who will serve thee with more understanding, fidelity, and affection than before*."

And in the note on the 2nd verse the commentator saith that " By telling Philemon that he would now have Onesimus forever, the Apostle intimated to him his firm persuasion that Onesimus *would never any more run away from him*."

These extracts are abundantly sufficient to prove the general accordance of the author with the primitive school of the ancient fathers. And little more remains to complete the list of our modern Protestant annotators.

CHAPTER XXV.

RIGHT REVEREND BROTHER: From the well-known volumes of the Presbyterian divine, Dr. Macknight, I proceed to the critical and exegetical commentary on the Greek Testament, by Henry Alford, B.D., Dean of Canterbury, Third London Edition of 1857, a work of extraordinary learning and most extensive research. Here I find an interesting passage in which the old interpretation of St. Chrysostom is vindicated, in opposition to the majority of the modern expositors. The text is in St. Paul's first Epistle to the Corinthians, ch. 7 : 21: "*Art thou called being a servant? Care not for it; but if thou mayest be made free, use it rather.*" And this is Dean Alford's exegesis, viz. :

"Wert thou called (converted) a slave, let it not be a trouble to thee, but if thou art even able to become free, use it (*i. e., remain in slavery*) rather. This rendering, which is that of Chrys., Theodoret, Theophyl., Oecum., Phot., Camerar., Estius, Wolf, Bengel, Meyer, De Wette, and others, is required by the *usage of the particles.*—It is also required by the *context*, for the burden of the whole passage is : 'Let each man *remain* in the *state in which he was called.*'—It would be quite inconsistent with the teaching of the Apostle that in Christ *freeman and slave are all one*, (Gal. 3 : 28,)—and with his remarks on the urgency and shortness of the time in this chapter, to turn out of his way to give a precept merely of worldly wisdom, that a slave should become free if he could.—Christ's service is *perfect freedom*, and the Christian's *freedom* is the *service* of Christ. But here the Apostle takes, in each case, one member of this double antithesis from the *outer world*, one from the *spiritual.* The (actual) slave is (spiritually) free. The (actually) free is a (spiritual) slave. So that the two are so mingled, in the Lord, that the slave need not trouble himself about his slavery, nor seek for this world's freedom, seeing he has a more glorious freedom in Christ, and seeing also that his

brethren, who seem to be free in this world, are in fact Christ's servants, as *he* is a servant."

In the Prolegomena of the same author on the Epistle to Philemon,
(vol. iii. p. 113,) we read as follows, viz. : " Onesimus, a native of
Colosse, the slave of Philemon, had absconded, after having, as it
appears, defrauded his master, (ver. 18.) He fled to Rome and there
was converted to Christianity by St. Paul. Being *persuaded by him
to return to his master,* he was furnished with this letter to recommend him, now no longer *merely* a servant, but a brother also, to
favorable reception by Philemon."

I conclude this long array of authorities with some eloquent and
very admirable extracts from the late work of the Rev. Chr. Wordsworth, D.D., Canon of Westminster, entitled, " *The New Testament
of our Lord and Saviour Jesus Christ, in the original Greek, with
Notes,*" London Edition of 1859, where he speaks thus, on the Epistle to Philemon, in Part iii, p. 327 :

" Some persons in ancient times expressed surprise that this short
Epistle, addressed to a private person on a private occasion, should
be publicly read in the Church, and be received as a part of Canonical
Scripture."

" But the world's history has fully justified the Church in this
respect."

" In the age when it was written, Europe was filled with slaves.
Wheresoever the word ' servants ' occurs in the New Testament, we
must understand ' slaves '—slaves purchased with money or taken in
war, or reared from slaves in the house of their master. Phrygia,
in which Colossæ was situated, was the land of slaves. A Phrygian
was another word for a slave. Nothing could be more miserable
than their condition."

" But Christianity was for all. How would it affect them ? What
would it do for them ? Would it leave them in their present misery ?
Would it mitigate the rigor of their sufferings ? And if so, by what
means ?"

" The answer to these questions is supplied by the Epistle to
Philemon."

" That short letter, dictated from ' the hired house ' of the aged
Apostle, a prisoner at Rome, may be called a divine Act of Emancipation ; one far more powerful than any edict of Manumission promulgated by sovereigns and senates; an Act, from whose sacred

principles all human statutes for the abolition of slavery derive their virtue ; an Act which, by its silent influence, such as characterizes all genuine reformations, gradually melted away and thawed the hardships of slavery, by softening and warming the heart of the master with the pure and holy flame of Christian love ; an Act which, while it thus ameliorated the condition of the slave, not only *did not impair the just rights of the master, but greatly improved them,* by dignifying service, and by securing obedience to man as a duty done to Christ, and to be hereafter rewarded by him, and by changing the fearful slave into an honest servant and a faithful brother, and by binding every Onesimus in bonds of holy communion with every Philemon, in the mystical body of Christ, in the fellowship of the same prayers, and of the same Scriptures and sacraments, in the worship of the same Lord, and in the heritorship of the same heaven."

" Therefore the writing of this short letter was like a golden era in the history of mankind. Happy is it for the world that this Epistle, dictated by the Holy Ghost, has ever been read in the Church as Canonical Scripture. And every one who considers the principles laid down in this Epistle, and reflects on the reformation they have wrought in the domestic and social life of Europe and the world, and on the felicitous results which would flow from them in still greater abundance if they were duly received and observed, will acknowledge, with devout thankfulness to God, that inestimable benefits, civil and temporal as well as spiritual, have been conferred on the world by Christianity."

" St. Paul did not constrain Philemon to emancipate his slave Onesimus, but he inculcated such principles as divested slavery of its evils. The Gospel of Christ, as preached by the holy Apostle, did not exasperate the slave-owner by angry invectives, and by contumacious and contemptuous sarcasms. It did not embitter him against the slave, and injure the interests of the slave himself by an acrimonious advocacy of his rights, and by a violent and intemperate partisanship, and thus inflict damage and discredit on the sacred cause of Emancipation. But, by Christianizing the master, the Gospel enfranchised the slave. It did not legislate about mere names and forms, but it went to the root of the evil, it spoke to the heart of man. · When the heart of the master was filled with divine grace, and was warmed with the love of Christ, the rest would soon follow.

The lips would speak kind words, the hand would do liberal things. Every Onesimus would be treated by every Philemon as a beloved brother in Christ."

"Here is the genuine specific for the abolition of slavery. Here also is the true groundwork for the extinction of caste in India. It is to be found in the Incarnation of the Son of God, and in the incorporation of all nations and families of the earth in the mystical Body of Christ. Wise will be the Sovereigns, Senates, and States, who recognize this truth."

To this quotation, which is worthy of all praise, I shall only add the comments of the same author on St. Paul's first Epistle to Timothy, ch. 6 : v. 1: "*Let as many servants as are under the yoke, count their own masters worthy of all honor,*" etc.

"St. Paul here," saith Dr. Wordsworth, "combats and condemns that false teaching which, under color of preaching the doctrines of Universal Liberty, Equality, and Fraternity in Christ, enlisted the passions of slaves against masters, and subjects against their rulers, and thus exposed the Name of God and the doctrine of the Gospel to reproach and blasphemy from the Heathen, as if it were a religion of anarchy and sedition, and ministered to man's evil appetites and love of lucre, under the name of piety and godliness."

"These anarchical doctrines were a natural product of a diseased Judaism. The Jews, supposing themselves to be the favored people of God, resented all secular rule as an usurpation on the prerogatives of Jehovah. Their Rabbis taught that it was a *sinful thing* to own any mortal master, and to be bond-servants to heathens."

"They might, therefore, in hatred to Christianity, maliciously pervert the doctrines of the Gospel to purposes congenial to their own notions; or they might, even unwittingly, so misunderstand and misinterpret them, as to render them hateful to society, and subversive of civil government and of domestic peace."

"The great Apostle had, therefore, a difficult task to perform, in vindicating and maintaining, on the one side, the great doctrine of *Christian Liberty* against *some of the Judaizers ;* and in asserting and upholding the duty of *Christian subjection*, on the other hand, against those of the same class who abused the sacred name of Liberty into a plea for licentiousness."

"How beautifully does the divine wisdom, charity, and courage, with which the holy Apostle was endued, shine forth in the execution of this difficult work in his Epistles !"

" The relative duty of masters and slaves is to be borne by both parties. Each of the two takes hold of it at its own end, and like the fruitful cluster of the grapes of Eshcol, (Num. 13 : 23,) it is to be carried on the shoulders of both. And, like that cluster, this *burden* is also a *benefit*. St. Paul will not flatter masters at the expense of their slaves, nor slaves at the expense of their masters. Each is to be a benefactor to the other. The master owes food and wages to the slave; the slave owes faithful service to the master."

" The force and wisdom of this Apostolic teaching will be more evident and impressive, when it is borne in mind that these words of St. Paul, addressed to the Bishop of Ephesus, would be listened to by masters and slaves, *gathered together in the Church*, and hearing this Epistle *publicly read* in the religious congregations at Ephesus and other great cities of the world."

" *If any man*, under color of *Christian liberty*, *teaches otherwise*, and exempts slaves from obedience to their masters, St. Paul, in holy indignation, inveighs against such a man, as one that is *proud and knoweth nothing, but doteth about questions and strifes of words.*"

" The false teachers ingratiated themselves with slaves, and other dependents, by flattering them, that because all men are equal and brethren in Christ, therefore they need not be subject to their masters; or that, if they were subject, they had a claim to greater temporal advantages than they enjoyed; and thus they excited slaves to disobedience, and made the profession of the Gospel to be a matter of secular traffic and worldly lucre."

" St. Paul commands masters to give to their slaves what is just and equal, (Col. 4 : 1,) but he also teaches slaves this lesson: If a man have food and raiment, let him be therewith content."

With these excellent comments of the Rev. Canon Wordsworth, I concur most heartily; in fervent thankfulness to God, that up to the year 1859, our venerated mother Church of England has proclaimed none other but the pure doctrine of the Apostles, and that her latest utterance is in harmony with the only divine standard of wisdom, truth, and peace.

CHAPTER XXVI.

RIGHT REVEREND BROTHER : Before I conclude the survey of the Scriptures, it may be well to notice a perversion, which it is becoming quite common to urge, as a convincing argument, on behalf of ultra-abolitionism.   I allude to the favorite quotation from the prophet Isaiah, 58 : 6 : "*Is not this the fast that I have chosen ?   To loose the bands of wickedness, to undo the heavy burdens, and to let the oppressed go free, and that ye break every yoke ?* "   This is applied, without hesitation, to the case of the slaves ; and some of our modern wise men even consider it to be a divine *repeal* of the law previously laid down, for the perpetual bondage of the heathen races, by the express authority of the God of Israel !

There is something so absurd in the idea that a formal law, set forth repeatedly by the Almighty, should be repealed by words like these, which do not refer to it all, and are susceptible of quite a different application, that I should not have thought it worthy of notice, if it were not manifest that it passes for sound reasoning with the popular mind.   It is indeed a sad proof of the low state of reverence towards the Word of God which permits such a wresting of the Scriptures, not only by laymen, but by many of those who are the commissioned servants of the sanctuary.

I shall show, therefore, by direct proof, that this novel commentary on the language of the prophet is totally unwarranted.   The true state of the matter is this.   The Israelites were expressly directed, by the divine law, to buy slaves of the heathen, and to hold them as an inheritance for themselves and their posterity forever.   Hence, as we have seen, those slaves were not set free at the Jubilee, the benefits of which were wholly confined to the children of Israel, who had a family and a possession in the land to which they might return.   But with respect to the servitude of their own brethren, they were as expressly forbidden to hold them in bondage longer than six years ; and at the expiration of that time they were commanded to set them free, either at the seventh year, which was the year of release, or, if that season intervened, at the year of Jubilee. It often happened, however, that the Jews violated this law, and continued the yoke of bondage over their own brethren, and grievously oppressed them, long after the period when they were entitled to their freedom. This was the abuse against which the prophets uttered their strong denunciations, by the direction of the Lord. The case of the heathen races, whom they were authorized by the Almighty to retain in perpetual slavery, was not contemplated in any way. And hence we may see the glaring inconsistency of this modern misapplication, because it makes the Deity contradict himself, and sets one part of his Word in direct opposition to the other.

In order to place this matter, therefore, in its proper light, we have only to look at the case as it stands fully exemplified in the book of the prophet Jeremiah 34 : 8–17. The passage is long, but I shall present it in its own integrity :

"This is the word that came unto Jeremiah from the Lord, after that the King Zedekiah had made a covenant with all the people which were in Jerusalem, to proclaim liberty unto them, that every man should let his man-servant, and every man his maid-servant, *being an Hebrew or a Hebrewess*, go free, that none should save himself of them, to wit, *of a Jew his brother*. Now when all the princes and all the people which had entered into the covenant heard that every one should let his man-servant, and every one his maid-servant go free, that none should save themselves of them any more, *then they obeyed and let them go*. But afterwards they turned, and caused the servants and the handmaids whom they had let go free, to *return, and brought them into subjection for servants and for handmaids*. Therefore the word of the Lord came to Jeremiah from the Lord, saying : Thus saith the Lord, the God of Israel : I made a covenant with your fathers in the day that I brought them forth out of the land of Egypt, out of the house of bondmen, saying : At the end of seven years, let ye go every man *his brother an Hebrew which hath been sold unto* thee, and when he hath served thee six years, thou shalt let him go free from thee; but your fathers hearkened not unto me, neither inclined their ear. And ye were now turned and had done right in my sight, in proclaiming liberty every man to his neighbor, and ye had made a covenant before me in the house that is called by my name. But ye turned and polluted my name, and

10

caused every man his servant, and every man his handmaid, whom he had set at liberty at their pleasure, to return, and brought them into subjection, to be unto you for servants and for handmaids. Therefore thus saith the Lord : Ye have not hearkened unto me, in proclaiming liberty, every one to his brother, and every man to his neighbor ; behold I proclaim a liberty for you, saith the Lord, to the sword, to the pestilence, and to the famine, and I will make you to be removed into all the kingdoms of the earth," etc.

Here we have a plain statement of the oppression for which the Jews were so often rebuked by the prophets. It was oppression practiced upon *their own brethren the Hebrews*, against the express law of the Almighty, and had no relation whatever to the slaves of the heathen races, whom they were directly authorized to hold in bondage, as an inheritance for themselves and their children, in perpetuity. Thus we find that there is no inconsistency in the Bible. It is only those modern interpreters, choosing, in the very face of the sacred record, to set the Old Testament at variance with itself on this subject, who are unhappily employed, however unconsciously, in bringing confusion into the Word of God, and forging weapons for the use of infidelity.

So plain is this matter, that it is hardly necessary to state the opinions of commentators. Yet, to remove all possibility of doubt, I shall set down a few.

Thus, in D'Oyly and Mant, we read, (Jer. 34 : 8,) "By the law of Moses, (Exod. 21 : 2, Deut. 15 : 12,) the Israelites were not allowed to detain *their brethren* in perpetual bondage, but were required to let them go free after having served six years. This law, it seems, had fallen into disuse ; but King Zedekiah, upon the approach of the Chaldean army, whether from religious motives, or a political view to employ the men who were set free in the service of the war, engaged the people to act conformably to the law, and they released their brethren accordingly. But no sooner were their fears abated by the retreat of the Chaldeans, than, in defiance of every principle of religion, honor, and humanity, they imposed the yoke of servitude anew upon those unhappy persons."

So in Scott's commentary on the same passage : "The law of liberating Hebrew slaves, at the end of seven years, was an express condition of the national covenant. The seventh year was the year of release, (Deut. 15 : 9,) consequently servants were to continue in service but six years, and at the beginning of the seventh, were to be let go free."

So Clarke's commentary, on the eleventh verse: "They had agreed to manumit them at the end of the seventh year, but when the seventh year was ended, they recalled their engagement, and detained their servants." And on the seventeenth verse, *I proclaim a liberty for you*, etc., the paraphrase of Clarke is this, "You promised to give liberty to your *enslaved brethren :* I was pleased and *bound* the sword in its sheath. You broke your promise, and brought them again into bondage. I gave liberty to the sword," etc.

So in the Comprehensive Commentary, "When Jerusalem was closely besieged by the Chaldean army, the princes and people agreed on a reformation in one thing, and that concerning their servants. The law of God was very express—that *those of their own nation* should not be held in servitude above seven years, whether they had sold themselves into servitude for the payment of their debts, or were sold by the judges for the punishment of their crimes. Whereas *those of other nations, taken in war or bought with money, might be held in perpetual slavery, they and theirs,*" etc.

So Henry, in his commentary, and in his remarks on Is. 58 : 6, saith, the Jews "were as covetous and unmerciful as ever. '*Ye exact all your labors* from your servants, and will neither *release them according to the law,* nor relax the rigor of their servitude.' This was their fault before the captivity. (Jer. 34 : 8–9.) It was no less their fault after their captivity." (Neh. 5 : 2.)

So far, then, was this passage about *breaking every yoke* a repeal of the divine law, that the sin of the Israelites consisted in their disobedience to that law precisely as it stood ; and for that disobedience the Almighty, by the mouth of His prophets, strongly rebukes them. Even the commentators who have written since the abolition excitement in England, and who show, here and there, its powerful influence, do not intimate the slightest wish to wrest the true meaning of those texts. *That* seems to have been the task of a still later period, and is one of the newest inventions in Biblical interpretation which threaten the welfare of the Church and of the country. For I can imagine no transgression more odious in the sight of God, and more sure to forfeit His blessing, than the willful determination to distort His revealed Word, and *make it speak, not as it truly is,* but as

men, in their insane pride of superior philanthropy, fancy that *it
ought to be.*

. I have now, my Right Reverend Brother, gone over the list which
I promised, and more; showing the general sense of the Church
from the time of the Apostles to our own, with the exception of the
Church of Rome, which some persons claim as being, at this day, en-
listed on the side of ultra-abolitionism. That this is a total mistake,
I shall prove in the next chapter.

CHAPTER XXVII.

RIGHT REVEREND BROTHER: The Church of Rome, as you are perfectly aware, ruled almost the whole continent of Europe, from the seventh to the sixteenth century, and, since the Reformation, still retains nearly one half of the Christian world. In very many important questions of faith, of government, and of worship, I need hardly say that we differ from the Papal communion, and claim a far more complete accordance with the primitive Church of the first four centuries. But in matters of Christian morality, there is happily no serious difference of opinion sanctioned amongst the professed disciples of the blessed Redeemer. And in the lawfulness of slavery, as now established in the Southern States, the doctrine of the Roman Catholic is precisely the same with that of Protestants, as I shall proceed to prove, by the best testimony.

The work of the late Right Reverend John England, first Bishop of Charleston, entitled "Letters to the Hon. John Forsyth, on the subject of Domestic Slavery," shall be my text-book, because I consider it of unquestionable authority. The writer was one of the most learned and accomplished prelates of his Church, and no one can fairly doubt his competency. His personal sympathies, like my own, were not partial to the institution, while his high official position, and his acknowledged eminence in literary character, give assurance that his statements are worthy of implicit confidence. My quotations are from the third volume of his works, published in Baltimore, A.D. 1849.

The ultra-abolitionists who say that slaveholding is a deadly sin, under any circumstances, are accustomed to rely on the Apostolic letter of Pope Gregory XVI. dated December 3d, 1839. In that letter the Pontiff refers to the action of his predecessors, namely, of Pope Paul III, May 29, 1537, of Pope Urban VIII, April 22, 1639, of Pope Benedict XIV, Dec. 20, 1741, and also of Pope Pius VII, all directed against the *slave-trade*, which our laws pronounce to be *Piracy*.

Speaking of the last of these Apostolic letters, Bishop England saith that "it is not at all applicable to what is known amongst us, as *domestic slavery*. Our holy father, Pope Gregory XVI, is not the associate of the abolitionists." (Letter 1, p. 116.)

"At the late Council in Baltimore," continues our author, "that document was formally read and accepted by the prelates of the United States. If it condemned our domestic slavery as an unlawful and consequently immoral practice, the bishops could not have accepted it, without being bound to refuse the sacraments to all who were slaveholders, unless they manumitted their slaves; yet if you look to the prelates who accepted the document unanimously, you will find that the majority of the Council were those who were in charge of the slaveholding portion of the Union. Amongst the most pious and religious of their flocks, are large slaveholders. The prelates under whose charge they are, have never, since the day on which they accepted this letter, indicated to them the necessity of adopting any new rule of conduct respecting their slaves. Nor did the other six prelates, under whose charge neither slaves nor slaveholders are found, express to their brethren any new views upon the subject, because they all regarded the letter as treating of the *slave-trade*, and not as touching domestic slavery." (Let. 2, p. 116.)

This seems to me altogether conclusive upon the construction properly belonging to the apostolic letter of Pope Gregory XVI. For while there are expressions in that document which an ordinary reader might readily construe as relating to the Southern institution, especially if his own mind was inclined toward the doctrine of ultra-abolitionism, yet it must be admitted that the Bishops of the Church of Rome are the only rightful judges of their own laws; and the Council of Baltimore, consisting of all the prelates in the Union, and unanimously agreeing as to the true meaning of the Pontiff, with whom they held personal intercourse every three years in their official visits to Rome, could not be mistaken in a matter which concerned their pastoral duty.

But our author proceeds to state the principles of his Church at large, and I shall set before you several other extracts from his treatise, which are worthy of attention.

"The abolitionists assert," saith he, "generally, that slavery is contrary to the natural law. Our theological authors lay down the principle that man, in his natural state, is master of his own liberty, and may dispose of it if he thinks fit, as in the case of a Hebrew, (Exod. 21 : 5,) who preferred remaining with his wife and children, as a slave, to going into that freedom to which he had a right; and as in the case of the Hebrew, (Lev. 25 : 47,) who, by reason of his poverty, would sell himself to a stranger." (Letter 2, p. 117–18.)

"The existence of slavery is considered by our theologians to be as little incompatible with the natural law, as the existence of property. The sole question will be, in each case, whether the title, on which the dominion is claimed, is valid." (Letter 2, p. 118.)

Speaking of his personal experience, Bishop England saith as follows, viz. :

"I know many slaves who would not accept their freedom. I know some who have refused it. And although our domestic slavery must upon the whole be regarded as involuntary, still the exceptions are not so few as are imagined by strangers." (Ib. p. 118.)

And again, "It may be asked," saith our author, "why any one should prefer slavery to freedom. I know many instances where the advantages to the individual are very great. Yet I am not in love with the existence of slavery, I would never aid in establishing it where it did not exist. But the situation of a slave, under a humane master, insures to him food, raiment, and dwelling, together with a variety of little comforts. It relieves him from the apprehensions of neglect in sickness, from all solicitude for the support of his family, and in return, all that is required is fidelity and moderate labor. I do not deny that slavery has its evils, but the above are no despicable benefits. Hence I have known many freedmen who regretted their manumission." (Ib. p. 118.)

This is strong testimony from one who was an Irishman by birth, who was educated amongst a people to whom African slavery was unknown, and yet, after he had spent years in the midst of the Southern institution, and was well acquainted with its practical results, notwithstanding he still retained his original antipathy to it, he gives this candid judgment on its comparative advantages.

Bishop England thus sums up the position of his Church in another passage, which is well worth transcribing, viz. :

"Slavery, then, is regarded by that Church, of which the Pope is the presiding officer, not to be incompatible with the natural law, to be the *result of sin by divine dispensation*, to have been established by human legislation, and when the dominion of the slave is justly acquired by the master, *to be lawful*, not only in the sight of the human tribunal, *but also in the eye of Heaven*. But not so the *slave-trade*, or the reducing into slavery the African and Indian in the manner that Portugal and Spain sanctioned, which they continue still to perpetuate, and which the Apostolic letters have justly censured as unlawful." (Letter 2, p. 119.)

With respect to the Old Testament, we have the following clear and well-condensed view:

"The divine legislation of the Hebrews," saith our author, "is quite decisive."

1. "A man disposes of his own liberty." (Exod. 21 : 5, Levit. 25 : 39, Deut. 15 : 15.)

2. "A person is born in servitude." (Exod. 21 : 4, Levit. 25 : 45, 46.)

3. "Children sold by their parents." (Exod. 16 : 7, Isaiah 50 : 1.)

4. "Thieves, unable to make restitution." (Exod. 22 : 3.)

5. "Creditors taking the debtor and his children to pay the debt. (4 Sam. or 2 Kings ch. 4.)" (To this our Saviour refers in His parable, Matt. 18 : 25.)

6. "Purchase recognized throughout as a good title to the service of one already enslaved."

7. "Slaves made in war." (Deut. 20 : 14.)

"Thus, all the divines of the Roman Catholic Church acknowledge that they find, in the divine legislation for the Hebrew people, the recognition of slavery, and the enactment of provisions for its regulation." (Letter 2, 122.)

"The divine legislator of Christianity," saith Bishop England, "made no special law, *either to repeal or to modify the former and still subsisting right*, but He enforced principles which produced an extensive *amelioration*. Neither did the apostles consider the Christian master obliged to liberate his Christian servant. St. Paul, in his epistle to Philemon, acknowledges the right of the master to the services of his slave. Thus a runaway slave still belonged to his master, and though having become a Christian, so far from being thereby liberated from service, he was bound to return thereto, and submit himself to his owner. In the same manner that St. Paul sent Onesimus, did the angel send Hagar." (Gen. 16 : 6–9.) (Letter 3, p. 124–5.)

Again, saith our author, "The legislator of Christianity, while he admitted *the legality* of slavery, rendered the master merciful, and the slave faithful, obedient, and religious." (Ib. p. 127.) "The Church which He commissioned to teach all nations to the end of the world, has at all times considered the existence of slaves as compatible with religious profession and practice." (Ib. p. 128.)

"The principle which St. Augustine laid down was that observed, viz. : The State was to enact the laws regulating slavery ; the Church was to plead for morality, and exhort to practice mercy." (Ib. p. 130.)

"The right of the master, the duty of the slave, the lawfulness of continuing the relation, and the benevolence of religion in mitigating the sufferings of those held in bondage, and releasing them by lawful means permitted by the State, are the results exhibited by our view of the laws and facts, during the first four centuries of Christianity." (Ib.)

These extracts from the work of this eminent representative of the Roman Catholic Church, are abundantly sufficient to establish her doctrine on the subject. It differs in no respect from the doctrine of our own, as I have proved most copiously by all the Commentators and divines, already quoted, up to the period when we find so strong a disposition to depart from the old paths, in this age of innovation. And it will not be pretended that the Church, in any other region of the world, has yet authorized the change.

For no man doubts that the Churches of the East still retain and practice slavery. The Greek Church, the Armenians, the Copts, the Nestorians, have promulgated no new rules upon the subject. And the Church of Russia, with her sixty millions, has never yet varied from her views of the moral and religious aspect of the question. The late emancipation of twenty millions of serfs was purely the act of the State, under the absolute authority of the Czar or Emperor, Alexander. And we have no reason to suppose that the Church had any thing to do with it, beyond the expression of a cheerful acquiescence in the imperial will.

10*

CHAPTER XXVIII.

RIGHT REVEREND BROTHER: The learned and very thorough work of Bishop England did not come under my notice, until I had collected my own list of authorities from the Fathers and the Councils. But I am indebted to it for two very interesting facts on the important subject of the marriage of slaves, which escaped my attention; and I gladly avail myself of his labors to record them here.

"One of the subjects," saith our author, "which at all times caused slavery to be surrounded with great difficulties, was the result of marriage. The interest of the owner frequently interfered with the affection of the husband and wife, and also was irreconcilable with the relation of parent and child. The liability to separation of those married was a more galling affliction in the Christian law, where the Saviour made marriage indissoluble; and it often happened that an avaricious or capricious owner cared as little for the marriage bond, as he did for the natural tie of affection. Hence as Christianity became the religion of the state, or of the great body of the people, it was imperatively demanded, by the very nature of the case, that some restraint should be placed upon that absolute power which the owners had, and sometimes abused, of wantonly making these separations."

"This was a strong temptation to both master and slave, to prefer concubinage to marriage. This is one of the worst moral evils attending slavery, where no restraint of law effects its removal." (*Let.* 12, p. 160.)

Bishop England proceeds to state that a remedy was provided, to a considerable extent, in the case of serfs, or *colonists*, (*coloni*, or *rustici*, as they were then styled, *i.e.*, slaves who had an allotment of land to work for the benefit of the master,) an edict being set forth by the Emperor Justinian, in A.D. 539, (*Novel.* clxii. c. 3,) of which our author gives the following translation, viz.:

"THE EMPEROR JUSTINIAN AUGUSTUS TO LAZARUS, THE COUNT OF THE EAST.

"Preamble.   We have learned by relation in various ways, that a delinquency quite unworthy of our times is allowed in the provinces of Mesopotamia and of Osdroene.   They have a custom of having marriage contracted between those born on different estates ; whence the masters endeavor to dissolve marriages actually contracted ; or to take away from the parents the children who are their issue ; upon which account that entire place is miserably afflicted, whilst country people, husbands and wives, are drawn away from each other, and the children whom they brought into light are taken away from them ; and that there needs for the regulation only our provision."

"Wherefore we enact, that otherwise the masters of the aforesaid keep their colonists (serfs) as they will ; but it shall not be allowed by virtue of any custom heretofore introduced and in existence, to put away from each other those who are married, or to force them to cultivate the land belonging to themselves," (that is, to force the serfs to labor on the other parts of their master's estate, outside of their allotted portion,) "or to take away children from their parents, under the color of colonial condition, (serfdom.)   And you will be careful that if any thing of this sort has haply been already done, the same be corrected and restitution made, whether it be that children were taken away from their parents, or women from their consorts of marriage.   And for any who shall in future act in this way, it shall be at the hazard of losing the estate itself."

"Wherefore, let marriages of servants be exempt from that fear which has hitherto hung over them, and from the issue of this order, let the parents have their children.   It shall not be competent for the lords of the estates to strive by any subtle arguments either to take away those who contract marriage, or their children." (*Letter* 12, p. 161.)

The same evil, however, prevailed in the ninth century, and our author quotes the 30th canon of the Council of Chalons, on the Saone, in France, A.D. 813, which was "confirmed by Charlemagne, and made a portion of the law of the empire," in order to correct it.   The translation of Bishop England is as follows, viz. :

"It has been stated to us that some persons, by a sort of magisterial presumption, dissolve the marriages of slaves ; not regarding that evangelical maxim, *What God hath joined together let man not separate.* Whence it appears to us, that the wedlock of slaves may not be dissolved, even though they have different masters ; but let them serve their masters remaining in one wedlock. And this is to be observed with regard to those where there has been a lawful union, and with the will of the owners." (*Let.* 15, p. 177.)

These enactments were wise and salutary, and clearly prove that the ancients were sensible of the great difficulty to which slavery has been more or less subject, and which legislation can never correct until the masters themselves become earnestly interested in the matter. For neither of these laws took away the practice of concubinage. Instead of this, they seem rather to have promoted it, as the easiest mode of avoiding the restraints which followed a lawful marriage. Yet it would seem that much might be done, by judicious legislation, to strengthen and increase a sound public sentiment on this important matter. And it is to be hoped that the clergy will not cease, wherever slavery exists, to use their best efforts in favor of a wise and thorough reformation, which shall do away effectually the most serious reproach now brought against the institution.

CHAPTER XXIX.

RIGHT REVEREND BROTHER: I have now, I trust, redeemed my pledge to establish the position taken in my *Bible View of Slavery* against the modern doctrine of ultra-abolitionism, namely, that the slavery of the negro race in the Southern States was *lawful*, not only by the Constitution of our country, but by the word of God and the voice of the Holy Catholic Church from the beginning. Of course it resulted that in the *relation* of master and slave there was no sin, because *sin is the transgression of the law ;* and I may safely defy my learned and zealous antagonist to point out any law of God or of the Church which forbids or condemns the institution.

But before I proceed to the general summing up of my authorities, there are some popular arguments which ought to be discussed for the better satisfaction of my readers. First, Polygamy ; second, Man-stealing ; and third, the golden rule of doing to others what we would they should do unto us, from which my opponents suppose that I ought to become a slave if I vindicate the lawfulness of slavery. I have touched on some of them already in my published letter, but I shall consider them again rather more at large.

Beginning with polygamy, my adversaries are very fond of confounding it with slavery, because it was permitted among the Jews. But the difference between the two is manifest to any candid and fair mind in these respects, viz. :

First, that slavery was the subject of divine prophecy and legislation, while no one pretends that the Almighty ever declared it to be His will that a man should have more wives than one. Our Saviour, speaking of the general laxity on the subject of the marriage relation, (Matt. 19 : 8,) expressly saith that " Moses " (not by the positive command of the Deity, but in his human discretion) "*suffered it because of the hardness of their hearts*," " *but from the beginning it was not so.*" And this forever settled the question. Therefore the Apostles everywhere maintain the rule, as St. Paul distinctly states it in the qualifications of a bishop, that he shall *be the husband of one wife.* (1 Tim. 3 : 2.) And this restriction is the more emphatic when it is remembered that polygamy was allowed, without reprehension, among the Jews.

Secondly, the voice of the Church of Christ, from the beginning, proclaimed the same distinction, defending and sustaining slavery, while polygamy was positively forbidden. This is distinctly proved by the following testimonies, viz. :

"If any one," say the Apostolic Canons, "after receiving holy Baptism, is connected with two wives, or has a concubine, he can not be a bishop, or a presbyter, or a deacon, or in any way of the number of the priesthood." (74)

And the first General Council of Nicea, which consisted of three hundred and eighteen bishops from every part of the Christian world, assembled A.D. 325, pronounces the rule to be of universal obligation. "No one," saith this Council, "ought to have two wives at the same time, nor bring in another woman to his wife, for the indulgence of carnal pleasure or appetite, thrusting himself into sin, by a commerce with many, for the indulgence of lust instead of the increase of progeny, according to the order of God. And whoever shall act thus, if he be a priest, he shall be prohibited from the ministry of sacrifice and the communion of the faithful until he sends away the second woman from his house, retaining the first one. *The same judgment is declared concerning the laity.*" (75)

So stringent was the law on this subject that St. Augustine considers it binding under every circumstance. For thus he writes, viz. :

"A man may desire to dismiss a wife who is barren, and take another by whom he may have offspring; yet nevertheless *it is not lawful,* nor can he, in our times and by the Roman custom, *have more than one wife living.*" (76)

Thus, likewise, declares St. Basil, the great authority amongst the Oriental churches, viz. :

"The Canon condemns bigamy, trigamy, and polygamy, a certain proportion being observed, viz., one year's penance for bigamy, but others say two years. Trigamy is punished by three years, and often by four, of excommunication." (74.) "The fathers have said little of polygamy, as being *a beastly thing, altogether foreign to humanity.*" (75)

Such is the law of the Christian Church. The attempt made to get rid of the authority which the Old Testament gives to slavery, on account of the practice of polygamy amongst the Jews, is not consistent with sound reason. In the case of slavery they had the *divine law* to sanction it. In the case of polygamy there was no law, and St. Paul plainly saith : " Where no law is, there is no transgression." (Rom. 4 : 15.) When my antagonists shall prove that it is the same thing whether men act *with* law or *without* it, they may make something of this argument, but not before.

With respect to the Church of Christ, however, the application of such sophistry is still more absurd and inexcusable, for we have seen that on the subject of slavery the Apostles, the fathers, the commentators, and the divines, sustain the lawfulness of the institution, although they nowhere approve of polygamy. Nay, more than this, for while they justify the one as the ordinance of divine Providence, they decree their positive prohibition and condemnation of the other.

It should be constantly borne in mind that the office which Moses sustained towards Israel, as their divinely appointed lawgiver, was committed to the inspired Apostles by the express authority of the Redeemer. " I appoint unto you a *kingdom*," saith He, " as my Father hath appointed unto me." (Luke 22 : 29.) " Go ye therefore and teach all nations, baptizing them in the name of the Father and of the Son and of the Holy Ghost, teaching them to observe *all things whatsoever I have commanded you ;* and lo, I am with you alway, even unto the end of the world. Amen." (Matt. 28 : 19, 20.) St. Paul asserts this same authority most clearly where he saith : " If any man think himself to be a prophet, or spiritual, let him acknowledge that the things that I write unto you are *the Commandments of the Lord.*" (1 Cor. 14 : 37.) Hence he delivers his precepts, throughout, as the *inspired organ of the divine Lawgiver*, and where he speaks merely of his own mind he states the distinction, as where he saith : " Now concerning virgins I have *no commandment of the Lord*, yet I give my judgment as one that hath obtained mercy of the Lord to be faithful." (1 Cor. 7 : 25.) But whenever he lays down his precepts without this distinction he exacts entire submission, under the penalty of exclusion from all ecclesiastical fellowship. For thus he writes to the Thessalonians : " If any man *obey not our word* by this epistle, note that man *and have no company with him*, that he may be ashamed." (2 Thes. 3 : 14.)

When, therefore, we find St. Paul, as the divinely appointed legislator, clearly commanding that the bishop shall be "the *husband of one wife*"—(1 Tim. 3 : 2)—when we see that, throughout all his epistles, he speaks of the wife in the singular number, never alluding to the possibility of Christians having more, and that this is in strict agreement with the principle laid down by Christ himself when He opposed the Jewish practice of divorces, and said that Moses had only allowed it "on account of the hardness of their hearts," (Matt. 19 : 3–9,) we can not doubt that polygamy was regarded as inconsistent with the law of holiness, which was designed for the more spiritual dispensation of the Gospel.   There is, however, an objection made by some, viz. that the restriction placed upon the bishop implies a greater license to the people.   And the argument can only be sustained by supposing that the laws of Christian morality were to be one thing for the priesthood and another for the laity.   But this is contrary both to reason and to Scripture.   To reason, because the priest and the layman are equally candidates for heaven, into which nothing unholy or impure can be allowed to enter.   And to Scripture, because St. Peter addresses the laity in these words, viz. : "Ye are built up a spiritual house, *an holy priesthood*, to offer up spiritual sacrifices, acceptable to God by Jesus Christ."   (1 Peter 11 : 5.)   And again : "Ye are a chosen generation, a *royal priesthood*, an *holy nation*, a peculiar people."—"Dearly beloved, I beseech you, as strangers and pilgrims, abstain from *fleshly lusts* which war against the soul."   (Ib. ver. 9–11.)   And again St. Paul saith : "Follow peace with all men, and *holiness*, without which *no man* shall see the Lord."   (Heb. 12 : 14.)

Since it must thus be manifest that holiness is as much enjoined on the people as on the priesthood, since the laity are even specially exhorted to *flee from fleshly lusts which war against the soul*, and since the whole Church is called a "holy priesthood," a "royal priesthood," a "holy nation," it seems plain that the restriction laid down to the bishop that he should be *the husband of one wife*, was the law intended for all.   There is but one straight and narrow path to the kingdom of heaven.   The clergy are the leaders in that path, but the people must follow or they can not lead.   There is but one saving faith and one code of pure morality.   The clergy are bound to teach the world, but the same truths which they are appointed to preach, both they and the people are alike bound to adopt, as the only rule of life and conversation.

Most justly, therefore, did the Church so expound the law laid
down by the great Apostle of the Gentiles, when the great Council
of Nicea applied the restriction of *one wife* to *all Christians*, without
exception. The *Holy Catholic Church*, in which the Apostles' Creed
requires us to believe, that is, the *Church Universal*, embraced this
rule throughout the whole extent of Christendom, and has always
maintained it to this day.   And such being the unanimous voice of
the Church of Christ, proving her *assent* to slavery and her *condemnation* of polygamy, I can not sufficiently wonder at the perversity
which affects to place them on the same foundation.

CHAPTER XXX.

RIGHT REVEREND BROTHER: I proceed, next, to the charge of man-stealing, which the ultra-abolitionist is so fond of bringing against the Southern institution. And I know of nothing, in the whole range of religious or legal controversy, which is more unjust and indefensible.

The argument stands thus, in the pages of one of the pamphlets which have honored me with their condemnation:

"In the year 1562, Sir John Hawkins set fire to a city in Africa and carried off two hundred and fifty slaves. And the king of Dahomy captured, quite lately, a town in which he slew one third of the population and took the remainder into captivity." This is assumed to be the mode in which all the slaves at the South were originally reduced to bondage; and as their masters can have no better title than those who sold them, therefore they are all involved in the sin of man-stealing!

Now, really, this sort of absurdity strikes me as a most extraordinary example of sophistical perverseness. If these facts were brought forward against the *slave-trade*, they might be deemed appropriate. But there we have no controversy. The slave-trade has been abandoned long ago, and pronounced piracy by the laws of the land. The Southern States maintain the same position that we occupy with respect to it. But what has that to do with their *domestic slavery?* Have they attacked the African towns, and slaughtered the inhabitants, and taken away the captives? At the time when this sort of work was held to be legitimate, it was done by Old England; and New-England carried on the trade, while the South had no share in it, although they received the Africans by fair purchase from the persons who imported them, without any direct participation in the mode by which they were obtained. But you may say that "the receiver is as bad as the thief." I grant it, *if the receiver knows that the property was stolen.* Two facts, however, must be proved in order to establish this offense. For in the first place it must be shown that the property *was stolen*. And in the second place, it must be testified that the purchaser was *aware of the felony*, neither of which can possibly be established at this day with respect to the original stock of Africans from whom the Southern negroes have descended.

No one can be farther than I am from justifying the barbarity of the African slave-trade. But to deal fairly with that, as I suppose we should deal fairly with the worst kinds of criminality, it should be remembered that it involved two elements, of which one was *the mode* in which the slave-traders obtained the slaves, and the other was the horrid *treatment* to which they were subjected in what was called the *middle passage*, or the voyage from Africa to the destined port of delivery.

With respect to the first of these alone, our present topic is concerned. We are told, by Malte Brun, that in Africa *two thirds of the population are slaves*, which, as the whole is estimated at ninety millions, would give *sixty millions* for the present number of the *native slaves*, independent of any new war between the rulers of that heathen continent.

Suppose then, that the slave-traders, applying to the king of Dahomey, were supplied with their sad cargo of human beings from the multitude who were *slaves already*, could they, by any propriety of speech, be called *men-stealers ?* By all that I have read upon the subject, I presume that those traders found the slaves in the absolute power of their heathen master, and purchased them for whatever price he was willing to take, without having any thing to do with the mode by which *he* came into possession. And if they had inquired into that mode, the barbarian despot would most probably have replied that it was none of their business. The slaves were his, and they might buy them or let them alone, just as they pleased. I do not see, under such circumstances, how we could convict the traders themselves as having *stolen* the slaves ; much less, as having burned the towns and carried off the captives, in the style of Sir John Hawkins, or any other man.

Suppose, again, that these degraded and wretched beings were brought to Boston, to Bristol, or to Salem, in the days when such traffic was permitted, and sold again to the planters of the South, how were they to know that they were certainly stolen ? If the traders themselves had no information of that fact, how could they communicate it to the second purchaser? And by what process of reasoning can it be shown that these Southern purchasers had any thing to do with *man-stealing?*

But, perfectly plain as the matter appears to my mind, by this simple course of common-sense and justice, I shall go further, and maintain, that even if the first slaves imported had been stolen, and the traders knew it and communicated the knowledge to the purchasers, it would be neither lawful nor reasonable to charge the sin of such an act upon their heirs and descendants, who have come into possession regularly and legally, without the slightest complicity in the original wrong.

For look at the title by which you, with every other man in the community, must hold the lands and houses in your possession. What is its origin? The country once belonged to the Indian tribes, and the claim set up to it by England was based upon the right of discovery. What sort of right is that? Does my discovery of property which belongs to another man make it mine? It would be mere absurdity to pretend it. If I can not find the true owner, I may be authorized to keep it; but as soon as he appears I am bound to surrender it, or I become a transgressor. Manifestly, therefore, there is no law of natural justice that authorized Queen Elizabeth or her royal successors to confer the lands of the Indians on their subjects, in the charters granted by the crown to the Virginia colonists, or to the Pilgrim fathers, as it is the fashion to call them, or to Lord Baltimore, or to William Penn. All this was taken for granted by the European maxims of those days, which assumed the right of claiming any land inhabited by *savage heathen tribes*, and calling it their own; precisely in the same way that they assumed the right of taking the natives themselves, and reducing them to bondage.

Now the ultra-abolitionist holds his property by the same title precisely, that the Southern planter claims in his slaves. The way in which the real Indian owners of the soil were divested of it is stamped on the page of history. It was done by force or fraud. Battle after battle had to be waged against them. And when the poor wretches were compelled to submit to the superior knowledge and arms of the invaders, the treaties of peace by which they consented to give up their lands were in most cases, if not in all, the results of a dire necessity.

When our ultra-abolitionist talks about the negro, he tells us that all men are brothers, and is pathetically eloquent upon the Christian rule of doing to others as we would that they should unto us. But when his subject is the Indian, he has no idea that the rule is applicable. Then it was all right that the strong hand should take possession of their property, drive them away from their homes and the burial-places of their fathers, and gradually exterminate the savage race, if they stood in the way of advancing civilization.

The effects of these operations, however, on the Indian and the negro, have been widely different; though justice and humanity can say very little in favor of their commencements. The Indians have been left to their barbarism, without any attempt on the part of government to convert or civilize them. The Africans, on the contrary, have been elevated from the most degraded state, far more degraded than that of the Indians, and changed from heathen savages into Christian men. The Indians have been diminished in number until they have become a mere remnant, and the whole will probably disappear in a few generations more; while the Africans have multiplied in eighty years from seven hundred thousand to four millions. The Indians are wronged, dissatisfied, unhappy, and hostile. The Africans are contented, affectionate, and attached to their masters. The prospect open to the Indian is dark and gloomy, with nothing to cheer or console him. The prospect of the African is bright and hopeful, for a portion of his race have been enabled to plant Liberia, and he can turn his eyes to the sunny land of his forefathers with a reasonable expectation that he or his children may rise, in time, to a fair condition amongst the citizens of a civilized community. So marked, indeed, is the contrast between the practical working of the event in the cases of these two savage races, that no reflecting mind can contemplate them without surprise. Can any Christian believer in the providence of God fail to see that a blessing to the African has followed in the train of Southern slavery, while a blight has rested on the system adopted for the Indian? Is it possible to doubt that if the Indians could have been successfully subjected to the white man, it would have been infinitely better for them at the present day?

But it is unnecessary to pursue this train of reflection any farther. My object in adverting to it is only to show that the original violence, fraud, and injustice by which the Indians were dispossessed, have nothing to do with the *title* of those who now claim what was once their property. It would be an absurdity for any man to ask that our citizens should surrender their farms and their city lots to some Indian tribe, because the land was originally torn from the lawful owners. The past can not be recalled, nor do the evil acts of other days admit of any remedy. It is enough that each man has now a valid title, transmitted from the first settlers or under a patent from the established government in each State. What would you think of an attempt to invalidate this, on the ground that the tract in question was originally the seat of an Indian village, that the white men attacked it, burned the huts, killed many of the savages, drove off the rest, and seized the land as their own; and that property thus acquired by robbery and murder could not be lawfully held by those who derived it from such a bloody and cruel invasion of natural right and justice? Have you any doubt that the lawyer who should try to nullify a regular conveyance, by a plea like this, would be laughed at for his folly? Yet such is precisely the course of the abolitionist, who persuades himself that because the Africans were originally seized by violence, and enslaved by the strong hand, therefore the present owners of the Southern slaves have no valid title; although they hold it by transmission or regular purchase under the same established law of their country.

On this point, therefore, though it be such a favorite with most of my antagonists, their agument is simply ridiculous. The title now held to the greater part of the landed property in these United States rests on the same foundation with that of the Southern slaveholder. Pennsylvania, indeed, under the pacific policy of William Penn, may have been an exception, so far as force was concerned. Whether it was an exception with respect to the skill manifested in cheating the simplicity of the Indian, would be a different question. We read, for example, of a bargain in which an Indian agreed with a worthy Quaker to take a handful of glass beads for as much land as an ox-hide would cover. But the wily Friend cut the hide into strips as narrow as ten to the inch, and laying these end to end upon the ground, surrounded a comfortable lot of almost four acres. The poor Indian attempted to remonstrate against a construction of the contract so very different from the natural meaning of the terms employed. But it was in vain. Yet no jury of honest men would hesitate to condemn such a trick, as a fraudulent imposition.

I do not vouch for the truth of this small specimen. Nor is it of any importance. For no reasonable man has any doubt that the superior sagacity and power of the Anglo-Saxon race were fully exercised in every practicable way, to despoil the poor savages of their rights in the soil, throughout the whole extent of our vast territory. And this is enough to prove that even if the first Southern purchasers of the Africans could be charged with the sin of man-stealing, they would be in no worse condition than the first settlers, who robbed the Indians of their land and exterminated the owners without pity or compunction. I have shown, however, that there is no testimony which can bring home this accusation against the Southern purchasers of the imported negroes; while the whole strain of history establishes the charge with respect to the Indians. And, therefore, notwithstanding the zeal of the ultra-abolitionist in urging this popular argument, it must be perfectly manifest that the title of the present generation to their property in the slaves is even less liable to impeachment on this score, than the title to the soil itself, on a fair comparison.

CHAPTER XXXI.

RIGHT REVEREND BROTHER : The next ground of accusation, and one which the eloquent declaimers against Southern slavery find most convincing with the multitude, is derived from their management of the " Golden Rule," as it is often called, laid down by our Saviour, namely, " Whatsoever ye would that men should do to you, do ye even so to them, for this is the law and the prophets." (Matt. 7 : 12.) I have touched briefly on this topic in my *Bible View of Slavery*, but it deserves a more extended examination. Before I enter upon it, however, I must call your attention to the important fact that it was no *new* rule of Christian practice. Our divine Redeemer expressly saith, " *This is the law and the prophets*," plainly referring to the existing system of the Mosaic economy, in which the slavery of the heathen races was sanctioned by the Word of God. And this of itself should be enough to satisfy any candid mind that the " Golden Rule," properly understood, could not have been intended to interfere with the institution.

But in examining the true meaning of this law, it is evident that a qualification is necessary ; and this is usually expressed by understanding the circumstances of the parties to be taken into consideration. Thus, for example, the master of the negro can have no doubt that *if he were in the condition of a slave* he would desire to be free, and therefore, according to the " Golden Rule," he is bound to emancipate his bondman. This is the view which suits the ultra-abolitionist exactly ; and it must be admitted that it is, at first sight, sufficiently plausible to convince the ordinary understanding, when there is no motive of personal interest on the other side of the question. To test its truth, however, let us examine how it would apply to the other relations of civilized society.

Take the case of a wealthy father, whose favorite daughter has fixed her affections on some worthless rake, gifted with a handsome person and a flattering tongue, but utterly destitute of the qualities necessary to secure her safety or her comfort in the married relation.

He knows that *if he were in her place*, he would desire beyond all things the gratification of her wishes, and the " Golden Rule" is appealed to, as his law of duty. Is it, indeed, his law of duty ? Not at all. On the contrary, having a far clearer view than she can form of what is best for her own happiness, he firmly refuses her passionate prayer, turns the unprincipled fortune-hunter from his doors, and thus proves himself the real guardian of his daughter's welfare.

Take the case of the judge or the juryman, sitting on the trial of some unhappy culprit at the bar of justice. They know perfectly well, that if *they were in the place of the prisoner*, it would be their heart's desire that the judge would be favorable in his charge, and the jury favorable in their verdict. And the " Golden Rule" is again brought forward. Has it any proper application ? None whatever. The judge and the jury are bound to act according to the law and the testimony, without any regard to the wishes of the prisoner. For if these were to be taken for their rule, society would be unhinged, and justice would become an empty name, signifying nothing.

Take the case of a fashionable and extravagant wife, who is earnestly bent upon a lavish display in dress, furniture, and parties of pleasure, which her husband knows to be quite unsuited to his circumstances. He understands her feelings perfectly well, and has no doubt that if *he were in her place*, he would desire to be indulged with all the money required for her gratification. But does the " Golden Rule" demand his compliance with her solicitations ? By no means. It is his duty to restrain her foolish vanity and pride, to deny her wishes, nay, to countermand her orders if necessary, notwithstanding it may produce no small amount of reproach and mortification ; since otherwise, the result would probably be that, in a little while, he might become a bankrupt, without house or home.

Or, take the common case of the poor beggar, who once enjoyed the sunshine of prosperity, but now stands at your door, asking for aid to relieve his destitution. He sees your tasteful dwelling, filled with the best products of art and the appliances of modern refinement and luxury. He compares his lot with yours, and is tempted to upbraid the partial Providence which has placed so vast a difference between the conditions of men, notwithstanding the Declaration of Independence has pronounced that they are all created " FREE

11

AND EQUAL." You give him, perhaps, a meal in your kitchen, and even add to it a small sum in money. But you mark his eye, as it gazes on the opulence around him ; and you have no doubt that *if you were in his place*, you would desire to have a fair partition of the whole. Does the "Golden Rule" convince you that you ought to make him a sharer in your prosperity ? You would as soon think of committing suicide. On the contrary, you feel quite satisfied that you have already displayed a commendable amount of Christian charity; and sit down at your well-covered board, without the slightest idea that you have violated one of the most comprehensive precepts of your divine Master.

An abundance of cases might be thus adduced, proving, beyond the possibility of doubt, that the "Golden Rule" must be qualified by another restriction : "Whatsoever ye would that men should do to you, do ye even so to them," *provided it be just and reasonable.* And as this restriction is really understood and acted upon, in all the other relations of life, it is certainly fair that it should be equally applicable to the relation of slavery.

When, therefore, the master is required to manumit his slave, on the ground, that *if he were in the condition of the slave*, he would desire to be free, and that, consequently, according to the "Golden Rule," he is obliged to give liberty to his bond-servant, we are assuredly obliged to apply the precept on the same principles. For, in no other way can we escape the reproach which our Lord administered to the Pharisees : "They bind heavy burdens and grievous to be borne, and lay them on men's shoulders ; but *they themselves will not move them with one of their fingers.*" (Matt. 23 : 4.) In such a case, the master is really under no more obligation than all other men ; which is, as we have shown, to obey the precept when it demands nothing but what is *just and reasonable.* And as, in every other instance, he is compelled to judge what would be just and reasonable, so it is in this, that he must reflect whether the grant of freedom would be an advantage to the slave, and compatible with the paramount duty which he owes to his own family, and the community around him.

If, therefore, he believes that the slave is not fit for freedom—if he knows, by experience, that in the majority of instances, the free negroes have proved to be made worse and more miserable by their liberty than they were before—he would be not only authorized but obliged, by the true rule of duty, to deny the request, on the same principle which compels the father to refuse indulgence to the child, when his compliance would only work mischief to the object of his affection.

Or if the master thinks that there is no reason for granting this supposed privilege to one slave, more than to many others, while the extension of it would be ruin to himself and his family, justice to them would make it his duty to refuse.

Or if, living in a slave State, to whose laws and customs he is bound as a faithful citizen, he knows that the indiscriminate emancipation of his slaves would spread discontent amongst the servants of his neighbors, and produce an excitement likely to cause serious trouble and perhaps danger to the public peace,—in such case, even if his circumstances could bear the loss of his property, he would be justified in refusing to emancipate, lest, in yielding to the dictates of his private feelings, he should violate the higher duty which he owes to the general good of the community.

Thus we see that the " Golden Rule," fairly interpreted, would only effect the freedom of the slave in those cases where the master was persuaded that it was *just and reasonable.* And in all such cases, the Southern slaveholders have pursued it, as I believe, with a liberal kindness, which has not always worked happily even to the slaves themselves; though I rejoice to think that in many instances it has been wisely applied, especially when it has been connected with the noble enterprise, planned and executed by themselves, of planting the colony of Liberia. If the tenth part as much had ever been done for the negro race, by the leaders of ultra-abolitionism, I should have a far higher respect for the character of their philanthropy.

CHAPTER XXXII.

RIGHT REVEREND BROTHER : Some of the profound theologians who have honored my humble pamphlet with so many rebukes, are apparently convinced, that in order to be consistent with my argument, I should be myself a slave. And, notwithstanding the puerile folly of the intended sarcasm, it may be as well to devote a short chapter to its consideration.

I have called it a puerile folly, because it has nothing to do with the question ; and only reminds one of the style in which children in a passion reproach their best friends, when they happen to offend them. But the question in dispute has no relation to the propriety of making *slaves of freemen.* On the contrary, the only point at issue is upon the religious duty of making *freemen of slaves.* The negro race at the South have never been free, so far as we have any knowledge. Their ancestors were slaves in Africa, and the millions of their posterity now in bondage, were born and bred in the same condition, only elevated, to a vast extent, by their intercourse with the white race, and the influence of the Gospel. The question whether it is best for the true interests of both races that they should continue as they are, until the wisdom of Providence opens the way for the gradual abolition of slavery and the extradition of the negroes to their parent soil of Africa, on the one hand ; or whether, on the other, the United States should be drenched in blood, in the wild hope of forcing their immediate emancipation, and raising them to a perfect equality with their former masters on their own soil—this, indeed, is a question of tremendous magnitude. But what it has to do with the suggestion that I should become a slave, who have been born and bred a freeman, is quite too deep for my poor understanding.

Yet nevertheless, as the proverb declares that it is sometimes expedient to answer even " a fool according to his folly," I shall first remind these gentlemen that I am, in the highest sense, a *slave* already, and my master is the Lord Jesus Christ. " Ye are *bought with a price,*" saith St. Paul to the Corinthians, "therefore glorify God in your body and in your spirit, which are God's." (1 Cor. 6 : 20.) And again saith the same Apostle: "He that is called in the Lord, being a *slave*, is the Lord's freeman; likewise also, he that is called, being free, is Christ's *slave*." (1 Cor. 7 : 21.) And devoutly do I thank Him, who has thus purchased my redemption with His own precious blood, and saved me from being a slave to the world, the flesh, and the devil, and brought me into His own family—the Church—to serve Him forever!

If that divine and sovereign Lord had so determined in His wise, though often mysterious providence, that I should also be the slave of a Southern master, I trust that He would have given me grace to bear it with a spirit of cheerful obedience to His will. In that case, however, he would have fitted me for my condition. I should have been born of the negro race, bred up in bondage, surrounded by the associations best adapted to my lot, accustomed to its necessary toils, and willing to take my part in its simple recreations, while, under the care of a kind and Christian master, I should have learned to congratulate myself on the security from want, the certainty of a home, and food and clothing, nursing in sickness, benevolent regard in old age, and perfect freedom from the fear of being abandoned, when my strength should fail, to the "tender mercies" of the poor-house. And I should have had, perhaps as fully as I now have, the blessed assurance, that in the sight of God, through the redemption of Christ Jesus, I was *His* slave yet more than my earthly master's, that this slavery was the only perfect freedom, that my human bond-age would be ended in due time, and that I should then be released, at His Almighty Word, to be one amongst the spirits of the just and the society of angels, in His glorious and celestial kingdom.

But the Lord has not so ordered my condition, and therefore I am not a fit subject for Southern slavery. He has chosen to place me in a different sphere—a much higher sphere in the estimation of man-kind, although it is possible that many a Christian slave may be exalted far above me, in the kingdom of heaven. My faith teaches me that these earthly differences in the conditions of men are the work of His providence. "He setteth up one, and putteth down another." He "divideth severally to every man as He will," and no one is authorized to say unto Him, What doest thou? For, in the language of the Apostle, "Who art thou that repliest against God?

Shall the thing formed say to Him that formed it, Why hast thou made me thus ? Hath not the potter power over the clay of the same lump, to make one vessel unto honor, and another to dishonor ?" (Rom. 9 : 20–1.) These distinctions, therefore, are all ordered by the divine Master. And if my condition in life is a subject of thankfulness, because it is exempt from the humiliation of a slave, I have none the less reason to fear the final result, if I fail to discharge the far more difficult duties which devolve upon the freeman.

My objections to being a slave, however, might be extended much further. I should be unwilling to be a blacksmith, a tailor, a shoemaker, a hatter, a sailor, or a soldier. Nay, I should be unwilling to be a politician or a statesman. And why ? Precisely for the same reason. I am not *fitted* for any of them. It is not because I lack respect for these various conditions. On the contrary, I honor them all, as necessary and laudable parts of the vast system of society which composes the nation. But I am only qualified for the condition in which it has pleased God to place me. And probably you may think me not very well qualified for that. If so, there is one point, at least, in which we shall not differ.

And this brings me to the fundamental principle which determines the fitness of men for their respective stations in the community, namely, the *power of habit.* A certain measure of capacity must of course be taken for granted, for without it, no habit could be formed. But beyond that, all the rest is dependent on the repetition of the same round of study, of labor, and of duty, which, by degrees, moulds the whole mind, desires, and actions of the individual into the form adapted to his circumstances. And this, for the most part, requires many years, before the result can be accomplished. I speak of the general rule, to which we all know that there are occasional exceptions. Still, with respect to the great bulk of mankind, nothing is more true than the fact, that habit alone can fit them fully for their specific situations. And when that habit is completely established, all experience proves how dangerous it is to make any serious change. The character of thought once fixed, the circle of knowledge once filled, the routine of occupation once settled, it is rarely possible for the individual to succeed in any new and strange relation to society. And the attempt to accomplish any sudden revolution in the established course of life, seldom fails to injure the powers both of the mind and of the body.

But if this be true in the case of the individual, much more must it be true in the case of nations. All history proves that changes in the fixed habits of whole communities can never be effected wisely or well, except it be done *gradually and slowly*, by the insensible progress of feeling and education *amongst the people themselves*. For habit has been justly termed our *second nature*, in most cases stronger than the first. Hence the well-known difficulty of overcoming old habits in the individual. Hence the vastly greater difficulty of eradicating the old habits of society at large. And hence the perilous character which marks the wild theory of ultra-abolitionists. That the Southern States can be revolutionized in their social habits by a single stroke of power—that the relations of master and slave, fixed firmly by the habits of generations, can be suddenly torn asunder— that millions of slaves can be safely set free before they are fitted for freedom—that millions of the governing race can be forcibly reduced to an equality with those who were so lately their servants, and the whole condition of the community totally subverted and thrown into confusion, without any of the wise guards and careful preparation which so vast a change requires—such a scheme as this appears to be so contrary to every dictate of experience, every lesson of history, every law of justice, and every rule of common-sense and reason, that its acceptance on the part of so many enlightened minds can only be accounted for as a sort of *monomania* on the part of its zealous originators, while the crowd of their followers have never taken the trouble to examine for themselves, seriously and calmly, the real merits of the question.

I have already said, and have frequently published my own hope and persuasion, that the time will come for the total abolition of slavery. But when it comes, it will not be by the insane projects of politicians, through blood and desolation. The Supreme Ruler of nations, in whose hand are the hearts of men, will incline the minds of the South, when He sees it to be right, to institute and carry on the process, in the only safe and effectual way, which has been pursued by the other States in relation to it. Since the world began, slavery has never been abolished by external force and violence. It has only been done away by *internal action* on the part of those who are directly concerned. Of this we have two very different examples. The first was that of St. Domingo, where the slaves, excited by the pestilent orators of the French Revolution, rose against their masters, and attained their horrid triumph by the most savage butchery which history has recorded. The other was the abolition movement of England, where the result was regularly effected by the peaceful action of Parliament, after the discussion of more than twenty years, with compensation to the masters, and the restraints of apprenticeship upon the slaves, in order to avoid the dangers anticipated from a sudden and complete change. Yet neither of these examples suits our ultra-abolitionists. They are *philanthropists*, and of course would not desire that the South should suffer under a bloody and inhuman massacre, like that of St. Domingo. But they have quite as little inclination to imitate the course of England, because they are determined to condemn slave-holding as a *sin*, and they could not be partakers in the sin, by paying the masters for their slaves, for that would be acknowledging that they had a right to hold them. Moreover, such payment would be rather costly, and therefore their view is not only *philanthropic*, but withal it is *economical*—and economy is a virtue! Hence, according to their theory, the emancipation of four millions of slaves must be accomplished on a *new principle*, which they have the sole merit of inventing. It is not in the Bible. It is not in history. It is not in justice, nor in reason, nor in common-sense. But they cling to it, like a fond mother to a deformed bantling, because it is *their own ;* and argument, and authority, and experience, though sustained by the Scriptures and the unanimous voice of all Christendom, fail to convince them of their gross delusion.

The results, however, of these two cases in history, namely, that of St. Domingo, and the more recent one of England, may aid the intelligent reader, who is not infected by the mania of ultra-abolition-ism, to understand the practical aspects of the question, and to them I shall proceed in the next chapter.

CHAPTER XXXIII.

RIGHT REVEREND BROTHER: As philanthropy is the acknowledged motive of the ultra-abolitionist, and he holds it to be self-evident that the deliverance of the African race from slavery is the one thing needful to raise them to an equality with the best and most favored portions of mankind, it is fair to inquire how the experiment has succeeded in the case of St. Domingo, which has been, for two generations, entirely under negro domination.

On this subject, we have had conflicting statements, on none of which reliance can be placed, because the writers were so largely influenced by their particular prejudices. But I shall set the matter before you in the words of the eminent Alison, whose "History of Europe" is one of the most trustworthy productions of modern literature, and who, as a native of Scotland, surrounded by English sympathies, and naturally inclined to favor abolition, is altogether unlikely to fall into any error on the Southern side of the question.

"St. Domingo," saith this distinguished historian, "the greatest except Cuba, and, beyond all question, the most flourishing of the West-India Islands before the Revolution, is about three hundred miles long, and its average breadth about ninety miles. The Spaniards possessed two thirds, and the French the remainder. In the French portion, the inhabitants consisted of about forty thousand whites, sixty thousand mulattoes, and five hundred thousand negro slaves. This French colony was immensely productive, exceeding all the British islands together. Its exports, including the Spanish portion, were £18,400,000, and its imports £10,000,000 sterling. Eighteen hundred vessels and 27,000 sailors were employed in conducting the vast colonial traffic. It was this splendid and unequaled colonial possession which the French nation threw away and destroyed at the commencement of the revolution, with a recklessness and improvidence of which the previous history of the world had afforded no example."

11*

"Hardly had the cry of liberty and equality been raised in France," continues our historian, "when it responded warmly and vehemently from the shores of St. Domingo. The slave population were rapidly assailed by revolutionary agents and emissaries, and the workshops and fields of the planters overrun by heated missionaries, who poured into an ignorant and ardent multitude the new-born ideas of European freedom. The constituent Assembly of March 8, 1790, had empowered the colonies to make known their wishes on the subject of a Constitution, by Colonial Assemblies, freely elected by their own citizens. And on the 15th of May, 1791, the privileges of equality were conferred by the same authority on all persons of color, born of a free father and mother. The planters openly endeavored to resist the decree, and civil war was preparing, when, on the night of the 26th August, 1791, the negro insurrection, long and silently organized, at once broke forth, and wrapped the whole northern part of the colony in flames. The conspiracy embraced nearly the whole negro population of the island. The cruelties exercised exceeded any thing recorded in history. The negroes marched with spiked infants on their spears instead of colors. They sawed asunder their male prisoners, and violated the females on the dead bodies of their husbands," etc.

"Louis XVI. was condemned January 15th, 1793. On the 21st of January he was executed. The Democratic passions of St. Domingo were roused to the highest pitch by this event. Twenty thousand negroes rushed in and completed the work of ruin. And the universal freedom of the blacks was proclaimed June 3d, 1793."*

"By the expulsion of the French from St. Domingo," saith this historian, "it has been nominally independent, but slavery has been far indeed from being abolished, and the condition of the people any thing but ameliorated by the change. Nominally free, the blacks have remained really enslaved. Compelled to labor by the terrors of military discipline, for a small part of the products of the soil, they have retained the severity without the advantages of servitude. The industrious habits, the flourishing aspect of the island, have disappeared, and the inhabitants, reduced to half their former amount, and bitterly galled by their republican task-masters, have relapsed into the indolence and inactivity of savage life."†

* *Alison's History of Europe.* Vol. ii. p. 240. Harper's Ed. 1843.
† Ib. p. 251.

"The revolution of St. Domingo," continues our author, "has demonstrated that the negroes can occasionally exert all the vigor and heroism which distinguish the European character; but there is yet no reason to suppose that they are capable of the continued efforts, the sustained and persevering toil, requisite to erect the fabric of civilized freedom. An observation of Gibbon seems decisive on the subject: 'The inaction of the negroes does not seem to be the effect either of their virtue or of their pusillanimity. They indulge, like the rest of mankind, their passions and appetites, and the adjacent tribes are engaged in frequent acts of hostility. But their rude ignorance has never invented any effectual weapons; they appear incapable of forming any extensive plan of government or conquest, and the obvious inferiority of their mental faculties has been discovered and abused by the nations of the temperate zone.' If the negroes are not inferior, either in vigor, courage, or intelligence, to the European, how has it happened that they have remained, for six thousand years, in the savage state? It is impossible to arrive at any other conclusion but that, in the qualities requisite to create and perpetuate civilization, the African is decidedly inferior to the European race, and if any doubt could exist on this subject, it would be removed by the subsequent history and present state of the Haytian republic."

"The following table contains the comparative wealth, produce, and trade of St. Domingo, before 1789, and in 1832, after forty years of nominal freedom."*

1789.	1832.
Population,..............600,000.	Population, ...280,000.
Sugar exported,....672,000,000 lbs.	Sugar exported,.............none.
Coffee, do. .....86,789,000 lbs.	Coffee, ...32,000,000.
Ships employed,............1,680.	Ships employed,................1.
Sailors, ...27,000.	Sailors,......................167.
Exports to France,.....£6,720,000.	Exports to France,...........none.
Imports, ...£9,890,000.	Imports, ...none.

Now here, my Right Reverend Brother, we have a very sad but very instructive account of the results of sudden and complete emancipation, presented by one of the most enlightened historians of the age, without any conceivable bias to incline him against the prevailing sentiment in England, which is universally known to be in favor

* *Alison's History of Europe.* Vol. ii. p. 251. Harper's Ed. 1843.

of negro equality. And it is perfectly clear that even if we set aside the horrible cruelties and fiend-like atrocities which marked the revolution, the island has been almost ruined, while the African race have lost, instead of gaining, by the change. The population reduced from 600,000 to 280,000, less than half; the sugar exported reduced from 672,000,000 of pounds to nothing; the coffee reduced from nearly 87,000,000 of pounds to 32,000,000, less than half; the ships reduced from 1680 vessels to one; the sailors reduced from 27,000 to 167; the exports reduced from thirty-one millions of dollars to nothing; the imports reduced from forty-six millions of dollars to nothing! What a commentary does this exhibit on forty years of negro liberty, produced by a sudden change, under the doctrine proclaimed by the atheists of France, which is identical with that now advocated by our own school of ultra-abolitionism! In one point, however, our philanthropists surpass the French Directory, namely, in the discovery that slaveholding is a *sin*, yea, the sum of all villainies! That was left out of the Gallican programme, because they were open infidels, denouncing religion, and silencing the priests, and closing the churches, and denying the God of truth, while they worshiped an infamous courtesan under the name of the goddess of reason! Whether it is more consistent to renounce the Bible altogether, or to quote it in such a way as to subvert its teaching and set its divine Author in opposition to His own Word, is a question which I do not profess to determine. To my mind, it is like deciding between Scylla and Charybdis. The true Christian will carefully shun them both, without troubling himself to inquire whether it is best to be dashed upon the rock, or swallowed in the whirlpool.

CHAPTER XXXIV.

My Right Reverend Brother : Having now set before you the result of the first example recorded by history, in which negro slavery was abolished by immediate emancipation, I turn next to the course pursued in England, where the persevering efforts and eloquence of the distinguished Wilberforce, employed against a powerful opposition for more than twenty years, were at length crowned with such triumphant success.

But here we must take special notice that the whole of his assaults were at first directed against the barbarity and cruelty of the *slave-trade*, without the slightest intention of interfering with the established relations of the planters in the British colonies. The notion that the holding of a negro in bondage was a sin *per se*, had never entered into his scheme of philanthropy, for he was a devout Christian, and had no sympathy whatever with that class who trim the Bible down to their own judgment of what it *ought to be*, and, under the name of Christianity, are as really worshipers of *reason* as the open infidels of the French Directory. The faith of Wilberforce was the faith of the Church, and therefore the Church accorded with his noble work in abolishing the slave-trade.

I was disappointed and sorry to find, in reading the minute and voluminous biography of this celebrated man, published by his sons, in five volumes, that none of his speeches were preserved entire, and that only a few passages occurred in which this broad and important distinction was noticed plainly. But we have enough of these scattered through the work, to prove the great difference between his principles and those of the ultra-abolitionists, who are so fond of thinking that they are the same.

Thus, in Vol. 1 of his biography, p. 293, we have this note belonging to the year 1791. Speaking of the pamphlets published by the abolitionists in answer to the evidence given by the advocates for the slave-trade, the author, quoting from his father's memoranda, saith :

" It was necessary, in refuting this evidence, to show the mode of obtaining the slaves in Africa, the effect of the trade upon African manners ; the cruelty of the mode of transport ; the waste of life which it caused in the colonies ; the *practicability of maintaining the number of slaves on the West-Indian estates by breeding ;* the injurious effects of the Guinea trade upon our own seamen ; and the *possibility of substituting for it a more advantageous as well as humane traffic.* All these points the witnesses for the abolition completely established." And he adds :

" *The bar were all against us.* Fox could scarcely prevent Erskine from making a set speech in favor of the trade."

Again, in 1815, (vol. iv. p. 241,) the biographer states that Wilberforce reproved one of his colleagues for going so far. "You," he tells Mr. Stephen, " are full ten degrees above me." He was resolved, in the first instance, to strengthen the ameliorating influence of the Act of Abolition by preventing the illicit introduction of fresh laborers. But he and others around him saw not as yet to what they should be led. They had never acted on the claim of abstract rights, and they reached emancipation at last only because it was the necessary conclusion of a series of practical improvements. " They looked," says Mr. Stephen, " to an emancipation of which *not* the slaves, but *the masters themselves* should be the *willing authors.*"

That is precisely the ground on which Wilberforce then stood, and on the same ground I should be perfectly willing to stand with him.

Again, in a letter addressed to Lord Liverpool, March 17, 1815, this eminent man expresses himself as follows, (vol. iv. p. 252 :) " Life is wearing away, and I should indeed be sorry if mine were to terminate before at least a foundation had been laid of a *system of reformation,* which I verily believe would scarcely be more for the *comfort of the slaves* and free colored population, than it would be for the ultimate security of the West-India colonies themselves."

Again, in an extract from one of his speeches in Parliament, 1816, Wilberforce makes these statements, (vol. iv. p. 287 :) " Ever since the year 1789, those persons who resist all improvement in the condition of the negroes have been reiterating the cry against us : ' What, then, you mean to *make the slaves free !* You intend to *emancipate them at once,* and without the least notice !' It might be supposed that our opponents would have abandoned this position *after we had gone on for twenty-seven years constantly refuting it.* But no ; they still persevere. Nor have they confined their assertions to this House, or to this country, but they have actually printed and published in the West-Indies that the design of the friends of the abolition was to make all slaves instantly free. In short, there is nothing, *however monstrous, however dangerous to the tranquillity of our islands,* which they have not laid open to the eyes and ears of all the inhabitants of the West-Indies."

Again, in a letter to Hannah More, 1816, (vol. iv. p. 295,) Wilberforce saith : "I have much to say to you about my Registry Bill, or rather about its object, the *amelioration of the state of the poor slaves.* Alas ! alas ! it grieves me to see the Bristol people so misled, but it really is entirely the effect of misinformation."

And, so late as the year 1818, we find him using these decisive words, (vol. iv. p. 365 :) "Our grand object and our universal language *was* and *is* to produce by abolition (of the trade) a disposition to *breed instead of buying.* This is the *great vital principle* which would work in every direction, and produce reform everywhere."

In 1822, addressing the House of Commons, (vol. v. p. 131,) Wilberforce gave the first intimation of his ultimate views for the West-Indies. "Not I only," he said, "but all the chief advocates of the abolition declared from the first that our object was, by ameliorating regulations, and by stopping the influx of uninstructed savages, to *advance slowly* toward the period when these unhappy beings might exchange their degraded state of slavery for that of a free and industrious peasantry. To that most interesting object I still look forward."

The following year, 1823, produced an order from the English ministry that the whip should no longer be used in the correction of the slaves, and an insurrection broke out in Demarara, causing the death of some white men. "These results," saith the biographer, (vol. v. p. 201,) "Mr. Wilberforce had dreaded, as soon as he heard the measures which government had taken. 'What !' he at once exclaimed, 'have they given such an order without preparation, and without explaining its purpose to the slaves—why, it is *positive madness.*'"

Speaking on the same subject in a letter to Z. Macaulay, (vol. v. p. 252,) he saith : "I am clear that we should become the assailants, and charge government with provoking the insurrection. As to the mode of carrying reforms into operation, I have thought precisely with you. The slaves, it appears to me, should be called together and told that henceforth they would not be flogged at the time, (in the field,) *but at night, after the day's work*, if they had not conducted themselves properly."

And in the same year, 1823, (vol. v. p. 204,) we have this statement : " The conduct of St. Paul, in sending back the fugitive Onesimus, was brought against him in one of those attacks. ' St. Paul,' he answers, ' directed Philemon to regard him as a brother. He *did not rend the civil tie that bound him to his master* by individual power. *No more do we ;* but by directing him to be treated as a brother, did he not substantially claim for him even more than we ask for negro slaves ?' "

Finally, when he heard that the bill for emancipation had passed in 1833, though near his end, he exclaimed : " Thank God that I should have lived to witness the day in which England is willing to give twenty millions sterling for the abolition of slavery." (Vol. v. p. 370.)

I have been thus particular in gleaning, from these volumes, the passages which distinctly prove the substantial agreement of Wilberforce with the principles which I, in my humble way, have always advocated. He attacked the *slave-trade*, and on this all are of the same mind, the Southern States included. He advocated the *breeding of the slaves* in order to keep up the requisite number for the colonies. And such is the Southern system. He denied and repudiated the intention of emancipating the slaves for twenty-seven years together. He advocated *the use of the whip*, only desiring that, instead of employing it in the field, it should be applied, if required, at night, when the work was over. He wished to ameliorate the condition of the slaves, without disturbing the institution itself, until near the close of his parliamentary course : and after emancipation was declared, he approved the paying a hundred millions of dollars to the masters. But even when he was led to intimate the final result to which he had looked forward, he stated his policy to be a *slow advance* to the point of ultimate freedom, and *that* he hoped would be accomplished *with the consent of the planters themselves.*

Where, in all this, do we find the dogmas of our ultra-abolitionists, that slaveholding is a *sin* under any circumstances ; that it is a sufficient reason for debarring Christians from the Communion ; that it is a duty to disobey the laws of the land by refusing to return the fugitive slave to his master ; that the Constitution which sanctions slavery "is a covenant with death and an agreement with hell," and must be done away; that the negroes are entitled to immediate emancipation without any equivalent paid the owners; that they have a right to a perfect equality with the European race; that it is lawful to induce them to run away, and if the master presumes to apprehend them, that they are justified in killing him, so that they may thus obtain their freedom? And, finally, that a desolating civil war, which owes its main origin to these very dogmas, shall be continued until fire and sword shall force the Southern States to bow down to their authority?

No, no, my Right Reverend Brother, not a trace of all this can be defended on the principles of Wilberforce. The British Parliament, under his guidance, proceeded carefully and cautiously, step by step, and were more than forty years before they arrived at the conclusion; although they were not living, as we are, under a Constitution which stipulated for the existence of slavery, and confined the consideration of its policy to the government of the States concerned. The Church of England has never proclaimed her ban upon the institution, nor been known to make the holding of slaves a bar to her communion. And when, at last, emancipation was decreed, it was done, not only with true British justice and magnanimity, under the stipulation of payment to the masters, but also of apprenticeship to the freed slaves, which bound them, for five years, to the service of their former owners, and made the transition from bondage to liberty more gradual and secure.

Yet, with all these guards, the results of the measure have been far from satisfactory. And to the proof of this, I shall invite your attention in the next chapter.

CHAPTER XXXV.

My Right Reverend Brother: The eminent historian, Alison, in his *History of Europe*, gives us the following statement of the arguments employed by Wilberforce, Lord Howick, and Earl Grenville, for the abolition of the slave-trade, in A.D. 1806, before the British Parliament, and I commend the extract to the attention of all who are disposed to advocate the perilous dogma of immediate emancipation:

"The grand, the decisive advantage," said they, "which recommends the abolition of the slave-trade, is, that, by closing that supply of foreign negroes to which the planters have hitherto been accustomed to trust, we will compel them to *promote the multiplication of the slaves on their own estates*, and it is obvious that this can not be done, without *improving their physical and moral condition*. The dangers so powerfully drawn, as likely to result from this measure, are really to be apprehended, not from it, but from *another with which it has no connection*, viz. the *immediate emancipation of the negroes*. That would produce horrors similar to those which have happened in St. Domingo. But nothing of that kind is in contemplation. On the contrary, it is expressly to exclude them, and induce that *gradual emancipation* which is called for, alike by justice to the planters and the interests of the slaves themselves, that the measure under discussion is proposed."*

Nothing can prove, more decisively, the difference between the views entertained by those true Christian philanthropists of Old England, and the course which is so strongly urged by the school of our ultra-abolitionists in New-England. But if the dangers of *immediate* emancipation were deprecated so earnestly by Wilberforce and his colleagues, when the question only concerned the comparatively small number of negroes in their West-Indian Colonies, how much more would they have shrunk from incurring those dangers if they

* Alison's *History of Europe*, 2 vols. p. 407.   Harper's Ed. 1843.

had been placed in our circumstances, with the safety of fourteen States, and the condition of four millions of slaves, depending on the issue!

I proceed, however, to the remarks of the historian upon the results which followed the English movement, guarded as it was by so much of cautious wisdom.

"There can be no question," saith our author, "that this great step was recommended by every consideration of justice and humanity. Nevertheless its effects hitherto have been in the highest degree deplorable. The prophecy of Mr. Hibbert and the opponents of the abolition, that the slave-trade, instead of ceasing, would only change hands, and at length fall into the management of desperate wretches who would double its horrors, has been too fatally verified, and to an extent even greater than they anticipated. From the returns laid before Parliament it appears that the slave-trade is now four times as extensive as it was in 1789, and twice as great as it was when the efforts of Mr. Wilberforce procured its abolition in the British dominions. Nearly 200,000 captives now annually cross the Atlantic. Their former sufferings in the large and capacious Liverpool slave-ships were as nothing compared to those which they now endure, in the hands of the Spanish and the Portuguese. And they are brought, not to the comparatively easy life of the British West-India Islands, but to the desperate service of Cuba or Brazil, in the latter of which they are worked like animals, in droves of several hundreds, without a single female among them, and without any attempt to perpetuate their race. They are thus worn down to the grave by a lingering process, which, on an average, terminates their existence in seven years."

"The precipitate and irretrievable step of emancipation, forced on the Legislature in 1834, by benevolent but incautious, and perhaps, mistaken feeling, has already occasioned so great a decline in the produce of the British West-Indies, and excited such general expectations of a still greater and increasing deficiency, that the impulse thereby given to the foreign slave-trade to fill up the gap, has been unbounded, and, it is to be feared, almost irremediable."*

"It is the multitude who forced on those measures," continues the historian, "who frustrated all the benevolent efforts of Mr. Wilber-

* *Alison's History of Europe*, vol. ii. p. 499.

force and Mr. Fox, and rendered the abolition of the slave-trade in the British dominions the remote and innocent cause of boundless misfortunes to the negro race. The British slaves, since the slave-trade was abolished, had become fully equal to the wants of the colonies; their numbers were on the increase, their condition was comfortable and prosperous *beyond that of any peasantry in Europe,* and large numbers were annually purchasing their freedom from the produce of their own industry. But now all these admirable effects of the abolition of the slave-trade have been completely frustrated, and the humane but *deluded inhabitants of Great Britain* are bur-dened with twenty millions, to ruin, in the end, their own planters, consign to barbarism their own negroes, cut off a principal branch of their naval strength, and double the slave-trade in extent, and quad-ruple it in horrors throughout the world."*

I shall close my extracts from this distinguished writer with a passage of great force, which adds the profound wisdom of the phi-losopher to the truth of the historian. Speaking of the system of Russian slavery, which has since been done away, he saith:

"The laborers on an estate constitute, as they formerly did in the West-Indies, the chief part of its value, and thus the proprietor is induced to take care of his slaves by the same motives which prompt him to do so with his buildings or his cattle. Relief in sickness, care of orphans, maintenance of the maimed, or in old age, are im-portant advantages to the laboring classes, even in the most favorable circumstances, and with all the facilities for rendering themselves independent, which the habits of civilized life, and the power of ac-cumulating and preserving capital arising from the interchange of com-merce, afford.—In rude periods, when these advantages are unknown, and the means of providing during the vigor for the weakness of life do not exist, they are of inestimable value.—Stripes, insults, and compulsory labor, are no light evils, but they are as nothing com-pared to the wasting agonies of famine, and the violence of ill-directed and ungovernable passions, which never fail to seize upon prema-turely emancipated man. The servitude and forced industry of the serf fills up the interval, the long and important interval, between the roving independence of the savage, who lives by the chase, or the milk of his herds, and the voluntary toil of the freeman, around whom artificial wants have thrown the unseen but riveted chains of civilized life. But for its existence, this wide chasm could never have been passed, *for man will never labor voluntarily till he has acquired the habits and desires of an advanced state of society;* and those habits, when generally pervading the community, can exist only from the effect of *previous centuries of compulsory labor.*"*

Such are the opinions of an author who occupies a high place amongst the most enlightened and thoroughly informed historians of the age, and whose proclivities, from his birth, his education, and his natural sympathy with the tone of sentiment around him, would all tend to an exaggerated estimate of the evils of slavery, and the advantages of freedom. I could add a large amount of other testimony, to prove the correctness of his views upon the dangers of sudden and hasty emancipation. But it is unnecessary. The statements of this eminent writer are enough for any candid mind, and to those who are fond of their delusion, and determined to maintain it, all the facts and arguments which could be heaped together would be addressed in vain.

* *Alison's History of Europe*, vol. iv. p. 12–13. Harper's Ed. 1843.

CHAPTER XXXVI.

RIGHT REVEREND BROTHER: The favorite argument of our ultra-abolitionists is derived from the assumption that the slave-system of the South is in direct contrariety to the Gospel, and that the extinction of slavery in Europe was owing to the influence of Christianity. No statement can be more utterly unsupported by the facts of history, although it is repeated, over and over again, by writers and orators, who ought to know better. But I am sorry to say that it is the fashion of too many to repeat these declarations with as much confidence as if they were self-evident, and, like the axioms in mathematics, needed no demonstration; because they are perfectly aware that they are always acceptable to those who have no personal interest in the institution, and that very few will object to the eloquence which seems to honor religion, when it costs them nothing more than an empty tribute of applause.

I have already shown, by the most abundant testimony, that the Church of Christ, from the beginning, recognized slavery as a system established by the laws of the State, in accordance with the wisdom of Divine Providence; and I have now to prove, by the best writers of law and history, that the causes which led to its extinction in Europe were entirely of a civil and not of a religious character. This, indeed, would be a necessary result from the evidence which I have so largely furnished; but I desire to set it forth with the full force of many concurrent witnesses.

The system of slavery, as it formerly existed amongst our European ancestors, is thus stated by the historian Hume. (Appendix to vol. i. p. 136.)

"The most numerous rank by far, in the community, seems to have been the slaves or villeins who were the property of their lords, and were consequently incapable of possessing any property. The power of the master was not unlimited among the Anglo-Saxons, as it was among their ancestors. If a man beat out his slave's eye or teeth, the slave recovered his liberty ; if he killed him, he paid a fine to the king, provided the slave died within a day after the wound or blow ; otherwise he passed unpunished.   The selling of themselves or children to slavery was always in practice among the German nations, and was continued by the Anglo-Saxons."

Blackstone, in his commentaries, is more express.   " Under the Saxon government," saith he, " there were, as Sir William Temple speaks, a sort of people in a condition of downright servitude, used and employed in the most servile works, and belonging, both they, their children, and effects, to the lord of the soil, like the rest of the cattle or stock upon it.   On the arrival of the Normans here, it seems not improbable that they who were strangers to any other than a feudal state, might give some sparks of enfranchisement to such wretched persons as fell to their share, by admitting them, as well as others, to the oath of fealty ; which conferred a right of protection, and raised the tenant to a kind of estate superior to downright slavery, but inferior to every other condition.   This they called villenage, and the tenants villeins, either from the word *vilis*, or else, as Sir Edward Coke tells us, *a villa*, because they lived chiefly in villages, and were employed in rustic works of the most sordid kind."   (Bl. Com. b. ii. ch. vi. sec. 3, p. 92.)

" These villeins, belonging principally to lords of manors, were either villeins *regardant*—that is, annexed to the manor or land—or else they were *in gross*, or at large—that is, annexed to the person of the lord, and transferable by deed from one owner to another.   They could not leave their lord without his permission, but if they ran away, or were purloined from him, might be claimed and recovered by action, like beasts or other chattels."   (Ib. p. 93.)

" The children of villeins were also in the same state of bondage with their parents.   The law, however, protected the persons of villeins, as the king's subjects, against atrocious injuries of the lord ; for he might not kill or maim his villein, though he might beat him with impunity."   (Ib. p. 93–4.)

" When tenure in villenage was virtually abolished by the statute of Charles II., there was hardly a pure villein left in the nation. For Sir Thomas Smith testifies that in all his time (and he was Secretary to Edward VI.) he never knew any villein *in gross* throughout the realm, and the few villeins *regardant* that were then remaining were such only as had belonged to bishops, monasteries, or other ecclesiastical corporations, in the preceding times of popery." (Ib. p. 96.)

Here then, we see that this sort of English slavery died out by degrees, without any direct assault either by Church or State. The villeins were of the same race of Anglo-Saxons, and there was no barrier of color to prevent their gradual emancipation. But to prove conclusively that Christianity had nothing to do with the change, the last of the villeins that remained were those who belonged to *the bishops, the monasteries, and other ecclesiastical corporations.* It is perfectly manifest that if the Church had disapproved the system, as being inconsistent with the Gospel, the bishops and the monasteries would have been the first, instead of the last, to let their bondmen go.

CHAPTER XXXVII.

RIGHT REVEREND BROTHER: The next witness to the state of slavery during the first centuries of the Christian era, is the historian Gibbon, from whose luminous and accurate pages I shall quote a highly interesting statement on the subject, for my readers' satisfaction.

After giving a masterly sketch of the Roman polity and law, this admirable writer proceeds as follows, viz. :

" It was by such institutions that the nations of the empire insensibly melted away into the Roman name and people. But there still remained, in the centre of every province and of every family, an unhappy condition of men who endured the weight, without sharing the benefits of society. In the free states of antiquity, the domestic slaves were exposed to the wanton rigors of despotism. The slaves consisted, for the most part, of barbarian captives, taken in thousands by the chance of war, purchased at a vile price, accustomed to a life of independence, and impatient to break and avenge their fetters. Against such internal enemies, whose desperate insurrections had more than once reduced the republic to the brink of destruction, the most severe regulations and the most cruel treatment seemed almost justified by the great law of self-preservation. But when the principal nations of Europe, Asia, and Africa, were united under the laws of one sovereign, the source of foreign supplies flowed with much less abundance, and the Romans were reduced to the milder but more tedious method of propagation. In their numerous families, and particularly in their country estates, they encouraged the marriage of their slaves. The sentiments of nature, the habits of education, and the possession of a dependent species of property, contributed to alleviate the hardships of servitude. The existence of a slave became an object of greater value, and though his happiness still depended on the temper and circumstances of the master, the humanity of the latter, instead of being restrained by fear, was encouraged by the

12

sense of his own interest. The progress of manners was accelerated by the virtue or policy of the emperors; and by the edicts of Hadrian and the Antonines, the protection of the laws was extended to the most abject part of mankind. The jurisdiction of life and death over the slaves—a power long exercised and often abused—was taken out of private hands, and reserved to the magistrates alone. The subterranean prisons were abolished, and upon a just complaint of intolerable treatment, the injured slave obtained either his deliverance or a less cruel master."

"Hope, the best comfort of our imperfect condition, was not denied to the Roman slave; and if he had any opportunity of rendering himself either useful or agreeable, he might very naturally expect that the diligence and fidelity of a few years would be rewarded with the inestimable gift of freedom. The benevolence of the master was so frequently prompted by the meaner suggestions of vanity and avarice, that the laws found it more necessary to restrain than to encourage a profuse and undistinguishing liberality, which might degenerate into a very dangerous abuse. It was a maxim of ancient jurisprudence, that as a slave had not any country of his own, he acquired with his liberty an admission into the political society of which his patron was a member. The consequences of this maxim would have prostituted the privileges of the Roman city to a mean and promiscuous multitude. Some seasonable exceptions were therefore provided; and the honorable distinction was confined to such slaves only as, for just causes, and with the approbation of the magistrate, should receive a solemn and legal manumission. Even those chosen freedmen obtained no more than the private rights of citizens, and were rigorously excluded from civil or military honors. Whatever might be the merit or fortune of their sons, they likewise were esteemed unworthy of a seat in the Senate; nor were the traces of a servile origin allowed to be completely obliterated till the third or fourth generation." (*Gibbon's Decline and Fall*, etc., vol. i. pp. 51–2. New-York ed. 1822.)

"The youths of a promising genius," (among the slaves,) continues our author, "were instructed in the arts and sciences, and their price was ascertained by the degree of their skill and talents. Almost every profession, either liberal or mechanical, might be found in the house of an opulent senator. It was more for the interest of the merchant or manufacturer ·to purchase than to hire his workmen;

and in the country, slaves were employed as the cheapest and most laborious instruments of agriculture. Four hundred slaves were maintained in a single palace of Rome. The same number belonged to an estate which an African widow, of a very private condition, resigned to her son, while she reserved to herself a much larger share of her property. A freedman, under the reign of Augustus, though his fortune had suffered great losses in the civil wars, left behind him three thousand six hundred yoke of oxen, two hundred and fifty thousand head of smaller cattle, and, what was almost included in the description of cattle, four thousand one hundred and sixteen slaves." (Ib. pp. 52–3.)

With regard to the immense number of the slaves, the historian makes the following estimate :

"After weighing with attention every circumstance which could influence the balance, it seems probable that there existed, in the time of the Emperor Claudius, about one hundred and twenty millions of persons, a degree of population which possibly exceeds that of modern Europe, and forms the most numerous society that has ever been united under the same system of government. The slaves were at least equal in number to the free inhabitants of the Roman world." (Ib. p. 53–4.)

On this copious extract from our eminent historian, I would suggest a few points worthy of special observation.

1. That these sixty millions of slaves included a vast multitude, equal, in capacity and intellect, to their masters. Descended as they were from all the nations with whom the Romans had ever been at war, there were doubtless some Africans, but the greater part, by far, were Asiatics and Europeans; and Greeks, Germans, Gauls, and Britons were in abundance amongst them. Their system was not confined to one savage and barbarous race, taken from the most degraded portion of the human family, as it is in the Southern States. And hence it is easy to account for the fact that they were far more liable to insurrections, and that those insurrections were much more formidable ; because the great majority of the slaves possessed a full amount of native energy and talent. The most serious of these revolts had for its leader Spartacus, a Greek, who was a noted gladiator. To such men as these, slavery must indeed have been a galling debasement. While, to the negro race, it has been the means of improve-

ment and elevation, greatly superior to any condition which they enjoyed before.

2. I would remark, in the next place, the checks which the Roman government thought necessary to prevent indiscriminate emancipation, and the restraints which they placed on the freedmen, not permitting them to be admitted into the army, nor to hold any civil office, until the third or fourth generation. Notwithstanding their equality of race, and the progress of many amongst them in art and science, the idea that a newly-emancipated slave was forthwith fit for the full privileges of freemen, was regarded, by these wise ancients, as an utter absurdity.

3. And lastly, I must charge the historian with a very unfair omission, where he speaks of the causes which produced so great an amelioration in the treatment of the slaves. For these causes were mainly the results of the Gospel. We have seen, in the early fathers and councils of the Christian Church, how earnestly they set forth the precepts of the Apostles in the duty of the masters, to be just, and kind, and merciful to those whom they held in bondage. It was the proper office of the Church, from the beginning, not to make the slightest effort to *abolish* the institution, but to render its practical *administration* as consistent as possible with justice and with love. This gifted historian, however, was an infidel philosopher; and much as we may admire his learning, his accuracy, and his style, we could hardly expect from his pen a willing tribute to the humane and purifying influence of Christianity.

CHAPTER XXXVIII.

RIGHT REVEREND BROTHER : The next historical testimony bearing on the subject, is that of Robertson, whose celebrated work on the reign of Charles V. gives a clear statement of slavery in Europe, anterior to the sixteenth century.   I quote from Note ix. vol. 1, p. 191, of Hosford's ed. 1822 :

" The *servi*, or slaves," saith this author, " seem to have been the most numerous class, and consisted either of captives taken in war, or of persons, the property in whom was acquired in some of the various methods enumerated by Du Cange, voc. *servus*, v. 6, p. 447. The wretched condition of this numerous class will appear from several circumstances.   1. Their masters had absolute dominion over their persons.   They had the power of punishing their slaves capitally, without the intervention of any judge.   This dangerous right they possessed not only in the more early periods, when their manners were fierce, but it continued as late as the twelfth century.   Even after the jurisdiction of masters came to be restrained, the life of a slave was deemed to be of so little value, that a very slight compensation atoned for taking it away.   They were not originally permitted to marry.   During several centuries after the barbarous nations embraced the Christian religion, slaves who lived as husband and wife were not joined together by any religious ceremony, and did not receive the nuptial benediction from a priest.   When this conjunction came to be considered as a lawful marriage, they were not permitted to marry without the consent of their master ; and such as ventured to do so, without obtaining that, were punished with great severity, and sometimes were put to death.   When the manners of the European nations became more gentle, and their ideas more liberal, slaves who married without their master's consent were subjected only to a fine.   All the children of slaves were in the same condition with their parents, and became the property of their masters ; and that so entirely, that they could sell them at pleasure.   Slaves had a title to nothing but subsistence and clothes from their master; all the profit of their labor accrued to him. Conformably to the same principle, all the effects of slaves belonged to their master after death, and they could not dispose of them by testament.—It was enacted in the laws of almost all the nations of Europe, that no slave should be admitted to give evidence against a freeman in a court of justice."

"The *villani* (or serfs) were *adscripti glebœ or villœ*, (bound to the soil or village,) from which they derived their name, and were transferable along with it. But in this they differed from slaves, that they paid a fixed rent to their masters for the land which they cultivated, and after paying that, all the fruits of their labor and industry belonged to themselves."

"Such was the spirit of tyranny, however, which prevailed among the great proprietors of lands, and so various were the opportunities of oppressing those who were settled on their estates, or of rendering their condition intolerable, that many freemen, in despair, renounced their liberty, and voluntarily surrendered themselves as slaves to their powerful masters. This they did in order that their masters might become more immediately interested to afford them protection, together with the means of subsisting themselves and their families. It was still more common for freemen to surrender their liberty to bishops or abbots, that they might partake of the security which the vassals and slaves of churches and monasteries enjoyed, in consequence of the superstitious veneration paid to the saint under whose immediate protection they were supposed to be taken. The number of slaves in every nation of Europe was immense. The greater part of the inferior class of people, in France, were reduced to this state at the commencement of the third race of kings. The same was the case in England."

In another part of this volume, (Note 20, § 1, p. 229,) the historian, Dr. Robertson, states the practice of manumission on religious motives which actuated individuals, and then (p. 232) proceeds to say that "as sentiments of religion induced some to grant liberty to their fellow-Christians who groaned under the yoke of servitude, so mistaken ideas concerning devotion led others to relinquish their liberty. The *oblati*, or *voluntary slaves of churches or monasteries were very numerous. How zealous the clergy were to encourage the opinion which led to this practice* will appear from a charter by which one gives himself up as a slave to a monastery. Great, however, as the power of religion was, it does not appear that the enfranchisement of slaves was a frequent practice while the feudal system preserved its vigor.   On the contrary, there were laws which set bounds to it, as detrimental to society.   The inferior order of men *owed the recovery of their liberty to the decline of that aristocratical policy,* which lodged the most extensive power in the hands of a few members of the society, and depressed all the rest.   When Louis X. issued his ordinance, several slaves had been so long accustomed to servitude, and their minds were so much debased by that unhappy situation, that they refused to accept of the liberty which was offered them.   Long after the reign of Louis X. several of the French nobility continued to assert their ancient dominion over their slaves.   It appears from an ordinance of the famous Bertrand de Guesclin, Constable of France, that the custom of enfranchising them was considered a pernicious innovation.   There is no general law for the manumission of slaves in the statute-book of England, similar to that of the kings of France.   Though the genius of the English Constitution seems early to have favored personal liberty, personal servitude, nevertheless, continued long in England in some particular places.   In the year 1514, we find a Charter of Henry VIII. enfranchising two slaves belonging to one of his manors.   As late as the year 1574, there is a Commission from Queen Elizabeth with respect to the manumission of certain bondmen belonging to her."

I have extracted the whole of these passages at great length, because I wish to give the reader the fullest information in my power. But their evidence is clear on two points, which properly belong to my argument.   First, that large numbers of *freemen* became *voluntary slaves to the churches and monasteries* in Europe, and that *the clergy were zealous to encourage the practice;* a very decisive proof that *no sin* was attached to the relation in their judgment.   And secondly, that the inferior order of men owed the recovery of their liberty, *not,* as is commonly supposed, to the influence of Christianity, but to the *decline* of the aristocratic feudal system.   Here, therefore, we have another proof of the same fact, viz. that the Church did not consider it a religious duty to meddle with the law of the State on this subject, but took a full share in the existing institution, while her influence was used to ameliorate and improve the treatment of the slaves, both by precept and example.   Hence, freemen, who were disposed to seek the greater protection which slavery gave them, during those turbulent ages of baronial strife and contention, preferred to have the Church or the monastery for their master; because they knew that they would there experience a milder and kindlier exercise of authority than they could expect elsewhere.

CHAPTER XXXIX.

RIGHT REVEREND BROTHER: There are some interesting statements of our distinguished American historian, Mr. Motley, in his "Dutch Republic," to which I shall next invite your attention.

Thus, speaking of the Gauls, in the time of Julius Cesar, he saith: that "the people were all slaves. The knights or nobles were all trained to arms. The people had no rights at all, and were glad to assign themselves as slaves to any noble who was strong enough to protect them. In peace, the Druids exercised the main functions of government." (Vol. 1, p. 7–8.)

"The Anglo-Saxon Willibrod, in the eighth century, destroyed the images of Woden in Walcheren, and founded churches in North Holland. Charles Martel rewarded him with extensive domains above Utrecht, together with many slaves and other chattels. Soon afterwards he was consecrated Bishop of all the Frisians. Thus arose the famous episcopate of Utrecht." (Ib. p. 31.)

Describing the condition of the Netherlands in the tenth century, the historian saith that "slavery was both voluntary and compulsory. Paupers sold themselves that they might escape starvation. The timid sold themselves that they might escape violence. These voluntary sales, which were frequent, were usually made to cloisters and ecclesiastical establishments, for the condition of Church slaves was preferable to that of other serfs. Persons worsted in judicial duels, shipwrecked sailors, vagrants, strangers, criminals unable to pay the money-bote imposed on them, were all deprived of freedom ; but the prolific source of slavery was war. Prisoners were almost universally reduced to servitude. A free woman who intermarried with a slave, condemned herself and offspring to perpetual bondage. The number of slaves throughout the Netherlands was very large; the number belonging to the Bishopric of Utrecht, enormous." (Ib. pp. 32–3.)

12*

Tracing the progress of society, Mr. Motley gives the following masterly sketch: "The Crusades," saith he, "made great improvement in the condition of the serfs. He who became a soldier of the Cross, was free on his return, and many were adventurous enough to purchase liberty at so honorable a price. Many others were sold or mortgaged by the crusading knights, desirous of converting their property into gold, before embarking upon their enterprise. The purchasers or mortgagees were in general churches or convents, so that the slaves thus alienated obtained at least a preferable servitude. The place of the absent serfs was supplied with free labor, so that agricultural and mechanical occupations, now devolving on a more elevated class, became less degrading, and, in process of time, opened an ever-widening sphere for the industry and progress of freemen. Thus a people began to exist. It was, however, a miserable people, with personal but no civil rights whatever. Their condition, although better than servitude, was almost desperate." (Vol. 1, p. 33–4.)

And the change which gradually brought about the general decline of the feudal system of vassalage, is rightly stated by Mr. Motley to have been *not* religion but *commerce*. "In the fifteenth century," saith he, "commerce had converted slaves into freemen, freemen into burghers, and the burghers were daily acquiring a larger hold upon the government." (Ib. p. 42.)

And to prove, still further, how little the change had to do with the idea that slavery was inconsistent with religion, we find the following historical fact, a hundred years later. At the battle of Lepanto, in A.D. 1545, our author states correctly that "the Turks taken prisoners were made slaves to the victorious Spaniards."

"The Turkish slaves," saith he, "were divided among the victors in the proportion of one half to Philip, and one half to the Pope and Venice. Don John received, as a present, one hundred and seventy-four slaves. Alexander of Parma received thirty slaves; Requesens thirty. To each general of infantry was assigned six slaves; to each colonel, four; to each ship's captain, one. The number of slaves in chains allotted to Philip was 3600. Seven thousand two hundred Turkish slaves, therefore, at least, were divided among Christians." (Dutch Republic, v. 3. p. 140, in note.)

These extracts serve to demonstrate the universal judgment of Christendom, that there was *no sin in holding slaves.* In their *treatment* there might be, and doubtless was, an abundance of sin. And amongst fallen creatures like ourselves, there is no relation of society in which we are not compelled to say the same. It is the result of Christianity to *improve the administration* of all the relations of life, by bringing mankind under the government of heaven. And slavery was thus improved, among the rest. But to abolish it was another matter, which belonged to the State, and not to the Church. Hence we find that the Church has never meddled with it, because the Church is the Kingdom of Christ, which is "not of this world." And therefore she leaves the State to manage its temporal interests in its own way, always willing to "render unto Cæsar the things that be Cæsar's," while she "renders unto God the things that be God's."

CHAPTER XL.

RIGHT REVEREND BROTHER : The celebrated case of the negro Somerset, as you probably know, produced, in the year 1772, a new era
of thought in England on the subject of slavery; and doubtless aided
powerfully, under the great authority of Lord Mansfield, to attach
many influential minds to the side of Wilberforce, in his subsequent
assault upon the slave-trade.

On the side of the negro, who claimed his freedom from West-Indian slavery on the ground that his master had brought him to England, where slavery was no longer known, the eminent lawyer Hargrave, with others, was engaged, and his written argument is in the
State Trials. (Vol. 11 and 12, app. p. 340.) From this very learned
and interesting specimen of legal and historical research, I shall extract another testimony which well deserves attention. Of course
you will remember on which side this accomplished jurist was retained.

"Notwithstanding," saith Mr. Hargrave, "the force of the reasons
against the allowance of domestic slavery, there are civilians of great
credit who insist on its utility. This opinion is favored by Puffendorf, and Ulricus Huberus. In the dissertation on slavery prefixed
to Potgiesserus on the German law, *De Statu Servorum*, the opinion
is examined minutely and defended."

"The great origin of slavery is captivity in war, though sometimes
it has been commenced by contract. It has been a question much
agitated, whether either of these foundations of slavery is consistent
with natural justice. It would be engaging in too large a field of inquiry
to attempt reasoning on the *general lawfulness* of slavery. I trust,
too that the liberty for which I am contending does not require such
a disquisition, and am impatient to reach that part of my argument
in which I hope to prove slavery reprobated by the law of England
as an *inconvenient thing*. Here, therefore, I shall only refer to some

of the most eminent writers, who have examined how far slavery, founded on captivity or contract, is conformable to the law of nature, and shall just hint at the reasons which influence their several opinions."

"The ancient writers suppose the right of killing an enemy vanquished in a just war, and thence infer the right of enslaving him. In this opinion, founded, as I presume, on the idea of punishing the enemy for his injustice, they are followed by *Albericus Gentilis, Grotius, Puffendorf, Bynkershoeck*, and many others. But in *The Spirit of Laws* (Montesquieu) the right of killing is denied, except in case of absolute necessity, and for self-preservation. However, when a country is conquered, the author seems to admit the conqueror's right of enslaving for a short time, that is, till the conquest is effectually secured. Dr. Rutherford, not satisfied with the right of killing a vanquished enemy, infers the right of enslaving him from the conqueror's right to a reparation in damages for the expenses of the war. The lawfulness of slavery by contract is assented to by *Grotius* and *Puffendorf*, who found themselves on the maintenance of the slave, which is the consideration moving from the master."

"But however reasonable it may be to doubt the justice of domestic slavery, however convinced we may be of its ill effects, it must be confessed that the practice is ancient, and has been almost universal. Its beginning may be dated from the remotest period, in which there are any traces of the history of mankind. It commenced in the barbarous state of society, and was retained, even when men were far advanced in civilization. The nations of antiquity most famous for countenancing the system of domestic slavery, were the Jews, the Greeks, the Romans, and the ancient Germans, amongst all of whom it prevailed, but in various degrees of severity. By the ancient Germans it was continued in the countries they overran; and so was transmitted to the various kingdoms and states which arose in Europe out of the ruins of the Roman Empire. At length, however, it fell into decline in most parts of Europe. The history of its decline in Europe has been traced by many eminent writers, particularly *Bodin, Albericus Gentilis, Potgiesserus, Dr. Robertson*, and *Mr. Millar*. It is sufficient here to say that this great change began in Spain, according to *Bodin*, about the end of the eighth century, and was become general before the middle of the fourteenth century. *Bartolus*, the most famed commentator on the Civil Law, in that period, represents slavery as in disuse, and the succeeding commentators hold much the same language. However, they must be understood with many restrictions and exceptions, and not to mean that slavery was completely and universally abolished in Europe. Some modern civilians, not sufficiently attending to this circumstance, rather too hastily reprehend their predecessors for representing slavery as disused in Europe. The truth is that the ancient species of slavery, by frequent emancipations, became greatly diminished in extent, the remnant of it was considerably abated in severity; and the disuse of the practice of enslaving captives taken in the wars between Christian powers, assisted in preventing the future increase of domestic slavery."

"Such was the expiring state of domestic slavery in Europe at the commencement of the sixteenth century, when the discovery of America and of the western and eastern coasts of Africa gave occasion to the introduction of a new species of slavery. It took its rise from the Portuguese, who, in order to supply the Spaniards with persons able to sustain the fatigue of cultivating their new possessions in America, particularly the islands, opened a trade between Africa and America for the sale of negro slaves. This disgraceful commerce in the human species is said to have begun in the year 1508, when the first importation of negro slaves was made into Hispaniola from the Portuguese settlements on the western coasts of Africa. In 1540 the Emperor Charles V. endeavored to stop the progress of the negro slavery, by orders that all slaves in the American isles should be made free; and they were accordingly manumitted by *Lagasca*, the governor of the country, *on condition of continuing to labor for their masters*. But this attempt proved unsuccessful, and on Lagasca's return to Spain, domestic slavery revived and flourished as before. The expedient of having slaves for labor in America was not long peculiar to the Spaniards, being afterwards adopted by the other Europeans as they acquired possessions there. In consequence of this general practice, negroes are become a very considerable article in the commerce between Africa and America, and domestic slavery has taken so deep a root in most of our American colonies, as well as in those of other nations, that there is little probability of our seeing it generally suppressed."

"The law of England," continues Mr. Hargrave, "never recognized any species of domestic slavery except the ancient one of villenage, now expired; and has sufficiently provided against the introduction of a new slavery under the name of villenage, or any other denomination whatever."

"The condition of a villein had most of the incidents belonging to slavery in general. His service was uncertain, and indeterminate, such as his lord thought fit to require—he was liable to beating, imprisonment, and every other chastisement his lord could devise, except killing and maiming. He was incapable of acquiring property for his own benefit, the rule being, *quicquid acquisitur servo, acquisitur domino*. He was himself the subject of property; as such saleable and transmissable. If he was a *villein regardant*, he passed with the manor or land to which he was annexed, but might be severed, at the pleasure of his lord. If he was a *villein in gross*, he was an hereditament or a chattel real according to his lord's interest, being descendible to the heir when the lord was absolute owner, and transmissible to the executor when the lord had only a term of years. Lastly, the slavery extended to the issue if both parents were villeins, or if the father only was a villein; our law deriving the condition of the child from that of the father, contrary to the Roman law, in which the rule was, *Partus sequitur ventrem*."

"The origin of villenage is principally to be derived from the wars between our British, Saxon, Danish, and Norman ancestors, whilst they were contending for the possession of the country."

"After the Conquest, many things concurred happily, first, to check the progress of domestic slavery in England, and finally to suppress it. The cruel custom of enslaving captives in war being abolished, from that time the accession of a new race of villeins was prevented; and the humanity, policy and necessity of the times were continually wearing out the ancient race. Sometimes, no doubt, manumissions were freely granted, but they probably were much oftener extorted during the rage of the civil wars, so frequent before the reign of Henry VII., about the forms of the constitution or the successions to the crown. Another cause which greatly contributed to the extinction of villenage, was the discouragement of it by the courts of justice. They always presumed in favor of liberty, throwing the *onus probandi* upon the lord. And manumissions were inferred from the slightest circumstances of mistake or negligence in the lord, from every act or omission which legal refinement could strain into an acknowledgment of the villein's liberty. I shall not attempt to follow villenage in the several stages of its decline, it being sufficient to mention the time of its extinction, which, as all agree, happened about the latter end of Elizabeth's reign, or soon after the accession of James. From the fifteenth of James I., being more than one hundred and fifty years ago, the claim of villenage has not been heard in our courts of justice: and nothing can be more notorious, than that the race of persons who were once the objects of it, was about that time completely worn out by the continued and united operation of death and manumissions."

The conclusion of Mr. Hargrave was, that "the law of England *excludes every slavery not commencing in England, every slavery, though commencing there, not being ancient and immemorial.* Villenage is the only slavery which can possibly answer to such a description, and that has long expired by the deaths and emancipations of those who were once the objects of it. Consequently there is now no slavery which can be lawful in England, until the legislature shall interfere to make it so."

Lord Mansfield decided the case in accordance with this argument, as you doubtless know, and the slave was pronounced to be a freeman. But I have quoted so largely from Mr. Hargrave, in order to show the perfect accordance of his statements with the position which I have maintained.

For he does not say one word about the *sinfulness* of slaveholding, nor claim any action of the Church against it, as being inconsistent with religion or morality. He admits that the great majority of the most eminent writers were in favor of it on the ground of natural justice. He attributes its extinction in England, not to any direct opposition by Church or State, but to its gradual decay, by death and manumission; and while he contemplates the establishment of negro slavery in the colonies as a settled practice, he contents himself with opposing its introduction into England as an *inconvenient thing*, not warranted by law, nor agreeable to modern usage, since slavery had ceased to exist there, in any form, one hundred and fifty years before.

CHAPTER XLI.

RIGHT REVEREND BROTHER: The public feeling in England, with respect to negro slavery, at the time when our Constitution was established, is set forth with great ability in a manuscript defense of the decision of the Supreme Court in the case of Dred Scott, which has been sent to me by a friend. And from this I shall take a few additional facts, in corroboration of the preceding statements.

The treaty of Utrecht, which crowned the victories of Marlborough, in the reign of Queen Anne, A.D. 1713, was distinguished by a special regard to the slave-trade, securing to the English African company a monopoly in the introduction of negroes into the several ports of Spanish America, for the term of thirty years. And the first Article of this treaty stipulated that this company should bring into the West-Indies one hundred and forty-four thousand negroes, within that period, being at the rate of four thousand eight hundred in every year, *one fourth part of the commercial profits being reserved to the King of Spain, and another fourth part to the Queen of England.* The negro race was then held to be a proper subject of commerce by the universal sentiment of Europe. The transferring them from their deplorable savage state to the mastership of civilized men, was considered to be a benefit of the highest value to the negroes themselves. And had it been otherwise, the "good Queen Anne," who was certainly a religious and excellent woman, would never have been an actual partner in the trade of the English African company.

The provisions of the treaty of Utrecht on this subject were kept in view by the subsequent treaties, in the reigns of George I. and George II., clearly proving that there was no change of English sentiment down to 1749, when the monopoly of the English company having expired, the slave-trade was thrown open to every British subject who chose to embark in it. This was done by statute twenty-third George Second, chapter thirty-one. And the result produced so great an influx of negroes into the colonies, that the Legislature of South-Carolina passed an act prohibiting the further importation. But the British government disallowed this act, and reprimanded the governor for having assented to it.

The American Revolution having been successfully accomplished, and peace proclaimed in 1783, we find the British Parliament passing another act, granting certain privileges of trade to the ports of the West-Indies. The fourth section of this, (statute twenty-seven, George Third, chapter twenty-seven, 1787,) authorizes the exporting of merchandise from the English islands to any foreign colony, and in this merchandise there is special mention of *rum* and *negroes*. This was thirteen years after the decision of Lord Mansfield in the case of Somerset, and only two years before the adoption of our present Constitution.

In the year 1773, when that famous case was decided, there were no less than fourteen thousand negro slaves in London alone. And the opinion of Lord Mansfield was denied to be law by several great authorities, Lord Hardwicke and Lord Stowell being clearly opposed to it. We have seen the statement of Mr. Wilberforce, that all the lawyers were against him, and we know that it cost more than twenty years of struggle before the slave-trade was abolished, while it was not until 1833 that emancipation was granted to the British slaves in the West-Indies, through the pressure, as the historian Alison states, of the new popular feeling.

The success of the Republican theory in the establishment of the United States was undoubtedly the first great step which led the minds of men in this direction. But that went no further than the abolition of the slave-trade, leaving the domestic institution alone, and even providing for its protection. The great blow against slavery was reserved for the French Revolution, which freed the negroes of St. Domingo, and led to the horrid massacre of the whites, and threw all Europe into alarm and consternation by the conflicts which arose in every quarter, between popular rights and the old systems of monarchy. In all this the Church of Christ took no part, save by prayer and loyal sufferance. The atheism of France, which uprooted slavery, did not spare the altar. Liberty, equality, and fraternity became the new trinity which men adored, instead of the God of the Bible. And hanging, drowning, and the guillotine were the prompt punishment of those who refused to bow down and worship them.

That the Church of England held slavery to be perfectly lawful in itself, as well as the Church of Rome and all the Christian denominations of Europe and America, through the whole period of their history, down to the end of the last century, and far into the present, is therefore as incontrovertible as any fact can be. The bishops of that Church saw no sin in the treaty of Utrecht, to which the religious Queen Anne was a party. They concurred in the Act of Parliament under George the Third, which regarded the negroes as lawful merchandise. The Puritans of New-England sold the Indians as slaves, and were the chief importers of the Africans for the Southern market. Even the Quakers of Pennsylvania had slaves, and William Penn was a slaveholder, though that was the first State which passed an act of gradual abolition, and this estimable people have been among the most ardent and constant friends of the measure. Their principles, however, were in no substantial respect at variance with my own. They did not denounce slavery as a *sin* in itself, and the "sum of all villainies." They did not denounce the Constitution as "a covenant with death and an agreement with hell." They did not insist on *immediate emancipation*. And, above all, they sought to accomplish their object only by the use of kind persuasion and friendly argument, on the ground of a *wise expediency*, without bringing it into the region of party politics, without kindling hatred, discord, and strife between brethren, and with that love of "peace and good-will to men" which has so honorably marked their character.

CHAPTER XLII.

RIGHT REVEREND BROTHER: I now come to consider the *treatment* of the Southern slaves, which, in the popular mind, constitutes the main ground of the horror expressed by so many persons with regard to the institution. And here, I trust that I may claim as strong an antipathy to all cruelty and oppression, as becomes the character of a Christian minister. But this charge of cruelty concerns the religious consistency of thousands amongst my brethren : men who, though now unhappily separated from us by this deplorable war, are yet belonging to the same spiritual fraternity. Justice is due to those slaveholders, as well as to the slaves. I only ask that the evidence brought against them shall be tested fairly, by the same rules which apply to human conduct in general. And this can only be done by a comparison of the evils which the slaves suffer from their masters, with those to which the laboring classes are liable in the state of freedom.

The Journal of Mrs. Kemble, during her residence on the Georgia plantation of her husband, is one of the most popular books on the evils of negro slavery; and deservedly so, not only from its literary merits, and the wide-spread reputation of the writer, but mainly because it deals in facts, with actual knowledge, on the spot, of the practical results of the institution. And yet, passing from its perusal to the recent work of Joseph Kay, Esq., on the social condition of the people of England, no intelligent and candid mind can avoid the conviction that her picture of misery and degradation amongst the slaves falls far short of the delineations of brutalized licentiousness and debasement amongst the lower class of English freemen. I shall make a copious selection of extracts from this sadly interesting book, to prove the assertion.

"I speak it," saith Mr. Kay, "with sorrow and with shame, but with not the less confidence, that our peasantry are more ignorant, more demoralized, less capable of helping themselves, and more pauperized, than those of any country in Europe, if we except Russia,

Turkey, South Italy, and some parts of the Austrian Empire." (p. 24, Harper's New-York ed.)

" The laborer has no longer any connection with the land he cultivates; he has no stake in the country; he has nothing to lose, nothing to defend, and nothing to hope for," (p. 16.) "His position is one of hopeless and irremedial dependence. The work-house stands near him, pointing out his dismal fate if he falls one step lower," (p. 17.) " In the civilized world there are few sadder spectacles than the present contrast in Great Britain of unbounded wealth and luxury, with the starvation of thousands and tens of thousands, crowded into cellars and dens, without ventilation or light, compared with which *the wigwam of the Indian is a palace*. Misery, famine, brutal degradation, in the neighborhood of stately mansions which ring with gayety and dazzle with pomp and unbounded profusion, shock us as no other wretchedness does.—It is a striking fact that the private charity of England, though almost incredible, makes little impression on this mass of misery," (p. 28.)

The writer gives the following statement on the amount of *pauperism*, which is truly astounding:

" Before the enactment of the new poor-law," saith he, " we were expending annually between six and seven millions of pounds sterling for the relief of abject pauperism in England and Wales alone. Since then, we have been expending, in the same cause, between four and five millions per annum — without reckoning the vast sums which have been sunk in the administration of the poor-law in the different Unions, or the immense sums which have been given away annually by charitable individuals and societies. All this, be it remembered, has been required to alleviate the miserable condition of our laboring population, and to keep crowds from actual starvation. *Their independence is destroyed;* they can not live unless they depend upon the charity of the higher classes," (p. 29.)

Our author proceeds to show, from a carefully prepared table, the comparative increase of crime in the agricultural districts. " The proportional amount of crime to population," saith he, " in 1841 and 1847 was greater in almost all the agricultural counties of England than it was in the manufacturing and mining districts." This table " also shows how fearfully the amount of crime is increasing in the agricultural districts of Westmoreland, Lincoln, Cambridge, Huntingdon, Leicestershire, Rutland, Bedfordshire, Buckinghamshire, Wor-

cestershire, and Devonshire."—" Does not this show that the peasants of England must be subjected to a singularly demoralizing system, to produce so strange, so almost incredible a result?" (p. 44–5.)

He next passes on to the "awfully wretched state of the children
of London," and our author observes that "although this singular
account refers to London alone, it does in reality give a very correct
picture" of other cities. "In the towns of Lancashire," saith he,
"and in all the larger of the manufacturing and provincial towns,
the life and character of an equal proportion of the whole number of
the children is precisely similar to that of the juvenile population of
the back streets of London," (p. 45.)

They may be seen everywhere; "but in Lambeth and Westminster
we find the most flagrant traces of their swarming activity. There
the foul and dismal passages are thronged with children of both
sexes, and of every age from three to thirteen. Though wan and haggard, they are singularly vivacious, and engaged in every sort of occupation but that which would be beneficial to themselves and credit-
able to the neighborhood. Their appearance is wild; the matted hair,
the disgusting filth, that renders necessary a closer inspection, before
the flesh can be discerned between the rags which hang about it, and
the barbarian freedom from all superintendence and restraint, fill the
mind of a novice in these things with perplexity and dismay. Visit
those regions in the summer, and you are overwhelmed with the ex-
halations; visit them in the winter, and you are shocked by the
spectacle of hundreds shivering in apparel that would be scanty in
the tropics; many are all but naked; those that are clothed are gro-
tesque; the trowsers, when they have them, seldom pass the knee;
the tail-coats very frequently trail below the heels. In this guise
they run about the streets, and line the banks of the river at low
water, seeking coals, sticks, corks, for nothing comes amiss as
treasure trove," (pp. 60–1.)

" A large proportion of those who dwell in the capital, and all the
larger towns of the British empire, are crammed into regions of filth
and darkness, the ancient but not solitary reign of the newts and
toads."

" Here are the receptacles of the species we investigate; here they
are spawned, and here they perish. Can their state be a matter of
wonder? We have penetrated alleys terminating in a *cul-de-sac*,
long and narrow, like a tobacco-pipe, where air and sunshine were

never known. On one side rose walls several feet in height, blackened with damp and slime; on the other side stood the dwellings, still more revolting, while the breadth of the wet and bestrewed passage would by no means allow us the full expansion of our arms! We have waited at the entrance of another, of similar character and dimensions, but forbidden by the force and pungency of the odors to examine its recesses. The novelty of a visit from persons clad like gentlemen, gave the hope that we were official; and several women, haggard, rough, and exasperated, surrounded us at once, imploring us to order the removal of the filth, which had poisoned their tenements, and to grant them a supply of water, from which they had been debarred for many days. Pass to another district, you may find it less confined; but there you will see, flowing before each hovel, and within a few feet of it, a broad, black, uncovered drain, exhaling at every point the most unwholesome vapors. If there be not a drain, there is a stagnant pool; touch either with your stick, and the mephitic mass will yield up its poisonous gas like the coruscations of soda-water."

"The children sit along these depositories of death, or roam through the retired courts, in which the abominations of years have been suffered to accumulate. Here reigns a melancholy silence, seldom broken but by an irritated scold, or a pugnacious drunkard. The pale, discolored faces of the inhabitants, their shriveled forms, their abandoned exterior, recall the living skeletons of the Pontine marshes, and sufficiently attest the presence of a secret agency, hostile to every physical and moral improvement of the human race."

"The interior of the dwelling is in strict keeping; the smaller space of the apartments increasing, of course, the evils that prevail without—damp, darkness, dirt, and foul air. Many are wholly destitute of furniture; many contain nothing except a table and a chair; some few have a common bed for all ages and both sexes, but a large proportion of the denizens of these regions lie on a heap of rags more nasty than the floor itself. Happy is the family that can boast of a single room to itself, and in that room, of a dry corner."

"The children that survive the noxious influences and awful neglect, are thrown, as soon as they can crawl, to scramble in the gutter, and leave their parents to amusement or business." . . . .

"The '*duris ingens in rebus egestas*' stimulates these independent urchins; and at an age when the children of the wealthy would still be in leading-strings, they are off, singly or in parties, to beg, borrow, steal, and exercise all the cunning that want and a love of evil can stir up in a reckless race."

"This is a fair picture of the state of things in all our larger towns," (p. 61–3.)

The author gives a sad account of what he rightly calls "a very singular and very melancholy proof of the degradation and pauperism of a great part of the laboring population. Large and ever-increasing hordes of vagrants or wandering beggars infest all the highways of England and Wales. These poor wretches are miserably clothed, filthily dirty, covered with vermin, and generally very much diseased; sometimes from debauchery, and sometimes—though this would appear to be the exceptional case—from the want of food. These vagrants consist, in some parts of the country, of nearly equal parts of Irish and English; while, in other parts, two thirds of them are Irish, and the other third English. They are composed of persons of both sexes, and of all ages. Very few are married. The women, of whom there are great numbers, are nearly all prostitutes. Each man is generally attended by one or two such companions in misery and crime."

"To nearly every work-house there are attached-what are called vagrant-wards, or buildings which are specially set apart for the reception of tramps, such as those I have described. In some places, such is the filthy state of the poor wretches who are admitted at night, that it is necessary to have the framework of the beds whitewashed every day. In many places it is found impossible to give them beds, because the tramps swarm so horribly with vermin. In those cases, a rug is allowed to each, and the rug is washed in the morning."

"Men are kept, in order to guard these foul receptacles every night, but it is needless to observe that nothing can prevent scenes which I may not attempt to describe," (p. 73–5.) "The conduct of the poor wretches is reported to be bad in the extreme. They are described as being noisy and turbulent; as making the wards resound with the vilest songs and language; as being ungrateful and refractory towards the ward-officers, and as having habits too filthy and indecent to be named," (p. 76.)

"If I were only to state," saith our author, "that 16,000 of such poor wretches were wandering about our roads begging alms in 1848,

I should give no idea of the magnitude of this plague. Hitherto, I have only spoken of those who seek shelter for the night in the work-house vagrant-wards. But besides these, there are vast numbers who sleep every night in the vagrant lodging-houses in the towns. These lodging-houses, which are to be found in most of our towns, consist of long low rooms, filled with beds or mattresses, upon which the vagrants of all ages and of both sexes sleep, two or three in one bed or upon one mattress. These rooms are unventilated, seldom cleaned, filthy and close beyond comprehension to those who have not been into them. In these dens, the vagrants, pickpockets, beggars, and, in fine, all the houseless wanderers of the streets, sleep, crowded together—old men and young men, old women and young women, and children of all ages, from the infant at the breast, to the boy who is just ripening into the felon. The scenes which take place are horrible. In one bed sleeps a man with two women ; in another, a woman with two men ; in another, two or three women or men ; in another, a poor mother and her children. Drunkards, pickpockets, prostitutes, and beggars, covered with vermin, are packed in together. Foul songs, oaths, drunken yells, and groans mingle every night in one sad chorus, until sleep closes the eyes of all," (p. 79–80.)

"One of the city missionaries, describing the state of the Mint district in London, says : ' It is utterly impossible to describe the scenes which are to be witnessed here, or to set forth, in its naked deformity, the awful characters sin here assumes. . . . *In Mint street alone, there are nineteen lodging-houses*, the majority of which are awful sinks of iniquity. Quarrels and fights are very common, and the cry of murder is frequently heard. The public-houses in this street are crowded to excess, especially in the Sabbath evenings," (p. 80–81.)

"If the nightly inmates of these dens are added to the tramps who seek lodging in the vagrant-wards of the work-houses, we shall find that there are at least between 40,000 and 50,000 tramps daily infesting our roads and streets," (p. 81.)

Now all this is revolting enough, but the next set of facts which this author sets forth is still more so. "Another sad symptom of the condition of the poor," saith he, "is the use they make of the ' burial clubs.' In some of our towns the degradation of many of the poor is such, that parents often cause the death of their children in

13

order to obtain the premiums from the societies. It appears that in our larger provincial towns the poor are in the habit of entering their children in what are called 'burial clubs.' A small sum is paid every year by the parent, and this entitles him to receive from three to five pounds from the club, on the death of the child. Many parents enter their children in several clubs. One man in Manchester has been known to enter his child in nineteen different clubs. On the death of such a child, the parent becomes entitled to a large sum of money, and as the burial of the child does not necessarily cost more than one pound and ten shillings, the parent realizes a considerable sum after all the expenses are paid."

"It has been clearly ascertained that it is a common practice among the more degraded classes of poor in many of our towns, to enter their infants in these clubs, and then to cause their death, either by starvation, ill-usage, or poison! What more horrible symptom of moral degradation can be conceived? One's mind revolts against it, and would fain reject it as a monstrous fiction. But alas! it seems to be but too true," (p. 82.)

This awful statement is proved by numerous cases, which occupy twelve pages of the book. And the author concludes by saying: "There can be no doubt that a great part of the poorer classes of this country are sunk into such a frightful depth of hopelessness, misery, and utter moral degradation, that even mothers forget their affection for their helpless little offspring, and kill them, as a butcher does his lambs, in order to make money by the murder, and therewith to lessen their pauperism and misery," (p. 94.)

Mr. Kay passes on from this terrible statement to the "great numbers and miserable condition of the inhabitants of the cellars."

"In all our larger towns," saith he, "and especially in those in which manufactures are carried on, there are a great number of cellars beneath the houses of the small shopkeepers and operatives, which are inhabited by crowds of the poor. These rooms measure, in Liverpool, from ten to twelve feet square. In some towns they are rather larger. They are generally flagged. The flags lie directly upon the earth, and are generally wretchedly damp. In wet weather they are very often not dry for weeks together. Within a few feet from the windows rises the wall which keeps the street from falling in, darkening the gloomy rooms, and preventing the sun's rays from penetrating into them."

"Dr. Duncan, in describing the cellar-houses of the manufacturing districts, says: 'The cellars are ten or twelve feet square, generally flagged, but frequently having only the bare earth for a floor, and sometimes less than six feet in height. There is frequently no window, so that light and air can gain access to the cellar only by the door, the top of which is often not higher than the level of the street. In such cellars, ventilation is out of the question. They are of course dark, and, from the defective drainage, they are very generally damp," (pp. 95-6.)

"They have never more than two, and generally only one room each, but small as they are, they are crowded to excess. It is no uncommon thing for two and three, and sometimes for four families, to live and sleep together in one of these rooms, without any division or separation whatever for the different families or sexes. There are very few cellars where at least two families do not herd together in this manner. Their beds are made sometimes of a mattress, and sometimes of straw in the corners of the cellar, and upon the damp, cold, flag floor; and on these miserable sleeping-places, the father, mother, sons, and daughters crowd together in a state of filthy indecency, and *much worse off than the horses in an ordinary stable.* In these cellar-houses, no distinction of sex and age is made. Sometimes a man is found sleeping with one woman, sometimes with two women, and sometimes with young girls; sometimes brothers and sisters of the age of eighteen, nineteen, and twenty, are found in bed together, while at other times the husband and wife share the bed with all their children."

"The poor creatures who inhabit these miserable receptacles are of the most degraded species; they have never learned to read; have never heard of the existence of a Deity; have never been inside a church, being scared from the door by their own filth and wretchedness, and have scarcely any sense of a distinction between right and wrong."

"I have heard gentlemen who have visited these kinds of dens in London say, that they have found men and women sleeping together, three and four in a single bed, that they have not disturbed or shamed them in the least by discovering them in these situations, but that, on the contrary, *their remonstrances have been answered only by a laugh or by a sneer,*" (p. 96-7.)

"In the twelve wards forming the parish of Liverpool, there are

6294 inhabited cellars, containing 20,168 inhabitants, exclusive of the inhabited cellars in courts, of which there are 621, containing probably 2000 inhabitants." And these numbers Dr. Duncan thinks are "under the mark." "The whole of the cellar population of the parish, upwards of 20,000, are absolutely without any place of deposit for their refuse matter," (p. 97–8.)

"But what," continues our author, "is the condition of the houses of the poor in our towns and villages? The further we examine, the more painful, disgusting, and incredible does the tale become!"

"We see on every hand stately palaces, to which no country in the world offers any parallel. The houses of our rich are more gorgeous and more luxurious than those of any other land. Every clime is ransacked to adorn them. The soft carpets, the heavy rich curtains, the luxuriously easy couches, the beds of down, the services of plate, the numerous servants, the splendid equipages, and all the expensive objects of literature, science, and the arts, which crowd the palaces of England, form but items in an *ensemble* of refinement and magnificence which was never imagined or approached in all the splendor of the ancient empires. But look beneath all this display and luxury, and what do we see there? A pauperized and suffering people."

"To maintain show, we have degraded the masses, until we have created an evil so vast, that we now despair of ever finding a remedy. The Irish poor have drunk the dregs of the cup of misery, and are hardly kept from revolution by the strong arm of the soldiers and police; while the English poor are only saved from despair and its dread consequences, by the annual expenditure of MANY MILLIONS in relief, which our own neglect and misgovernment have rendered necessary," (p. 99–100.)

If this dreadful picture were confined to the condition of the poor in the cities and towns, it would be a very melancholy spectacle. But unhappily it extends to the country at large. For thus our author proceeds with his sad narration.

"Miserable," saith he, "as the habitations of a great part of the poor of our towns are, the cottages and the cottage life of the peasants are still worse, and, what is more, they have been for some time past, and still are, rapidly deteriorating. The majority of the cottages are wretchedly built, often in very unhealthy sites; they are miserably small, and are crowded to excess; they are very low, seldom drained, and badly roofed; and they scarcely ever have any cellar or space under the floor of the lower rooms. The floors are formed either of flags, which rest upon the cold, undrained ground, or, as is often the case, of nothing better than a mixture of clay and lime, which receives, day after day, and year after year, water and droppings of all kinds, and gives back pestilential vapors, injurious to the health of the inhabitants. Such cottages are fit abodes for a peasantry pauperized and demoralized by the utter hopelessness of their situation," (p. 115–6.)

"The accounts we receive from all parts of the country show that these miserable cottages are crowded to an extreme, and that the crowding is progressively increasing. People of both sexes, and of all ages, married and unmarried, parents, brothers, sisters, and strangers, sleep in the same rooms and often in the same beds. Women have been delivered in bed-rooms crowded with men, young women, and children, and facts are witnessed much too horrible to be alluded to. Nor are these solitary instances, but similar reports are given by gentlemen writing in ALL parts of the country," (p. 117–8.)

"The landlords are unwilling to increase the number of the cottages in the rural districts, because they fear to increase the numbers of the resident laboring population, and the amount of their poor-rates; and they are generally unwilling, even when they are able, to spend money in improving the size or character of the cottages, because they know that they can easily let any of the existing cottages, no matter how wretched, owing to the great demand for house-room."

"The crowding of the cottages has, therefore, of late, been growing worse and worse. The promiscuous mingling of the sexes in the bed-rooms has been increasing very much, and is productive of worse consequences every year. Adultery is the very mildest form of the vast amount of crime which it is engendering. We are told by magistrates, clergymen, surgeons, and union officers, that *cases of incest, and reports of other cases of the same enormity, are becoming more and more common,*" (p. 119.)

"Such is the hideous social system to which we have subjected our poor," (p. 123.)

The apathy with which this matter is regarded by all the parties, is strongly stated by our author.

"One singular thing is," saith he, "that this state of things has existed so long, that *the poor have sunk below complaining*, and that the landlords and richer classes are quite surprised, if you talk to them of the miserable condition of the peasants' cottages. They have learned to think it a *necessary state of things*, and ridicule the idea of its being the result of a system of defective legislation. Many go much further and boldly maintain that *it is better that the peasants should not be educated*, as education would make them thoroughly discontented with their present position in life," (p. 126.)

With respect to the diseases of the English peasantry, we have the following statement :

"Fever, and scrofula in all its forms, prevail under such circumstances," (p. 134.) And the nourishment is of the humblest quality. "Persons living in these cottages are generally very poor, very dirty, and usually in rags, *living almost wholly on bread and potatoes, scarcely ever tasting animal food*, and consequently highly susceptible of disease, and very unable to contend with it," (p. 135.)

"It is impossible," says a writer quoted by Mr. Kay, "fully to estimate the wretchedness to which the inmates of the hovels, which meet the eye at all points, are exposed, without a close personal inspection of them. We are accustomed to associate with the idea of a country village, or with a cottage situated in a winding vale, or hanging upon the side of a rich and fertile slope, nothing but health, contentment, and happiness. A rural dwelling of this class, with its heavy thatch and embowering trees, makes such a nice pencil-sketch, that we are naturally inclined to think it as neat and comfortable as it appears. But to know it aright, it must be turned inside out, and its realities exposed to the gaze of the observer. How often does the cot which looks so attractive and romantic upon paper, conceal an amount of wretchedness, filth, squalor, disease, privation, and frequently of immorality, which, when exposed in their reality, are perfectly appalling? It is high time that people divested themselves of the false impressions too generally entertained of the character of our rural cottages. They are chiefly drawn from descriptions which at one time may have suited the reality, when the condition of the agricultural laborer was much better than it is now ; for that it was much better than at present, is evident from the information derived from a variety of valuable sources. To go a considerable way back : we find Fortescue alluding to their condition in his day, as one of great comfort and happiness ; inasmuch as they lived chiefly upon butcher meat, of which they had plenty, and had abundance of good ale, with which to accompany it at their meals. In regard to their diet, at least, their condition now seems the very reverse of what it was then; and as it is impossible that they could have fallen back so much in this important element of their physical condition, without having all the others deteriorated in the same proportion, it is fair to infer that their house accommodation was better formerly than now. It was better in this, if in no other respect—that fewer people were to be found under one and the same roof,—a state of things much more favorable to health, cleanliness, and good morals, than that which now prevails. We must therefore judge of the laborer's condition, not from past descriptions of it, but from the sad realities of the present hour," (142–4.)

Describing one of the parish houses on the borders of Devonshire and Cornwall, our author saith, that "In each room there lived a family, night and day, the space being about twelve feet square. In one were a man and his wife and eight children; the father, mother, and two children lay in one bed, the remaining six were huddled 'head and foot,' (three at the top and three at the foot,) in the other bed. The eldest girl was between fifteen and sixteen, the eldest boy between fourteen and fifteen! Is it not horrible to think of men and women being brought up in this *foul, brutish manner* in civilized and Christian England? The *lowest of savages are not worse cared for than these children of a luxurious and refined country*," (p. 151.)

"It is, perhaps, worthy of remark, that dishes, plates, and other articles of crockery seem almost unknown. There is, however, the less need for them, as *grist bread forms the principal and, I believe, the only kind of food that falls to the laborer's lot.*" In no single instance did I observe meat of any kind during my progress. The furniture is such as may be expected — a rickety table and two or three foundered chairs generally forming the extent," (p. 153.)

"This misery," says another country rector, "is not confined to Dorsetshire. If you go to Devonshire, Wiltshire, and the hill country of Gloucestershire, you will find the peasant *at the point of starvation*," (p. 154.)

"We need not wonder," continues our author, "if we find that the amount of crime in counties, where the peasants are in such a horrible social condition, is alarmingly and terribly increasing. The *Times* of the 30th of November, 1849, shows this terrible increase of crime in the last few years in Dorsetshire. 'We yesterday published,' saith the editor, 'in a very short compass, some grave particulars of the unfortunate county of Dorset. It is not simply the old story of wages inadequate for life, hovels unfit for habitation, and misery and sin alternately claiming our pity and our disgust. This state of things is so normal, and we really believe so immemorial, in that notorious county, that we should rather deaden than excite the anxiety of the public by a thrice-told tale. What compels our attention just now is a sudden, rapid, and, we fear, a forced aggravation of these evils, measured by the infallible test of crime. Dorsetshire is fast sinking into a slough of wretchedness, which threatens the peace and morality of the kingdom at large. The total number of convictions which, in 1846, was seven hundred and ninety-eight, in 1847, eight hundred and twenty-one, in 1848, nine hundred and fifty, mounted up in 1849 to the astonishing number of one thousand three hundred for the whole year! Unless something is done to stop this flood of crime, or the tide happily turns of itself, the county will have more than *doubled* its convictions within four years!" (p. 156-7.)

Again, speaking of the hovels of the peasants, the author saith: "During the present century, we have been building dwellings for the poor, as if we were *running up sties for pigs*," (p. 162.)

"The food of the laborer and his family in Norfolk and Suffolk is principally bread, potatoes, and the Norfolk dumpling, which consists of the dough of which the bread is made. *In none of the cottages that I have visited in either of the three counties have I ever seen such a thing as a piece of fresh butcher's meat,*" (p. 164.)

"One species of immorality, which is peculiarly prevalent in these counties, is that of bastardy—being fifty-three per cent above the average of England or Wales. *There appears to be a perfect want of decency among the people.* 'The immorality of the young women,' said the rector of the parish to me, ' is literally horrible, and I regret to say it is on the increase in a most extraordinary degree. When I first came to the town, the mother of a bastard child used to be ashamed to show herself. The case is now quite altered; *no person seems to think any thing at all of it.* When I first came to the town, there was no such thing as a common prostitute in it; now, there is an enormous number of them. When I am called on to see a woman confined with an illegitimate child, I endeavor to impress upon her the enormity of the offense; and *there are no cases in which I receive more insult from those I visit than from such persons.* They generally say: 'They'll get on as well, after all that's said about it, and if they never do any thing worse than that, they shall get to heaven as well as other people.' There appears to be, among the lower orders, a perfect *deadness of all moral feeling* upon this subject," (p. 169.)

With respect to the mining and manufacturing populations in Wales, the evidence is nothing better. Thus the Rev. John Griffith saith : "Nothing can be lower, I would say more degrading, than the character in which the women stand relative to the men. The men and women, married as well as single, sleep in the same room. *Promiscuous intercourse is most common, is thought of as nothing, and the women do not lose caste by it*," (p. 183.)

Again, saith Edward W. Seymour, Esq., speaking of the mining districts : " The vices of lying, thieving, swearing, and drunkenness, and the vastly increasing crime of illicit intercourse between the sexes, prevail to a great extent, and these are by no means confined to the uneducated," (p. 189.)

The Rev. James Denning, Brecknock, saith that " the poor seem ignorant on most subjects, except how to cheat and speak evil of each other. They appear not to have an idea what the comforts of life are. There are at least two thousand persons living in this town in a state of the greatest filth, and to all appearance they enjoy their filth and idleness, for they make no effort to get rid of it. From my experience of Ireland, I think there is a great similarity between the lower orders of Welsh and Irish—both are dirty, indolent, bigoted, and contented."—"The number of illegitimate children, when compared with England, is astounding," (p. 190.)

" Morals are generally at a low ebb, but want of chastity is the giant sin of Wales."

But others say that " the lower classes of Wales are far superior to the same class in other parts of the kingdom," (p. 192.)

Speaking of the mining population of Monmouthshire, Mr. Symons says : " Evil in every shape is rampant in this district, demoralization is everywhere dominant, and all good influences are comparatively powerless. They drink to the most brutal excess. They have little regard to modesty or the truth, and even the young children in the streets, who can scarcely articulate, give utterance to imprecations. The bodies and habits of the people are almost as dirty as the towns and houses of the swarthy region in which they swarm. The whole district, with the exception of Newport, teems with crime,

and all the slatternly accompaniments of animal power and moral
disorder, with scarcely a ray of mental or spiritual intelligence.
The people are savage in their manner, and mimic the repulsive rude-
ness of those in authority over them," (p. 199.)

"The Rev. St. George Armstrong Williams testifies that the moral
principles of the Welsh people are totally corrupt and abandoned in
this respect. *While the sexes continue to herd like beasts, it were
idle to expect that they can be restrained by religion or conscience.*
I assert with confidence as an undeniable fact, that fornication is not
regarded as a vice, scarcely as a frailty, by the common people in
Wales. *It is avowed, defended, and laughed at, without scruple, or
shame, or concealment, by both sexes alike,*" (p. 211.)

On the state of education, the assertions of our author are what
might be expected from the foregoing. Thus he saith, that "about
one half of our poor can neither read nor write, have never been in
any school, and know little, or positively nothing, of the doctrines of
the Christian religion, of moral duties, or of any higher pleasure than
beer or spirit-drinking and the grossest sensual indulgence. They
live *precisely like brutes,* to gratify, as far as their means allow, the
appetites of their uncultivated bodies, and then die, to go they have
never thought, cared, or wondered, whither. Brought up in the
darkness of barbarism, they have no idea that it is possible for them
to attain any higher condition; they are not even sentient enough to
desire, with any strength of feeling, to change their situation; they
are not intelligent enough to be perseveringly discontented; they are
not sensible to what we call the voice of conscience; they do not understand the necessity of avoiding crime, beyond the mere fear of the
police and a jail; they do not in the least comprehend that what is
the interest of society is their own also; they do not in the least understand the meaning, necessity, or effect of the laws—they eat, drink,
breed, work, and die; and while they pass through their brute-like
existence here, the richer and more intelligent classes are obliged to
guard them with police and standing armies, and to cover the land
with prisons, cages, and all kinds of receptacles for those who, in
their thoughtlessness or misery, disturb the quiet and happiness of
their more intelligent and consequently more moral and prosperous
neighbors, by plunder, assault, or any other deed which the law is
obliged, for the sake of the existence of society, to designate a 'crime,

although most of those who commit it do not in the least comprehend its criminality," (pp. 2, 16, 17.)

"Let it not be said that this picture is too strongly drawn. *The subject is one which does not admit of exaggeration*," (p. 219.)

"It has been calculated that there are at the present day, in England and Wales, nearly *eight millions of persons who can not read and write*."

"Of all the children in England and Wales, between the ages of five and fourteen, more than the half are not attending any school."

"Even of the class of the farmers, there are great numbers who can not read and write."

"Of the teachers who are officiating in many of the village schools, there are many who can not read and write correctly, and who know very little of the Bible which they profess to explain."

"A very great part of our present village and town schools are managed by poor and miserably instructed dames, who thus seek to gain a livelihood, and who literally do no good to the children, except it be by keeping them for a certain number of hours in the day, out of the dirt, and out of worse society," (p. 252–3.)

"In most of our schools, it is necessary, in order to provide salaries for the teacher, and funds for the support of the school, to charge from twopence to fourpence a week per head, for the instruction of scholars. This absolutely excludes the children of all paupers and of all poor persons, who can not afford to pay so much out of their small earnings," (p. 255.)

I conclude these multiplied extracts with a few strong words of serious warning, on the inevitable results of the awful condition of the masses in Great Britain.

"We stand," saith Mr. Kay, "on dangerous ground. We know not now how far the mine has been excavated. We know not how strong the enemy is; but certain it is that a spirit omnipotent for evil, a spirit of revolution, irreverence, irreligion, and recklessness, and, more dangerous than all, a spirit of unchecked, unguided, and licentious intelligence, is abroad, which will be the most dangerous enemy with which Christianity has hitherto had to cope. If religious teachers are not found, and that soon, for this people, where will the Church be fifty years hence? Where the French Church was in 1796—overthrown by an infidel multitude. Can any one look on, for the next half century, without dismay?" (p. 294.)

"I repeat that the great majority of the people in the great towns of this kingdom *have no religion*," (p. 298.)

"Here, with our vast accumulated masses; with a population increasing by 1000 per diem; with an expenditure on abject pauperism which amounts to £5,000,000 per annum; with a terrible deficiency in the numbers of our churches and of our clergy; with the most demoralizing publications spread through the cottages of our operatives; with democratic ideas of the wildest kind, and a knowledge of the power of union daily gaining ground among them;—here, too, where the poor have no stake whatever in the country,—where the most frightful discrepancy exists between the richer and the poorer classes; where the poor fancy they have nothing to lose and every thing to gain from a revolution;—where the majority of the operatives have no religion;—where our very freedom is a danger, unless the people are taught to use and not abuse it,—and here, too, where the aristocracy is richer and more powerful than that of any other country in the world—*the poor are more depressed, more pauperized, more irreligious, and very much worse educated than the poor of any other European nation, solely excepting Russia, Turkey, South Italy, Portugal, and Spain.* Such a state of things can not long continue!" (p. 322–3.)

CHAPTER XLIII.

RIGHT REVEREND BROTHER: The book of Mr. Kay, from which I have made so many extracts, is a perfect demonstration that millions of people, descended from the superior races of mankind, are in a worse condition, by far, in free England, than the negro slaves of the South, in their social habits, in their sense of morality and religion, and in every other element of human comfort.

But the Southern slaves are subject to the lash of the overseer, if they are insubordinate! Suppose they are, no man doubts that some kind of discipline is necessary for those who are idle and refractory; and the only question is whether the summary punishment of twelve stripes* is more cruel than the substitute of imprisonment, which modern philanthropy prefers, on the ground of its greater humanity. I confess that I am more than doubtful of the assumption that the wisdom of our age has made any improvement on the practice of former times in this matter. The Mosaic law, which was divine, ordered forty stripes even for the free Israelite; and children were to be corrected by the rod, as a necessary element in their moral and religious training. I shall quote the words of Scripture, however, not for your information, of course, but for my other readers; as a familiarity with the language of the Bible on these subjects is by no means common, at this day. Thus then we read in Deut. 25 : 1–3 :

"If there be a controversy between men, and they come unto judgment, that the judges may judge them, then they shall justify the righteous, and condemn the wicked. And if the wicked man be worthy to be beaten, the judge shall cause him to lie down, and to be beaten before his face, according to his fault, by a certain number. Forty stripes he may give him and not exceed, lest if he should exceed, and beat him with many stripes, then thy brother should seem vile unto thee."

* This is all, according to Mrs. Kemble, which are allowed to be given in the field. In bad cases, the head overseer may extend the punishment to fifty, which is rarely exceeded.

The same kind of discipline is recognized in the book of Proverbs. Thus, ch. 10, v. 13 : "A rod is for the back of him that is void of understanding." Again, ch. 26, v. 3 : "A whip for the horse, a bridle for the ass, and a rod for the fool's back."

And we find it most expressly laid down in the education of children, Prov. 13 : 24: "He that spareth the rod, hateth his son; but he that loveth him, chasteneth him betimes." Again, ch. 22, v. 15: "Foolishness is bound in the heart of a child, but the rod of correction shall drive it far from him." Again, ch. 23, v. 13-4, "Withhold not correction from the child, for if thou beatest him with the rod, he shall not die. Thou shalt beat him with the rod, and shalt deliver his soul from hell."

Here there is no restriction laid upon the parent with respect to the number of stripes, because the affection of the father was a sufficient guard against excess. And in the case of the slave, there was no restriction, since the interest of the master was enough, as a general rule, to prevent undue severity, which could only deprive him of the labor of the servant, and thus prove to be a loss to himself, independent of the feelings of humanity.

But the strongest evidence in favor of bodily correction is that which our blessed Saviour gave in person. For thus we read, (John 2 : 13–5:) "And the Jews' Passover was at hand, and Jesus went up to Jerusalem, and found in the temple those that sold oxen, and sheep, and doves, and the changers of money sitting ; and when he had made a *scourge of small cords*, he drove them all out of the temple," etc.

I have briefly referred to these passages in the *Bible View of Slavery*, but I set them forth here in full, because there is nothing which I regard with more regret than the disposition, so manifest in our day, to regard such precepts as only fit for a barbarous age, and totally inconsistent with the mild precepts of the Gospel. It is a slander on the character of God to charge His laws with any thing like cruelty, or unnecessary harshness. On the contrary, I maintain that His system, as laid down for His chosen people, paid more regard to love, and tenderness, and consideration for the poor, than any code of laws which has ever existed, or now exists, in the boasted refinement and philanthropy of the nineteenth century. And I shall proceed to prove this statement by positive testimony from the same book of Deuteronomy, which commands the use of the scourge, even to the free Israelite. Thus, then, we read:

" Thou shalt love the Lord thy God with all thine heart, and with all thy soul, and with all thy might." (Deut. 6 : 5.)

" The Lord did not set his love upon you, nor choose you, because ye were more in number than any people, for ye were the fewest of all people; but because the Lord loved you, and because he would keep the oath which he had sworn unto your fathers." (Deut. 7 : 7–8.)

" He doth execute the judgment of the fatherless and widow, and loveth the stranger in giving him food and raiment. Love ye therefore the stranger, for ye were strangers in the land of Egypt." (Deut. 10 : 18–9.)

" At the end of every seven years thou shalt make a release. Every creditor that lendeth aught unto his neighbor shall release it; he shall not exact it of his neighbor, or of his brother; because it is called the Lord's release. Of a foreigner thou mayest exact it again : but that which is thine with thy brother thine hand shall release." (Deut. 15 : 1–3.)

" If there be among you a poor man of one of thy brethren within any of thy gates in thy land which the Lord thy God giveth thee, thou shalt not harden thy heart, nor shut thy hand from thy poor brother, but thou shalt open thine hand wide unto him, and shalt surely lend him sufficient for his need, in that which he wanteth."

" Beware that there be not a thought in thy wicked heart, saying : The seventh year, the year of release, is at hand, and thine eye be evil against thy poor brother, and thou givest him nought; and he cry unto the Lord against thee, and it be sin unto thee. Thou shalt surely give him, and thine heart shall not be grieved when thou givest unto him; because that for this thing the Lord thy God shall bless thee in all thy works, and in all thou puttest thine hand unto. For the poor shall never cease out of the land : therefore I command thee, saying, thou shalt open thine hand wide unto thy brother, to thy poor, and to thy needy, in thy land." (Deut. 15 : 7–11.)

" Thou shalt observe the feast of tabernacles seven days, after that thou hast gathered in thy corn and thy wine. And thou shalt rejoice in thy feast, thou, and thy son, and thy daughter, and thy man-servant, and thy maidservant, (thy *bondman* and thy *bondmaid* in the

Hebrew,) and the Levite, the stranger, and the fatherless, and the widow, that are within thy gates." (Deut. 16 : 13–4.)

These passages clearly prove that the great law of love to God and love to man was the fundamental principle in this divine system. The release of all debts every seventh year, the benevolence and liberal charity to the poor, and the special regard paid to the stranger, the orphan, and the widow, stand preëminent above the legislation of the whole Christian world, and claim our highest reverence and admiration.

But now I pass to the divine rule in time of war, which is marked with such peculiar regard for human feelings, viz. :

"When thou goest out to battle against thine enemies, and seest horses, and chariots, and a people more than thou, be not afraid of them, for the Lord thy God is with thee, which brought thee up out of the land of Egypt. And it shall be, when ye are come nigh unto the battle, that the priest shall approach and speak unto the people, and shall say unto them: Hear, O Israel, ye approach this day unto battle against your enemies ; let not your hearts faint; fear not, and do not tremble, neither be ye terrified because of them ; for the Lord your God is he that goeth with you, to fight for you against your enemies, to save you."

"And the officers shall speak unto the people, saying: What man is there that hath built a new house and hath not dedicated it ? Let him go and return to his house, lest he die in the battle, and another man dedicate it. And what man is he that hath planted a vineyard, and hath not yet eaten of it ? Let him also go unto his house, lest he die in the battle, and another man eat of it. And what man is there that hath betrothed a wife, and hath not taken her ? Let him go and return unto his house, lest he die in the battle, and another man take her."

"And the officers shall speak further unto the people, and they shall say : What man is there that is fearful and faint-hearted ? Let him go and return to his house, lest his brethren's heart fail as well as his heart." (Deut. 20 : 1–9.)

Here we see a contrast between the laws of God and the laws of men, which is a wonderfully impressive proof of the tenderness to natural human feeling, manifest throughout this divine system. There is no dragging of the unwilling soldier from his house, his vineyard, or his betrothed bride, against his will. Even the shrinking of the coward is respected, instead of shooting him for a defect which is rooted in his physical temperament, and beyond his control. Indeed it is remarkable, that in the whole Bible there is no praise bestowed on mere physical courage, for this belongs only to the animal part of human nature. We see it in the brutes, and even in the insects. The hornet and the enraged bee will follow a man for a mile, and attack him with fury. But what human being would venture to assault a creature as much superior to himself in size and strength, as the man is superior to the insect? So we see it in the dog, that some of the species are endowed by nature with the most obstinate courage, as the mastiff and the bull-dog; while others, like the spaniel, could never be made to fight, by any training. So with the birds. Some are made for violent assaults, as the eagle and the hawk, but who would expect the dove to manifest the same ferocity? All these varieties of natural temperament may be found in man, who is the head and complement of the creation in our lower world. And hence, the courage which belongs merely to our physical constitution is no just subject of praise from the Almighty. It is the animal nature, and nothing more. The *moral courage of the soul* is quite another thing, because it is the result of spiritual principle. This, therefore, and this only, is properly a virtue. Such was the courage of David when he offered himself to the combat against Goliath, in faithful reliance on the God of Israel. Such was the courage of the noble three, who were ready for the fiery furnace, rather than bow down before the idol of the Babylonian king. Such was the courage of the blessed Apostles, who endured scourging, imprisonment, and death, in the service of their divine Master. Such was the courage of the martyrs in all ages. And such is the courage which alone may claim the admiration of the Christian, and the approval of the divine Redeemer, in the judgment of the great day.

But this code of laws contains several other commandments, bearing on the same subject of a kind and affectionate spirit, which distinguish it above all other systems as the work of the God of love. For thus we read in the twenty-second chapter:

" Thou shalt not see thy brother's ox or his sheep go astray, and hide thyself from them; thou shalt in any case bring them again unto thy brother. And if thy brother be not nigh unto thee, or if thou know him not, then thou shalt bring it unto thine own house, and it shall be with thee until thy brother seek after it, and thou

shalt restore it to him again."—"And with all lost things of thy
brother's, which he hath lost and thou hast found, shalt thou do likewise ; thou mayest not hide thyself."

"Thou shalt not see thy brother's ass or his ox fall down by the
way, and hide thyself from them ; thou shalt surely help him to lift
them up again."

"If a bird's-nest chance to be before thee in the way, in any tree,
or on the ground, whether they be young ones or eggs, and the dam
sitting upon the young or upon the eggs, thou shalt not take the dam
with the young ; but thou shalt in any wise let the dam go, and take
the young to thee, that it may be well with thee, and that thou mayest prolong thy days."

"When thou buildest a new house, then thou shalt make a battle-
ment for thy roof, that thou bring not blood upon thine house, if any
man fall from thence." (Deut. 22 : 1–8.)

"When a man hath taken a new wife, he shall not go out to war,
neither shall he be charged with any business ; but he shall be free
at home one year, and shall cheer up the wife which he hath
taken."

"No man shall take the nether or the upper mill-stone to pledge ;
for he taketh a man's life to pledge."

"When thou dost lend thy brother any thing, thou shalt not go
into his house to fetch his pledge : thou shalt stand abroad, and
the man to whom thou dost lend shall bring out the pledge abroad
unto thee."

"And if the man be poor, thou shalt not sleep with his pledge : In
any case thou shalt deliver him the pledge again when the sun goeth
down, that he may sleep in his own raiment, and bless thee ; and it
shall be righteousness unto thee before the Lord thy God."

"Thou shalt not oppress an hired servant that is poor and needy,
whether he be of thy brethren, or of thy strangers that are in the
land within thy gates. At his day thou shalt give him his hire,
neither shall the sun go down upon it, for he is poor and setteth his
heart upon it : lest he cry unto the Lord, and it be sin unto thee."

"When thou cuttest down thine harvest in thy field, and hast forgotten a sheaf in the field, thou shalt not go again to fetch it ; it shall
be for the stranger, the fatherless and the widow : that the Lord thy
God may bless thee in all the work of thine hands."

"When thou beatest thine olive-tree, thou shalt not go over the boughs again : it shall be for the stranger, the fatherless, and the widow."

"When thou gatherest the grapes of thy vineyard, thou shalt not glean it afterwards ; it shall be for the stranger, the fatherless, and the widow."

"And thou shalt remember that thou wast a bondman in the land of Egypt ; therefore I command thee to do this thing." (Deut. 24 : 5–6, 10–5, 19–22.)

Now we may search in vain through the whole legislation of the world for any thing to be compared with these laws of the God of Israel, so full of tender compassion for the poor, of brotherly kindness in the acts of social interest, and even of pitiful consideration towards the birds and beasts ; the least performance of mercy being regarded by Him, without whom the sparrow can not fall to the ground, and His favor being only assured to those who cherish, in their daily life, the spirit of benevolent affection.

When, therefore, we find that the same God of love directs offend- ers to be chastised with the scourge, and even orders the rod to be used in the education of children, we can not, without absolute im- piety, suppose that these punishments are cruel, or liable to be charged with inhumanity. On the contrary, we are bound to believe that they were dictated by the unerring wisdom of Him who thor- oughly understands the requirements of human nature, and who com- manded them precisely because he knew that they were best adapted to secure the proper objects of all punishment, namely, the reforma- tion of the offender, and the warning of others against the offense. To show how this should be understood by every Christian believer, will be my labor in the next chapter.

CHAPTER XLIV.

RIGHT REVEREND BROTHER: In the divine system laid down for the chosen people, we read nothing of imprisonment for debt, or for crime, or for any offense against established authority. The debtor might be sold for six years, in order to pay the creditor by his labor, and if this did not suffice, the remainder of the debt was canceled, and the creditor was obliged to let him go free. The thief was compelled to make restitution fourfold, and if this was not in his power, he likewise was sold into bondage. The murderer, adulterer, ravisher, etc., were to be stoned by the whole multitude, the witnesses beginning the work of punishment. The man-slayer who was not guilty of murder, because the death was unintentional, was forced to betake himself to a city of refuge, and remain there until the decease of the High Priest. The transgressor in small matters was ordered to be chastised with the scourge, according to the discretion of the judges. And in cases of injury by maiming, the culprit suffered the loss of the same member of which he had deprived his neighbor, "an eye for an eye, a tooth for a tooth," etc. But we read of no jails, no penitentiaries, no imprisonments for years or for life, no shutting up of men from the free light and air of heaven, and from social intercourse with their families and the community around them.

Now the special question to be considered is this, viz., whether the infliction of the scourge or the lash was, or was not, more safe, more merciful, and more effectual, than the modern substitute of imprisonment, which so many philanthropic minds imagine to be a vast improvement upon the divine system.

I am perfectly aware that in justifying the law of God in this matter, I run counter to the prevailing habits and notions of our country. In the last century it was otherwise. The punishment of scourging was then the established course for all the lighter misdemeanors. Flogging was the chastisement of the soldier in the army, of the sailor in the navy, of the pupil in the school, of the child in the family. But so rapidly have the ideas of society advanced about what they are pleased to call the *dignity of human nature*, that this sort of discipline has become discreditable and even odious. In the administration of justice the old common-law maxim, *Qui non habet in crumena, luat in corpore*—i.e., "He that has no money in his purse, must pay in his body," has entirely disappeared. Flogging in the army and the navy is abolished by the Legislature. Schools are managed as they may be, without the rod, and the *dignity of human nature* must not be violated by giving *twelve* stripes even to the Southern slave, although the law of God directed *forty* to be administered to the Jewish freeman !

It is no part of my present purpose to set forth the results already apparent from this rapid change in public sentiment, though I think it would be easy to show that it has produced a serious deterioration in the old reverence for law and order, without which freedom must degenerate into anarchy, and prosperity into corruption. But I confine myself to my proper object by considering it in its relation to the authority of the Word of God. In the progress of these new ideas, Christianity has been made to bow down to the popular opinion, until the Bible has almost ceased to be the standard of truth. Men have discovered that the ancient Jews were a *barbarous race*, and therefore the law laid down to them by the wisdom of the Almighty is regarded as a *barbarous code*, no longer entitled to religious veneration. The tone and spirit of a godless literature have infected even the professed ministers of the sanctuary ; and too many are found doing the work of Bishop Colenso in another way, by denying the meaning and the application of the Old Testament, because "the people love to have it so."

I thank God, however, that the Church has not yet been forced to change her system. The Old Testament is still read along with the New, according to her Calendar. The Psalms of David still hold their place, as her chief songs of praise. And there are still left, I trust, a goodly number amongst her bishops, her clergy, and her laymen, willing and able to resist the encroachments of modern infidelity, and maintain the preëminence of the whole Bible, as the Word of inspiration.

But I return from this digression to the specific point which I have undertaken to discuss, namely, whether the punishment of the scourge, ordered by the authority of the divine and Omnipotent

Lawgiver, is not more safe, more merciful, and more effectual, than the modern substitute of imprisonment. That it is so, I should be willing to assume, because it was the system appointed by the Almighty for His chosen people. But I think it may be proved to any reflecting and candid mind, for the following reasons:

First, then, it is more *safe* for the offender, both in mind and in body. In mind, because it is universally conceded that a residence for some time in a jail or a work-house rarely fails to make the prisoner, morally and socially, a far worse man when he leaves, than he was when he entered it. His companionship, during the time of his confinement, is with men, many of whom are deeply depraved, and familiar with iniquity. He finds no one trying to cure him of his errors, while the leading spirits are disposed to make light of his fault, to teach him to curse the law, and to sink him to their own level. Thus the prison becomes a school of vice, and the punishment of a light offense prepares him for a much more perilous course of future criminality.

But imprisonment is also less safe for the body, because the change of his habits, from daily exercise in the open air, to the unwholesome atmosphere of the jail, with its wretched fare, and its contaminating associations, must soon reduce his strength, and lay the foundation, at least, for disease and suffering, perhaps to the total ruin of his constitution.

In the second place, the punishment of the scourge is more *merciful* than imprisonment, because, though sharper at the time, it is soon over. The culprit is not cut off from the kind sympathy of his humble home, his accustomed friends, and his affectionate family. He suffers nothing from the unfeeling jests and often insulting taunts of such companions as he would have found in the jail. The conduct of those around him is adapted to soothe and comfort him. And he returns to his labor without any loss of health or moral principle.

In the third place, I consider the punishment of the scourge to be much more *effectual* than imprisonment, both as it respects the offender himself, and the community to which he belongs. For the temper of insubordination or rebellion which calls for chastisement is very apt to be rather inflamed than put down by confinement. The culprit broods over the hardship of his case, with sullen wrath; and regards the law which shuts him up with the feeling of indignation. Whereas the summary infliction of the lash humbles his pride and subdues his temper, and thus reforms him by the strong hand, which is the most convincing argument with ordinary human nature. This, therefore, effects, much more surely than the prison, the first object of punishment, which is the correction and amendment of the offender. And the second object, namely, the warning given to others, in order to save them from transgression, is evidently better accomplished; because the lesson is given publicly, and operates on all who witness the infliction. If he were imprisoned, on the contrary, he would be taken out of sight; and what he suffered, or whether he suffered at all, would excite comparatively but little interest in others. On the whole, therefore, I can see no reason whatever for doubting the superior effects of the punishment prescribed by the law of God, and universally retained by all Christendom for eighteen centuries together. And thus far, the practice of the Southern slaveholder, in the usual mode of keeping his servants in subordination, seems abundantly sanctioned by the highest authority. For it is certain that the Bible, the Church, and the State, everywhere, concurred upon the subject, until the present era of sensitive transcendentalism raised against it the reproach of cruel barbarity, and in so doing, set itself in opposition to every previous rule of discipline, whether human or divine.

That it is liable to abuse, is no argument against its reasonable and just application. For so is every other kind of discipline, and none more so than the favorite plan of imprisonment. But it has this advantage on its side, namely, that it is public in its administration; and this very publicity is one of the surest guards against excessive severity. Whereas the abuses of imprisonment are private of necessity, and the sufferers are exposed to all the impositions, exactions, and caprices of their keepers, with the least probable chance of exposure. No class of men in the community are more liable to be led into every practice of petty tyranny than the officers of prisons, from the very nature of their employment. And no offense against humanity is more difficult to prove than the maltreatment to which the prisoners must needs be subject, if those who are virtually their masters should be lacking in conscience or in moral principle.

But this privacy protects them from reproach, because the wise philanthropists of our day see and hear nothing of any abuse, and therefore take it for granted that their favorite system is open to no suspicion. The Southern masters, on the contrary, are sheltered by no secrecy. All the punishments which they inflict, and a vast deal which they do *not* inflict, are sure to be wafted on the wings of the wind, to every quarter of the land, and across the ocean, and dressed up in eloquent oratory, in pathetic poetry, and in exciting novels, to stir the generous pulse of public sympathy and indignation. We have seen that by the Jewish law, the Roman law, the English law, and, in fine, by the law of every other people, the testimony of slaves could not be received on any trial. But to make amends for this, the mere statements of every slave, without any oath at all, are received by all our modern philanthropists in the most absolute confidence, while the contrary statements of freemen, bishops, clergy, and laity, are set at nought, as perfectly unworthy of regard. And this is what our ultra-abolitionists call *justice !*

It was thus with Mrs. Kemble, whose journal of six months' residence upon a Georgia plantation is accepted as so conclusive a description of the treatment of the slaves throughout the whole Southern population. I entertain the utmost respect for this lady's talents, for her very attractive style, and for her perfect sincerity. But I demur to the sufficiency of the testimony, because the greater part of it rested on the veracity of the slaves, in opposition to her husband and his overseer; and was besides strongly influenced by her own previous prejudices, by her exceedingly susceptible temperament, and by her manifest ignorance of the state of brutal depravity which Mr. Kay sets forth as the condition of the poorer classes in her own beloved England, where the substance of slavery remains, under the form of freedom.

Granting, therefore, most willingly, all that can be claimed for the personal character of this lady, I can not admit that she was properly qualified for the work which she had undertaken. The daughter of a distinguished tragedian, herself highly educated and accomplished for the stage, brought up in the midst of affluent indulgence, a fascinating actress and refined gentlewoman, what opportunity had she to learn the debased condition of the laboring poor in her own country? And when she came, in her bloom of youth and loveliness, to dazzle her admiring audiences in the United States, knowing nothing about the negro beyond the popular voice of English abolitionism, what time and attention could she possibly devote to the thorough investigation of the problem, which had tasked the abilities of the ablest statesmen, North and South, to understand its true political and social character? Had she ever looked into the awful degradation and heathenism of the colored race, on their native soil in Africa? Had she taken any pains to investigate the condition of the free negroes in the great cities? Did she belong to the class of those angels of mercy who ply their religious task amongst the degraded and demoralized masses of our own country? Had she, in a word, acquired any degree whatever of the experience, observation, and practical wisdom, necessary for the formation of a calm and reliable judgment on such a question?

Not at all! She passed through a brilliant course of histrionic celebrity, and then married a gentleman of great wealth, residing in Philadelphia, but owning a large plantation in Georgia. She lived and moved in the most luxurious and aristocratic circle. And when she accompanied her husband on a visit to his property, where he had not been for some years, she brought with her all her strong English prejudices against slavery, all her refined disgust towards the ordinary habits of English and Irish as well as African laborers, all her impulsive and gushing sensibilities, all her fixed resolution to open her ears and eyes to one side, while she closed them fast against the other, and all her ignorance of the wide field of facts and experience the knowledge of which is absolutely essential, before even a cool and masculine mind can be fully prepared to form a fair estimate of the Southern institution.

A worse qualified witness, therefore, on such a subject, it would be difficult to imagine. I should as soon think of appointing a boarding-school girl to frame a code of laws, or to inspect the management of our colleges, as of selecting Mrs. Kemble to settle the administration of a social system, embracing four millions of slaves, and involving the interests of nearly half the States on our vast continent.

Yet even under the strong bias of her habits, her feelings, and her prejudices, she informs us of much which places the condition of the slaves on this Georgia plantation far above the debased state of the English peasantry, as it is described by Mr. Kay. She found amongst them no promiscuous licentiousness of all ages and both sexes, herding like brutes in the same wretched den of filth and darkness. She found no drunkenness, no oaths, no obscene and wanton songs, no blasphemy, no fighting or violence, no midnight cries of murder, no stolid ignorance of the simplest religious truth, no children brought up

14

to be thieves and pickpockets, no fathers and mothers poisoning or starving their little ones to obtain the burial-fees, no wandering beggars, no work-houses to be the miserable refuge of cast-off old age, and no necessity for an annual tax, to keep body and soul together. All this, and more, I have proved to exist throughout the laboring masses in England, by the testimony of Mr. Kay, transcribed from the speeches of Lord Ashley, the committees appointed by the British Parliament, the letters of magistrates, rectors, and curates, from every quarter of the land, the author of the book being himself appointed by the great University of Cambridge as a commissioner, to collect the facts ; and having spent a long period in traveling throughout the kingdom, in the execution of his sad but most important mission.

But there is one fact recorded by Mrs. Kemble, which I confess astonished me. And as it is one which is equally likely to surprise my readers, I shall transcribe her words in full.

On her visit to St. Simon's Island, she saith : " At the door, I found another petitioner, a young woman named Maria, who brought a fine child in her arms, and demanded a present of a piece of flannel. Upon my asking her who her husband was, she replied, without much hesitation, that she did not possess any such appendage. I gave another look at her bonny baby, and went into the house to get the flannel for her. I afterwards heard from Mr. —— that *she and two other girls* of her age—about seventeen—were the *only instances on the island* of women with illegitimate children," (pp. 134–5, Harper's ed. 1863.)

When we look back at Mr. Kay's statement of bastardy amongst the English peasantry, where he informs us that the cases amount to fifty-three per cent ; and then compare with it the condition of the negroes on this plantation, containing some hundreds of slaves, and yet having only *three* girls who were the mothers of illegitimate children ; we can not fail to see the vast superiority on the side of this much-abused institution, even in that special point, which its adversaries assume to be most open to reprobation.

Nor is this the whole of Mrs. Kemble's statements. She praises the docility and affectionate temper of the slaves. She praises their devout spirit, their readiness to receive religious instruction, and their attention to the teaching of their own pious colored preacher. She praises the attainments and character of the slave who was the engineer, and conducted the mills of the establishment. She praises the deportment of the young slave who was her special attendant. She describes the ball which the slaves got up in honor of her arrival. She tells her readers that the slaves profess, at least, to be contented, and had no wish to run away. She sets forth their music and their songs — not very poetical, indeed, but free from any thing like corruption. And while she complains that the driver was allowed to carry a whip into the field, and to give *twelve* lashes, but no more, to the disobedient or the lazy, she forgets, or is ignorant, that in her own beloved country, the schoolmaster carried his rod, and laid it on his pupils, at his discretion; that the system of *fagging*, in which every younger pupil is a servant to the senior, still prevails in England; that flogging remains in the army in Canada; that eight millions exist in that happy kingdom, who can not read or write; that five millions sterling are expended every year, to keep them from starving; and that they are sunk, by wretchedness and poverty, to the lowest degree of immorality and degradation.

And, above all, she forgets to compare the condition of these slaves in Georgia with that of the savages of Dahomey, from which they were descended. She forgets that slavery was the only means by which they could have been raised to their present degree of light and civilization. She forgets that three thousand slaves are emancipated by their masters, on an average, every year. She forgets that out of these emancipated slaves the State of Liberia has sprung into existence, and that the future extension of the same noble work will be the great instrumentality, through which the providence of the All-wise God will redeem, in time, the whole vast continent of heathen Africa, thus making this much-abused institution a blessing, not only to the slaves, but to the world.

The bondage of Egypt was appointed to the Israelites, as the preparatory state for their establishment in Canaan. There was no attempt to free them by rising against their masters, or inciting them to rebellion, although their numbers attained to six hundred thousand men, able to bear arms. Moses undertook the work, supposing, as St. Stephen saith, that "his brethren would understand how that God by his hand would deliver them, but they understood not." (Acts 7 : 25.) The time had not yet come. Moses was obliged to flee from the wrath of the king, and spend forty years in humble labor as a shepherd, before he was commissioned as their leader. And then the work was effected, by the power of the Most High, without war, or tumult, or violence. The Lord turned the hearts of Pharaoh and the Egyptians, and His people were commanded to depart, with gifts and offerings, from " the land of bondage."

So, when the Israelites were doomed, by the divine decree, to the captivity in Babylon, the Almighty, at the time predicted by the prophet Jeremiah, inclined Cyrus to send them back into Judea, and it was accomplished in concord and in peace.

So, when slavery died out in the nations of Europe, it was by the providence of God, through the various changes of society. No war was made upon it, by Church or State. But it faded gradually away, without trouble or commotion.

So, when the slaves were emancipated in the West-Indies, it was done by the British Parliament, peaceably and legally, with an apprenticeship of five years to the negroes, and a fair price paid to the masters.

The only instance in which slavery was abolished, in war and blood, is the horrible case of the St. Domingo butchery, and that was the work of an infidel French Directory, when every atrocity was committed in Paris, under the names of liberty, equality, and fraternity. The historian Alison has told us the wretched result to the negroes themselves.

Contemplating these facts, and looking to Liberia, I anticipate the time when the same Almighty Ruler will give emancipation to the negro race in the Southern States, by inclining the minds of their masters to adopt it on a gradual scale of peaceful and beneficent enlargement. Not by the red hand of war; not by a bloody and cruel insurrection; not by arming the blacks against the whites, which would be most likely to produce a general massacre of the colored population; not by keeping up a bitter and unceasing assault upon an institution which is preparing a Christian host to regenerate the barbarous hordes of heathen Africa; not by degrading the pulpits of the North, in order to elevate the dogmas of ultra-abolitionism; and not by hostile attacks upon the Word of God, the testimony of the Church, and the Constitution of the country. But by a faithful and patient trust in the government of divine Providence, which orders every change among the nations by the counsels of unerring wisdom; by kindness and charitable forbearance towards the principles and feelings of those who are placed in different circumstances from our own; by a quiet abstinence from a busy intermeddling with evils

which we have no power to correct; and by a hopeful assurance
that, if we do not thwart the course of things by a dangerous precipi-
tancy, the grace and mercy of the Almighty will accomplish all that
is best for the negro race, in His own appointed time. And then
there will be no blood, no desolations, no groans, nor sighs, nor tears,
to stain the triumph of emancipation. Ethiopia will stretch out her
hands to the divine Redeemer, and His faithful disciples will be ready
to proclaim, " Glory to God in the highest, and on earth peace, good-
will towards men."

CHAPTER XLV.

Right Reverend Brother: I shall now invite your attention, and that of my readers in general, to the positive testimony of the Southern clergy, on the subject of the treatment and condition of the slaves; not derived from a residence of six months on a single plantation, but drawn from an intimate and life-long familiarity with all the facts connected with the institution.

The first evidence is entitled to serious consideration and respect, being an extract from an "Appeal of Southern Clergymen, addressed to Christians throughout the world," signed by ninety-five ministers, and representing all the principal Protestant denominations. It was published in England, in the *Edinburgh Review*, as well as in the Southern States, and bears date at Richmond, April 22, 1863. I omit all that portion of this interesting document which discusses the war, and confine my extract to the paragraphs which concern my special subject.

"We are aware," saith this Appeal, "that in respect to the moral aspects of the question of slavery, we differ from those who conceive of emancipation as a measure of benevolence, and on that account we suffer much reproach which we are conscious of not deserving. With all the facts of the system of slavery, in its practical operations before us, 'as eye-witnesses and ministers of the Word, having had perfect knowledge of all things' on the subject of which we speak, we may surely claim respect for our opinions and statements. Most of us have grown up from childhood among the slaves; all of us have preached to and taught them the Word of Life; have administered to them the ordinances of the Christian Church; sincerely love them as souls for whom Christ died; we go among them freely, and know them in health and sickness, in labor and rest, from infancy to old age. We are familiar with their physical and moral condition, and alive to all their interests; and we testify in the sight of God, that the relation of master and slave among us, however we may deplore abuses in this, as in other relations of mankind, is not incompatible with our holy Christianity, and that the presence of the Africans in our land is an occasion of gratitude in their behalf, before God, seeing that thereby Divine Providence has brought them where missionaries of the Cross may freely proclaim to them the word of salvation, and the work is not interrupted by agitating fanaticism. The South has done more than any people on earth for the Christianization of the African race. The condition of slaves here is not wretched, as Northern fictions would have men believe, but prosperous and happy, and would have been yet more so, but for the mistaken zeal of abolitionists. Can emancipation obtain for them a better portion ?"

"The practicable plan for benefiting the African race must be the providential plan—the Scriptural plan. We adopt that plan in the South, and while the States should seek, by wholesome legislation, to regard the interest of master and slave, we, as ministers, would preach the Word to both, as we are commanded of God. This war has not benefited the slaves. Those that have been encouraged or compelled to leave their masters have gone, and we aver can go, to no state of society that offers them any better things than they have at home, either in respect to their temporal or eternal welfare. We regard abolitionism as an interference with the plans of Divine Providence. It has not the signs of the Lord's blessing. It is a fanaticism which puts forth no good fruit: instead of blessing, it has brought forth cursing; instead of love, hatred; instead of life, death; bitterness and sorrow, and pain and infidelity, and moral degeneracy, follow its labors. We remember how the Apostle has taught the minister of Jesus upon this subject, saying, 'Let as many servants as are under the yoke count their own masters worthy of all honor, that the name of God and his doctrine be not blasphemed. And they that have believing masters, let them not despise them because they are brethren; but rather do them service because they are faithful and beloved, partakers of the benefit. *These things teach and exhort.* If any man teach otherwise, and consent not to wholesome words, even the words of our Lord Jesus Christ, and to the doctrine which is according to godliness, he is proud, knowing nothing, but doting about questions and strifes of words, whereof cometh envy, strife, railings, evil surmisings, perverse disputings of men of corrupt minds, and destitute of the truth, supposing that gain is godliness; from such withdraw thyself."

"This is what we teach, and obedient to the last verse of the text, from men that 'teach otherwise'—hoping for peace—we 'withdraw' ourselves."

In the notes appended to this "Appeal," the following facts are stated, and we can not have a better authority for their truth.

"From the best sources of information, it is ascertained that the whole number of communicants in the Christian Churches of the Confederate States is about two millions and fifty thousand."

"Of these, the number of white communicants is about one million five hundred and fifty thousand. Supposing the total white population to be eight millions, and one half that number to be over eighteen years of age, a little more than one third of the adult population are members of the Church of Christ."

"The number of colored communicants is about five hundred thousand. Assuming the colored population to be four millions, there would be, upon the same method of computation, one fourth of the adult population in union with the Church of Christ. Thus has God blessed us in gathering into his Church from the children of Africa more than twice as many as are reported from all the converts in the Protestant missions throughout the heathen world."

I regard this testimony as conclusive as any evidence can be, when we remember that there is no proof of the contrary which can be at all compared with it in number or in value. And I proceed to another statement published by Bryan Tyson, Esq., of North-Carolina, at Washington, 1863, which is important on the two most serious charges concerning evil treatment and marriage.

"We shall look at the institution of slavery," saith this writer, "in a family where there are some thirty or forty servants. We find among them a good many women and children, and some old men and women who are not able to do regular field labor. So, out of the whole, we shall probably not get more than four ninths who are regular field-hands. The children play about at their sports, the white and black almost invariably together, until they reach a proper age to be put to work, which is light at first, but as they grow older, gradually assumes a heavier form, until they can do any work belonging to the farm. They thus continue to labor, and in the course of time, declining years set in, and they cease to be regular field-hands any longer. They have now some light work assigned to them, such as boiling food, feeding stock, looking after the children, etc. Thus, of the three stages, youth, maturity, and old age, through which the servants pass, there is but one in which they are relied on as regular laborers. In childhood and in old age, they are well taken care of, and thus the whole slave population is rendered self-supporting. So, of the 3,953,760 slaves that were in the United States in 1860, there was not one supported by a public tax. Such an instance, I presume, is unknown among an equal number of the industrial classes, anywhere in the civilized world. I will ask where else on the face of the globe could you go to find, in a population of nearly four millions, no paupers?" (*Pamphlet on the Institution of Slavery, etc., by Bryan Tyson*, p. 8–9.)

"The servants at the South, for the most part, receive good treatment, as is evident from the census returns of 1860. During that year there were 3000 servants manumitted, and 803 escaped to the North, making a total loss to the slave population of 3803. Taking this as the average for the past decade, there would have been a loss to the slave population of 38,030. But with these odds against them, the slave population at the South increased during the decade ending in 1860 no less than 23.39 per cent, while the free blacks, after being augmented by about 38,030, increased only 12.33 per cent. The women, at times when their health is delicate, are not required to labor, being taken about as good care of as a member of the white family under similar circumstances."

"The servants at the South are not only, generally speaking, well treated, but becoming respect is also shown to them in old age. The white children are even taught to call the elderly servants uncle or aunt, as the case may be. I was thus brought up myself, and it still appears natural for me to do so." (Ib. p. 10–1.)

"As regards evil treatment, I admit that there are a few who do not treat their servants well, but the number is small in comparison with those who do treat them well. The time has never been, and probably never will be, when, in a population of four millions of people, whether they be bond or free, there will not be some acts of violence committed on the weak and inoffensive." (Ib. p. 27.)

"The past summer, a year ago, I was at a friend's house in Chatham County, North-Carolina, who owned a good many servants. It was in time of wheat-harvest. About dusk, the hands came in from their laborious work. It would seem that all might have been tired enough without seeking farther exercise in diversions; but not so.

14*

After supper the banjo was brought forth, and preparations made for a social dance. They soon struck up in high glee. I remarked to my friend that negroes enjoyed a great deal of satisfaction and pleasure. Yes, said he, the most of any people in the world. He told me that wishing to finish a certain field of grain, they had labored very hard that day. But one would not have judged so from present appearances. When I went to rest, they were still in the midst of their glee, their busy feet keeping time to the music." (Ib. p. 12.)

The writer states another fact, which gives a stronger proof of the estimation attached by the negroes to their condition. " The comfort of the bond-servant is such," saith he, " that I have actually known free persons of color to choose their masters and voluntarily enslave themselves. This may appear very singular to us, but unless they expected to better their circumstances it is still more strange that they should thus voluntarily give away their liberty." (Ib. p. 13.)

In answer to the prevailing opinion at the North that the slaves are never legally married, Mr. Tyson makes the following statement, which is worthy of great attention :

" A great many of the servants are married after book form ; and they all, so far as my knowledge extends, have their choice in this matter, whether to be married after book form, or cohabit under a vow. The essential part of the marriage contract consists in a solemn vow between the parties, and a faithful observance thereof. The servants that cohabit under a vow are fully as faithful to their companions as those who are married after book form, and in both cases they are generally true to their engagements." (Ib. p. 22–3.)

And with regard to the separation of families, the writer saith : " In a sojourn of over twenty years at the South, I have known but very few cases where a man and his wife were parted. There is a disposition among the people to keep them together as much as possible. But I should be glad to see laws passed at the South to prohibit a man and his wife from being separated under any and all circumstances, and such is now the case in some of the States." (Ib. p. 26–7.)

On the comparative advantages to the slave over the free laborer, the writer remarks as follows :

" It should be borne in mind that the relations existing between a master and his servant are quite different from those existing between the same person and a hired servant. In the one case he is considered and treated as a member of the family; in the other, but little regard is manifested for him after receiving his wages, and he is able to obtain but few favors—only such as he can purchase with his money—which in many instances are fewer than the bond-servant enjoys." (Ib. p. 26.)

Of the feelings expressed by the freed negroes, the writer gives some instances which fell under his own observation:

" A negro man (one of the lately emancipated servants) told me in the streets of Newbern, that he was not as free now as he was before he came into the Federal lines. And also that he fared better, particularly in sickness, for, said he, when I got sick, I had some person to bring medicine to me; but it is not so now."

" A woman that had belonged to a gentleman who owned some three hundred of those people, said she fared better and was better contented before obtaining her freedom than she had been since."

" And an old colored person with whom I conversed at the market-house, in this city, (Washington,) but a few days ago, said that a good many years before, his master, living in South-Carolina, emancipated himself and family, consisting of his wife and seven children—four boys and three daughters—and gave them money to pay their expenses to a free State. He said that at first he hailed this change with much joy, as he expected to get aid from his children; but they had all scattered off, his wife was dead, and he was dependent on his own labor for support, and now, being very old, he was ill able to labor. I asked him which situation he would prefer, to be back with his master, or live the way he was now living? He said that his master was a good and kind man, and if he was now back with him, he would never consent to leave him again. Said he, I then had some time to rest, but I have none now." (Ib. p. 31-2.)

This testimony from a witness who speaks with a perfect knowledge of the truth, is more minute than the Appeal from the 95 Southern clergy, but it is in entire accordance with it, and must go far, with any impartial mind, to correct many of the most popular prejudices against the Southern institution. But I shall add one more extract from a different quarter, before I dismiss the topic, and then hasten to my conclusion.

CHAPTER XLVI.

RIGHT REVEREND BROTHER: Amongst the great number of discourses published on the subject of slavery in the Southern States, I shall select for my readers a portion of one which was delivered by the Rev. George D. Cummins, D.D., in St. Peter's Church, Baltimore, January 4, 1861. The title of this able and eloquent sermon expresses the leading idea of most of the Southern clergy: "THE AFRICAN A TRUST FROM GOD TO THE AMERICAN." And I shall confine myself to that part of it in which this position is maintained.

"By the light of Scripture, and the history of the early Church," saith Dr. Cummins, "a Christian man whose lot is cast amidst slavery in this age and nation, is enabled to ascertain his duty towards it—and that is:"

" *To regard the African race in bondage (and in freedom too) as a solemn trust committed to this people from God, and that He has given to us the great mission of working out His purposes of mercy and love towards them.* The Anglo-American, the tutelar guardian of the African—this is the lofty view to which we now rise. It is a study of intense interest to trace the workings of God's Providence in the mode He has chosen to effect His purposes concerning these children of Ham. He has linked together, by a counsel of infinite wisdom, the destiny of two races, more diverse from each other than any two upon the globe. By the silver thread of His Providence the weakest race on the earth has been joined to the strongest, the oldest to the newest, the most repulsive barbarism to the highest civilization, the darkest superstition to the brightest and purest Christianity."

"Other races have at different periods of history been brought into close and intimate relations with the African race, as the Roman and the Castilian, but not to these has God intrusted this great work. To the Anglo-Saxon and the American has he reserved the high honor."

"God has brought these people to our doors, and placed them in our homes, and said to us by His Providence: 'Take this child and nurse it for me, and I will give thee wages.' It is a sublime trust, a stupendous work worthy of the genius of this Christian nation, to train, to discipline a race, to prepare them to work out the destiny of a continent of one hundred and fifty millions of the same race. We believe this to be the design of God, in the presence and condition of the African in this land. And it is for us to decide whether we will fulfill this high mission, or fail ignominiously under it. We can not decline the trust; it is ours by inheritance, and not by our seeking. We can not escape from its responsibilities if we would. But how shall we best fulfill that trust? This question involves and determines our duty towards the African in servitude. How shall we prove ourselves their truest friends—their best guardians? How discharge our duty towards them in the light of our duty to the Master whom we serve? Will it be by seeking hastily and violently to change their condition, and bid them go forth from under our guardianship? As well might we turn from our doors our children of tender years, and send them forth, helpless, into the world, exposed to every evil. It has been well and truthfully said that 'if the South should, at this moment, surrender every slave, the wisdom of the entire world, united in solemn council, could not solve the question of their disposal.' But we may add, that the Providence of God will solve it, in His own time, if we do not rashly thwart His plans, by our short-sighted schemes. It may, indeed, be a long time before He develops all His purposes towards the African race, and, like ancient Israel, He may prolong the time of their discipline. But in all His sublime arrangements, there is ever the same slow and stately movement, ever the absence of all haste. It required four thousand years to prepare the world for the advent of Christianity ; and it may require four thousand more to extend its triumphs over the whole earth.—But we can well be patient and wait on Him, with whom a thousand years are as one day," (p. 19–22.)

After giving a full account of the great attention paid at the South to the religious instruction of the slaves, Rev. Dr. Cummins proceeds to make the following interesting statement :

"To a Christian slaveholder, his slaves occupy a relation scarcely inferior to that of children ; they form part of his household, and for their temporal and eternal welfare he feels himself responsible to God.

How profound is this feeling of responsibility, I can attest from a personal residence among the pious masters of Virginia; I 'speak that which I know, and testify that which I have seen.' It was my lot to minister at the altar of a church where, along with three hundred whites, fifty slaves knelt by them to receive the sacrament of the Lord's supper. I have seen the master standing at the chancel of the church to act as sponsor in baptism for a faithful slave who came forward to receive the sacred rite. I have seen Christian women of the highest refinement and social position, sitting down on every Lord's day in the midst of the classes of a Sunday-school of slaves, to instruct them in the knowledge of salvation. I have known the slave girl in consumption to be taken into the chamber of her mistress, and nursed with a care equal to a mother's tenderness, and the passage to the grave illumined by the light of Christian sympathy and love. And I have seen a congregation of three thousand slaves presided over by their regular pastor, the President of a College, at the close of each sermon responding to the catechetical instruction concerning the truths preached."

"But it will be said that, according to the example of the Apostles and the early Christians, our whole duty towards slavery is not fulfilled until we do our part to correct its abuses and remove the evils attendant upon it—and we freely admit this. It is our part and duty, following in the steps of the Apostles, to tell both masters and servants of their mutual duties, and to warn them against abusing the relation in which they stand to each other—to say to the servant, 'Obey your master in singleness of heart, as unto the Lord'—to say to the masters, 'Give unto your servants that which is just and equal.' And we firmly and earnestly believe that there is not an evil connected with slavery, as it now exists in the Southern States, which in due time would not be corrected and removed by the force of Christian sentiment, enlightened by the Holy Spirit, and guided by the Word of God. *There is power enough in the Christianity of the South to grapple with and solve all the difficulties of this great question, if left unhindered by interference from without*," (p. 25–6.)

I might fill a volume with similar testimony from bishops, clergymen, and laymen; but this may suffice to prove the general fact, to which there are few exceptions, namely, that the Southern slave-holders are just and kind to their slaves, and that the negro race, under their care, are far better provided for, both temporally and spiritually, than the laboring classes in England, or the free negroes among ourselves.

My own personal acquaintance with the institution is very trifling, being limited to a residence of three weeks in St. Louis and New-Orleans, during the delivery of a course of lectures—about as long in Richmond, at our General Convention, in 1859, where you were also present, and afterwards, some three months in Tennessee. All the slaves with whom I came in contact on these occasions were house-servants; but a superior class of domestics I have never seen, nor has it ever been my lot to witness so much kindliness of feeling towards servants as seemed to exist towards these, from all the members of the family.

I can not, however, pretend to any knowledge personally of the condition of the slaves upon the plantations. But I conversed largely on the subject with our episcopal and clerical brethren, in whose statements I could place the most absolute confidence; and it was impossible to avoid the conclusion that the generous credulity of the North had been grossly deluded with respect to the treatment of the slaves; that the cases of severe or inhuman usage were rare and exceptional, and that, as a general rule, the negroes were really what the Southern people esteemed them—the happiest laborers in the world.

But what then, it may be asked, are we to make of the strong dislike expressed towards slavery by Washington, Jefferson, and many of the eminent men who formed the Constitution? What of the efforts made, after their day, to abolish it in Virginia and Kentucky? And what of the array of facts collected and published, in positive proof of the terrible barbarity connected with the system?

I answer that all this is freely admitted as a very reasonable ground for objecting to the institution, if it were an original question. And it may also warrant a strong desire that it might be abolished as soon as it can be, peaceably, justly, and wisely for the interests of all concerned. But it furnishes no ground for denouncing it as a *sin* to hold a slave, when he is properly treated—no ground for supposing that the slaves are not generally treated well—no ground for abusing the Constitution which provides for slavery, and which Washington and all his colleagues approved; and especially no ground for imputing iniquity to a social relation which was sanctioned both by the Old and the New Testament, which was held to be lawful before God by the voice of the Universal Church for more than eighteen centuries, and which is still allowed by the vast majority of Christians at the present day. Let us examine the objections, however, a little more particularly.

With respect to the wish expressed for the abolition of slavery by Washington, Jefferson, and others, I have over and over again maintained the same opinion, that such a measure was highly expedient and desirable, and have further endeavored to show how it might be effected. But did these great men esteem it a *sin* to hold slaves? The notion is absurd, because it is notorious that they were slaveholders themselves to the end of their days. Or did they even make any systematic effort in Virginia to have slavery abolished? They certainly did not. And if they had made such an effort, is it possible to suppose that they would have insisted, like the ultra-abolitionist, upon *immediate emancipation*, and have thus nullified the provisions of the Constitution which they had just approved? Surely such folly and inconsistency could never be imputed to those distinguished patriots by any one who has not himself lost his reason.

The truth is that the abhorrence of these great men was most probably produced by the *slave-trade*, which was not given up until 1808, and which brought into the South, every year, fresh importations of the wretched Africans, in their savage state, the civilizing and instructing of whom must have been a very distressing and difficult task to the planters at the South—a task which, doubtless, they would gladly have avoided if it had been in their power. But it is against all reason to suppose that the fathers of the American Constitution could ever have given the slightest countenance to our modern ultra-abolitionism, which was not heard of until some years after they were in their graves. Washington died in 1799, Jefferson in 1826, and the emancipation of the slaves in the British West-Indies, which gave birth to ultra-abolitionism, did not take place until 1834, eight years afterwards.

The plan of abolition advocated in Virginia and Kentucky by Mr. Randolph and Mr. Clay, was not rested on the modern absurdity that slaveholding was a *sin*, because they also, as well as Washington and Jefferson, were slaveholders all their lives. Neither was it a plan of *immediate* but of *gradual* abolition, like that which Pennsylvania and many other States had adopted long before. Between their views and my own there is no difference.

And with regard to the array of facts collected by the gifted Mrs. Stowe and others, I do not question their truth; but I deny that they afford any ground for impeaching the *lawfulness* of the institution, so far as the *relation* of master and slave is concerned, because they are all cases of *abuse*, which are not the proper, much less the necessary results of the institution; on the contrary, they are transgressions against the rules laid down to the master in the Word of God, and therefore *sins* before heaven. No maxim is better settled than this, namely, that the *abuse* of a thing does not take away the *use* of it. If it were otherwise, every relation in life would be destroyed, for there is not one amongst them that is not abused continually.

Suppose, for example, that the same industry were applied to the relation of man and wife, and that some feminine advocate of the Free-love notion were to advertise in the city of New-York that she was ready to listen to the complaints of every poor woman who had a cruel, a dissipated, or a faithless husband, and give her relief. Is there any doubt that such a philanthropist would be thronged with visitors, and that the tales of domestic suffering—many of them most sad and heart-breaking—would be numerous enough to fill a volume in a very short time? Fifty such stories would make a respectable book, and if related with the talent of Mrs. Stowe or Mrs. Kemble, would certainly be painfully interesting. What then? Granting that they were all true, as many of them unquestionably would be, could they authorize any man to conclude that *all the other wives* in the city were equally abused, that *abuse* is therefore *inseparable from marriage*, that marriage is consequently a *sin against humanity*, and hence, that the *institution itself* should be *abolished without delay?*

The population of New-York is about eight hundred thousand. I presume that amongst the whole there must be at least one tenth who are married women, which would give us eighty thousand wives to be sent adrift, on account of the abuse suffered by fifty or one hundred! Is there any reason, justice, or even common-sense in this? Yet such is precisely the logic of the ultra-abolitionist when he makes the narrative of some hundred instances of cruelty a reason for the immediate emancipation, not of eighty thousand, but four million of Southern slaves.

But judging fairly by the rules of evidence, notwithstanding my own habits and sympathies are in nowise partial to the institution, I can not doubt that these cases of abuse are mere exceptions, and that

the general treatment which the slaves receive is such as would become a Christian people. For such, as we have seen, is the positive
evidence of the most competent witnesses. And I can see no reason
why it should be otherwise. It is natural that the master should use
them kindly, because they are a part of his own family; and harsh
treatment would not only prevent their laboring cheerfully and pro-
fitably, but would provoke them to mischief or tempt them to run
away. It is natural that he should regard them with affection, and
desire that they should regard him with affection in return; for how
can a man, who loves even his horse and his dog, fail to love a human
being who works for his benefit, and looks up to him for protection
and support? And when, to the ordinary sympathies of nature, we
add the duty of religion in the case of those who are Christians, how
manifest does it seem that the treatment of the slave, as a general
rule, must be in accordance with justice, benevolence, and conscientious care?

That it is so, is proved by the direct testimony of the Southern
clergy, and by these unquestionable facts besides: First, that notwithstanding all the inducements held out by ultra-abolitionists, only
eight hundred and three slaves out of four millions, (or one in five
thousand,) abandoned their master in the year 1860, while three thousand were voluntarily emancipated. Secondly, that during the three
years of this mournful war, the great body of the slaves have been
faithful and attached. There has been no taking advantage of the
absence of the male members of the family—no rising into insurrections—and no apprehensions entertained by the white population that
any disturbance would occur, unless they were alienated and perverted by hostile influences from some other quarter. This fact alone
is worth more than a volume of individual testimony, and ought to
be decisive on the question.

It may be said, indeed, that the declarations of Southern men should
be put out of view, because they are interested in the maintenance of
slavery, and it is a sound rule of law that no man is a competent witness in his own cause. But this rule is limited to matters of private
and individual dispute, and operates only on the parties who appear
before a court of justice. Whereas this controversy involves an institution which affects the whole of the Southern States, and therefore
the people of the South are the proper judges of its practical results
among them. If it were a Northern institution, the men of the North

would be the best witnesses. But being a Southern institution, the men of the South must know it far better than we do. It is thus that we deal with all great questions. We do not expect a foreign traveler to do justice to our American system. We say, and say truly, that he does not understand it; and we claim the right to be its exponents ourselves. We say that even the different portions of these United States can not form a fair estimate of each other; that Southern men do not and can not appreciate the merits of the North-ern character, while Northern men are just as liable to err concerning the South. There is, indeed, nothing more rare amongst the best and most enlightened persons, than the disposition to make a kindly and liberal estimate of customs, laws, or habits with which they have not been thoroughly familiarized; and the difficulty is greatly increased when the institutions of a country are opposed to the ideas and sym-pathies which we have cherished from infancy. Hence, in order to be really just to other states of society, we must try to put ourselves, as much as possible, in their position; and this we can only do by placing all reasonable confidence in what they say of themselves, in those open and public documents which they set before the world.

Instead of this, however, the ordinary course is to regard the insti-tution from our own stand-point, as if it were a controversy about the propriety of making slaves of freemen. Hence the popular ques-tion, which so many take for a convincing argument: "How would you like to be a slave?" They forget that the history of the matter has nothing to do with the enslaving of any freeman. They forget that these Southern slaves, so far as we know, have never been free, at least for centuries—that their ancestors were slaves amongst the barbarous and heathen tribes of Africa—that their Southern masters have not deprived them of any right which they possessed before, but have, on the contrary, raised them up from the lowest depths of pagan darkness to be Christian men and women, and have bestowed liberty upon thousands every year, from whom the State of Liberia has taken its rise, giving the best ground for hope that millions of these Southern negroes will in due time issue from the South, to be the missionaries to their fatherland, and regenerate that savage con-tinent by the power of the Gospel. And they forget that the South, having in truth done more to elevate the African race than all the world besides, have a right to consider the work as belonging to themselves, in the order of Providence, and should be permitted to carry it on, without reproach or interference, in their own way.

There is another popular notion which does very little credit to our Northern understanding, and that is the strangely absurd statement that the negro slave gets nothing for his labor! On the contrary, it is demonstrable that he receives a larger compensation, on the whole, than any of us would choose to pay, in the support of himself from his birth to his burial, and the support besides of his wife and children, in sickness and in health, in childhood and old age, without any danger of the poor-house, or of begging, or of starvation. Mrs. Kemble herself states that the slaves had not only a regular allowance of food and clothing, but also had a garden-spot attached to their cottages, and were free to raise all sorts of fowls, except turkeys, for their own use, while a regular physician was employed to attend to their diseases. I doubt whether any Northern farmer or manufacturer would be willing to make the same bargain with his laborers. I doubt whether he would think himself likely to clear as much profit from their work as he does now, when he only pays for what is actually done, and is at no expense for house, or lot, or food, or clothing, or children, or old age, or sickness, or burial. And the superiority of advantage to the negro is sufficiently plain, if the reader considers the immense amounts paid yearly in our Northern States for the support of the poor, and then remembers that *among the four millions of Southern slaves there is not one pauper dependent on public charity.*

CHAPTER XLVII.

RIGHT REVEREND BROTHER : Amongst the prominent and admired antagonists of the Southern institution, the late Theodore Parker occupied a conspicuous place ; and a few extracts from his autobiography may be instructive as a convincing proof, that the philanthropy of the great leaders in ultra-abolitionism has no affinity with the religion of the Bible.   I quote from the recent volumes containing his "Life and Correspondence, by John Weiss," published by the Messrs. Appleton.

Speaking of the results of his theological studies, while preparing for the ministry, Mr. Parker presents us with this frank statement of infidelity, in the appendix to the second volume, p. 454, viz. :

"I studied," saith he, "the historical development of religion and theology amongst Jews and Christians, and saw the gradual formation of the great ecclesiastical doctrines which so domineered over the world.   As I found the Bible *was the work of men*, so I also found that the Christian Church was *no more divine than the British State, a Dutchman's shop, or an Austrian farm.*   The miraculous infallible Bible, and the miraculous infallible Church, *disappeared when they were closely looked at ;* and I found the fact of history quite different from the pretension of theology."

Here we have the open avowal of sheer infidelity.   This man of superior talents, energy, and influence, professing to be a minister of the Gospel, attaches no importance to the express words of Christ : "Upon this Rock I will build MY CHURCH, and the gates of hell shall not prevail against it."   (Matt. 16 : 18.)   He takes no account of our Lord's declaration : "If he neglect to hear THE CHURCH, let him be unto thee as an heathen man and a publican."   (Matt. 18 : 17.)   And the multiplied statements of the Apostles, of course, go for nothing. St. Paul might say that "Christ is the head of THE CHURCH," (Eph. 5 : 23 ;) that Christ "loved THE CHURCH, and gave Himself for it," (Eph. 5 : 25 ;) that THE CHURCH is "the pillar and ground of the truth," (1 Tim. 3 : 15.) And St. Luke might declare that the Lord added to THE CHURCH daily, " such as should be saved." (Acts 2 : 47.) All these, together with a large number of similar passages, were of no weight in the judgment of Mr. Parker, because he had satisfied himself that the Bible was " the work of men," and that " the Church was no more divine than a Dutchman's shop, or an Austrian's farm !" And this is the teaching which thousands of deluded minds accept, as if it were the utterance of an infallible oracle !

The highly-gifted Mr. Emerson seems to have as little confidence in the Church as Mr. Parker. " I and my neighbors," saith he, " have been bred in the notion, that unless we came soon to some good Church—Calvinism, or Behmenism, or Romanism, or Mormonism— there would be a universal thaw and dissolution. No Isaiah or Jeremy has arrived. *Nothing can exceed the anarchy that has followed in our skies. The stern old faiths have all pulverized !* 'Tis a whole population of gentlemen and ladies out in search of a religion." *

This is tolerably strong ; but he exceeds it in the startling declaration that " God builds His temple in the heart on the *ruins of Churches and religions.*"†

And his estimate of the *masses* is remarkable for its severity. " Shall we judge a country by the majority," saith he, " or by the minority ? By the minority, surely. Leave this hypocritical prating about the masses. Masses are rude, lame, unmade, pernicious in their demands and influence, and need not to be flattered, but to be schooled. I wish not to concede any thing to them, but to tame, drill, divide, and break them up, and draw individuals out of them. The worst of charity is that the *lives you are asked to preserve are not worth preserving.* Masses ! the *calamity is the masses.* I do not wish any mass at all, but honest men only ; lovely, sweet, accomplished women only ; and no shovel-handed, narrow-brained, gin-drinking, million stockingers or lazzaroni at all. If Government knew how, I should like to see it check, not multiply the population."‡

In this extraordinary effusion of transcendental philosophy, the nerves of Mr. Emerson seem to have gotten the mastery of his understanding. The society of the uncultivated " masses " might not be agreeable to his refined and sensitive habits ; but how would his in-

---

* See Emerson's *Conduct of Life*, p. 177, Boston ed. of 1861.
            † Ib. p. 178.   ‡ Ib. p. 218-9.

tellectual "minority" of men, and his "lovely, sweet, accomplished women," contrive to live in such a world as ours, without the "hewers of wood and drawers of water," the laborers, the artisans, the "shovel-handed" tillers of the soil, and the operatives of the mine and of the workshop? Where would they find the food that sustains, or the garments that clothe, or the dwellings that shelter them? What means would they employ to build the ships and navigate the ocean? Nay, how would they supply their minds with their favorite literature, if the "masses" had not reduced the ores of lead and iron, and formed the printing-press, and raised the flax, and made the paper, and tanned the leather, and bound the book, and performed the whole of the mechanical but indispensable work, which gives the best means of earthly fame to the successful author? And what would our mighty Republic be at this day, if Mr. Emerson's policy had been adopted, by "checking" instead of encouraging the increase of those "masses," who are, in truth, the very bone, and sinew, and muscle of our country?

But strange as such extravagance appears in the eyes of common-sense, it seems much worse than strange when we regard it in contrast with the spirit of Christianity. The Saviour of the world looked down upon "the masses," not with philosophical contempt, but with loving compassion, "as sheep having no shepherd." He did not reserve His Gospel for the intellectual "minority" of men, nor for the "sweet, accomplished women," but preached it freely to the multitudes. He did not praise the self-righteous Pharisee who thanked the Lord that he was "not as other men," but rather justified the despised publican, who "smote upon his breast, saying: God be merciful to me, a sinner." He even chose His own earthly lot among "the masses," aided His reputed father, Joseph, in the labors of a carpenter, and after He entered on His sacred ministry, and had refused the offer of a kingly throne, yet He still continued His work of mercy to the "common people," from whom He had selected, as His favored Apostles, the fishermen of Galilee. Is it possible to conceive a more striking contrast than the whole life and doctrine of Christ present, to the conscious pride of this transcendental philosopher? Is it possible that we can suppose him to be influenced by religious truth when we hear him exclaiming: "The masses! The calamity is the masses. *The worst of charity is that the lives you are asked to preserve are not worth preserving;*" and then listen to the divine

Saviour, saying: " To the poor the Gospel is preached. Blessed are the poor in spirit, for theirs is the kingdom of heaven ? "

But I pass on to some further developments of this admired writer's sentiments. In an eloquent Address to the Senior Divinity Class connected with Harvard University, delivered July 15th, 1838, this passage occurs:

" It is my duty to say to you that the need was never greater of *new revelation* than now. From the views I have already expressed, you will infer the sad conviction, which I share, I believe, with numbers, of the *universal decay* and now *almost death of faith* in society. The soul is not preached. *The Church seems to totter to its fall, almost all life extinct.*"[*]

And he enlightens his readers by an intimation of his system in the following propositions, which he seems to have drawn from that grand old heathen slave, the philosopher Epictetus:

" That is always best," saith he, " which *gives me to myself.* The sublime is excited in me by the great stoical doctrine, OBEY THYSELF. That which shows God in me, fortifies me. That which shows God out of me, makes me a wart and a wen. There is no longer a necessary reason for my being."[†]

Speaking, in the same volume, of the decay of religion, Mr. Emerson makes the following statement, viz. :

" Certainly there have been periods when, from the inactivity of the intellect on certain truths, a greater faith was possible in names and persons. The Puritans in England and America found, in the Christ of the Catholic Church, and in the dogmas inherited from Rome, scope for their austere piety, and their longings for civil freedom. *But their Creed is passing away, and none arises in its room.* It is already beginning to indicate character and religion, to *withdraw* from the *religious meetings.* I have heard a devout person, who prized the Sabbath, say, in bitterness of heart: ' On Sundays, it seems wicked to go to Church.' And the motive that holds the best there, is only a hope and a waiting."[‡]

These passages, which might be greatly multiplied, prove sufficiently the results of Mr. Emerson's experience within his special sphere of observation. And these results appear to my mind to be

---

[*] *Emerson's Miscellanies*, p. 131.   [†] Ib. p. 127.

[‡] *Emerson's Miscellanies*, p. 138-9.

the necessary consequence of indulgence in the same self-will, which began by a wanton separation from the apostolic system of the Church of England, and went on, by degrees, to question the divine authority of the Bible. The commencement was Puritanism. The next step was Socinianism. And the end was a departure, farther and farther, from the Standard of religious truth, until the Word of God was regarded as the word of man, and all real faith was set aside, in the worship of the individual reason. " Obey *thyself*," saith this modern philosopher. " That which shows God *in me*, fortifies me. That which shows God *out of me*, makes me a wart and a wen." Here is the doctrine which deifies the human mind, and seeks for salvation, not in the humble and grateful acceptance of the atoning sacrifice and mediation of the glorious Redeemer, offered to us in mercy by the free grace of the Holy Spirit; but in the proud reliance on our own inward light, which scorns to submit itself to any other teacher, however celestial and divine!

But the ideas of this gifted, though sadly erroneous writer, are yet more developed in the following passages, viz:

" The religion which is to guide and fulfil the present and coming ages, whatever else it may be, must be intellectual. The scientific mind must have a *faith which is science*. 'There are two things,' said Mohammed, ' which I abhor, the learned in his infidelities, and the fool in his devotions.' Our times are impatient of both, and especially of the last. *Let us have nothing now which is not its own evidence.* There is surely enough for the heart and the imagination in the religion itself. Let us not be pestered with assertions and half truths, with emotions and snuffle."

" There will be a *new church founded on moral science*, at first cold and naked, a babe in a manger again, the algebra and mathematics of ethical law, the church of men to come, without shawms, or psaltery, or sackbut; but it will have heaven and earth for its beams and rafters; science for symbol and illustration; it will fast enough gather beauty, music, picture, poetry. Was never stoicism so stern and exigent as this shall be. It shall send man home to his central solitude, shame these social, supplicating manners, and make him know that much of the time he must have himself to his friend. He shall expect no coöperation, he shall walk with no companion. The nameless Thought, the nameless Power, the superpersonal Heart,—he shall repose alone on that. He needs only his own verdict. No good fame

15

can help, no bad fame can hurt him. The Laws are his consolers, the good Laws themselves are alive, they know if he have kept them, they animate him with the leading of great duty, and an endless horizon. Honor and fortune exist to him who always recognizes the neighborhood of the great, always feels himself in the presence of high causes."*

Here, then, we have Mr. Emerson's ideal of what religion should be. He had told us before that the old faiths "have all pulverized"— that "God builds his temple in the heart *on the ruins of churches and religions*"—that "the need was never greater of *new revelation* than now." And he predicts, accordingly, a *new church*, not founded on the Bible, nor on tradition, nor on the authority of miracles and prophecy, nor on the recorded Word and work of Christ; but on what he calls MORAL SCIENCE. The evidence of the old truth is of no further value. We must have "*nothing now which is not its own evidence !*"

The sympathy of Mr. Emerson with Mr. Parker is exhibited very plainly in a letter, acknowledging the receipt of a book which the latter had dedicated to him. This letter is worth transcribing, as a fair exponent of the growing power of ultra-abolitionism, in connection with infidelity, viz.:

"CONCORD, MASS., March 19, 1853.

"MY DEAR PARKER: Before that book came to me, though not until several weeks after it was sent, I read the inscription, if with more pride than was becoming, yet not without some terror. Lately I took the book in hand, and read the largest part of it with good heed. I find in it all the traits which are making your discourses material to the history of Massachusetts; the realism, the power of local and homely illustration, the courage and vigor of treatment, and the masterly sarcasm—now naked, now veiled—and I think with a marked growth in power and *coacervation*—shall I say?—of statement. To be sure, I am in this moment thinking also of speeches out of this book, as well as those in it. Well, you will give the times to come the means of knowing how the lamp was fed, which they are to thank you that they find burning. And though I see you are too good-natured by half in your praise of your contemporaries, you will neither deceive us nor posterity, nor—forgive me—yourself, any more,

* *Conduct of Life*, p. 210.

in this graceful air of laying on others your own untransferable laurels."

"We shall all thank the right soldier whom God gave strength and will to fight for Him the battle of the day."

"Ever new strength and victory be to you!"

"R. W. EMERSON."

I shall now return to Mr. Parker, whose course is made perfectly plain in his own letters, so copiously published by his admiring biographer. Thus he writes to the Hon. S. P. Chase, in 1854. (Vol. ii. p. 226.)

"I have studied this matter of the Divine origin of the Bible and the Divine Nature of Jesus of Nazareth all my life. If I understand any thing, it is that. I say *there is no evidence—external or internal —to show that the Bible or Jesus had any thing miraculous in their origin or nature, or any thing divine in the sense that word is commonly used.* The common notion on this matter I regard as an error —one, too, most *fatal to the development of mankind.* Now in all my labors I look to the general development of mankind, as well as to the removal of every such special sin as *American slavery,* as *war, drunkenness,* etc., therefore I introduce my *general principle* along with my *special measures.* I become personally unpopular, *hated* even; but the *special measures* go forward obviously; the *general principle* enters into the public ear, the public mind, and what is true of it will go *into the heart of mankind and do its work.* I think I work prudently—I know I do not rashly, and without consideration."

"Here let me say that the thing I value most in a man is *fidelity to his own nature,* to his mind and conscience, heart and soul."

No language can be more clear, in proving that this professed minister of the Gospel had utterly abandoned the old faith of Christianity. And we shall see the political and philanthropic working of *his* religion, in the following extracts:

Thus, in a letter to the Hon. Horace Mann, June 27, 1856, (vol. ii. p. 188,) Mr. Parker saith: "What a state of things we have in politics! The beginning of the end! I take it we can elect Fremont; if so, the battle is fought and the worst part of the contest is over. If Buchanan is elected, I don't believe the Union holds out three years. *I shall go for dissolution.*"

---

* See *Life and Correspondence of Theodore Parker.* Vol. ii. p. 45.

In another letter, addressed to Professor Desor, during the same year, he saith: "If Fremont is not elected, then I look forward to what is worse than civil war in the other form, viz., a long series of usurpations on the part of the slave-power, and of concessions by the North, until we are *forced to take the initiative of revolution at the North.* That will be the worst form of the case, for then the worst fighting will be among the Northern men—between the friends of freedom and the Hunkers. *I expect civil war, and make my calculations accordingly."* (Ib. 189.)

And again, in a letter to Hon. J. P. Hale, dated Oct. 21, 1856, we have this declaration, viz.:

"If Buchanan is President, I think the Union does not hold out his four years. *It must end in civil war, which I have been preparing for these six months past.* I buy no books, except for pressing need. Last year I bought fifteen hundred dollars' worth. This year I shall not order two hundred dollars' worth. *I may want the money for cannons.* Have you any plan in case we are defeated? Of course the principles and measures of the administration will remain unchanged, and the mode of execution will be the more intense and rapid."

The views of Mr. Parker are yet more clearly set forth in the following extract from his Journal, (2 vol. p. 190,) written on the day when President Buchanan was elected:

"This day is not less critical in our history for the future than 4th July, '76, was for the past. At sunrise there were three alternatives:"

"1. Freedom may put down slavery peacefully by due course of law."

"2. Slavery may put down freedom in the same way."

"3. The friends of freedom and its foes may draw swords and fight."

"At sunset the people had repudiated the first alternative. Now America may choose between Nos. 2 and 3. *Of course we shall fight. I have expected civil war for months;* now I buy no more books for the present. Nay, I think affairs may come to such a pass, that my own property may be confiscated; for who knows that we shall beat at the beginning—and I *hung as a traitor!* So I invest property accordingly. Wife's will be safe. I don't pay the mortgage till 1862."

And once more, I quote from Mr. Parker's letter to Miss Hunt, in Europe, Nov. 17, 1856, (vol. 2, p. 191,) viz. :

"At New-York and elsewhere, Banks said the election of Fremont would settle the slavery question, and stop agitation for thirty years ! I opened my eyes when I went out West, and saw that the hands of the Republicans are not yet quite clean enough to be trusted with power. There has a deal of bad stuff come over to the Republican party. I am more than ever of opinion that we must settle this question in the old Anglo-Saxon way—*with the sword.*"

"There are two Constitutions for America—one writ on parchment and laid up at Washington ; the other also on parchment, but on the *head of a drum.* It is to this we *must appeal, and before long.* I make all my pecuniary arrangements—with the *expectation of civil war.*"

I must confess that I read these declarations of Mr. Parker with astonishment, and should not believe them on any evidence less satisfactory than that of his admiring biographer. How a professed minister of Christ, however he had wandered from the true faith of the Gospel, could continue to proclaim, Sunday after Sunday, even the moral doctrines of religion, and yet hail with satisfaction the bloody horrors of civil war—how a zealous philanthropist, in his fervent devotion to the abolition of negro slavery, could resolve that it must be accomplished by the sword of slaughter—how a native American, bound by his allegiance to support the Constitution, could coolly determine, almost five years before the crisis arrived, that the Union should be destroyed by an appeal to the other constitution *written on the head of a drum*, and make all his pecuniary arrangements with a view to the possibility that he might himself be *hung as a traitor*—all this seemed to me so little in accordance with the principles and feelings of common humanity, that I could only regard it as a kind of monomania—a terrible delusion, proceeding from the Prince of Darkness, and in direct hostility to the precepts of that Divine Redeemer who is the Prince of Peace.

But Mr. Parker was consistent with all this in his theory of natural ethics, where he justifies the maxims of supposed right which led to the horrid butchery of St. Domingo. For thus he writes in a letter to Francis Jackson, dated at Rome, in 1859, (vol. ii. p. 170):

"In my best estate," saith he, "I do not pretend to much political wisdom, and still less now while sick ; but I wish yet to set down a few thoughts for your private eye, and it may be, for the ear of the fraternity. They are, at least, the result of long meditation on the subject; besides, they are not at all new nor peculiar to me, but are a part of the *public knowledge of all enlightened men.*"

"1. A man held against his will as a slave, has a *natural right to kill every one* who seeks to prevent his enjoyment of liberty. This has long been recognized as a self-evident proposition, coming so directly from the *primitive instincts of human nature*, that it neither required proofs, nor admitted them."

"2. It may be a *natural duty* of the slave to develop this *natural right* in a practical manner, and *actually kill* all those who seek to prevent his enjoyment of liberty. For if he continues patiently in bondage—First, he entails the foulest of curses on his children; and, secondly, he encourages other men to commit the *crime against nature* which he allows his own master to commit," etc.

"3. The freeman has a *natural right* to help the slaves to recover their liberty, and in that enterprise to do for them all which they have a right to do for themselves. This statement, I think, requires no argument or illustration."

"4. It may be a *natural duty* for the freeman to help the slaves to the enjoyment of their liberty, and as means to that end, to *aid them in killing all such* as oppose their natural freedom."

"5. The performance of this duty is to be controlled by the freeman's power and opportunity to help the slaves. The impossible is never the obligatory.—If I *could* help the bondmen in Virginia to their freedom as easily and effectually as I can aid the runaway at my own door, *then I ought to do so.*"

"These five maxims have a direct application to America at this day, and the people of the free States have a certain *dim perception* thereof, which, fortunately, is becoming clearer every year."

Here, then, we have a full display of the new *revelation*—the gospel of ultra-abolitionism which anticipated our mournful war as the true means to emancipate the negro, and seeks to accomplish this favorite object through a deluge of blood, and at any sacrifice of life and treasure. The Union is nothing, for Mr. Parker is for "dissolution." The Bible is nothing, for it is "the work of men." The Church is nothing, for it has no more sanctity about it than "a Dutchman's shop or an Austrian's farm." The Constitution is only "a piece of parchment laid up in Washington," and the real constitution is written on the "*parchment on the head of a drum!*" The power of established law, the safety and contentment of the negro race, the advancement of our national prosperity in the path marked out by the revolutionary patriots, the oath of office, the feelings of civilized humanity, the connections and relationships of families spread abroad, North and South, throughout the land—all these are nothing in the scale of social consideration. The one thing needful is the *destruction of slavery*, no matter at what cost of fearful consequences. The negroes must be roused *to kill their masters*. The freemen must be roused *to help them*, as in the case of John Brown, who honestly acted on this theory. And the millennium of the *new Church* must be inaugurated in the victory of infidelity, the ruin of all the old faith, the contempt of every civil obligation, the groans and tears of suffering millions, and the threatened reign of bloody anarchy; ending, too probably, in the worst form of military despotism, over a once happy, prosperous, and peaceful people!

CHAPTER XLVIII.

RIGHT REVEREND BROTHER: With the exhibition of the infidel principles, the sanguinary plan of abolitionism, and the frank desire to disunite the States, which were so plainly professed by Mr. Theodore Parker, (a great leader in this dangerous school,) I shall close my extracts, saving only the matters which the reader will find in the Appendix. And I think it will be admitted that I have amply redeemed my promise in the answer to your *Protest*. The doctrines laid down in the *Bible View of Slavery* have been sustained by abundant testimony, and nothing more remains but to bring my work to its conclusion.

To this end, I would recall to your memory the precept delivered by St. Paul to Timothy, the Bishop of Ephesus: "*Rebuke not an elder, but intreat him as a father.*" (1 Tim. 5 : 1.)

I am your elder, in years, and especially in office. You have not merely rebuked, but much more, *denounced* me, without warning, examination, or the slightest effort to practice the ordinary rules of justice, and far less of Christian courtesy. And your denunciation accuses me of a grave offense against the laws, amounting to *misprision of treason*, although, for this preposterous charge, you had not a shadow of proof, or even of probable presumption. This false and insulting accusation, moreover, you induced your clergy to indorse, and proclaimed it in handbills, far and wide, to be used in your political election. And all for what? Simply because, at the request of some of your own gentlemen in Philadelphia, nearly five months before, I sent them a pamphlet containing my opinions on the lawfulness of slavery, which I had published substantially several times within the last thirteen years. And this pamphlet I gave them my consent to have reprinted at their expense, and made no objection, two months afterwards, to have it circulated by the Democratic party. And this is the whole of my course, which you denounce in your protest as "unworthy of any servant of Jesus Christ," and challenging your "indignant reprobation."

The spirit and the action which become me, under this extraordinary provocation, are marked out by another precept of the Apostle: "We *command* you, brethren," saith he, "in the name of our Lord Jesus Christ, that ye *withdraw yourselves* from every brother that walketh disorderly, and not after the tradition which he received of us, and have no *company with him.* Yet count him not as an enemy, but *admonish him* as a brother." (2 Thes. 3 : 6, 14–5.)

I might, with perfect propriety, according to the rules of worldly justice, prosecute you and your clergy, for a gross and scandalous libel. I might also take measures to have you presented before a court of Bishops for your transgression; which I consider to be of a far more dangerous character to the law and order of the Church, than any of the charges brought in former years before that tribunal. But I have no desire to trouble our brethren or myself with any hostile proceeding. As a lover of peace, I take the mildest possible view of your conduct, by calling it "disorderly," and not "after the tradition" or rule of the Apostle. And therefore, in obedience to his command, I *withdraw myself* from your company, not counting you as an enemy, but *admonishing you as a brother.*

For you are still my brother in Christ, notwithstanding you are so thoroughly alienated by your course of public and libelous denunciation, that I can not look forward to any future association with you on earth, however I may hope to meet you in His heavenly kingdom. But this is of small importance. The time of my sojourn in this troublesome world is not likely to be very long; and, since it must be so, I can finish my humble course in the Church below, without any renewal of my former fraternal intercourse with the Diocesan of Pennsylvania.

With this brief statement of the matter, I proceed, in obedience to the precept of St. Paul, to complete my unwelcome duty, trusting that it may be useful to others, if not to you.

1. In the first place, I admonish you to remember your ORDINATION vows, which are registered in heaven. When you were ordained a priest, you were asked: "Will you give your faithful diligence always so to minister the doctrine and sacraments and the discipline of Christ, as the Lord hath commanded and as *this Church* hath received the same?" And you answered: "I will so do, by the help of God."

Again you were asked: "Will you be ready, with all faithful diligence, to banish and drive away from the Church all erroneous and strange doctrines contrary to God's Word?" And you answered: "I will, the Lord being my helper." The same question and answer were repeated, when you were consecrated a bishop.

Now I maintain that it is utterly impossible to tolerate the dogmas of ultra-abolitionism, or to bring them into the sanctuary of God, or to recommend them to His people, without a direct infraction of these vows of ordination. For the Church never held that it was a *sin* to buy, or sell, or hold a slave; much less that it was the *worst of all sins*, and "the sum of all villainies." On the contrary, she has ever repudiated it as false doctrine. She has even placed slaveholders, as bishops, in her highest seats of honor; and up to the commencement of this mournful conflict, you professed as much esteem for the piety and Christian consistency of those bishops, as any man.

But I would further observe, that between these two doctrines there can be no middle ground of compromise. Slaveholding is either a sin, or it is not. If it is a sin, the Northern Methodists were right in excommunicating their Southern brethren; for it is manifestly forbidden to administer the sacrament to any one who is living openly in sin, and refuses to forsake it. If it is not a sin, these Northern Methodists were wrong, and stand chargeable themselves with the sin of schism, by casting off their brethren without any justification.

And here, in truth, was the fatal act which lighted up the torch of *religious discord* amongst the Christian societies of the land, and thus furnished material to the politicians, who brought about, in due time, the *civil war* now raging through our unhappy country. The ultra-abolitionists, who had previously been regarded as a small body of absurd and deluded enthusiasts, suddenly rose to dignity and importance, under the powerful wing of Northern Methodism. The pulpits of the various denominations began to ring with the *sin* of slaveholding, the wrongs of the poor Africans, and the barbarities of the tyrants who held them in bondage. The excitement spread from sect to sect, with a few individual exceptions, until at length our Church was the only ark of refuge among Protestants for the old faith of the Bible, where the Word of Christ and the doctrine of His inspired Apostles could be heard, unpolluted by the eloquent ravings of a very sincere but utterly mistaken philanthropy. The novel-writers, the magazines, and the editors, all echoed the new cry of the *equal rights of man*, and the infidel reformer, the ambitious statesman, and the intriguing demagogue worked in loving unity with the fervent and earnest preachers, who had unhappily been persuaded to change the Gospel of peace into the trumpet-blast of war and confusion.

But has this mournful work of philanthropy, run mad, discharged *you* from your vows of ordination? Not so, my Right Reverend Brother; for you are still bound as much as ever to maintain "the doctrine and discipline of Christ as the Lord hath commanded and as this Church hath received the same." I can not conceive that the false light which has deluded the Christian sects should have any influence on you; and therefore it is that I admonish you to remember your solemn obligation.

2. In the next place, I admonish you to ponder seriously the divine authority of the HOLY SCRIPTURES on this subject. I contend that every Christian man must adhere to the language of the Bible, in speaking of slavery. He may desire and promote its peaceable abolition, on the score of *expediency*, if he will; but he can never justify its *abolition by force*, on the ground that it is a *sin* to hold a slave, without a direct conflict with the plain teaching of both the Old and the New Testament. Such a course would be at war with the faith even of a private Christian. How much more must it be inconsistent with your office, as a bishop over the flock of the Redeemer!

3. In the third place, I admonish you to remember the reverence which you owe to the VOICE OF THE CHURCH. You repeat the ancient creed every Sunday, in which you profess your *belief in the holy catholic Church*, meaning thereby the universal Church of Christ, in the first pure centuries of the Christian era, before it was divided; and taking for your guide the rule of St Vincent, *Quod semper, quod ubique, quod ab omnibus*—what was believed "always, everywhere, and by all"—as the only sure standard of Scriptural interpretation. I have proved, by many indisputable witnesses, that this rule recognized the *lawfulness of slavery*, as it existed in the old Roman empire. And I have also proved that, up to the period of the English Act of Emancipation, there was no variance on the subject in any part of the Christian world. Hence, if there could be a doubt concerning the meaning of the Bible, the voice of the Holy Catholic Church must be decisive on the question. And against that authority no Bishop is at liberty to rebel.

4. In the fourth place, I admonish you to remember your ALLE-

GIANCE TO THE CONSTITUTION OF THE UNITED STATES, which every naturalized foreigner is sworn to support, as well as every officer in the Government. The same allegiance, as you must be aware, devolves on every native citizen by virtue of his birth; and therefore you are bound as fully as if you had taken the oath, and to an equal extent, precisely. This, however, is not only a civil, but also a religious obligation; because the Constitution is the "supreme law of the land," and the Saviour commands us to "render unto Cæsar the things that be Cæsar's," and the Apostle lays down the precept: "Let every soul be subject unto the higher powers." By the terms of this Constitution, slavery is made *lawful.* And therefore I do not see how you can deny its lawfulness, without opposing the "supreme law of the land," which you are solemnly bound to support; and thus becoming the patron of treason in sentiment, if not in action.

5. In the fifth and last place, I admonish you not to rush again, through your zeal for political expediency, into a libelous assault on a brother bishop; nor to bring your clergy into a false position, without at least some decent regard to the usual course of previous inquiry and consultation. The mode in which you did this thing would be a disgrace to the lowest court of justice, in deciding upon the act of the most worthless individual. Even the self-appointed tribunal which is called "Lynch law" gives an opportunity to the culprit to make his defense before a jury, and imitates, to some extent, the order established in every civilized community. But your clergy were not summoned to meet together. Your intended victim was not notified. The false and defamatory sentence was drawn up by your own hand, and a committee of three were deputed to obtain the subscribers; the object being to accomplish the work in the least possible time, in order that the placards containing your Protest might be posted at the corners of the streets before the day of election!

And yet your proceeding was nothing short of a public judgment, pronounced on a brother bishop, your senior in years and in office, who had labored at least as hard in the service of the Church, who had published more books in defense of her principles than all your diocese together, and who had some little character to lose, and some few friends to be disgusted and amazed by the total want of justice and propriety, of feeling and courtesy, which marked the whole extraordinary transaction.

As the party whom you have thus publicly defamed, I have justified my pamphlet by an appeal to the highest authority; and I challenge yourself and your phalanx of "indignant reprobationists" to prove that I am in error, by any argument worthy of a consistent Christian or a loyal citizen. The position which I occupy is impregnable, for it is defended by the Word of God, the voice of the Church, and the Constitution of the country. Your zealous adherents may continue to assail it, as some of them have already done, by invective, by abuse, and by misrepresentation. But like the waves which dash against the rock, such assaults will make no impression; and even though their violence may be favored for a while by the strong wind of popular excitement, it will end in nothing more substantial than froth and foam.

I conclude with a brief summary of the whole. To slavery under the domination of any human master, I am as much opposed as you or your clergy, by birth, education, and the habits of a long lifetime. I desire to see the Southern institution abolished as soon as it can be, peaceably, lawfully, and with a just regard to the best interests of all concerned. I have put forth my argument many years ago, in favor of such abolition, on the principles of Thomas Jefferson, of Rufus King, of President Harrison, and others; being the constant advocate of a gradual emancipation connected with the planting of the freedmen in Africa, after the model of Liberia. Hence, I contend that I have never been in favor of the *perpetual bondage* of the negro race, and never have opposed their peaceable and gradual enfranchisement, and their future elevation to the highest development which they may be able to attain. To charge me with such sentiments is a sheer calumny, in the face of those publications which were issued and repeated years before the commencement of our present national warfare.

But along with this I have maintained, and shall always maintain that the *relation* of the master to the slave in the Southern States involves no sin, provided the *treatment* of the slave be in accordance with the Scriptures; because the slavery of the heathen races was sanctioned by the divine law in the Old Testament, and the system of Roman slavery was allowed to Christians by the apostles in the New Testament; and it was regarded as a providential arrangement of society by the fathers, the councils, the theologians, and commentators in every branch of the Church for more than eighteen centuries; so that there is no question on which the Holy Catholic Church was

more perfectly unanimous—that by necessary consequence the modern doctrine of ultra-abolitionists is an impious error, because it
opposes the Bible and the Church—that it is a dangerous error, because it divides Christian communities into hostile sects, bitterly warring against each other—that it is rebellious to the State as well as to
the Church, because it tramples on the Constitution, calling it a
"covenant with death and an agreement with hell," and has driven
the old Union of the States into discord and strife, of which no man
can foretell the issue—that to the negro race, slavery in the hands of
their Southern masters has been a blessing; because it has been the
means appointed in wisdom by divine Providence to redeem them from
a far more bitter bondage in Africa, in the midst of savage barbarism
and heathen degradation, to train them up to the civilization of the
Gospel, to qualify a portion of them to plant the State of Liberia, and
to enrol five hundred thousand communicants amongst the professed
Christians of the South—that if there had been no such arrangement
opened to them through the Southern institution, all these, with other
millions of their ancestors, must have lived and died in African bondage and in the darkest paganism—that the same Providence which has
thus far produced so vast a benefit to a portion of the negro race, will
doubtless incline the masters to their ultimate emancipation on a
much larger scale, when the Almighty sees that the proper time has
come, if His designs are not rashly opposed by human presumption—
that, meanwhile, the Church has no right to interfere with the institution, warranted as it is not only by the "supreme law of the
land," laid down in the Constitution, but by the word of God and the
unanimous judgment of Christendom—that we have no reason to
question the assurances of the Southern clergy, concerning the justice
and kindliness of the treatment which the slaves receive, as the general rule, notwithstanding occasional exceptions, nor to doubt that
the Christians of the South are quite as sensible of their responsibility,
and as indulgent and humane as we are—that the ultimate result will
be the preparation, in due time, of a vast host of missionary laborers,
able, by their physical peculiarities, to enjoy the climate of Africa,
which few of the white race can endure: and that these will multiply
the influence of Liberia a thousand fold, regenerate, by the light of
Christian truth, the whole of that barbarous and benighted continent,
and open a rich field of civilization to the commerce of the world.

Such, my Right Reverend Brother, is the view which I have taken, on this most important and deeply interesting subject. Thus believing, I claim the right of every American freeman to proclaim my belief, and utterly deny the justice or propriety of your denunciation for the maintenance of sentiments which have been held substantially by the best and most devoted men in all preceding ages. But while I have plainly expressed my sense of the grievous wrong which you and your clergy have committed, both in the fact and in the style of your false and libelous Protest, yet I should be blameworthy if I omitted to mention the Christian and manly course of those who refused to set their names to that most unwarrantable document. I thank God that there were more than sixty of your clergy who had the honesty and courage to resist the pressure of the popular political current, though it carried you and so many others away. I thank God that two of those who were induced to sign had afterwards the magnanimity to withdraw their names, from motives of honor and of conscience. And I doubt not that all of these just and independent men, who had the firmness to withstand the force so strongly used to warp their true Church principles, will be rewarded, not only by their consciousness of religious duty, but by the increased respect of all candid minds, when the excitement of strife and passion shall have cooled down, and given place, once more, to the counsels of sober sense and reason.

With respect to yourself and those who acted with you, although I am compelled, in obedience to the Apostolic precept, to withdraw from your fellowship and to admonish you, yet I wish you to remember that I do so without any personal feelings of resentment. I know how to make all charitable allowance for the delusions produced by the warmth of political zeal; and I regard your course with the indulgence due to the extravagance of good men, who are for a time demented. I have lived too long and experienced too much, to be ignorant of the devices of our spiritual adversary, who understands so well how to appear as an angel of light. Were not the most pious ministers in New-England carried away into acts of horrid injustice during the times of the Salem witchcraft? Did they not banish the zealous Roger Williams into the wilderness, in the depth of a severe Northern winter, only because he had become a Baptist? Did they not publicly whip his followers at the cart's tail from village to village, and hang the Quakers, for the glory of God? It was the accepted notion of those good old Puritans, that *tolera-*

tion of religious errors was the *doctrine of the devil;* and in all these acts, and hundreds of the same character, they were perfectly *conscientious,* though perfectly *deluded.* Nay, we have a still more awful instance of the adversary's power, when we remember that even the great Apostle Peter was led, by the temptation of Satan, to deny his Divine Lord and Master! And what a trifling case of delusion does your Protest against the poor Bishop of Vermont present in comparison with examples like these!

True indeed, it is, that persecution for religious opinions has long ceased to trouble the peace of society. It is not religion, but politics, which now excites the passions of men; and our subtle enemy adapts himself adroitly to the change of circumstances, wearing the robe of Christian philanthropy to give him influence with pious minds, but relying on *political zeal* to stir them up to action. That is the reason why my publications against the heresy of ultra-abolitionism attracted no notice from you or your clergy, until the Democratic party thought fit to use them in your election. Then, the doctrines which were previously suffered to pass without the slightest sign of disapproval started forth to your excited minds under a new aspect, as if they were the very utterances of treason. Then, the ecclesiastical thunder began to roll in the Vatican of Pennsylvania. And then, the lightning flash of your redoubtable Protest, was launched at my devoted head without delay, under the powerful excitement of *political expediency!*

So be it, while it pleases God to suffer this popular frenzy to prevail. I have no difficulty in forgiving the act, as a small example of the delusions to which the best men are liable, and which, sooner or later, are certain to pass away. Meanwhile, it has no effect on my old partiality for the Diocese and State of Pennsylvania. I can not forget that Philadelphia was the principal scene of my education; and the memories of those youthful years are all associated with persons and with places on which I look back with peculiar affection. Pittsburgh and its vicinity were the witnesses of my early manhood. It was there my married life began. There, my elder children were born. There, I passed through the struggles which prepared me for success in the practice of the law. There, I entered into the ministry, and became the architect and first rector of the present Trinity Church— the mother of so many of your western parishes. There, I passed eight years of prosperous labor, under the wise and indulgent government of the venerable Bishop White; when as yet there was no ultra-abolitionism to raise its voice against the Word of God, and the Constitution of our country. And although I was then induced to accept a call to Boston, and soon afterwards was elected as the Bishop of Vermont, yet I still looked on Pittsburgh and Philadelphia with special attachment, as the residence of many personal friends, who esteemed me for my work, and whom I regarded with cordiality and confidence. During the thirty years which have since elapsed, I have paid numerous visits to your Diocese; some in its service, and more in the service of the Church Institutions belonging to my own. And the warm hospitality, the generous liberality, and the kindly greetings which marked those visits, have left a grateful impression on my heart, too deep and strong for a hundred protests to obliterate. Your action, of necessity, destroys my former intercourse. But the old feeling remains unchanged. And I am as constant as ever in my prayer that the blessing of God may rest, in rich abundance, on the clergy and laity of Pennsylvania!

And here, my Right Reverend Brother, I close my unwelcome labor. Frankly and unreservedly, but I trust not unkindly, I have set forth "the truth wherein I stand." It is the same truth which was held from the beginning, founded on the absolute Will of the Almighty and all-wise Creator, taught by Moses and the prophets, sanctioned by the inspired Apostles, and maintained by the Holy Catholic Church throughout the world, even to our own day. It is none the less true, because, in many portions of the land, it has become distasteful. And, therefore, being myself the "bond-servant of Christ," our divine Redeemer, I can not be diverted from my obligations to contend, under his banner, for the authority of His Word, for the judgment of His Church, and, in harmony with these, for the allegiance which I owe to the Constitution of my country. Relying on His strength, which is "made perfect in weakness," I hope to persevere in the fearless and honest performance of my duty, whether popular or unpopular, whether "in honor or in dishonor," looking for no human praise, and dreading no human censure, but depending, with all humility, yet with all confidence, on Him who is "the way, the truth, and the life," whose Word is the only standard of right, and whose power alone can secure the final victory.

APPENDIX.

NOTE 1.

The proper meaning of the Hebrew word עֶבֶד being sometimes denied, I have made the following extracts from *Bagster's Polyglot*, showing the true sense of the Hebrew, as it was given by the Jews themselves, in the Septuagint version of the Fourth Commandment, to which I have added the Vulgate and others.

Thy man-servant and thy maid-servant. (Ex. 20 : 10.)

ὁ παῖς σου καὶ ἡ παιδίσκη σου, *Septuagint.*

Servus tuus et ancilla tua, *Latin Vulgate.*

dein knecht, noch deine magd, *German.*

ton serviteur ni ta servante, *French.*

tuo servo, ne la tua serva, *Italian.*

ni tu siervo, ni tu sierva, *Spanish.*

Now the word used here by the old Jews of Alexandria, viz., παῖς, signifies a child, a son, a daughter, a young MALE OR FEMALE SLAVE. See *Donnegan's* Greek and English Lexicon, and also Liddell and Scott, edited by Professor Drisler.

The appropriate signification, therefore, must be that of bondman and bondmaid, or male and female *slaves ;* because the son and the daughter were already mentioned just before. And this is, accordingly, the meaning given in the Latin, Italian, and Spanish versions.

The Tenth Commandment has the same words as the Fourth, both in the original Hebrew, and in all the versions. Thus we have *slave or bondman* in the Hebrew, Greek, Latin, Spanish, and Italian, and *servant* in the German, French, and English versions.

Levit. 20 : 44. *Both thy bondmen and thy bondmaids which thou shalt have, shall be of the heathen,* etc.

Here the Hebrew has the same words as in the Fourth and Tenth Commandments, עבד ואמה.

The Septuagint has the same, παῖς καὶ παιδίσκη.

The Latin has the same, servus et ancilla.

The German has the same, knecht und magd.

The French has *esclave* et servante.

The Italian has the same, servo ed alla tua serva.

The Spanish has the same, siervo y sierva.

The true meaning is given in this text, by all the versions save the German, which uses the doubtful word knecht, as before.

To these I shall add the following, from Robinson's Gesenius: "עֶבֶד a *servant*, who among the Hebrews was also a slave."

"In addressing superiors, the Hebrews, from modesty or humility were accustomed to call themselves *servants*, and those whom they addressed, *lords*."

And this extract from Robinson's edition of Calmet's Dictionary of the Holy Bible agrees with all the rest, viz.: "*Servant*. This word, in Scripture, generally signifies a *slave*, because, among the Hebrews and the neighboring nations, the greater part of the servants were such, belonging absolutely to their masters, who had a right to dispose of their persons, and in some cases, even of their lives."

"*Slavery*, compulsory servitude. To punish the indignity received from his son Ham, Noah foretold the slavery of his descendants. Gen. 9 : 25."

"Moses notices two or three sorts of slaves among the Hebrews; who had foreign slaves, obtained by capture, by purchase, or born in the house. Over these, masters had entire authority ; they might sell them, exchange them, punish them, judge them, and even put them to death without public process. In which the Hebrews followed the rules common to other nations."

The meaning of δουλος, in the New Testament, is hardly susceptible of a cavil. It signifies *a slave*, according to Donnegan, to Liddell and Scott, edited by Professor Drisler, to Parkhurst, and, in a word, to all the authorities. Of course, examples may be found in which both these words are applied in another sense than that of strict bodily servitude for life. Thus, no word is better understood than our English term *slave*, yet we use it constantly in a larger sense, as when we say, a slave to lust, a slave to drink, a slave to fashion, a slave to popularity. So, too, we say of an overtasked wife: "She is a perfect slave to her husband." But this license does not interfere with the proper meaning of the term, which is as firmly fixed as language can be.

On the meaning of the Latin word *servus*, which is invariably applied in the sense of *slave*, there is and can be no dispute whatever.

Note 2.

From the foregoing examples it will appear manifest that the proper meaning of the Hebrew *Ebed*, and the Greek *doulos*, and the Latin *servus*, is a *bond-servant* or slave. The hired servant is expressed in all these languages by a different word — *sakir* in the Hebrew, *misthotos* or *misthophoros* in the Greek, and *mercenarius* in the Latin. Our translators have not been precise in our English Bible. In some places they have translated the very same word by *bond-servant*, and in a far greater number they have employed the general term *servant*, while, in almost all, they have avoided the word *slave*, doubtless because slavery had died out in England before the reign of James I., when their translation was published, and they wished to secure the advantage of the precepts in the Scriptures for the relation of master and servant, in the form which was customary at the time. The Southern slaveholders and their slaves continue the same practice of avoiding the word *slave*. The milder word, *servant*, is the only one in common use among them. But if our English Bible had been translated with a view to the present question, which had not then been contemplated in its moral and religious aspect, the authority of the Scriptures would have appeared, as it really is, perfectly free from any ambiguity.

NOTE 3.

De Jure personarum.

Summa itaque divisio de jure personarum hæc est : quod omnes homines aut liberi sunt aut servi. Et libertas quidem (ex qua etiam liberi vocantur) est naturalis facultas ejus, quod cuique facere libet, nisi si quid vi aut jure prohibetur. Servitus autem est constitutio juris gentium, qua quis dominio alieno contra naturam subjicitur.

Servi autem ex eo appellati sunt, quod Imperatores captivos, *vendere* ac per hoc *servare*, nec occidere solent : qui etiam *mancipia* dicti sunt, quod ab hostibus *manu capiuntur.*

Servi autem aut nascuntur, aut fiunt : nascuntur ex ancillis nostris : fiunt aut jure gentium, id est, ex captivitate, aut jure civili, cum liber homo major xx annis ad pretium participandum sese venundari passus est. In servorum conditione nulla est differentia : in liberis autem multæ : aut enim sunt ingenui, aut libertini.—*Inst. Justin. L.* 1. *Tit. III. Corpus Juris Civilis. Ed. Amstel.* 1663.   *Tom.* 1, p. 4.

NOTE 4.

Libertini sunt, qui ex justa servitute manumissi sunt. Manumissio autem est de manu datio, nam quamdiu aliquis in servitute est, manui et potestati suppositus est: manumissus, liberatur potestate. Quæ res à jure gentium originem sumpsit: utpote cum jure naturali omnes liberi nascerentur, nec esset nota manumissio, cum servitus esset incognita. Sed postquam jure gentium servitus invasit, sequutum est beneficium manumissionis : et cum uno communi nomine omnes homines appellarentur, jure gentium tria hominum genera esse cœperunt: liberi, et his contrarium servi, et tertium genus libertini, qui desierant esse servi. Multis autem modis manumissio procedit: aut enim ex sacris constitutionibus in sacrosanctis Ecclesiis, aut vindicta manumittitur, aut inter amicos, aut per epistolam, aut per testamentum, aut per aliam quamlibet ultimam voluntatem.—*Inst. Justin. Corp. Juris Civilis, Tom* 1, p. 4.

Note 5.

Sequitur de jure personarum alia divisio. Nam quædam personæ sui juris sunt, quædam alieno jure subjectæ. Rursus earum, quæ alieno juri subjectæ sunt, aliæ sunt in potestate parentum, aliæ in potestate dominorum.—In potestate itaque dominorum sunt servi, quæ quidem potestas, juris gentium est. Nam apud omnes peræque gentes animadvertere possumus, dominis in servos vitæ necisque potestatem fuisse: et quodcumque per servum adquiritur, id domino adquiri.

Sed hoc tempore nullis hominibus, qui sub imperio nostro sunt, licet sine causa legibus cognita, in servos suos supra modum sævire. Nam ex constitutione divi Antonini, qui sine causa servum suum occiderit, non minus puniri jubetur, quam si alienum servum occiderit. Sed et major asperitas dominorum ejusdem principis constitutione coërcetur: nam Antoninus consultus a quibusdam præsidibus provinciarum de his servis, qui ad ædem sacram, vel ad statuam principum confugiunt, præcipit, ut si intolerabilis videatur sævitia dominorum, cogantur servos suos bonis conditionibus vendere, ut pretium dominis daretur: et recte: expedit enim reipublicæ, ne sua re quis malè utatur.—*Corpus Civilis, (Inst. Justin.) Tom.* 1., p. 5.

Note 6.

§ 17. Item ea quæ ex hostibus capimus, jure gentium statim nostra fiunt: adeò quidem, ut et liberi homines in servitutem nostram deducantur, qui tamen, si evaserint nostram potentiam, et ad suos reversi fuerint, primum statum recipiunt.—*Corpus Civilis, (Instit. Justin.) Tom.* 1, p. 10.

Note 7.

Tit. iv. De injuriis.

§ 3. Servis autem ipsis quidem nulla injuria fieri intelligitur, sed domino per eos fieri videtur: non tamen iisdem modis quibus etiam per liberos et uxores: sed ita, cum quid atrocius commissum fuerit, et quod aperte ad contumeliam domini respicit: veluti si quis alienum servum atrociter verberaverit: et in hunc casum actio proponitur. At si quis servo convicium fecerit, vel pugno eum percusserit: nulla in eum actio domino competit. —*Corpus Civilis, (Institut. Justin.) Tom.* 1, p. 32.

Note 8.

Servos sane sociari clericorum consortiis, volentibus atque consentientibus dominis, modis omnibus prohibemus : cum liceat eorum dominis, data prius servis libertate, licitum cis ad suscipiendos honores clericorum iter (si hoc voluerint) aperire.—*Corpus Juris Civilis, (Codex Justin.) Tom.* 11, p. 16.

Note 9.

Si servus, sciente domino, et non contradicente, in clericum ordinatus fuerit ab Episcopo : ex hoc ipso, quod constitutus est, liber et ingenuus erit. Si vero, ignorante domino, ordinatus fuerit ; liceat domino, intra anni unius spatium, et servilem fortunam probare, et servum suum accipere. Si vero servus, sciente vel nesciente domino (sicut diximus) ideo quod in clero constitutus, liber est factus, ministerium ecclesiasticum reliquerit, et ad secularem vitam transierit ; suo domino ad serviendum tradatur.—*Corpus Juris Civilis, (Codex Justin.) Tom.* 11, p. 16.

Note 10.

Quoniam igitur de servis fugitivis ad vitam monasticam devenientibus, statutum a superioribus est, ut si intra tres annos fugitivus manifestus fiat; illum habitu nudatum recipiendi facultatem dominus habeat : si vero usque in tertium annum incognitus manserit, tametsi postmodum agnoscatur, ut domini potestati non obnoxius sit, præterque illius voluntatem liber nuncupetur : et vero inde multos fugiendi dominos suos occasionem cepisse, ac re honesta monasticæ vitæ professione, ad tegendam malitiam abuti videmus, (cuilibet enim servo perfacile est, ut ad triennium se occultet, deindeque libertatem consequatur,) jubemus, *ut quantocunque* tempore servus tali consilio monachus factus delituerit, si ipsum aliquando dominus inveniat, nihilominus is quem malo proposito habitum sumpsit, hoc exuatur, rursumque in domini potestatem subigatur.—*Corpus Juris Civilis, (Imp. Leonis Constit. X.) Tom.* 11, p. 242, *pars* 2.

Note 11.

De illis servis quibus nesciente domino ad primarii sacerdotii honores conscendere visum est, statuimus : ut videlicet secundum ecclesiasticæ constitutionis voluntatem exauthorati, honore in quem clam irrepserint, priventur, et ad suum servilemque statum revocantur.—*Imp. Leonis Const. XI. Corpus Juris Civilis. Tom.* 11, *pars* 2, p. 242.

Note 12.

Testimonium cum magni momenti, necessariaque ad tuenda communis vitæ negotia res sit, non a quibuslibet, sed ab iis qui extra ignominiam vivunt, ferri æquum est. Recte ergo exquisita ratione de hoc disceptant leges, et non simpliciter ad dicendum testimonium cuique aditum præbent. Verumtamen, quia nonnullæ leges servilis conditionis hominibus in quibusdam rebus testari concesserunt ; visum nobis est, hoc nota inducendum

esse, ut qui liberæ vitæ participes non sunt, in universum ad testandum non
admittantur, lexque Novellarum Constitutionum obtineat, et de quocunque
simpliciter testimonio statuat, idque in quacunque re, sive testamenta, sive
aliam humanæ vitæ actionem testimonium complectatur. Si enim illis qui
cum liberæ vitæ sint, vitam ingenue, eaque libertate quam nacti sunt digne
non degunt, neque quantum fieri potest animi magnitudinem a servitute
liberam conservant, sed in illicitarum actionum servitutem subiguntur, testimonium dicere non licet : neque his quorum vitam non esse liberam
constat, ferre testimonium concedetur. Nam tametsi alius hic servitutis
modus sit, attamen ea servitus est, quam libertatis dignitate participem esse
indignum sit.—*Imper. Leonis Constit. XLIX. Corpus Juris Civilis, Tom.*
11, *pars* 2, p. 257.

Note 13.

Si quis ita demens sit, ut libertatem servitute commutans seipsum ven-
dat, ne is contractus validus sit, sed evertatur, et simul ipse libertatis suæ
proditor, simul is qui cum ipso id facinus designavit, verberibus castigen-
tur, nihiloque minus vesaniæ mancipio libertas in pristino suo statu ser-
vetur.—*Imp. Leonis Constit. LIX. Corpus Juris Civilis. Tom.* 11, *pars*
2, p. 260.

The reasons assigned for this imperial change in the civil law make no
allusion whatever to religion.

Note 14.

Servitus quædam animi, quædam corporis dicitur ; corporibus dominantur
homines, animis affectus et vitia.—*Phil. Jud.* p. 867.

Note 15.

At lex divina regulas juris non fortunæ sed naturæ accommodat. Ideo
decet dominos non abuti sua potestate contra famulos, cavereque ab inso-
lencia, contemptu atque sævitia. Nam ista non sunt indicia placidi animi,
sed impotentiæ tyrannicæ, exercentis licentiam pro arbitrio.—*Phil. Jud.
Liber de Special. Leg.* p. 798.

Note 16.

Quid enim injustius, quid iniquius, et improbrius, quàm ita alieno bene-
facere servo, ut domino eripiatur, ut alii vindicetur, ut adversus caput domini subornetur, et quidem, quo indignius, in ipsa adhuc domo domini, de
ipsius adhuc horreis vivens, sub ipsius adhuc plagis tremens ? Talis adser-
tor etiam damnaretur in seculo, nedum plagiator.—*Tertul. adv. Marcion.
Lib.* 1, § *XXIII.* p. 377, C.

Note 17.

*Quicunque sunt sub jugo servi Dominos suos omni honore dignos arbi-
trentur.* Non solum bonos, sed etiam infideles. Ne vidieantur per religionem

in deterius profecisse. Ne sibi æqualem contemnant. Si serviebant infidelibus timore odioso, quanto magis debent servire fidelibus quorum charitatis
participes esse merentur.—*Hieron. Op. T. IX.* p. 314.

Note 18.

Christianæ religioni conditio non potest obesse servilis, ne dicas ergo, quo
modo Deo possum placere, qui servus sum ? Deus enim non conditionem
aspicit, sed voluntatem quærit et mentem. Usque adeo non prodest libertas,
nec servitus nocet—Qui hominis servus est, liber est Deo, et qui hominibus
liber est, servus est Christi. Ambo ergo unum sunt.—*Op. Hieron. Tom. IX.*
p. 249.

Note 19.

Providet sanè hic Apostolus, ne doctrina Dei in aliquo blasphemetur, si
credentes servi suis dominis inutiles fiant. Et qui forte permissurus erat
alios servos fieri Christianos, de ipsis jam factis incipiat pœnitere. Si vero
viderit eos in melius profecisse, et ex infidelibus fideles effectos, non solùm
alios optabit credere famulos suos, sed etiam ipse fortasse salvabitur.—
Hieron. Op. T. IX. p. 294.

Note 20.

Sed hoc mundi iniquitate factum est, ut dum alter alterius fines invadit,
tunc captivos ducit ingenuos, unde et manu capti dicti sunt a veteribus, inde
mancipia. Hic casus et conditio etiam nunc apparet, alii redimuntur, alii
remanent servi. Apud Deum autem hic servus habetur, qui peccaverit.
Denique peccati causâ Cham servus audivit : Maledictus puer Chanaan, servus servorum erit fratribus suis.—*S. Ambros. Supp. Comm. in Epist. ad
Coloss. Tom.* 2 *Op. p. in app.* 274.

Note 21.

Servorum obsequiis dominos Deo gratias vult referre, cùm enim per Dei
disciplinam fidelia illis exhibuerint servitia, forte huic etiam ipsi se subjicient
disciplinæ. Si profanis dominis serviendum tota solicitudine imperat, quanto
magis fidelibus ? Tunc enim probat se timori Dei subjectum, si fideli et
temporali domino toto animo fuerit obsequtuus.—*App. Op. S. Ambros.
Tom.* 2, p. 302. Com. in 1 Tim. 6 : 1-2.

Note 22.

Tu (*i. e.* Ecclesia Catholica) dominis servos, non tam conditionis necessi-
tate, quàm officii delectatione doces adhærere. Tu dominos servis, summi
Dei communis Domini consideratione placabiles, et ad consulendum quàm
coërcendum propensiores facis.—*Augustini Op. Tom. I.* p. 527, *f.*

Note 23.

Timet servus offendere dominum suum ne jubeat illum verberari, jubeat in compedes mitti, jubeat carcere includi, jubeat eum pistrino contineri. Hæc timens servus non peccat.—*Augustini Op. Tom. V.* p. 542, D.

Note 24.

Servum autem hominem homini, vel iniquitas vel adversitas fecit; iniquitas quidem, sicut dictum est: Maledictus Chanaan, erit servus fratribus suis: adversitas vero, sicut accedit ipsi Joseph, ut venditus a fratribus servus alienigenæ fieret. Itaque primos servos, quibus hoc nomen in Latina lingua inditum est, bella fecerunt. Qui enim homo ab homine superatus jure belli possit occidi, quia servatus est, servus est appellatus; inde a máncipia, quia manu capta sunt. Est etiam ordo naturalis in hominibus, ut serviant feminæ viris, et filii parentibus: quia et illic hæc justitia est, ut infirmior ratio serviat fortiori. Hæc igitur in dominationibus et servitutibus clara justitia est, ut qui excellunt ratione, excellant dominatione.—*Aug. Op. Tom. III.* p. 311, C.

Note 25.

Quae de servo Hebræo præcipiuntur, ut sex annos serviat, et dimittatur liber gratis, ne servi Christiani hoc flagitarent a dominis suis, Apostolica auctoritas jubet servos dominis suis esse subditos, ne nomen Dei et doctrina blasphemetur. Illud enim ex hoc satis constat in mysterio præceptum, quia et pertundi subulâ ejus aurem ad postem, præcipit Deus, qui libertatem illam recusasset.—*Aug. Op. Tom. III.* p. 333, E.

Note 26.

Prima et quotodiana potestas hominis in hominem domini est in servum. Propè omnes domus habent hujusmodi potestatem. Sunt domini, sunt et servi, diversa sunt nomina; sed homines et homines paria sunt nomina. Et quid dicit Apostolus, docens servos dominis suis subditos esse? Servi obaudite dominis vestris secundum carnem: quia est Dominus secundùm Spiritum. Ille est verus Dominus et æternus, illi autem temporales secundùm tempus. Tu cùm ambulas in via, cùm vivis in hac vita, non vult te facere superbum Christus. Contigit tibi ut Christianus efficeris, et haberes dominum hominem; non ideo Christianus effectus es, ut dedigneris servire. Cùm enim Christo jubente servis homini, non illi servis, sed illi qui jussit. Et hoc ait, Obaudite dominis vestris secundùm carnem, cum timore et tremore, in simplicitate cordis, non ad oculum servientes, quasi hominibus placentes, sed quasi servi Christi, facientes voluntatem Dei ex animo, cum bona voluntate. Ecce non fecit de servis liberos, sed de malis servis bonos servos. Quantum debent divites Christo, qui illis componit domum?—*August. Op. Enar. in Ps.* 124, *Tom. IV. Pars Prima,* p. 1059, *C.*

Note 27.

Porro quicumque servi sub jugo detenti, ad fratrum conventum confugiunt,

16

admoniti et meliores effecti, ad dominos suos remittendi sunt: in quo imitandus est beatus Paulus, qui, cum genuiset Onesimum per evangelium, eum ad Philemonem remisit.—*S. Basil. Op. T.* 2, p. 353, *D. et T.* 3, p. 479, *A. B.*

Note 28.

Regula LXXV.

Quòd oportet servos, cum omni benevolentia ad Dei gloriam suis secundum carnem dominis obedire, in iis certe, in quibus mandatum Dei non solvitur.

Caput 1.

Servi obedite dominis carnalibus cum timore et tremore in simplicitate cordis vestri, sicut Christo : non ad oculum servientes, quasi homini placentes, sed ut servi Christi, facientes voluntatem Dei ex animo, cum benevolentia servientes, sicut Domino, et non hominibus : scientes quoniam unusquisque quodcumque fecerit bonum, hoc recipiet a Domino, sive servus, sive liber. Quicumque sunt sub jugo servi, dominos suos omni honore dignos arbitrentur, ne nomen Dei et doctrina blasphemetur. Qui autem fideles habent dominos, non contemnant, quia fratres sunt, sed magis serviant, quia fideles sunt et dilecti, qui beneficii participes sunt. Servos dominis suis subditos esse, in omnibus placentes, non contradicentes, non fraudentes, sed omnem fidem bonam ostendentes, ut doctrinam Salvatoris nostri Dei ornent in omnibus. —*S. Basil, Op. Om. T. II.* p. 310.

Note 29.

Aut enim potentia oppressi, sub jugum servitutis inducti sunt, velut in bello capti, aut ob paupertatem in servitutem edacti sunt velut Ægypti Pharaoni, aut juxta sapientem quandam et arcanam dispensationem, qui inter filios deteriores sunt, parentum voce, sapientioribus ac melioribus in servitutem addicti sunt, quam haudquaquam condemnationem, sed beneficium potius dixerit æquus rerum æstimator. Nam qui ob sensus inopiam, non habet in sese id quod natura imperat, huic utilius est alterius fieri mancipium.—*S. Basil, Op. Om. T. III.* p. 42–3.

Note 30.

Unusquisque .n qua vocatione vocatus es, in ea permaneat. Uxorem habens infidelem vocatus es, permane eam habens, ne propter fidem ejicias uxorem. Servus cùm esses, fuisti vocatus : ne sit tibi curæ, permane serviens. Cùm præputium haberes es vocatus, permane habens præputium. Credidisti cùm esses circumcisus, permane circumcisus. Quomodo nihil juvat circumcisio, neque lædit præputium, ita neque servitus neque libertas. Et ut ex abundantia hoc docerit evidentius, dicit : *Sed si potes fieri liber, magis utere.* Hoc est, magis servi. Et cúrnam eum qui potest liberari, jubet manere servum ? Volens ostendere quòd nihil lædit servitus, sed etiam prodest.

Neque verò ignoremus, quod quidam illud, Magis utere, aiunt dictum esse de
libertate, dicentes, Si potes liberari, liberare. Modo autem Pauli hoc verbum
est valde contrarium, si hoc significat. Non enim consolans servum, osten-
dendo eum nulla esse injuria affectum, jussisset eum fieri liberum. Diceret
enim fortè quispiam, Quid verò si non possum, affectus sum injuria et dam-
num accepi. Non ergo hoc dicit, sed sicut dixi, volens ostendere quòd nihil
emolumenti ei obtingit qui factus est liber, dicit: Etiamsi sit in tua potestate
ut manumittaris et liber fias, permane potius serviens. Deinde subjungit
etiam causam. *Qui enim in Domino vocatus est servus, libertus est Domini.
Similiter qui liber vocatus est, servus est Christi.* In iis enim quæ sunt secundum Christum, ambo sunt pares.—Quomodo ergo qui est servus, est libertus?
Quoniam se liberavit, non solùm a peccato, sed etiam ab externa servitute,
manentem servum.—Et quomodo qui est servus est liber, manens servus?
Quando fuerit liberatus ab affectionibus et animi ægritudinibus. Quando
despexerit pecunias, iramque et ejusmodi alias animi perturbationes. *Pretio
empti estis: nolite fieri servi hominum.* Hoc dictum est non solùm servis sed
etiam liberis. Fieri enim potest ut et cùm sit servus, non sit servus, et cùm
sit liber, sit servus. Et quomodo cùm sit servus, non est servus? Quando
propter Deum omnia fecerit: quando non simularit neque fuerit hypocrita,
nec aliquid agat ut serviat oculis hominum: hoc est hominibus servientem
esse liberum. Aut quomodo rursus quispiam cùm sit liber, fiat servus?
Quando hominibus aliquod malum obit ministerium, aut propter ingluviem,
aut propter pecuniæ cupiditatem, aut propter potentiam. Nam qui est ejusmodi, est omnibus servilior, etsi sit liber. Utraque autem hæc considera.
Servus erat Joseph: sed non servus hominum. Quamobrem etiam in servitute erat omnibus hominibus liberior. Dominæ quidem certè non cessit in
iis quæ volebat quæ ipsum possidebat. Rursus illa erat libera, et omnibus
erat servilior, ut quæ servo assentaretur et eum rogaret et provocaret. Sed
non persuasit libero ut faceret quod noluit. Non erat ergo res illa servitus,
sed summa libertas. Quid enim illi ad virtutem impedimento fuit servitus?
Audiant servi et liberi.—Hoc quidem certè tacitè significat dicens, *Nolite
fieri servi hominum.* Si autem non ita est, sed jussit dominos relinquere, et
contendere ut fiant liberi, quomodo monebat dicens, *Unusquisque in eo
maneat in quo vocatus est?* et alibi, quicumque sunt sub jugo servi, suos
dominos omni honore dignos censeant.—Ad Ephesios quoque scribens et
Colossenses, eadem præcipit et statuit. Unde est perspicuum quod non
tollit hanc servitutem, sed eam quæ est a vitio, in qua sunt etiam liberi.—
S. Chrysostom, in Ep. ad. Corin. c. vii. Hom. xix. Ed. Paris, 1636. T. v.
p. 196–8.

NOTE 31.

Nomen et conditionem servitutis culpa genuit, non natura, et prima hujus subjectionis causa peccatum est; quia sicut scriptum est. *Omnis qui facit peccatum, servus est peccati.* Unde melior ejus status est qui famulatur homini, quàm qui suæ servit cupiditati.—*Prosper. Aquit. Op. Om.* p. 566.

Note 32.

Sciendum est duo genera esse bonæ servitutis: unum timoris, aliud dilectionis: unum timentium ancillorum et servorum, aliud diligentium et placentium filiorum, timet enim ancilla, ne flagelletur, timet matrona, ne offendat animum viri sui.—*S. Greg. Mag. Op. T. III. Par.* 2, p. 562.

Note 33.

"Admonitio VI.—Aliter admonendi sunt servi, atque aliter domini. Servi, scilicet, ut in se semper humilitatem conditionis aspiciant: domini vero, ut naturæ suæ qua æqualiter sunt cum servis conditi, memoriam non amittant. Servi admonendi sunt ne dominos despiciant, ne Deum offendant si ordinationi illius superbiendo contradicunt: domini quoque admonendi sunt, quia contra Deum de munere ejus superbiunt, si eos quos per conditionem tenent subditos, æquales sibi per naturæ consortium non agnoscent. Isti admonendi sunt ut sciant se servos esse dominorum; illi admonendi sunt ut cognoscant se conservos esse servorum. Istis namque dicitur: servi, obedite dominis carnalibus. Et rursum: quicumque sunt sub jugo servi, dominos suos omni honore dignos arbitrentur: illis autem dicitur: et vos, domini, eadem facite illis, remittentes minas, scientes quod et illorum et vester Dominus est in coelis."—*S. Greg. Mag. Op. Pastoralis Curæ, Pars* 3, *c.* 1.

Note 34.

" Gregorius Felici Episcopo Portuensi."

" Charitatis vestræ gratiâ provocati, ne infructuosi vobis videamur existere, præcipuè cum et minus vos habere servitia noverimus, ideo Johannem juris ecclesiastici famulum, natione Sabinum, ex massâ * Flavianâ, annorum plus minus decem et octo, quem nostra voluntate jam diu possidetis, fraternitati vestræ jure directo donamus atque concidemus; ita ut eum habeatis, possideatis, atque juri proprietatique vestræ vindicetis atque defendatis, et quidquid de eo facere volueritis, quippe ut dominus, ex hujus donationis jure libero potiamini arbitrio. Contra quam munificentiæ nostræ chartulam nunquam nos successoresque nostros noveris esse venturos. Hanc autem donationem a Notario nostro perscriptam legimus atque subscripsimus, tribuentes etiam, non expectatâ professione vestrâ, quo volueritis tempore alligandi licentiam legitima stipulatione et sponsione interpositâ. Actum Romæ."—*S. Greg. Mag. Op. Liber. X. Ep. LII.*

---

* The *massa* above mentioned was generally a farm or plantation.

Note 35.

Propter peccatum primi hominis humano generi pœna divinitus illata est servitutis, ita ut quibus aspicit non congruere libertatem, his misericordius irroget servitutem. Et licet peccatum humanæ originis per baptismi gratiam cunctis fidelibus dimissum sit, tamen æquus Deus ideo discrevit hominibus vitam, alios servos constituens, alios dominos : ut licentia male agendi servorum, potestate dominantium restringatur. Nam si omnes sine metu fuissent, quis esset qui a malis quempiam prohiberet? Inde et in gentibus principes regesque electi sunt, ut terrore suo populos a malo coercerent, atque ad recte vivendum legibus subderent.—Melior est subjecta servitus, quàm elata libertas. Multi enim inveniuntur Deo liberè servientes sub dominis flagitiosis, qui et si subjecti sunt illis corpore, prælati tamen sunt mente.—*Isidor. Hispal. Op. Om. Sentent. L. III. c. XLVII. p.* 471.

Note 36.

Servus in clerum provehi sine voluntate dominorum, non permittimus, ad eorum qui possident molestiam, domorum enim eversionem talia efficiunt. Siquando autem, etiam dignus servus visus est, qui ad gradum eligatur, qualis noster quoque Onesimus visus est, et domini concesserint ac liberaverint, et ædibus emiserint, fiat.—*Can. Apostol. Can. LXXXI.*

Note 37.

De famulis quid amplius dicamus, quam quod servus habeat benevolentiam erga dominum cum timore Dei, quamvis sit impius, quamvis sit improbus, non tamen cum eo religione consentiat. Item dominus servum diligat, et quamvis præstet ei, judicet tamen esse æqualitatem, vel quatenus homo est. Qui autem habet dominum Christianum, salvo dominatu, diligat eum, tum ut dominum, tum ut fidei consortem et ut patrem, non sicut servus ad oculum serviens, sed sicut dominum amans, ut qui sciat mercedem famulatûs sui a Deo sibi solvendam esse. Similiter dominus, qui Christianum famulum habet, salvo famulatu, diligat cum tanquam filium, et tanquam fratrem propter fidei communionem.—*Constit. Apostol. Clem. Lib. IV. ch.* 5.

Note 38.

Si quis servum, prætextu divini cultus, doceat dominum contemnere proprium, ut discedat ab ejus obsequio, nec ei cum benevolentia et omni honore deserviat, anathema sit.— *Concilium Gangrense,* A.D. 341. *Hardouini Concil. Tom.* 1, p. 534.

Note 39.

Si quos de servis ecclesiæ bene meritos sibi episcopus libertate donaverit, collatam libertatem a successoribus placuit custodiri, cum hoc quod eis manumissor in libertate contulerit.—*Concilium Agathense, Can. VII.* A.D. 506. *Hardouini Con. Tom.* 2, p. 998.

Note 40.

Servus qui ad ecclesiam pro qualibet culpa confugerit, si a domino pro admissa culpa sacramenta susciperet, statim ad servitium domini sui redire cogatur. — *Concilium Aurelianense* 1, *Can. III.* A.D. 511. *Hardouini Con. Tom.* 2, p. 1009.

Note 41.

Si quis servum proprium sine conscientia judicis occiderit, excommunicationis biennii effusionem sanguinis expiabit.—*Concilium Epaonense, Can. XXXIV.* A.D. 517. *Hardouini Con. Tom.* 2, p. 1051.

Note 42.

Ut servis ecclesiæ, vel sacerdotum, prædas et captivitates exercere non liceat : quia iniquum est, ut quorum domini redemptionis præstare solent suffragium, per servorum excessum disciplina ecclesiastica maculetur.—*Concilium Aurelianense IV. Can. XXIII.* A.D. 541. *Hardouini Con. Tom.* 2, p. 1439.

Note 43.

Ut servum, qui libertatem a dominis propriis non acceperit, aut etiam jam libertum, nullus episcopus absque ejus tantum voluntate, cujus aut servus est, aut eum absolvisse dignoscitur, clericum audeat ordinare.—*Concilium Aurelianense V. Can. VI.* A.D. 549. *Hard. Con. Tom.* 2, p. 1444–5.

Note 44.

Idcirco præsenti concilio, Deo auctore, sancimus, ut nullus Christianus, Judæo deniceps debeat deservire, sed datis pro quolibet bono mancipio duodecim solidis, ipsum mancipium quicumque Christianus, seu ad ingenuitatem, seu ad servitium, licentiam habeat redimendi ; quia nefas est, ut quos Christus Dominus sanguinis sui effusione redemit, persecutorum vinculis maneant irretiti. Quod si acquiescere his quæ statuimus, quicumque Judæus noluerit, quamdiu ad pecuniam constitutam venire distulerit, liceat mancipio ipsi cum Christianis, ubicumque voluerit, habitare.—*Concilium Matisconense* 1, A.D. 581, *Can. XVI. Hardouini Con. Tom. III.* p. 453.

Note 45.

Quoniam cognovimus per multas civitates ecclesiarum servos, et episcoporum, vel omnium clericorum a judicibus vel actoribus publicis diversis angariis fatigari, omne concilium a pietate domini nostri poposcit, ut tales deinceps ausus inhibeat : sed servi suprascriptorum officiorum, in eorum usibus vel ecclesiæ laborent.—*Con. Toletanum III. Can. XXI.* A.D. 589. *Hard. Con. Tom. III.* p. 483.

Note 46.

Ut omnis homo, tam ingenuus, tam servus, Gothus, Romanus, Syrus,

Græcus, vel Judæus, diei Dominico nullam operam faciant, nec boves jungantur; excepto si in metando necessitas incubuerit. Quod si quisquam præsumpserit facere, si ingenuus est, det comiti civitatis solidos sex; si servus, centum flagella suscipiat.— *Concilium Narbonense*, A.D. 589. *Can. IV. Hardouini Con. Tom. III.* p. 492.

Note 47.

Si quis servum suum ad altere mǎnumiserit, liber esto, et habilis sit ad gaudendum hereditate et wirgildo, et fas sit ei ubi volet sine limite versari. —*Con. Berghamstedense, Can. IX.* A.D. 697. *Hard. Con. T. III.* 1819.

Note 48.

Propter peccatum primi hominis, humano generi pœna divinitus illata est servitutis : ita ut quibus aspicit non congruere libertatem, his misericordius irroget servitutem. Et licet peccatum humanæ originis, per baptismi gratiam cunctis fidelibus dimissum sit, tamen æquus Deus ideo discrevit hominibus vitam, alios servos constituens, alios dominos, ut licentia male agendi servorum, potestate dominantium restringatur. Non est personarum acceptio apud Deum.—Unus enim Dominus æqualiter, et dominis refert consultum, et servis. Melior est subjecta servitus, quam elata libertas. Multi enim inveniuntur Deo libere servientes, sub dominis constituti flagitiosis : quo etsi subjecti sunt illis corpore, prælati tamen sunt mente. — *Concil. Aquisgranense Can. CIV.* A.D. 816. *Hard. Con. T. IV.* p. 1115.

Note 49.

De servorum vero ordinatione, qui passim ad gradus ecclesiasticos indiscretè promoventur, placuit omnibus cum sacris canonibus concordari debere : et statutum est, ut nullus episcoporum deinceps eos ad sacros ordines promovere præsumat, nisi prius a dominis propriis libertatem consecuti fuerint. Et si quilibet servus dominum suum fugiens, aut latitans, aut adhibitis testibus munere conductis vel corruptis, aut qualibet calliditate vel fraude ad gradus ecclesiasticos pervenerit, decretum est ut deponatur, et dominus ejus recipiat.—*Ludovici Pii Imperatoris Capitulare, anno imperii ejus editum. Hard. Con. Tom. IV.* p. 1214.

Note 50.

Si quis servum proprium sine conscientia judicum, qui tale quid commiserit, quod morte sit dignum, occiderit, excommunicatione vel pœnitentia biennii reatum sanguinis emundabit. — *Concilium Wormatense, Can. XXXVIII.* A.D. 868. *Hard. Con. Tom. V.* p. 743.

Note 51.

Si servus, absente vel nesciente domino suo, episcopo autem sciente quod servus sit, diaconus aut presbyter fuerit ordinatus, ipse in clericatus officio permaneat : episcopus tamen eum domino duplici satisfactione persolvat. Si vero episcopus eum servum esse nescieret et ita eum ad sacros ordines promovit, qui testimonium de illo perhibebant, aut eum postulabant ordinari, simili recompensatione teneantur obnoxii.—*Concilium Wormatense, Can. XL.* A.D. 868. *Hard. Con. Tom. V.* p. 743.

Note 52.

Ne quis illud nefarium negotium quo hactenus in Anglia solebant homines sicut bruta animalia venundari, deinceps ullatenus facere præsumat.

Note 53.

" Anselmus archiepiscopus Willelmo archidiacono dilecto suo, salutem et benedictionem.

Sententias capitulorum concilii expositas, nolo vobis aut alicui ad præsens mittere : quia quando in ipso concilio expositæ sunt, non potuerunt ad plenum et perfecté recitari, propterea quia subito sine præmeditatione, ac competenti tractatione, sicut oportuerat, sunt prolatæ. Unde quædam videntur addenda, et forsitan quædam mutanda, quod non nisi communi consensu coepiscoporum nostrum volo facere. Volo ergo eas dictare, et prius eisdem episcopis ostendere, cum primo convenerimus, quam per ecclesias Angliæ dictatæ et expositæ mittantur. Nomina tamen rerum, de quibus ibi locuti sumus, vobis mittimus, ut secundum quod recordari poteritis, nos de illis decrevisse faciatis." Then follows a list of subjects, but the topic of selling slaves is entirely omitted.—*Hard. Concil. Tom. VI. Pars.* 2, p. 1863–6.

Note 54.

Nous avons encore le testament de S. Gregoire de Nazianze, en date de dernier jour de Decembre de cette année 381. Il y prend le titre d'évêque de C. P.—Il conserve à une vierge nommée Russiene, la pension qu'il lui donnait pour sa subsistence, avec une habitation à son choix, et lui donne deux filles esclaves, qu'elle choisira, pour demeurer avec elle toute sa vie : il lui donne pouvoir de les affranchir, si non elles appartiendront à l'église de Nazianze.—*Hist. Ecc. de Fleury, Tome IV.* p. 419–420. *Ed. Paris.* 1758.

Note 55.

Saint Perpetuus vécut jusqu'en 491, et nous avons son testament fait vers le premier de Mai, l'an 475, par lequel il affranchit plusieurs esclaves, remet a ses debiteurs tout ce qu'ils lui doivent, et légue à son église plusieurs fonds de terre, et ses livres—*Hist. Ecc. de Fleury, Tome VI.* p. 555. *Ed. Paris.* 1758.

Note 56.

Alcuin avoit la disposition du revenu de ses abbayes, et comme leurs terres étoient peuplées de serfs, Elipand de Tolede lui reprochoit d'en avoir jusqu'à vingt mille.—*Hist. Ecc. de Fleury, Tome X.* p. 35. *Ed. Paris.* 1758.

NOTE 57.

Dans le Concile de Soissons, tenu A.D. 853. "Les évêques prioient le roi d'appuyer de son autorité, et pour cet effet il publia dans la septième session un capitulaire de douze articles. . . . Défense aux seigneurs d'empêcher les évêques de faire battre de verges les colons ou paysans serfs sujets des mêmes seigneurs, quand ils l'auront mérité pour leurs crimes.—*Hist. Ecc. de Fleury, Tome X.* p. 471. *Ed. Paris.* 1758.

NOTE 58.

Après cette préface, est le décret du pape (Benoit VIII. A.D. 1022,) divisé en sept articles. Il renouvelle la défense d'avoir ni femme ni concubine, et semble l'étendre à tous les clercs sans exception. Il déclare que les enfans des clercs sont serfs de l'église en laquelle servent leurs pères, quoique leurs mères soient libres, et prononce anathême contre le juge qui les déclarera libres. Aucun serf de l'église, clerc ou laïque, ne pourra faire aucune acquisition sous le nom d'un homme libre, sous peine de fouet et de prison, jusqu'à ce que l'église ait retiré tous les titres de l'acquisition.—*Hist. Ecc. de Fleury, Tome XII.* p. 405. *Ed. Paris.* 1758.

NOTE 59.

In sexto capite initio servis præceptum dat, ubi meminerint juniores communem regulam confirmari, quæ sæpè repetitur, Evangelium non abolet œconomias et politias, sed concionatur de aliis rebus, videlicet de æternis bonis, de æterna justicia et vita, quam Deus efficit in cordibus hominum, quos tamen, vult in hac vita mortali subjectos esse huic ordini, qui juxta voluntatem Dei convenit vitæ corporali. Vult nos cibo et potu sustentari, vult esse legitima conjugia, et propagationem. Vult esse consociationem ordinariam generis humani, distinctionem dominiorum, defensionem per imperia, contractus, leges, judicia, pœnas. Ita hûc videmus *approbari servitutem, qualis tunc in legibus descripta fuit.* Prodest autem et conscientiis et ad pacem intelligere hanc doctrinam de approbatione ordinis politici.—*Philip. Melanthonis, Com. in 1 Ep. ad Tim.* 6 : 1. *Ed.* 1564. *Pars IV.* p. 422.

NOTE 60.

Quincunque sub jugo.] Quia sibi quisque præstantiam falsa opinione arrogat, nemo est qui æquo animo ferat, alios sibi imperare. Qui effugere necessitatem nequeunt, parent illi quidem inviti superioribus : sed intus fremunt et indignantur, quia sibi putant fieri injuriam. Omnes ejusmodi disputationes uno verbo præcidit Apostolus, quum voluntariam subjectionem exigit ab omnibus qui sub jugo sunt. Significat enim non esse inquirendum sintne digni tali fortuna an meliore : quia sufficiat hac conditione esse obstrictos.—*Calvin's Com. on 1 Tim.* 6 : 1.

16*

Note 61.

Ne Dei nomen.] Semper in nostrum commodum plusquam oporteret inge-niosi sumus. Ita servis si infideles habeant dominos, prompta est objectio, indignum esse ut, qui diabolo serviunt, imperent filiis Dei. Paulus autem in contrariam partem retorquet argumentum, ideo infidelibus dominis paren-dum esse, ne malè audiat nomen Dei et Evangelium, quasi Evangelium con-tumaces reddat et præfractos, qui aliis subjecti esse debent.—*Ib.*

Note 62.

Quanta fuerit spiritus Paulini celsitudo, etsi ex gravioribus ejus scriptis perspici melius potest, hæc quoque Epistola testis est, in qua argumentum tractans humile alias et abjectum, suo tamen more sublimis ad Deum evehitur. Fugitivum servum et furem Domino remittens, pro illo deprecatur veniam. —*Calvin's Commentary on the Epistle to Philemon, introductory paragraph.*

Note 63.

Prolegomena.] Hæc epistola novo genere a Paulo scripta est, et sola verè proprièque epistola dici meretur. Ejus utilitas multiplex. Atonet enim nos. 1, neminem, quamvis imfimæ sortis, contemnendum : 2, de servorum ingenio non esse desperandum : 3, *Servos credentes in Christum non prop-terea liberos fieri, vel invitis eripi dominis :* 4, quodnam sit Episcopi officium, tum ergo inferiores, tum ergo nobiliores—Scribendi causa erat, ut servum hero reconciliaret. Quod cùm ei difficile videretur apud dominum justissimis de causis iratum, cùm et servus, rebus uti creditur, ablatis, profugisset omni orationis artificio eum aggreditur. Si quid in genere suasorio admirandum est, certè hoc epistolicum est.—*Poli Synopsis Criticorum, in Epist. Pauli ad Philemonem.*

Note 64.

Servi.] Non tollit morem tunc receptum servis utendi : habet enim sua commoda, et licet eo recté uti. Docet *libertatem Christianam consistere cum servitute politica, et per Christum non tolli, nec mutari, status politicos.*—*Poli Synopsis, in Epist. ad Ephesios* 6 : 5.

Note 65.

1 *Ep. ad Corinthos* 7 : 21. *Sed si potes liber fieri, potiùs utere.*] 1. Servi-tute utere : magìs servias, majoris boni causâ, scil, ad tuam exercitionem, et domini tui salutem. Syrus locum sic reddit. *Sed etiamsi* posses liber fieri, (tuis nempe artibus et fraudibus) *elige tibi ut servias.*—Huic sensui optimè quadrat sequens ratio consolatoria. *Nam qui servus vocatus est, libertus est Domini.* Non tamen hoc voluit, ut servitutem præferrent libertati *ab heris spontè oblatæ,* sed libertati illegitimæ per fugam, aut fraudem, etc.—*Poli Synopsis,* in 1 Epist. ad Corinthos, 7.

Note 66.

Gen 9 : 25. *Maledictus Canaan.*] Quidam subaudiunt אָבַר *pater.* Pater *Canaan.* Ita Ar.—quod paulò ante bis expressum est. Alii accipiunt de *Canaan.* Hunc populum maledictum fuisse eventus docuit. Hinc probabiliter colligitur eum fuisse paternæ iniquitatis socium. Nec tamen *Cham* immunis est a maledictione, quia filius ejus nominatur ; sicut *Semo* benedicitur, vers. sequente quamvis Deus nominetur, et Jacob dicitur *benedicere Josepho,* Gen. 48 : 15, quia liberis ipsius benedixit, v. 16. Punitur parens in filio, sceleris conscio, forsan et auctore et indice, ut volunt Hebræi et Theodoretus. Quidam observant maledicsisse Noe posteritati *Cham,* sed omissis reliquis filiis *Cham,* singulariter de *Canaan* expressisse Mosen, quia tantùm ea commemorâsse voluit quæ Israelitas confirmare et alacriores reddere possent ad capessendam terram promissam *Canaan.—Poli Synopsis, in loco.*

Note 67.

Servus Servorum,] *i. e.* Servus infimus et vilissimus.—*Ib.*

Note 68.

Gen. 17 : 12. *Tam vernaculus quam emptitius.*] Incircumcisus in terra Hebræorum vivere poterat sub bonis legibus, non item in domo Hebræi, ne mores exemplo confunderentur. Qu. An servi emptitii ad circumcisionem cogi poterant ? Affirmant multi ex hoc loco. Nam. 1. *Servus est possessio domini.* 2. Illud, *circumcidetur,* præceptum est, quod elides, si subaudias *si velit.* 3. Aliàs nulla distinctio esset inter mercenarium et servum nam mercenariis permissa erat (non præcepta) circumcisio, *Exod.* 12 : 44. Negant alii. Existimant nullum adultum servum obligari ad circumcisionem suæ aut prolis, nisi sponte consentiat. Nam sic sumenti (circumcisionem) imponeretur peccandi necessitas, et juberetur hypocrisis. Nec talis circumcisio sacramentum esset Dei fœderis, quod non nisi volentes amplectimur. Denique, vera religio suaderi debet, non imperari. Adde quod Maimonides sic explicat, de Circumcisione, cap. 1, sect. 6. *Si quis* (inquit) *servum jam adultum a Cuthæis comparavit, qui circumcidi nolit*—debet Cuthæis iterum venundari.—*Poli Syn.*

Note 69.

Exodus 20 : 10. *Servus tuus.*] Nec labores illis injungas, nec eos laborare patiaris. Intelligitur hoc de iis qui non erant Judæi, nam qui Judæi per precedentia erant prohibiti.—*Poli Syn. in loco.*

Note 70.

Ib. 17. *Non concupisses,* etc.] His legis verbis maximè stabilitur *dominium et proprietas* rerum quas ne concupiscere licet, *servitus* prætera et *herilis potestas.—Poli Syn. in loco.*

NOTE 71.

Deuter. 23 : 15. *Non trades servum,* etc.] Agit de domino extraneo. Sic terra Israelitica asylum fit. Intellige de servis qui ab Ethnicis dominis, prop ter tyrannidem, confugiebant ad Israelitas, Judaismi amplectendi gratiâ. — *Poli Synopsis in loco.*

NOTE 72.

Exod. 21 : 16. *Que furatus fucit hominem hominem et vendiderit.*] Nempe Israelitam. Patet ex Deut. 24 : 7. Quem Judæus aliquis vi vel fraude per-trahere posset in servitutem, et Gentilibus devendere.—*Poli Syn. in loco.*

NOTE 73.

Esdras 2d, c. 65. *Servi—septem millia,* etc.] Vide tenuem captivorum fortunam, cùm tot millia non haberent plures servos.—*Poli Syn. in loco.*

NOTE 74.

Qui post sanctum baptismum, duobus conjugiis fuerit implicitus, vel habuerit concubinam, non potest esse episcopus, vel presbyter, vel diaconus, vel omnino ex numero sacerdotali. — *Canones Apostolorum, Hardouini Concil. Tom.* 1, p. 14.

NOTE 75.

Nemo debet duas uxores simul ducere, nec uxori suæ alteram mulierem propter voluptatem et desiderium carnis subintroducere, projiciendo se in periculum peccandi, versando cum pluribus ad concupiscentiam, nec ad semen suscipiendum, sicut Deus ordinavit : et qui hoc fecerit, si fuerit sacerdos, prohibeatur ministerio sacrificandi, et communione fidelium, quousque ejiciat domo secundam : et debet retinere primam. Idem judicium est de laicis.—*Canon XXIV. Concilii Nicæni Versio Arabica. Hardouini Con. Tom.* 1, p. 467, *A.*

NOTE 76.

Polygamy.

Possit enim homo demittere sterilem uxorem, et ducere de qua filios habeat : et tamen non licet, et nostris quidem jam temporibus ac more Romano, nec superinducere, ut amplius habeat quam unam vivam.—*Augustin. Op. Tom. VI. De Bono Conjugali,* p. 237, *B.*

NOTE 77.

De trigamis et polygamis definiére eumdem Canonem, quem et de digamis, servata proportione, annum videlicet in digamis, alii vero duos annos. Tri-gamos autem tribus et sæpe quatuor annis segregant.—*Basil. Epistola* 188, *Canonica* 1, *Tom. III.* p. 271, *D.*

Note 78.

Polygamiam Patres silentio prætermisere, ut belluinam, prorsusque ab hominum genere alienam.—*Basil. Epist.* 217, *Canonica* 3, *Tom. III.* p. 329, *C.*

Note 79.

From the volume of Captain Canot, published by Appleton & Co., 1854,
I make the following extract, which gives a more graphic statement of the
atrocities committed by the native Africans than many books of much
greater pretension. See chapter LXI. p. 382–6.

"During my first visit to Digby," saith our author, "I promised my
trading friends—that I would either return to their settlement, or at least
send merchandise and a clerk to establish a factory."

"There were two towns at Digby, governed by cousins, who had always
lived in harmony. My mercantile venture, however, was unhappily destined to be the apple of discord between them. The establishment of so
important an institution as a slave-factory within the jurisdiction of the
younger savage, gave umbrage to the elder; and in a very short time, this
unlucky partiality ripened the noble kinsmen into bitter enemies."

"It is not the habit in Africa for negroes to expend their wrath in harm-
less words, so that preparations were soon made in each settlement for
defence as well as hostility. Both towns were stockaded and carefully
watched by sentinels, day and night. At times, forays were made into each
other's suburbs, but as the chiefs were equally vigilant and alert, the extent of harm was the occasional capture of women and children, as they
wandered to the forest and stream for wood and water."

"This dalliance, however, did not suit the ardor of my angry favorite.
After waiting a couple of months, he purchased the aid of certain *bushmen*,
headed by a notorious scoundrel named Jen-ken, who had acquired renown
for his barbarous ferocity throughout the neighborhood. Jen-ken and his
chiefs were *cannibals*, and never trod the war-path without a pledge to return laden with human flesh to gorge their households."

"Several assaults were made by this savage and his bushmen on the dissatisfied cousin, but as they produced no significant results, the barbarians
withdrew to the interior. A truce ensued. Friendly proposals were made
by the younger to the elder, and again a couple of months glided by in
seeming peace."

"Just at this time business called me to Gallinas. On my way hither I
looked in at Digby, intending to supply the displeased chieftain with goods
and an agent, if I found the establishment profitable."

"It was sunset when I reached the beach; too late, of course, to land my
merchandise, so that I postponed furnishing both places until the morning.

As might fairly be expected, there was abundant joy at my advent. The neglected rival was wild with satisfaction at the report that he, too, was at length favored with a 'white man.' His 'town' immediately became a scene of unbounded merriment. Powder was burnt without stint. Gallons of rum were distributed to both sexes; and dancing, smoking, and carousing continued till long after midnight, when all stole off to maudlin sleep."

"About three in the morning, the sudden screams of women and children aroused me from profound torpor! Shrieks were followed by volleys of musketry. There was a loud tattoo of knocks at my door, and appeals from the negro chief to rise and fly. 'The town was besieged— the head-men were on the point of escaping—resistance was vain—they had been betrayed—there were no fighters to defend the stockade.'"

"I was opening the door to comply with this advice, when my Kroomen, who knew the country's ways even better than I, dissuaded me from departing, with the confident assurance that our assailants were unquestionably composed of the rival townsfolk, who had only temporarily discharged the bushmen to deceive my entertainer. The Kroos insisted that I had nothing to fear. We might, they said, be seized and even imprisoned; but after a brief detention, the captors would be glad enough to accept our ransom. If we fled, we might be slaughtered by mistake."

"I had so much confidence in the sense and fidelity of the band that always accompanied me—partly as boatmen and partly as body-guard—that I experienced very little personal alarm when I heard the shouts as the savages rushed through the town, murdering every one they encountered. In a few moments our own door was battered down by the barbarians, and Jen-ken, torch in hand, made his appearance, claiming us as prisoners."

"Of course, we submitted without resistance, for although fully armed, the odds were so great in those ante-revolver days, that we should have been overwhelmed by a single wave of the infuriated crowd. The barbarian chief instantly selected our house for his headquarters, and dispatched his followers to complete their task. Prisoner after prisoner was thrust in. At times the heavy mash of a war-club and the cries of strangling women, gave notice that the work of death was not yet ended. But the night of horror wore away. The gray dawn crept through our hovel's bars, and all was still, save the groans of wounded captives, and the wailing of women and children."

"By degrees, the warriors dropped in around their chieftain. A *palaver-house*, immediately in front of my quarters, was the general rendezvous; and scarcely a *bushman* appeared without the body of some maimed and bleeding victim. The mangled but living captives were tumbled on a heap in the centre, and soon every avenue to the square was crowded with exulting savages. Rum was brought forth in abundance for the chiefs. Presently, slowly approaching from a distance, I heard the drums, horns, and war-bells ; and in less than fifteen minutes, a procession of women, whose naked limbs were smeared with chalk and ochre, poured into the palaverhouse to join the beastly rites. Each of these devils was armed with a knife, and bore in her hand some cannibal trophy. Jen-ken's wife, a corpulent wench of forty-five, dragged along the ground, by a single limb, the slimy corpse of an infant ripped alive from its mother's womb. As her eyes met those of her husband, the two fiends yelled forth a shout of mutual joy, while the lifeless babe was tossed in the air and caught, as it descended, upon the point of a spear. Then came the *refreshment*, in the shape of rum, powder, and blood, which was quaffed by the brutes till they reeled off, with linked hands, in a wild dance around the pile of victims. As the women leaped and sang, the men applauded and encouraged. Soon the ring was broken, and with a yell, each female leaped on the body of a wounded prisoner, and commenced the final sacrifice with the mockery of lascivious embraces !"

"In my wanderings in African forests, I have often seen the tiger pounce upon its prey, and with instinctive thirst, satiate its appetite for blood, and abandon the drained corpse ; but these African negresses were neither as decent nor as merciful as the beast of the wilderness. Their malignant pleasure seemed to consist in the invention of tortures that would agonize, but not slay. There was a devilish spell in the tragic scene that fascinated my eyes to the spot. A slow, lingering, tormenting mutilation was practised on the living as well as on the dead ; and, in every instance, the brutality of the women exceeded that of the men. I can not picture the hellish joy with which they passed from body to body, digging out eyes, wrenching off lips, tearing the ears, and slicing the flesh from the quivering bones ; while the queen of the harpies crept amid the butchery, gathering the brains from each several skull as a *bonne bouche* for the approaching feast !"

"After the last victim yielded his life, it did not require long to kindle a fire, produce the requisite utensils, and fill the air with the odor of *human flesh*. Yet, before the various masses were half broiled, every mouth was tearing the dainty morsels with shouts of joy, denoting the combined satisfaction of revenge and appetite ! In the midst of this appalling scene, I heard a fresh cry of exultation, as a pole was borne into the apartment, on which was impaled the living body of the conquered chieftain's wife. A hole was quickly dug, the stave planted, and fagots supplied ; but before a fire could be kindled, the wretched woman was dead, so that the barbarians were defeated in their hellish scheme of burning her alive."

" I do not know how long these brutalities lasted, for I remember very little after this last attempt, except that the bushmen packed in plaintain leaves whatever flesh was left from the orgie, to be conveyed to their friends in the forest. This was the first time it had been my lot to *behold the most savage development of African nature under the stimulus of war.* The butchery made me sick, dizzy, paralyzed. I sank on the earth benumbed with stupor ; nor was I aroused till nightfall, when my Kroomen bore me to the conqueror's town, and negotiated our redemption for the value of twenty slaves."

I had prepared a large number of other extracts from the works of the missionary, Rev. Mr. Moffat, of Dr. Livingstone, and especially of Captain Burton, whose book, entitled, *The Lake Regions of Central Africa*, presents, in the last chapter, the fullest and most satisfactory account of African character and habits that I have seen. But I have already exceeded the limits allotted to this volume, and shall only say, in conclusion, that I am not able to conceive how any Christian can seriously reflect on the awful depravity, the dark heathenism, the gross licentiousness, the cruel ferocity, and the worse than brutish degradation of the posterity of Ham, in their native country, and yet denounce, as *a sin*, the Southern institution, which has been the only means to raise millions out of that terrible abyss, and endow them with the knowledge of civilization, and of morality, founded on true religion. For my own part, as a friend to the negro race, and to the best interests of Africa, I can not hesitate to regard it as a dispensation of Providence ; through which the noble enterprise of the American Colonization Society, commencing with Liberia, will furnish, in due time, the best and most available instrumentality for the ultimate regeneration of that benighted continent. In the accomplishment of this grand design, the descendants of Canaan will have the largest scope for the development of all their faculties and powers. And looking forward to the result, which, sooner or later, will be effected, I consider the Constitution of the United States to be, not a " covenant with death, and an agreement with hell," but rather a covenant with life, and an agreement with the final purpose of divine mercy, for countless generations.

DISCARD